STYLE, COMPUTERS, AND EARLY MODERN DRAMA

Beyond Authorship

Hugh Craig and Brett Greatley-Hirsch extend the computational analysis introduced in *Shakespeare, Computers, and the Mystery of Authorship* (edited by Hugh Craig and Arthur F. Kinney; Cambridge University Press, 2009) beyond problems of authorship attribution to address broader issues of literary history. Using new methods to answer long-standing questions and challenge traditional assumptions about the underlying patterns and contrasts in the plays of Shakespeare and his contemporaries, *Style, Computers, and Early Modern Drama* sheds light on, for example, different linguistic usages between plays written in verse and prose, company styles, and different character types. As a shift from a canonical survey to a corpus-based literary history founded on a statistical analysis of language, this book represents a fundamentally new approach to the study of English Renaissance literature and proposes a new model and rationale for future computational scholarship in early modern literary studies.

HUGH CRAIG, University of Newcastle, Australia, has published on authorship attribution problems, mainly in Shakespeare, and on wider stylistic questions. He has ongoing collaborations in bioinformatics and speech pathology, resulting in articles in some leading science journals. He is on the Authorship Attribution Board for *The New Oxford Shakespeare* and is a Fellow of the Australian Academy of the Humanities.

BRETT GREATLEY-HIRSCH is University Academic Fellow in Textual Studies and Digital Editing at the University of Leeds. He is Coordinating Editor of Digital Renaissance Editions and co-editor of *Shakespeare*, the journal of the British Shakespeare Association. Before moving to the United Kingdom, he served as Vice President of the Australian and New Zealand Shakespeare Association.

STYLE, COMPUTERS, AND EARLY MODERN DRAMA

Beyond Authorship

HUGH CRAIG

University of Newcastle, Australia

BRETT GREATLEY-HIRSCH

University of Leeds

CAMBRIDGE
UNIVERSITY PRESS

CAMBRIDGE
UNIVERSITY PRESS

University Printing House, Cambridge CB2 8BS, United Kingdom

One Liberty Plaza, 20th Floor, New York, NY 10006, USA

477 Williamstown Road, Port Melbourne, VIC 3207, Australia

4843/24, 2nd Floor, Ansari Road, Daryaganj, Delhi - 110002, India

79 Anson Road, #06-04/06, Singapore 079906

Cambridge University Press is part of the University of Cambridge.

It furthers the University's mission by disseminating knowledge in the pursuit of education, learning and research at the highest international levels of excellence.

www.cambridge.org
Information on this title: www.cambridge.org/9781107191013
DOI: 10.1017/9781108120456

© Hugh Craig and Brett Greatley-Hirsch 2017

First published 2017

Printed in the United Kingdom by Clays, St Ives plc

A catalogue record for this publication is available from the British Library

ISBN 978-1-107-19101-3 Hardback

For John Burrows, who made
common words uncommon

Contents

List of Figures   *page* viii
List of Tables   xiv
Acknowledgements   xvi
Note on Texts   xviii

   Introduction   1

1 Methods   29

2 Prose and Verse: Sometimes 'transparent', Sometimes Meeting
   with 'a jolt'   53

3 Sisters under the Skin: Character and Style   79

4 Stage Properties: Bed, Blood, and Beyond   110

5 'Novelty carries it away': Cultural Drift   136

6 Authorship, Company Style, and *horror vacui*   164

7 Restoration Plays and 'the Giant Race, before the Flood'   202

   Coda   224

Appendix A: Play-Texts in the Full Corpus   227
Appendix B: Characters with ≥ 2,000 Words of Dialogue from 243
   Plays Performed on the Commercial Stage, 1580–1642   240
Appendix C: Plays First Appearing on the Commercial Stage
   1590–1609, with Totals for Prop-Types and Lines Spoken   247
Appendix D: Distribution of 691 Prop-Types across 160 Plays First
   Appearing on the Commercial Stage, 1590–1609   255
Appendix E: A List of 221 Function Words   261
Works Cited   262
Index   278

Figures

1.1 PCA scatterplot of 2,000-word non-overlapping segments of plays listed in Table 1.1, using the 500 most frequent words.   *page* 33

1.2 PCA scatterplot of 2,000-word non-overlapping segments of plays listed in Table 1.1, labelled by genre, using the 500 most frequent words.   36

1.3 PCA biplot of 2,000-word non-overlapping segments of plays listed in Table 1.1, labelled by genre, using the 500 most frequent words.   37

1.4 PCA biplot of 2,000-word non-overlapping segments of plays listed in Table 1.1, labelled by genre, using the 500 most frequent words and highlighting personal pronouns.   38

1.5 Binary decision tree diagram.   40

1.6 Diagram of a single binary decision tree populated for Random Forests classification of 2,000-word non-overlapping segments in a training dataset of 109 segments drawn from plays listed in Table 1.1, using the 500 most frequent words.   43

1.7 Delta distances between *Galatea* and four authorial sub-sets. 46

1.8 Delta distances for *The Jew of Malta* and four authorial sub-sets.   47

2.1 PCA scatterplot of prose and verse parts for 7 Shakespearean characters using the 100 most frequent function words.   60

2.2 PCA biplot of prose and verse samples from 7 Shakespearean characters, using the 100 most frequent function words, highlighting the 48 most weighted word-variables.   61

2.3 Column chart of word-variables exceeding the 0.01 probability threshold in the groups plays detailed in Tables 2.2–2.4.   69

2.4 Column chart of word-variables exceeding the 0.01
    probability threshold in the groups plays detailed in
    Tables 2.2–2.5.   72

2.5 Column chart of word-variables exceeding the 0.01
    probability threshold in the groups of plays detailed in
    Tables 2.2 and 2.5.   73

3.1 Distances between characters in plays and their sequels, using
    percentage counts of the 100 most common function words
    combined by Squared Euclidean Distance.   82

3.2 Histogram of distances between 666 characters based on
    percentage counts of the 100 most common function words
    (221,445 pairings in total).   83

3.3 The *z*-scores for the 20 most common function words for
    Orgilus and Ithocles in John Ford's *The Broken Heart*, using
    averages and standard deviations from the full set of 666
    characters with ≥ 2,000 words of dialogue.   85

3.4 Distances for the ten closest matches for ten characters with
    very close pairings with another character.   87

3.5 The 10 closest pairings for the 11 characters with dialogues
    ≥ 8,000 words, ordered by the distance to their closest
    match.   89

3.6 The *z*-scores for the 20 most common function words for
    Fluellen (*Henry the Fifth*), using averages and standard
    deviations from the full set of 666 characters with ≥ 2,000
    words of dialogue.   91

3.7 The *z*-scores for the ten closest matches for ten characters
    with very distant closest matches, ordered by distance to the
    closest match.   93

3.8 Total words spoken, number of and combined total words
    spoken by characters with ≥ 2,000 words of dialogue
    in 11 plays performed in 1599 by professional companies.   96

3.9 The *z*-scores for the 20 most common function words for
    Brutus and Cassius in Shakespeare's *Julius Caesar*, using
    averages and standard deviations from the set of 666
    characters with ≥ 2,000 words of dialogue.   97

3.10 Hierarchical cluster analysis of 35 character parts, using
     Ward's Linkage and Squared Euclidean Distance, based on
     counts of the 100 most common function words.   99

3.11 PCA scatterplot of 531 character parts from 197 plays
performed between 1580 and 1619, using the 100 most
common function words.   104

4.1 PCA scatterplot of 160 plays from the professional theatre,
1590–1609, using the 95 most common prop-types.   123

4.2 PCA biplot of 160 plays from the professional theatre,
1590–1609, using the 95 most common prop-types,
highlighting selected 'comedic' prop-types.   124

4.3 PCA biplot of 160 plays from the professional theatre,
1590–1609, using the 95 most common prop-types,
highlighting money-related prop-types.   126

4.4 PCA biplot of 160 plays from the professional theatre,
1590–1609, using the 95 most common prop-types,
highlighting prop-types associated with artificial light.   127

4.5 PCA biplot of 160 plays from the professional theatre,
1590–1609, using the 95 most common prop-types,
highlighting furniture and musical prop-types.   129

4.6 PCA biplot of 160 plays from the professional theatre,
1590–1609, using the 95 most common prop-types,
highlighting weapon prop-types.   131

4.7 PCA biplot of 160 plays from the professional theatre,
1590–1609, using the 95 most common prop-types,
highlighting selected prop-types.   132

5.1 Vertical chronological sequences arising from PC1 of a PCA
using the 50 most frequent function words in 243 plays from
the professional theatre grouped into 13 half-decades between
1580 and 1644.   140

5.2 PC1 weightings for the top 50 most frequent function words
in 203 plays from the professional theatre grouped into eight
half-decades between 1585 and 1624.   142

5.3 Boxplot of percentage counts for $that_{conjunction}$ in plays
between 1585 and 1624, grouped in half-decades.   143

5.4 Boxplot of percentage counts for *with* in plays between 1585
and 1624, grouped in half-decades.   144

5.5 Boxplot of percentage counts for *the* in plays between 1585
and 1624, grouped in half-decades.   145

5.6 Boxplot of percentage counts for *a* in plays between 1585 and
1624, grouped in half-decades.   146

5.7 Boxplot of percentage counts for $no_{adjective}$ in plays between
1585 and 1624, grouped in half-decades.   147

5.8 Boxplot of percentage counts for *that*~demonstrative~ in plays
between 1585 and 1624, grouped in half-decades. 148

5.9 PCA scatterplot of PC1 scores for Fletcher, Marlowe, and
Shakespeare plays by date, 1585–1624. 159

5.10 PCA scatterplot of PC1 scores for Shakespeare's plays by date. 160

6.1 PCA scatterplot of 2,000-word non-overlapping segments of
plays with well-attributed first companies, *c.*1581–94, using
the 500 most frequent words, labelled by company. 171

6.2 PCA scatterplot of 2,000-word non-overlapping segments of
plays with well-attributed first companies, *c.*1581–94, using
the 500 most frequent words, labelled by author. 172

6.3 PCA biplot of 2,000-word non-overlapping segments of plays
with well-attributed first companies, *c.*1581–94, using the 500
most frequent words, highlighting selected generic markers. 174

6.4 PCA biplot of 2,000-word non-overlapping segments of
plays with well-attributed first companies, *c.*1581–94, using
the 500 most frequent words, highlighting personal and
possessive pronouns. 175

6.5 PCA scatterplot of 2,000-word non-overlapping segments of
plays with well-attributed first companies, *c.*1581–94, using
the 500 most frequent words, labelled by genre. 176

6.6 PCA scatterplot of 2,000-word non-overlapping segments of
plays associated with the Admiral's (Nottingham's) Men,
Derby's (Strange's) Men, and Queen Elizabeth's Men,
*c.*1581–94, using the 500 most frequent words, labelled by
company. 179

6.7 PCA scatterplot of 2,000-word non-overlapping segments of
plays associated with the Admiral's (Nottingham's) Men,
Derby's (Strange's) Men, and Queen Elizabeth's Men,
*c.*1581–94, using the 500 most frequent words, labelled by
author. 180

6.8 PCA scatterplot of 2,000-word non-overlapping segments of
plays associated with Queen Elizabeth's Men, *c.*1581–94,
using the 500 most frequent words, labelled by play. 183

6.9 PCA scatterplot of 2,000-word non-overlapping segments of
plays associated with Queen Elizabeth's Men, *c.*1581–94,
using the 500 most frequent words, labelled by author. 184

6.10 PCA scatterplot of 2,000-word non-overlapping segments of
plays associated with Queen Elizabeth's Men, *c.*1581–94,
using the 500 most frequent words, labelled by genre. 185

6.11 PCA biplot of 2,000-word non-overlapping segments of
      plays associated with Queen Elizabeth's Men, *c.*1581–94,
      using the 500 most frequent words, highlighting
      demonstrative and relative pronouns.   186

6.12 PCA scatterplot of 2,000-word non-overlapping segments of
      Children of the King's Revels comedies, using the 500 most
      frequent words, labelled by play.   188

6.13 PCA scatterplot of 2,000-word non-overlapping segments of
      Children of the King's Revels comedies, using the 500 most
      frequent words, labelled by author.   189

6.14 PCA scatterplot of 2,000-word non-overlapping segments of
      9 comedies by Richard Brome, 1629–40, using the 500 most
      frequent words.   190

6.15 PCA scatterplot of 2,000-word non-overlapping segments of
      9 comedies by Richard Brome, 1629–40, using the 500 most
      frequent words, labelled by play.   192

6.16 PCA biplot of 2,000-word non-overlapping segments of 9
      comedies by Richard Brome, 1629–40, using the 500 most
      frequent words, highlighting thematic markers.   193

6.17 PCA biplot of 2,000-word non-overlapping segments of 9
      comedies by Richard Brome, 1629–40, using the 500 most
      frequent words, highlighting personal pronouns.   195

7.1   PCA scatterplot of 243 plays from 1580 to 1642 and 10
      comedies from the 1660s, using the 100 most common
      function words.   206

7.2   Scatterplot of PCA weightings for 11 prepositions in the 100
      most common function words across 243 plays from 1580 to
      1642 and 10 comedies from the 1660s.   207

7.3   Scatterplot of PCA weightings for 19 verbs in the 100 most
      common function words across 243 plays from 1580 to 1642
      and 10 comedies from the 1660s.   208

7.4   Scatterplot of PCA weightings for 23 pronouns and
      possessives in the 100 most common function words across
      243 plays from 1580 to 1642 and 10 comedies from the 1660s.   209

7.5   PCA scatterplot of 243 plays from 1580 to 1642 and 10
      comedies from the 1660s, using the 100 most common lexical
      words.   213

7.6   Scatterplot of PCA weightings for the 100 most common
      lexical words in 243 plays from 1580 to 1642 and 10 comedies
      from the 1660s.   214

7.7 PCA scatterplot of 243 plays from 1580 to 1642 and 8 tragicomedies from the 1660s, using the 100 most common function words. 215

7.8 PCA scatterplot of 243 plays from 1580 to 1642 and 8 tragicomedies from the 1660s, using the 100 most common lexical words. 217

7.9 Scatterplot of PCA weightings for the 100 most common lexical words in 243 plays from 1580 to 1642 and 8 tragicomedies from the 1660s. 218

7.10 Delta distances between a composite text of 10 1660s comedies and 15 playwrights with 4 or more pre-1642 plays, using the 100 most common function words. 219

7.11 Delta distances between a composite text of 10 1660s comedies and 15 playwrights with 4 or more pre-1642 plays, using the 100 most common lexical words. 220

7.12 Delta distances between a composite text of 8 1660s tragicomedies and 15 playwrights with 4 or more pre-1642 plays, using the 100 most common function words. 221

7.13 Delta distances between a composite text of 8 1660s tragicomedies and 15 playwrights with 4 or more pre-1642 plays, using the 100 most common lexical words. 222

Tables

1.1 A select corpus of plays.   *page* 32

1.2 Confusion matrix for Random Forests classification of
2,000-word non-overlapping segments in a training dataset of
109 segments drawn from plays listed in Table 1.1, using the
500 most frequent words.   44

1.3 Confusion matrix for Random Forests classification of 109
training and 29 test segments of plays listed in Table 1.1,
segmented into 2,000-word non-overlapping blocks, using the
500 most frequent words.   45

2.1 Prose and verse parts for seven Shakespearean characters.   59

2.2 Fourteen more or less 'all-prose' and fourteen more or less
'all-verse' comedies.   64

2.3 Paired sets of fourteen mixed prose–verse plays: comedies and
tragedies, plays by Jonson and Shakespeare, and plays dated
1600–4 and 1610–14.   66

2.4 Five randomly paired comparison sets of fourteen mixed
prose–verse plays.   67

2.5 Set of fourteen comedies with prose-to-verse ratios between 1:1
and 3:17.   71

2.6 Shannon entropies of 'all-prose' versus 'all-verse' comedies and
prose portions versus verse portions of mixed-mode comedies.   74

4.1 Distribution of props in 160 plays from the professional
theatre, 1590–1609.   120

5.1 Correlations between date of first performance and PC1 score
for 203 plays between 1585 and 1624, grouped by genre.   157

5.2 Correlations between date of first performance and PC1 score
for 203 plays between 1585 and 1624, grouped by author.   158

6.1 Plays with well-attributed first companies, *c.*1581–94.   168

6.2 Confusion matrix for Random Forests classification of 2,000-word non-overlapping segments of plays with well-attributed first companies, *c.*1581–94, using the 500 most frequent words. 178

6.3 Confusion matrix for Random Forests classification of 2,000-word non-overlapping segments of plays associated with the Admiral's (Nottingham's) Men, Derby's (Strange's) Men, and Queen Elizabeth's Men, *c.*1581–94, using the 500 most frequent words. 181

6.4 Confusion matrix for Random Forests classification of 2,000-word non-overlapping segments of 9 comedies by Richard Brome associated with Beeston's Boys, the King's Men, and King's Revels Company, 1629–40, using the 500 most frequent words. 197

Acknowledgements

A number of porcupines huddled together for warmth on a cold day in winter; but, as they began to prick one another with their quills, they were obliged to disperse. However, the cold drove them together again, when just the same thing happened. At last, after many turns of huddling and dispersing, they discovered that they would be best off by remaining at a little distance from one another. In the same way, the need of society drives the human porcupines together, only to be mutually repelled by the many prickly and disagreeable qualities of their nature.[1]

Arthur Schopenhauer

In writing this book, we somehow managed to avoid the porcupine's dilemma and collaborate entirely without insult or injury. We have also profited enormously from the warmth of many colleagues whom we wish to thank for their generous and invaluable feedback. Of course, any and all errors that remain are ours and ours alone, though we thank you, gentle reader-function, to forgive them. Remember: fellow porcupines don't read the footnotes.

Our principal debt is to John Burrows, the dedicatee of this book, for inaugurating computational stylistics as an area of scholarly inquiry and developing new data-driven methods for the study of literary style. This book is but one small product of his impressive critical legacy, and we hope we have done justice to his scholarship in the pages that follow.

We thank our wonderful colleagues for providing unwavering support while this book was in preparation, and for the challenging questions and apposite suggestions for improvement offered in response to earlier versions of the chapters presented at conferences and meetings. Chief among these are the scholars who participated in our *Beyond Authorship* symposium in Newcastle, Australia, 24–7 June 2014, whose contributions helped

---

[1] Arthur Schopenhauer, 'A Few Parables', *Studies in Pessimism: A Series of Essays*, trans. T. Bailey Saunders (London: Swann Sonnenschein & Co., 1893), 142.

us to formulate our ideas about applying computational stylistics in more descriptive areas: John Burrows, Douglas Bruster, Louisa Connors, Douglas Duhaime, Gabriel Egan, Jack Elliott, Heather Froehlich, Peter Groves, Jonathan Hope, MacDonald P. Jackson, Lynn Magnusson, Glenn Roe, Ros Smith, and Erica Zimmer.

We owe a debt of gratitude to Bill Pascoe for overseeing development of the Intelligent Archive software so crucial to this project. Likewise, we are especially beholden to our senior research assistant, Alexis Antonia, and to Jack Elliott, who served as a consultant analyst, developer, and sounding-board. Without their considerable contributions, this book would not have been possible.

For sage advice, timely provocation, and much-needed encouragement, we thank Michael Best, Lukas Erne, Oliver Gondring, Fen Greatley-Hirsch, Margaret Harris, Matthew Harrison, Yasmin Haskell, Tim Haydon, Peter Holbrook, Mark Houlahan, Fotis Jannidis, Laurie Johnson, Pete Kirwan, Ian Lancashire, Eleanor Lowe, Ruth Lunney, Kathleen Lynch, Willard McCarty, David McInnis, Jenna Mead, Philip Mead, Matt Munson, Sarah Neville, Catherine Oddie, Helen Ostovich, Trisha Pender, Steffen Pielström, Malte Rehbein, Tom Rutter, Christof Schöch, Tomoji Tabata, Gary Taylor, Justin Tonra, Lyn Tribble, Margaret Tudeau-Clayton, Bob White, Martin Wiggins, Pip Willcox, Owen Williams, Michael Witmore, the late Anne Wortham, and Chris Wortham.

We have also benefitted greatly from substantial institutional support. We are deeply grateful to the Australian Research Council for the award of a Discovery Project (DP120101955) grant, which funded necessary text preparation and software development, as well as the *Beyond Authorship* symposium. While working on this book, both authors also enjoyed invaluable research time through the award of research fellowships and visiting appointments. We wish to thank the University of Würzburg, which hosted Craig for sabbatical leave in 2013, and the Leverhulme Trust for a visiting research fellowship that allowed Greatley-Hirsch to work at the Centre for Textual Studies, De Montfort University, that same year. We are also grateful to the Moore Institute for Research in the Humanities and Social Studies at NUI Galway, the Institute for Advanced Studies at the University of Western Australia, and the Folger Institute of the Folger Shakespeare Library for the award of short-term fellowships in 2014 and 2015.

To our families, especially our better halves, we are eternally thankful for your unflinching love and support.

D.H.C. and B.D.G-H.

Note on Texts

For ease of reference, we quote from modern-spelling editions of early modern English materials wherever possible. These are cited in the notes upon their first appearance in each chapter, and then parenthetically in the text. Where such editions are not available, we silently modernise the spelling and punctuation of the early print or manuscript source, citing the relevant STC or Wing reference numbers.[1] Unless otherwise specified, all references to Shakespeare are from William Shakespeare, *The Complete Works*, ed. Stanley Wells and Gary Taylor, 2nd edn (Oxford University Press, 2005).

The 'Methods' chapter offers a thorough discussion of our principles of selection and the preparation of machine-readable texts used in this book. Standard bibliographical details for the plays we use are provided in Appendices A and B. Where additional details are required for a particular purpose, these are specified by the relevant tables in the chapters themselves.

---

[1] STC references are to A. W. Pollard and G. R. Redgrave, *A Short-Title Catalogue [. . .], 1475–1640*, 2nd edn, 3 vols. (London: Bibliographical Society, 1976–91). Wing references are to Donald Wing, *Short-Title Catalogue [. . .], 1641–1700*, 2nd edn, 4 vols. (New York: Modern Language Association of America, 1972–98).

Introduction

There is no such thing as a clearly defined historical field; facts are linked to other facts in all directions, and investigation merely leads to further and further questions.[1]

(W. W. Greg)

We are all disenchanted with those picaresque adventures in pseudo-causality which go under the name of literary history, those hand-books with footnotes which claim to sing of the whole but load every rift with glue.[2]

(Geoffrey Hartman)

It is generally admitted that a positivistic history of literature, treating it as if it were a collection of empirical data, can only be a history of what literature is not. At best, it would be a preliminary classification opening the way for actual literary study and, at worst, an obstacle in the way of literary understanding.[3]

(Paul de Man)

It is nearly ~~fifty years since the~~ most recent of these remarks were published, but the fragmentary nature of the evidence – to adapt the Porter's paradox in *Macbeth* – still provokes and unprovokes attempts towards a complete, unified literary history. This problem is particularly acute in relation to the literature and drama of the early modern period, for which, as Alexander Leggatt observes, 'the full picture can never be recovered', and the aim must be to draw plausible inferences from the available evidence, so that the literary and theatrical 'life of the time can be sketched in rough outline'.[4] A second inherent difficulty with literary history is where to draw boundaries:

---

[1] W. W. Greg, 'Preface', in Philip Henslowe, *Henslowe's Diary*, 2 vols. (London: A. H. Bullen, 1908), II: vii.
[2] Geoffrey Hartman, 'Toward Literary History', *Daedalus* 99.2 (1970), 355.
[3] Paul de Man, 'Literary History and Literary Modernity', *Daedalus* 99.2 (1970), 401.
[4] Alexander Leggatt, 'The Companies and Actors', in Clifford Leech et al. (eds.), *The Revels History of Drama in English*, 8 vols. (London: Methuen, 1975–83), III: 99.

changes and continuities in literary history pertain to the works themselves, but also relate to all the institutions that make publication and performance possible. As such, literary history is bound up with the histories of other art forms, as well as with political, social, and technological changes.

 Although the paucity of surviving historical and documentary evidence – as well as the resulting critical uncertainties and lacunae – remains an obstacle, the introduction of computing technologies and computer-aided quantitative methods in recent years has opened up possibilities to overcome some of the difficulties through new forms of evidence, critical frameworks, and vocabularies. The new methods offer comprehensiveness and evenness of attention, if at the cost of a radical narrowing of the data to those features that can be counted. A quantitative turn brings new models of literary history, combining large datasets and computerised statistical analysis to elicit otherwise hidden or only partially glimpsed patterns, which can then inform humanistic judgement and interpretation.

Some of the findings from this quantitative turn have been in areas where we might have despaired of ever getting an answer, such as the question of whether the style of the original writer survives in translations.[5] Others bring precision where we already knew the basic facts, as with the discovery that Henry James's style changed progressively with each new novel, with hardly a backward step, in the direction of his familiar late style.[6] A third variety reveals an unsuspected minuteness of patterning in literary texts, as in the distinctiveness of the speaking styles of the characters within a novel.[7]

The computer possesses some attributes of the ideal reader of narrative theory – such as the capacity to 'retain in memory and retrieve at will' the information provided by the text – while completely lacking others, such as 'the competence required to properly understand and interpret a literary work'.[8] Meanwhile empirical studies of actual readers show that they are quite unlike the ideal reader: for instance, they vary considerably over the course of reading a text in their engagement with the narrative.[9]

---

[5] Jan Rybicki, 'The Great Mystery of the (Almost) Invisible Translator: Stylometry in Translation', in Michael P. Oakes and Meng Ji (eds.), *Quantitative Methods in Corpus-Based Translation Studies* (Amsterdam: John Benjamins, 2012), 231–48.

[6] David L. Hoover, 'Corpus Stylistics, Stylometry, and the Styles of Henry James', *Style* 41.2 (2007), 174–203.

[7] John Burrows, *Computation into Criticism: A Study of Jane Austen and an Experiment* in Method (Oxford: Clarendon Press, 1987).

[8] Peter Dixon and Marisa Bortolussi, 'Fluctuations in Literary Reading: The Neglected Dimension of Time', in Lisa Zunshine (ed.), *The Oxford Handbook of Cognitive Literary Studies* (Oxford University Press, 2015), 543, 541.

[9] Dixon and Bortolussi, 'Fluctuations', 542–53.

The computer can read more, and more evenly, than any human reader, and this paradoxical situation – perfect evenness, unlimited memory, entire lack of comprehension – brings a capacity to offer results which might not be anticipated, which diverge from the conclusions of both ideal and actual readers, but which can be directly and completely related to the details of the text.

As the long history of the concordance demonstrates,[10] scholars since the Middle Ages have been both able and interested to count features of language in texts. To do so on a large scale, however, was simply impractical until the advent of computing, which, alongside the increasing availability of machine-readable transcriptions, as well as software applications for their processing and analysis, now allows us to consider more complex forms of evidence, such as multivariate patterns of language use and word distribution. Moreover, the application of quantitative methods and statistical reasoning to literary studies challenges scholars to situate their findings within degrees of probability, rather than making simple declarations of fact. Unexpectedly, perhaps, the quantitative approach leads to measured uncertainty rather than absolute findings. The methods foreground the possibility that a pattern is the result of chance, for instance. Tests for statistical significance frame the result: is it the sort of difference that we could expect to appear now and then, even when there is no genuine underlying contrast, or, on the other hand, is it so marked and persistent that it would take hundreds of trials of random data to come up with something similar – or thousands, or millions? (Admittedly, the authority we tend to give to numbers may obscure the other confounding possibility, that there is a hidden factor behind the results other than the one which has been targeted or detected, and investigators need to remind themselves constantly of this aspect.)

Our book does not seek to establish new certainties, but to present principled generalisations about literary history, drawn from datasets that are inevitably incomplete but nonetheless designed to bear specifically on the question at hand, and which would certainly exceed the possible span of an unaided reader. It is based on a conviction that Paul de Man, quoted above, was too pessimistic about quantitative studies of literature, which, in the decades since his remarks were published, have made valuable contributions to the discipline, by resolving some specific categorical questions like authorship and dating, and by providing some well-founded wider stylistic contexts in which particular examples can be placed. Quantitative

---

[10] David Leon Higdon, 'The Concordance: Mere Index or Needful Census?', *Text* 15 (2003), 51–68.

methods have distinct advantages in comprehensiveness, in giving equal attention to every instance of a feature under investigation, and in the use of well-established statistical techniques to counter potential biases. We do not suggest for a moment, however, that quantitative study can replace qualitative study. Any numerical analysis depends on previous scholarship to define the problem and the associated set of texts and variables for study, and its findings must then be interpreted in the light of a wider disciplinary understanding.

Style and Stylistics

Style is the key enabling concept in these studies. It implies a common factor linking a number of local instances and a number of markers. Writing in 1589, George Puttenham captures this sense of continuity and extent in *The Art of English Poesy*:

> Style is a constant and continual phrase or tenor of speaking and writing, extending to the whole tale or process of the poem or history, and not properly to any piece or member of a tale, but is of words, speeches, and sentences together a certain contrived form and quality, many times natural to the writer, many times his peculiar by election and art, and such as either he keepeth by skill or holdeth on by ignorance, and will not or peradventure cannot easily alter into any other.[11]

From the perspective of linguistics, style covers patterned variation within a language, an alternative to the usual focus of the discipline on the underlying syntactical rules and lexical resources of a language as a whole. For stylistics, style is a marked concentration or foregrounded under-representation of some linguistic items, and thus always a matter of relativities:

> Style is concerned with frequencies of linguistic items in a given context, and thus with *contextual* probabilities. To measure the style of a passage, the frequencies of its linguistic items of different levels must be compared with the corresponding features in another text or corpus which is regarded as a norm and which has a definite relationship with this passage. For the stylistic analysis of one of Pope's poems, for instance, norms with varying contextual relationships include English eighteenth-century poetry, the corpus of Pope's work, all poems written in English in rhymed pentameter couplets, or, for greater contrast as well as comparison, the poetry of Wordsworth.

---

[11] George Puttenham, *The Art of English Poesy*, ed. Frank Whigham and Wayne A. Rebhorn (Ithaca: Cornell University Press, 2007), 3.5 (233).

Contextually distant norms would be, e.g. Gray's *Anatomy* or the London Telephone Directory of 1960.[12]

In this strictly operational sense, it is possible for a given group of language samples to have a neutral style – that is, not to have any marked differences from a comparison set. Style is also something that is perceived by readers or hearers, who compare what they are reading or hearing with acquired standards for the genre.

When styles are detected in the quantitative way Nils Erik Enkvist describes above, their make-up can be precisely specified in terms of markers and frequencies. The researcher usually wants to go beyond this to a more qualitative description, but this is much more impressionistic. In this there is the risk of committing what Ernst H. Gombrich calls the 'physiognomic fallacy', that is, the mistaken belief that styles must have the unity of a human face, a singular combination of features adding up to a naturally occurring, recognisable, separately existing entity.[13] We can present a series of feature frequencies that have high or low correlations,[14] and claim that they represent the style of a given set of samples, but must acknowledge that these are only an arbitrary selection of the possible features and thus only one of the many possible views of the set and its contrast with other comparable sets. A further step, derided by Stanley Fish and exemplified in a recent article on *Double Falsehood*, is to go beyond metaphorical physiognomy to infer actual, personal, psychological characteristics from language features in a work.[15]

The interpreter has to avoid reckless leaps into fanciful interpretation but also do justice to a sense that, though quantitatively derived, and thus arbitrary in origin, some combinations of features can be associated with the intuitive experience of readers and can crystallise otherwise half-formed

---

[12] Nils Erik Enkvist, 'On Defining Style: An Essay on Applied Linguistics', in Nils Erik Enkvist, John Spencer, and Michael Gregory (eds.), *Linguistics and Style* (Oxford University Press, 1964), 29.

[13] Ernst H. Gombrich, 'Style', in David L. Sills (ed.), *International Encyclopedia of the Social Sciences*, 18 vols. (New York: Macmillan, 1968–79), XV: 359.

[14] In statistics, 'correlation' describes and measures the strength (low to high) and direction (positive or negative) of the association between two sets of counts. In meteorology these counts might be rainfall and temperature; in computational stylistics, they might be frequencies of the words *you* and *thou*. A positive correlation indicates the extent to which those sets of counts or 'variables' increase or decrease in parallel, whereas a negative correlation indicates the extent to which one variable increases as the other decreases.

[15] Stanley E. Fish, 'What Is Stylistics and Why Are They Saying Such Terrible Things about It?', in Seymour Chatman (ed.), *Approaches to Poetics: Selected Papers from the English Institute* (New York: Columbia University Press, 1973), 109–52; Ryan L. Boyd and James W. Pennebaker, 'Did Shakespeare Write *Double Falsehood*? Identifying Individuals by Creating Psychological Signatures with Text Analysis', *Psychological Science* 26.5 (2015), 570–82.

impressions about distinctive strands in language use. The ancient rhetoricians provide models for identifying styles in language in this way. They identify and analyse archaic versus modern and high versus low styles in particular.[16]

It is worth noting that we need to use the term 'style' without recourse to the idea of choice, which may underpin a more specific art-historical use.[17] The notion of 'style' we employ may not have been apparent either to practitioners or to consumers.

Classification and Description

Quantitative analysis of literary language can be applied to *classification* or *description*. Classification involves the principled categorisation of texts into discrete classes on the basis of established criteria (e.g. author, genre, period, and so on), whereas description involves analysis of numerical patterns to generalise (e.g. about the change in a given genre over time) or to reveal latent aspects of texts (e.g. an unexpected contrast between the speaking styles of protagonists and antagonists in novels). We adopt both approaches in this book but do not present any work in authorship attribution, which has been the commonest application of computational stylistics to date. Broadly our aim is to build on the striking advances in rigour and diversity in authorship attribution and apply similar methods to other aspects of literary history: questions about other kinds of classification – such as by repertory company, by era, by form (verse or prose) – and more descriptive generalisation, such as dialogue types and characters. Mostly our data is linguistic, profiles of word use in particular, but for one case study we look at another kind of data: the distribution of stage properties across the plays. This quantitative work can serve our discipline by arbitrating among possible answers to the more categorical questions – of which there are more than one might imagine – and by offering fresh perspectives through the power of statistics to generalise.

The application of quantitative methods to literary study is not without its critics, and the claims of 'distant reading' in particular have provoked a considerable reaction within and beyond the academy.[18] The accommodation between a scientific paradigm and humanistic approaches is fraught

[16] Gombrich, 'Style', 354.   [17] Gombrich, 'Style', 353.
[18] Representative examples include Maurizio Ascari, 'The Dangers of Distant Reading: Reassessing Moretti's Approach to Literary Genres', *Genre* 47.1 (2014), 1–19; Stanley E. Fish, 'Mind Your P's and B's: The Digital Humanities and Interpretation', *Opinionator* 23 Jan. 2012; essays in Jonathan Goodwin and John Holbo (eds.), *Reading Graphs, Maps, Trees: Responses to Franco Moretti* (Anderson: Parlor Press, 2011); Stephen Marche, 'Literature Is Not Data: Against Digital Humanities', *Los Angeles*

with difficulty, as the sweeping claims from one side are met with determined resistance from the other. The central proposition of literary Darwinism – that literature cannot be understood without taking into account the insights of evolutionary biology – has met with similar opposition.[19] Our position is that computational stylistics must take its place within the disciplinary framework of literary studies and is subject to an established understanding of the limitations of certainty in interpretation, but can nevertheless provide new insights through its power of principled generalisation. This is becoming clear in the cognate area of authorship attribution. Gary Taylor, for example, has argued that quantitative attribution work on William Shakespeare's early dramatic output has provided new opportunities for interpretation. Uncertainty about whether plays are collaborative, and which sections are written by which writer, inhibits criticism. If we know this part of *Titus Andronicus* is by George Peele, and this part by Shakespeare, we can see how they relate to the careers of these playwrights and are freed from the necessity to explain inconsistencies through textual corruption or the presence of prentice work.[20]

Quantitative Studies and the Counter-Intuitive

The ideal computational-stylistic finding is counter-intuitive but highly persuasive. In some cases, familiar critical assumptions are based on analysis of an inadequate sample of the whole or overly influenced by preoccupations and bias. A combination of empirical objectivity and expanded scale of sample opens the way to reassessing, and perhaps even invalidating, these views. The new methods may also detect patterns in certain features, which, though undeniably present, were invisible to the naked eye and thus hidden from qualitative literary-critical methods.

Inertia, ideology, and fashion have an influence on what works are studied, and what conclusions are reached – in terms both of what questions are deemed worthy of attention and what answers to the questions are preferred. Quantitative methods cannot escape the dilemmas of selectivity and bias in interpretation, but they do force the researcher to articulate a problem in objective terms and to expose a given claim to a test that can go

---

Review of Books 28 Oct. 2012; Adam Kirsch, 'Technology Is Taking over English Departments: The False Promise of the Digital Humanities', *New Republic* 2 May 2014; and Katie Trumpener, 'Paratext and Genre System: A Response to Franco Moretti', *Critical Inquiry* 36.1 (2009), 159–71.

[19] See Brian Boyd, 'Getting It All Wrong: The Proponents of Theory and Cultural Critique Could Learn a Thing or Two from Bioculture', *The American Scholar* 1 Sep. 2006; for a response, see Jonathan Kramnick, 'Against Literary Darwinism', *Critical Inquiry* 37.2 (2011), 315–47.

[20] Gary Taylor, 'The Fly Scene in *Titus*', paper presented at Shakespeare 450, Paris, 25 Apr. 2014.

either way. Experiment in literary interpretation, as elsewhere, can test and modify established assumptions.

Quantitative work provides an opportunity to be surprised: to back something other than the sentimental favourite and to reverse consensus views. It might have resonated better with early twenty-first-century disciplinary audiences if authorship had proved to be a muted aspect of style when analysed quantitatively. However, researchers in areas from ancient philosophy to contemporary mass-market romance have observed author-effects that cut across all the other groupings (e.g. genre and period) that can also be tested.[21] The authors of this book expected early modern repertory companies to have distinctive, identifiable styles, and that verse would constrain style whoever used it and whenever it was used. In fact, as detailed in the chapters that follow, these expectations – founded on a consensus of earlier scholarship – were consistently overturned by tests in which it was possible for the anticipated patterns to emerge. These examples suggest that the methods provide a way of avoiding confirmation bias, in which evidence supporting an established view tends to be favoured, and evidence tends to be interpreted so as to support a predetermined position. Often an established view has its own internal logic, seems plausible, and has the seductive appeal of opening up perspectives of special interest to the discipline at a given moment. A quantitative approach can offer a fresh start on the problem and challenge the researcher with unexpected findings, which in turn require further testing and explanation.

Quantitative language study works by concentrating on a select few of the manifested features of the text, ignoring the rest, as well as the context of the instances. This wilful blindness to all but a fraction of the signals to which readers and spectators respond allows all texts or text-segments to be put on exactly the same footing. The scale can be enlarged at will, limited only by the availability of suitably prepared text. A quantitative approach requires comparison to yield any results. A single reading only has significance in relation to another reading or to a standard derived from an *a priori* expectation. Comparison is built into the method. Practitioners are prevented from the sort of absolute, unanchored observations that treat a single instance in isolation, without reference to its context in comparable works.

[21] For example, Harold Tarrant and Terry Roberts, 'Appendix 2: Report of the Working Vocabulary of the Doubtful Dialogues', in Marguerite Johnson and Harold Tarrant (eds.), *Alcibiades and the Socratic Lover-Educator* (London: Bristol Classical Press, 2012), 223–36; and Jack Elliott, 'Patterns and Trends in Harlequin Category Romance', in Paul Longley Arthur and Katherine Bode (eds.), *Advancing Digital Humanities: Research, Methods, Theories* (New York: Palgrave, 2014), 54–67.

In a situation where we have a considerable collection of samples from a field such as early modern English drama, we can test how far the patterns of regularity go in particular cases. Some patterns we anticipate to be strong may prove weak in practice. The accumulation of readers' intuitions into a consensus on a given set of constraints – that a dramatic change in political régime was accompanied by a sea change in literary style, for example – may prove to be exaggerated: there was in fact only a minor change, or nothing detectable. Writing before and after this watershed is more variable than we thought – it is free to range and to innovate – and this fluctuation has for this purpose the same consequence as stability. That is, there is no marked and consistent contrast between texts either side of the divide. On the other hand, if there was a large change, it might be in a quite unexpected direction.

Authorship and Beyond

> People often say that it doesn't matter who wrote the works, we still have the works themselves . . . But it does matter. Utterly. To claim otherwise is to deny history, the nature of historical evidence, and also to sever from the works any understanding of the humanity and personality behind them. As people we want to know as much as possible about the artist responsible for the work. Even though we don't have as much personal information about Shakespeare of the kind we should like to have – diaries, letters, account-books – our desire to know as much as possible remains unabated. That is where the art of Shakespearian biography commences.[22]
>
> (Paul Edmondson and Stanley Wells)

Authorship has been the main focus of computational stylistics in studies of early modern drama to date. Since readers, playgoers, scholars, actors, and directors want to know who wrote the plays or parts of plays, it is unsurprising that new tools to classify texts have been applied first to questions of authorship. The findings have sometimes been controversial, but it is hard to imagine any new attribution now being made – or being persuasive – based entirely on a reader's sense of authorial affinities without any support from quantitative study. In 1968 Ernst Gombrich argued, 'For the time being, at any rate, the intuitive grasp of underlying *Gestalten* that makes the connoisseur is still far ahead of morphological analysis of style in terms of enumerable features' in the attribution of 'a painting, a piece of music, or a page of prose', but the balance would now seem to be

---

[22] Paul Edmondson and Stanley Wells, *Shakespeare Bites Back: Not So Anonymous* (Stratford-upon-Avon: Shakespeare Birthday Trust, 2011), 37.

reversed.[23] For the definition of authorial canons, the methods have become mainstream. *The New Oxford Shakespeare* (2016) is the first edition of the complete works to be predicated on a series of new inclusions and exclusions determined by quantitative study.

One side effect of the intense effort which has gone into specific, hotly contested questions of attribution is the discovery that authorial style is detectable in texts to a degree which surprises even traditional author-centred scholars. Such findings contradict many of the pronouncements of critics who prefer to see dispersed agency – through collaborative writing, or the influence of theatre or printing house participants in the process of transmission – as trumping the importance of the author.[24]

In our chapters, we take advantage of authorship work on particular questions and of the methods that have been developed and tested there. We also rely on the broader discovery about the pervasive authorial factor in linguistic style. We look beyond this powerful author-effect to other patterns in the plays, but the very strength of this effect means that we must always take it into account. We might notice a pattern of differentiation between a group of comedies and a group of tragedies, for instance, but if the majority of the comedies are by Jonson, and a majority of the tragedies by Shakespeare, then it is likely – based on the knowledge we have now accumulated – that the differences have more to do with authors than with genres. If we want to understand the nature and degree of important non-authorial considerations such as genre and era, then we must ensure that we account for any authorial effects. One simple way to do this is to observe the part played by a given grouping within the work of one author, or to make sure any one author does not dominate the sub-corpora we use for the tests.

Authorship is the prime example of a categorical question that is more important than we usually acknowledge. So much of our critical machinery will only function with a secure attribution, as the comparative neglect of anonymous and putatively collaborative works shows.[25] This is most obvious with a canonical writer: a bibliometric study would show that *A Funeral Elegy* was the object of extensive critical attention when it was (briefly) accepted as Shakespeare's, but now that it has been shown to belong to the

[23] Gombrich, 'Style', 360.
[24] Hugh Craig, 'Style, Statistics, and New Models of Authorship', *Early Modern Literary Studies* 15.1 (2009–10), 1–42; and Gabriel Egan, 'What Is Not Collaborative about Early Modern Drama in Performance and Print?', *Shakespeare Survey* 67 (2014), 18–28.
[25] For a recent survey of the editorial treatment of anonymous and collaborative plays, see Brett D. Hirsch, 'Moving Targets: Constructing Canons, 2013–2014', *Early Theatre* 18.1 (2015), 115–32.

canon of John Ford it has returned to the pack as just another early modern elegy of an obscure country squire.[26] As Shakespeare collaborations
become clearer following quantitative study, and the attribution of sections
to Shakespeare, Christopher Marlowe, Thomas Middleton, George Peele,
George Wilkins, and others, they enable sharper and better-founded analysis and resolve long-standing puzzles. Questions of authorship are matters
of classification and, in the absence of clinching documentary evidence,
best resolved through the objective numerical analysis of style.

Chronology is another crucial form of classification enabling literary
study not only to clarify individual literary careers and trajectories, but
also to estimate the direction of influence, to chart movements and inno-
vations, and to see works in synchronic contexts. Anywhere there is a firm
classification, such as genre, mode, gender of author, gender of character,
or theatrical company of first production, quantitative analysis has a role
in determining the soundness or otherwise of the classification and, thus
in turn, a role in enabling interpretation.

Where our questions relate to readily defined classes of literary works (or
parts of them), the usefulness of computational stylistics is easy to see. We
might wonder if two classes, readily defined by objective criteria, are in fact
different in style from each other, such as between the generic categories of
'tragedy' and 'comedy'. If the ascription of a given sample to one class or
another is disputed, we can seek in an objective way to distinguish between
the two classes and apply this to the disputed work. In their quantitative
analysis of Shakespeare's language classified by genre, for example, Jonathan
Hope and Michael Witmore provide linguistic confirmation of Susan Snyder's earlier argument – based on qualitative readings of the plays – that a
comic structure or 'matrix' underlies Shakespeare's tragedies, observing that
Othello shares more stylistic affinities with Shakespeare's comedies than his
other tragedies.[27]

The usefulness of quantitative methods in description is less obvious
than for classification, but we believe it is considerable. This is the province
of stylistics – the analysis of style on the basis of objectively observed

---

[26] On the controversy surrounding the Shakespearean attribution, see the individual essays by Richard Abrams, Stephen Booth, Katherine Duncan-Jones, Donald Foster, Ian Lancashire, and Stanley Wells in *Shakespeare Studies* 25 (1997), as well as Foster's essay and the rejoinders to it in *PMLA* 111.5 (1996) and (with Charles W. Hieatt et al.) 112.3 (1997). For a persuasive attribution to Ford, see G. D. Monsarrat, 'A Funeral Elegy: Ford, W. S., and Shakespeare', *Review of English Studies* 53.210 (2002), 186–203.

[27] Jonathan Hope and Michael Witmore, 'The Hundredth Psalm to the Tune of "Green Sleeves": Digital Approaches to Shakespeare's Language of Genre', *Shakespeare Quarterly* 61.3 (2010), 357–90; Susan Snyder, *The Comic Matrix of Shakespeare's Tragedies* (Princeton University Press, 1979).

features. Though we do not attempt it here, one aspect of this would be the analysis of authorial characteristics. If authors' styles are indeed distinctive and consistent, so that it is possible to detect the author of a sample of unknown origin with some confidence, then it follows that we should be able to highlight and discuss some differentiating features. Not all the features that serve to distinguish authors will necessarily prove to be stylistically interesting – just as a fingerprint may identify an individual with a high degree of accuracy but tell us nothing about that person's behaviour or predispositions – but it is likely that some of the features will have a literary interest.[28]

John Burrows, Very Common Words, and Principal Components Analysis

Although we use a range of data sources and procedures in this book, we also keep returning to the alliance of counts of very common words on the data side and Principal Components Analysis on the processing side. To put this combination in context – to help in understanding a disciplinary world where it did not yet exist, and thus to see it in perspective as an innovation – it may be helpful to rehearse the story of how the method evolved.

In the early 1970s John Burrows, author of a 1968 book presenting a close reading of the characters and local interactions of *Emma*,[29] developed an interest in the patterns of the use of words that occurred regularly and were relatively inconspicuous but carried ideological freight in the novels of Jane Austen – such words as *elegant* and *nonsense*. However, in 1973 Stuart M. Tave published a book on exactly this topic, *Some Words of Jane Austen*.[30] Burrows decided to look elsewhere, and to examine Austen's use of still more regularly occurring words, such as pronouns and articles. Burrows noted that such words as *we* and *the* varied between Austen's novels in ways that could be related to questions of critical interest, such as their characters' speaking styles.

Such words had been counted before, as in Frederick Mosteller and David L. Wallace's influential authorship attribution study of *The*

---

[28] See Hugh Craig, 'Authorial Attribution and Computational Stylistics: If You Can Tell Authors Apart, Have You Learned Anything about Them?', *Literary and Linguistic Computing* 14.1 (1999), 103–13.

[29] John Burrows, *Jane Austen's 'Emma'* (Sydney University Press, 1968).

[30] Stuart M. Tave, *Some Words of Jane Austen* (University of Chicago Press, 1973).

Federalist Papers (1964),[31] but the laborious nature of counting instances of a word like *the* by hand – there are six instances in the preceding paragraph of this Introduction alone, for instance – restricted its statistical use to a few well-funded studies. In any case, it was assumed that there was little to be learned from these counts of very common words, which mostly have a purely grammatical function and in these cases are known as 'function words'. In Italian they are known as *parole vuote*, that is, 'empty words'. In computer science they appear on most lists of 'stop words', that is, words to be ignored by the software.

Burrows was the first to see the potential of these words for literary analysis. By the 1980s he was well advanced with studies based on writers' use of very common words, and his 1987 book, *Computation into Criticism*, is a programmatic challenge to the orthodoxy about their role in literary meaning. He notes that linguists, concordance-makers, and lexicographers continue to hold that these words are used at stable rates and carry little, if any, stylistic significance. He comments on the generally tacit understanding:

> that, within the verbal universe of any novel, the very common words constitute a largely inert medium while all the real activity emanates from more visible and more energetic bodies. The falsity of any such assumption, the inappropriateness of any such model of a verbal universe, will be established in the course of the following discussion; and the far-reaching consequences that flow from the attempt to find a better model will be seen on every side. The neglected third, two-fifths, or half of our material has light of its own to shed on the meaning of one novel or another; on subtle relationships between narrative and dialogue, character and character; on less direct and less limited comparisons between novels and between novelists; and ultimately on the very processes of reading itself.[32]

With the computer, counting these words is a trivial matter, even in the longest text. They are easy for the machine to recognise, given that in modernised text at least they are separated from their neighbours by spaces or punctuation. Once an electronic text has been created, compiling tables of word frequencies is a simple exercise.

> Computer-based concordances, supported by statistical analysis, now make it possible to enter hitherto inaccessible regions of the language, regions where, to take an extreme case, more than 26,000 instances of 'the' in Jane

---

[31] Frederick Mosteller and David L. Wallace, *Inference and Disputed Authorship: The Federalist Papers* (Reading: Addison-Wesley, 1964).
[32] Burrows, *Computation*, 2.

Austen's novels defy the most accurate memory and the finest powers of dis-
crimination and where there is diversity enough within a single novel to cast
doubt on arguments based on supposedly typical specimens of Jane Austen's
prose.[33]

In Cambridge, on sabbatical leave from his native Australia in 1979–80,
Burrows had discussed his interest in these abundant but unevenly distributed lexical items with the Director of the University of Cambridge
Computer Laboratory, Nicholas (Nick) M. Maclaren. Maclaren suggested
using 'eigen-analysis', a technique for finding underlying patterns in a table
of counts of multiple variables in multiple observations. This procedure
was invented by Karl Pearson at the beginning of the twentieth century
and again (independently) by Harold Hotelling in the 1930s.[34] Hotelling
called it 'Principal Components Analysis' or 'PCA', and this name has been
generally adopted.

PCA is designed to be a way of making a table of multiple observations
for multiple variables comprehensible. If we take the sixty retail and hospi-
tality businesses operating in the central business district of a small city, and
collect statistics about weekly turnover, number of employees, borrowings
from banks, number of sales per day, average dollar value of a sale, ratio
of cash to credit sales, and number of wholesalers with a transaction every
month, we have a table of seven columns for the measures and sixty rows
for the businesses. A PCA will find the most important underlying factor
in clustering and separating the businesses. This might turn out to be low-
price, high-sales businesses like newsagents, cafes, and corner shops versus high-price, low-sales businesses like restaurants and whitegoods retail-
ers. Having accounted for most of the (otherwise bewildering) differences
between the businesses, the process then looks for a second independent
factor to help explain those differences not accounted by the first – which,
in this example, might turn out to be the difference between businesses
located uptown and businesses downtown. The analysis has provided a way
to see some simple but strong patterns in what is initially a confusing mass
of data.

In his book Burrows presents numerous striking examples of the fruit-
fulness of the analysis of very common words by PCA and other simpler
methods. The texts, often divided into segments, are mapped on charts
according to their scores on the principal components, reflecting each text

---

[33] Burrows, *Computation*, 3.
[34] Karl Pearson, 'On Lines and Planes of Closest Fit to Systems of Points in Space', *Philosophical Magazine* 2.6 (1901), 559–72; and Harold Hotelling, 'Analysis of a Complex of Statistical Variables into Principal Components', *Journal of Educational Psychology* 24.6 (1933), 417–41.

or segment's use of the chosen words and the weightings of those words. A PCA chart of the stages of Anne Elliot's dialogue and reported thoughts in *Persuasion* shows that the segments vary only a little in the early phases of the novel, in line with her confinement in what Mary Lascelles calls 'the prison that Sir Walter and Elizabeth have made of Kellynch'.[35] However, Burrows notes,

> As the gates of the prison begin to yield, the reader can see more room for hope than Anne has cause to do. But the movement from A4 to A6 [the fourth to the sixth of eight segments of her *spoken dialogue*] shows that she becomes free, at least, to talk more freely. For her as for Fanny, the last two phases show a more settled speech-idiolect. But her thinking changes still. Notwithstanding small fluctuations as her hopes of Wentworth rise and fall, her thought-idiolect increasingly approximates to the rhythms of speech. In a6 and a8 [the sixth and eighth of eight segments of her *reported thought*] especially, the accents of the inner voice are scarcely more stiff and formal than her speech-idiolect had been at the beginning. This is a mood of 'smiles reined in and spirits dancing in private rapture' (p. 240), a mood more exquisitely portrayed in its main lines and more fully realized in the very texture of Jane Austen's language than any of the moods that resemble it in the earlier novels.[36]

Burrows was careful to distinguish between the facts of numerical counts and the interpretations which follow. An early chapter in his book canvasses many instances of characters' use of the first-person plural pronouns, with detailed discussion of the local contexts. He notes that:

> The gulf in comparative incidence between the opposite extremities of the scale that underlies the foregoing discussion is a matter of demonstrable fact, to which we shall return. The differences between the actual pronoun idioms of the various characters lie in the more open ground of literary inference and interpretation. So far as literary interpretation is well founded, they can be seen as illuminating the 'personality' and 'situation' of each character that has been discussed. This, obviously, is not to suggest that my particular interpretations have any claim to be definitive. It is rather to insist that, even with such inconspicuous words as 'we', 'our', and 'us', worthwhile interpretative possibilities arise and that, in the further matter of literary evaluation, Jane Austen's long-standing reputation for exactitude and for 'density of texture' is given fresh support.[37]

---

[35] Mary Lascelles, *Jane Austen and Her Art* (Oxford: Clarendon Press, 1939), 181.

[36] Burrows, *Computation*, 211, referring to the edition of *Persuasion* in R. W. Chapman (ed.), *Jane Austen's Six Novels*, 5 vols., 3rd illus. edn (Oxford University Press, 1932–5).

[37] Burrows, *Computation*, 28.

Burrows' first experiments were with a form of PCA that started by cor-relating observations (businesses in our example). With words data – with frequencies declining very rapidly from the commonest, like *the* and *and*, to the less common words whose counts will be much lower – this means that the first principal component is dominant, accounting for most of the variation, and is largely a measure of how closely each text follows the average profile for word counts. A friend, the computer scientist Profes-sor Christopher (Chris) Wallace, later suggested that Burrows should use the correlation PCA. This starts by correlating the variables – that is, it first establishes how similar the frequency-patterns for different words are to one another – and then finds the principal components of the result-ing table of correlations. Each of the chosen word-variables therefore plays an equal part in the analysis, regardless of its comparative abundance or scarcity in the texts.

PCA gave Burrows access to the interactions of frequencies of very com-mon words in the texts. Some of these appear regularly together, such as *thou* and *thee* in early modern English. If the word *thou* appears regularly in a given set of texts, then *thee* is likely to appear too. Some less obvious pairings emerge as well. *The* and *of* tend to appear together. Where texts included a lot of nouns with *the* as determiner, the preposition *of* was likely to be common as well, in texts that specify and elaborate. In a set of novels, *the* and *of* could be a useful index, arranging texts from the most descrip-tive, with high scores, to the ones focusing on action, and dialogue, with low scores.

The combination of PCA and very common words was the key method for what came to be known as computational stylistics. It also proved useful in separating authors. In a review of the field in the 1990s, David I. Holmes described it as the 'standard first port-of-call' in quantitative authorship attribution.[38]

Function Word Frequencies and Style

At the core of computational stylistics as Burrows developed it is the claim that frequencies of the very common words are a useful index of style. These words, which tend to be function words, have advantages operationally. They are easy to count and appear regularly, so that they give access to deep-seated steady variation. In sheer bulk they account for a good chunk

---

[38] David I. Holmes, 'The Evolution of Stylometry in Humanities Scholarship', *Literary and Linguistic Computing* 13.3 (1998), 114.

of all the words in a text: the 221 function word forms (or 'types') on our usual list are approximately 58 per cent of all the word tokens in a 251-play dataset.[39] Lexical words bear more obvious meaning, and are much more likely to be noticed by a reader, but they appear sporadically and as the result of contingencies like topic and setting, and so are harder to link to a persisting and large-scale style. To pursue them runs the risk of taking too much account of the accidental and local. In this vein T. S. Eliot remarked that 'Comparison and analysis are the chief tools of the critic', tools 'to be handled with care, and not employed in an inquiry into the number of times giraffes are mentioned in the English novel'.[40]

As already noted, the persistence and commonness of function words means that they normally go unnoticed. Yet changes in frequencies of these words generally signal a significant change in construction or orientation. Thus the argument sometimes made that frequency does not mean salience – that an exceptional, foregrounded use of a linguistic item may have a larger effect of a series of repetitions – has less force with function words. Burrows offers some examples from the language of Jane Austen:

> However narrow the linguistic function of words like these, it is evident that if, as is indeed the case, disparities like these are typical of the language of Jane Austen's major characters, the effects must colour every speech they make and leave some impression in the minds of her readers. Even for the most attentive novel-reader, such an impression need not – and seldom does? – consist in a definite recognition that someone is peculiarly given, for example, to the use of 'I' and 'not' and has little recourse to 'the' or 'of'. It would ordinarily consist in an awareness, however inarticulate, of the larger implications – grammatical, semantic, psychological, social – that are marked by such peculiarities. Statistical analysis of the peculiarities of incidence makes it possible to approach the whole penumbra of 'meaning' in a new and fruitful way.[41]

English is what linguists call an 'analytic language', in that its grammatical relationships are mostly conveyed by function words rather than, as in so-called 'synthetic languages', being conveyed by lexical words inflected to indicate case, gender, tense, mood, and so on. This aspect has been underlined by cognitive grammar. The schema 'container' is signified by

---

[39] The 221 function words are listed in Appendix E. The terms 'type' and 'token' are used to differentiate between the word as an abstract entity and the concrete, particular instances of that word. Thus understood, the phrase 'to be or not to be' contains four types (*to, be, or, not*) and six tokens (because there are two instances of the types *to* and *be*).

[40] T. S. Eliot, 'The Function of Criticism' (1923), in *Selected Essays*, 2nd edn (London: Faber and Faber, 1932), 32–3.

[41] Burrows, *Computation*, 4.

the function word *in* in the prepositional phrase 'in the room'.[42] Potential versus actual is signified in English by the modal verbs *may* and *might*. As easy as these so-called 'small words' are for readers to ignore, their power to shape meaning has been demonstrated in recent years by Lynne Magnusson and Sylvia Adamson.[43]

The English pronoun system encodes number (*he* versus *they*), case (*he* versus *him*), person (*he* versus *I*), and intimacy (*thou* versus *you*), not systematically, but strongly. *Her* can be possessive or objective, and *you* can be singular or plural, but otherwise there is generally a pronoun form for each of the primary syntactic categories. Propositional verbs ('give up'), past and present modal forms (*are* versus *were*), and a complex article system (*the, a, an, some,* zero article [i.e., omitting the article entirely], and so forth) all contribute to the set of readily countable and meaning-heavy function words. In computer-aided analysis, the 'tagging' or 'marking up' of homograph forms – such as *to* as in 'to Sydney' and *to* as in 'to act', *her* as in 'her hand' and as in 'she promised her', and the three forms of *that* in 'he was able to tell her that that key was the one that opened the second box' – to formalise these distinctions further enhances the machine-readability of function words.

It is not immediately obvious that the frequencies of function words – simply counting occurrences, taking no account of the sequences in which they are placed – could serve to differentiate styles. Yet because of their structural roles in sentences they do bear traces of patterns of construction. Franco Moretti, for instance, found that titles of anti-Jacobin novels began with definite articles – *The Democrat, The Infidel Father* – far more often than those of New Woman novels, which favoured titles beginning with indefinite articles – *A Bluestocking, A Hard Woman,* and so on. Moretti argues that this can be explained by the different structural uses of the articles. The definite article is used with a known entity, fitting the anti-Jacobin defence of the status quo; the indefinite article, which typically introduces something new, serves the New Woman agenda of support for change.

> So: *A Girton Girl, A Hard Woman, A Mummer's Wife, A Domestic Experiment, A Daughter of Today, A Semi-detached Marriage*: what the article says

[42] Louisa Connors, 'Computational Stylistics, Cognitive Grammar, and *The Tragedy of Mariam: Combining Formal and Contextual Approaches in a Computational Study of Early Modern Tragedy*', Ph.D. thesis (University of Newcastle, 2013), 86–90.

[43] Sylvia Adamson, 'Understanding Shakespeare's Grammar: Studies in Small Words', in Sylvia Adamson, Lynette Hunter, Lynne Magnusson, Anne Thompson and Katie Wales (eds.), *Reading Shakespeare's Dramatic Language: A Guide*, (London: Arden Shakespeare, 2001), 210–36; and Lynne Magnusson, 'A Play of Modals: Grammar and Potential Action in Early Shakespeare', *Shakespeare Survey* 62 (2009), 69–80.

is that we are encountering all these figures *for the first time*; we think we know what daughters and wives are, but we actually don't, and must understand them afresh. The article announces the novel as a challenge to received knowledge. And instead, the democrat, the Parisian, the infidel father . . . We know these people! Anti-Jacobin titles don't want to change received ideas, they want to *use* them: the French Revolution has multiplied your enemies – beware.[44]

MacDonald P. Jackson provides another example of the way the frequencies of function words reflect different styles:

Consider two differently constructed sentences that convey the same information. Here is the first: 'As soon as we guests had finished dinner, we said goodbye to our kind hosts and drove to the theatre, where we saw a performance of *Twelfth Night*, which we greatly enjoyed.' And here is the second: 'Straight after dinner, we guests, saying goodbye to our kind hosts, drove to the theatre and saw a most enjoyable performance of *Twelfth Night*.' The two sentences each contain two examples of 'to' and one of 'a', 'and', 'of', 'our', and 'the'. But the first has three more instances of 'we' than the second, and also contains 'as' (twice), 'had', 'where', and 'which', none of which are found in the second sentence, which has instances of 'after' and 'most', both absent from the first. The two types of sentence construction entail the use of different function words. The first sentence uses a relative clause, introduced by 'which', whereas the second does not. The first sentence uses the conjunction 'and' to link co-ordinate clauses 'we said . . . and drove', whereas the second modifies 'we guests' by using the present participle 'saying'.[45]

The gist of Jackson's two invented sentences is the same, but they are constructed differently, and we can hazard a stylistic interpretation. The first sentence is more pedantic and more focalised through *we*, while the second follows a less predictable sequence and moves more decisively to the performance of the play as its destination. Jackson tallies the presence and absence of the various function words in the two constructions and their frequencies to illustrate the basis for the functioning of a typical computational-stylistics analysis, which happens in reverse: there we start with the patterns in the function word frequencies, and infer from them something of the style of the samples.

Quantitative Work on Style in Early Modern English Drama

Whatever the appeal of this and other computational-stylistic methods, the number of quantitative stylistic studies within the field of the present

[44] Franco Moretti, 'Style, inc. Reflections on Seven Thousand Titles (British Novels, 1740–1850)', *Critical Inquiry* 36.1 (2009), 154–6.
[45] MacDonald P. Jackson, *Determining the Shakespeare Canon: 'Arden of Faversham' and 'A Lover's Complaint'* (Oxford University Press, 2014), 42.

book – that is, early modern English drama – has been small, if strictly author-attribution work is excluded. A number of scholars have studied statistical patterns in dramatic verse.[46] Dolores M. Burton compared the grammatical styles of two Shakespeare plays.[47] Some individual function words have been studied in Shakespeare and elsewhere.[48] Two studies have challenged the traditional belief that Shakespeare's vocabulary was exceptionally large.[49] There is a corpus-based study of the rhetoric of *Hamlet*,[50] as well as studies of the interactions in the first scene of *King Lear* and of phrasal repetends in *Troilus and Cressida*.[51] Staying with Shakespeare, but ranging more widely across the canon, scholars have applied computational methods to analyse genre in Shakespeare,[52] to his late style,[53] to his characterisation,[54] and to the varying length of speeches in the plays.[55] There is quantitative work on the distribution of props in Shakespeare and

[46] Representative examples include Philip W. Timberlake, *The Feminine Ending in English Blank Verse* (Menasha: George Banta, 1931); Ants Oras, *Pause Patterns in Elizabethan and Jacobean Drama: An Experiment in Prosody* (Gainesville: University of Florida Press, 1960); Marina Tarlinskaja, *Shakespeare and the Versification of English Drama, 1561–1642* (Farnham: Ashgate, 2014); and Douglas Bruster and Geneviève Smith, 'A New Chronology for Shakespeare's Plays', *Digital Scholarship in the Humanities* 31.2 (2016), 301–20.

[47] Dolores M. Burton, *Shakespeare's Grammatical Style: A Computer-Assisted Analysis of 'Richard II' and 'Antony and Cleopatra'* (Austin: University of Texas Press, 1973).

[48] For example, Ulrich Busse, *Linguistic Variation in the Shakespeare Corpus: Morpho-Syntactic Variability of Second Person Pronouns* (Amsterdam: John Benjamins, 2002); and Hugh Craig, 'Plural Pronouns in Roman Plays by Shakespeare and Jonson', *Literary and Linguistic Computing* 6 (1991), 180–6, 'Grammatical Modality in English Plays from the 1580s to the 1640s', *English Literary Renaissance* 30.1 (2000), 32–54, and '*A* and *an* in English Plays, 1580–1639', *Texas Studies in Literature and Language* 53.3 (2011), 273–93.

[49] Hugh Craig, 'Shakespeare's Vocabulary: Myth and Reality', *Shakespeare Quarterly* 62.1 (2011), 53–74; Ward E. Y. Elliott and Robert J. Valenza, 'Shakespeare's Vocabulary: Did It Dwarf All Others?' in Mireille Ravassat and Jonathan Culpeper (eds.), *Stylistics and Shakespeare's Language: Transdisciplinary Approaches* (London: Continuum, 2011), 34–57.

[50] Thomas Anderson and Scott Crossley, '"Rue with a Difference": A Computational Stylistic Analysis of the Rhetoric of Suicide in *Hamlet*', in Mireille Ravassat and Jonathan Culpeper (eds.), *Stylistics and Shakespeare's Language: Transdisciplinary Approaches* (London: Continuum, 2011), 192–214.

[51] Dawn Archer and Derek Bousfield, '"See Better, Lear?" See Lear Better! A Corpus-Based Pragma-Stylistic Investigation of Shakespeare's *King Lear*', in Dan McIntyre and Beatrix Busse (eds.), *Language and Style* (Basingstoke: Palgrave, 2010), 183–203; Ian Lancashire, 'Probing Shakespeare's Idiolect in *Troilus and Cressida*, 1.3.1–29', *University of Toronto Quarterly* 68 (1999), 728–67.

[52] Hope and Witmore, 'The Hundredth Psalm'.

[53] Michael Witmore and Jonathan Hope, 'Shakespeare by the Numbers: On the Linguistic Texture of the Late Plays', in Subha Mukherji and Raphael Lyne (eds.), *Early Modern Tragicomedy* (Woodbridge: Boydell and Brewer, 2007), 133–53.

[54] Hugh Craig, '"Speak, That I May See Thee": Shakespeare Characters and Common Words', *Shakespeare Survey* 61 (2008), 281–8; Jonathan Culpeper, 'Keywords and Characterization: An Analysis of Six Characters in *Romeo and Juliet*', in David L. Hoover, Jonathan Culpeper, and Kieran O'Halloran (eds.), *Digital Literary Studies: Corpus Approaches to Poetry, Prose and Drama* (New York: Routledge, 2014), 9–34.

[55] Hartmut Ilsemann, 'More Statistical Observations on Speech-Lengths in Shakespeare's Plays', *Literary and Linguistic Computing* 23.4 (2008), 397–407.

the early modern drama,[56] and one attempt to apply computational methods to problems in the transmission of play-texts.[57]

Challenges to Stylistics

One fundamental objection to stylistics is based on the conviction that literature is always more than the sum of its constituent parts – that numerical methods, which are inevitably reductionist, can offer nothing useful for literary analysis.[58] Yet style does have a numerical aspect, and stylistics is founded on this truth. Each time a word is used, its meaning is created afresh, and is thus unique, yet it is also recognisably an instance of that word, a token of that word type. The quantitative analysis of style depends by definition on defining a language feature – at the simplest level, a word type – and then counting instances of that feature as if they were all the same. When the features are being used for a classifier this practice is easy to defend. If the feature-counts in whatever combination do serve to separate known members of the classes introduced as test samples, then the procedure is validated and scepticism about the categories is quietened.

Each time Prospero addresses Miranda, Caliban, Ariel, and Fernando as 'thou', this pronoun has a peculiar inflection more or less consciously apparent to audiences and readers, but it is also a choice within a system of pronoun types – most immediately, a choice between 'thou' and 'you' forms[59] – and therefore susceptible of a wider analysis in the context of other characters, plays, and canons. This is not the realm of classification but of a continuously varying spectrum of frequency, which can take its part in a network of variation with other words and other language features. How much such patterns illuminate literary questions is always a matter of debate. Language provides a rich source for statistics, as words are repeated or not, appear often or rarely near each other, and so on, but this abundance is no guarantee of interest. Independent of the methods employed, it is up to the literary critic to 'know when to compare and when to analyze',[60]

[56] Frances Teague, *Shakespeare's Speaking Properties* (Cranbury: Associated University Presses, 1991); Douglas Bruster, 'The Dramatic Life of Objects in the Early Modern English Theater', in Jonathan Gil Harris and Natasha Korda (eds.), *Staged Properties in Early Modern English Drama* (Cambridge University Press, 2002), 67–96.

[57] Lene B. Petersen, *Shakespeare's Errant Texts: Textual Form and Linguistic Style in Shakespearean 'Bad' Quartos and Co-Authored Plays* (Cambridge University Press, 2010).

[58] See de Man, 'Literary History', and Willie van Peer, 'Quantitative Studies of Literature: A Critique and an Outlook', *Computers and the Humanities* 23.4–5 (1989), 301–7.

[59] See Roger Brown and Albert Gilman, 'The Pronouns of Power and Solidarity', in Thomas A. Sebeok (ed.), *Style in Language* (Cambridge, MA: MIT Press, 1960), 253–76.

[60] Eliot, 'The Function of Criticism', 33.

guided by the accumulated understanding of the discipline in determining which among the plethora of possibilities is worthy of attention.

Another version of this objection is that features in literary study cannot be counted because meaning is constructed by the reader: instances of a given word on a page may appear to be stable or commensurate, the argument goes, but in fact they are 'relational', and counting them as if they were equivalent is misleading.[61] This is an important objection to consider. If sustained, it would invalidate all quantitative stylistics at a stroke. Indeed, Stanley Fish has repeatedly denounced stylistics in these terms since the 1970s.[62] As a blanket objection it is probably not sustainable, since to do so would rule out statistics in general – that is, any attempt to encapsulate events through counting. It is always possible to see individual variations in the instances accumulated, but there are important benefits in grouping them together. To sustain the objection, one would have to show that literary data is somehow intrinsically impossible to put into categories. This is, in essence, Fish's approach. One might respond that some features of literary data can be classified in categories, and some cannot. It is easy to think of cases in literary study where counting could be done in invalid categories. For example, counting instances of words with unrelated senses like *spring* or *lead*, or counting cases where a character waves a hand or any other action for which there are multiple and differing contexts and intentions. Since a sword and a pen have different associations in the literatures of various periods, counting instances and comparing the numbers indiscriminately would be of limited worth. On the other hand, one might defend counting instances of the word *all* on the grounds that each shares enough of a semantics to make them commensurate.

Burrows had already tackled this question in *Computation into Criticism*. He considers the objection that words 'mean nothing' if taken out of context:

> In answer to such an objection, a traditional grammarian would maintain that 'we', like other words, should be regarded as having incipient meaning, in a sort of Aristotelian potentiality, not realized until it is set in context. More recent authorities, following Roman Jakobson, would maintain that, for any speaker of English, 'we' bears a certain 'context' even before

[61] John Frow, *Genre* (New York: Routledge, 2006), 125. See also Tony Bennett, 'Counting and Seeing the Social Action of Literary Form: Franco Moretti and the Sociology of Literature', *Cultural Sociology* 3.2 (2009), 277–97.

[62] Fish, 'What Is Stylistics'; and, 'What Is Stylistics and Why Are They Saying Such Terrible Things about It? Part II', in *Is There a Text in This Class?* (Cambridge, MA: Harvard University Press, 1980), 246–67.

it is brought into use. It is among those words that can open a sentence. It is among those words that can stand as subject to a verb. It is among those words that allude to more than one referent (the speaker being among them) without actually naming those referents. Already it is distinct from 'John', 'I', 'you', and 'us' – to say nothing of 'although' and 'purple': for none of these words conforms even to this rudimentary set of constraints on meaning . . . As soon as it is mentioned, even if it is the opening word of a fresh discourse, 'we' takes on a more immediate meaning by identifying its referents: the bases of identification, not always unambiguous at first, are likely to be predominantly grammatical when other utterances have led on to the 'we', predominantly social when it initiates a fresh discourse. On either traditional or more recent doctrine, 'we', taken alone, is not devoid of meaning.[63]

Literary language, together with the paratextual materials of literary works, provides a wide range of features to count, and thus choices must be made. The choice must then influence results, and critics of quantitative work have argued that this undermines any claims to objectivity.[64] This is a fundamental critique of *any* quantitative study beyond the hard sciences, whether it is in ecology, sociology, or psychology. It is easy to show that there are cases where the choice of features does not determine the results, so there can be surprises and a definite gain in knowledge. If we were to ask, for instance, 'Do women write differently from men?', we have a way of validating the choice of features. If the pattern of use of a given feature shows a significant difference in balanced and commensurate sets of samples of the writing of women and the writing of men, then it does not matter how the unit was chosen. Here we have an external basis on which to discard some features and accept others: the difference between two objectively based classes.

There is a claim that Shakespeare's later verse is more informal and conversational than his earlier efforts. To investigate this claim, we might choose a group of units that intuitively seem to mark informality in verse (e.g. enjambment, contractions, hypermetric syllables, and second-person pronouns). We could then check this intuition by counting these features in groups of samples that are by consensus formal or informal. If we found that the first three are markedly and consistently more common in informal samples, but the last occurs about as often in both, we could count instances of the first three in early and late Shakespeare. The final stage would be to combine the three scores mathematically, say, by

---

[63] Burrows, *Computation*, 28–9.
[64] See, for example, Bennett, 'Counting and Seeing', esp. 290–1.

adding them together, to give a single value. If this separated later Shake-speare segments from earlier ones, we could show the extent of the difference between the two sets, as well as confirm that there is a genuine difference.

We can also proceed inductively. We look at all the word types used in *Jane Eyre* and a rewriting of this novel for late twentieth-century young adult audiences and determine which are used at significantly different rates between the two novels. The original set of features – the word types – has been our choice, but the selection within them is directed by patterns in the data. Then there are cases of classification, such as by author and by date. We can seek markers of the classes, check them with known members of the classes, and then find the patterns for the chosen markers in disputed cases. We have an objective way of validating the choice of features, so we do not care much about where they came from.

Computational stylistics generally counts the frequencies of particular words, which are as close as possible to a 'given'. Nevertheless, other linguistic features could be counted: the letters of which words are composed, for example, or punctuation; combinations of words; marked-up features, such as images and figures of speech, and so on.

Given 'world enough and time', quantitative analysis could perhaps proceed without having to select features to count and discard others. Even so, some features are not susceptible to counting, and thus the results can be characterised as representative but not universal. Stylistics captures significant aspects of style, but not the totality. Any findings are relative to the features chosen rather than absolute. In computational stylistics, practitioners sometimes speak of a style, referring to collective patterns of particular features. It is important to remember that literary style in the general sense encompasses so much more than that. If we make a profile of the usage of the 100 most common words, it may be revealing, but only in specific ways, and it certainly does not capture everything that might be included under 'style'.

The Variability and Predictability of Literary Language

Commentators on literary language, as on all language, may choose to focus either on the variability of language or its predictability. There is a premium on creativity in language. Even in commonplace exchanges we expect variation, as a guarantee of spontaneity and full and conscious investment in the present. Readers of literary texts expect to be surprised occasionally, even if against a background of probability.

Yet language is also a shared knowledge, so variation must be limited if it is to function as communication. Beyond that, economy of effort demands that most of what we read or hear must be already familiar. As soon as we recognise that a character is a Petrarchan lover, a large set of associations is invoked and can be used to create effects of familiarity or reversal. We are listening to a friend tell a story about what happened yesterday, but we are also listening for the familiar idiosyncratic characteristics of the speaker to be rehearsed and responding to a well-established framework of expectations which make the story work through surprise, amusement, or sympathy.

The language of literary texts is endlessly creative but also manifests some regularities, so that it is predictable in relation to some categories such as author, genre, period, mode, and so on. Each time an individual writer at a certain moment takes up a pen to write in a certain familiar genre, he or she is free to put old or new ideas in old or new ways, but also cannot help writing as that person at that time in that genre. It is impossible to predict with absolute precision what the resulting writing will be, but it is possible to formulate some ranges beyond which it is unlikely to go, and retrospectively, given an already written sample of unknown author, genre, date, and so on, these constraints allow the observer to place the sample with a good degree of reliability within some broad categories.

This balance of predictability and unstructured fluctuation puts literary language into the category of a 'stochastic' system, from the Greek στόχος, 'aim'. Some broad directions or regularities are evident, while each component step cannot be precisely predicted. The content of a sentence spoken in a play is certainly not precisely predictable – language is not a deterministic system – but those contents do take part in a pattern of regularity that constrains variation. The same can be said of many aspects of human activity. No one murder is entirely predictable, and citizens exercise free will, but the number of murders in a given large city in a year can be predicted with impressive accuracy.[65]

Immanuel Kant had already grasped this fundamental insight of statistics in the eighteenth century. In his 'Idea for a Universal History' (1784), Kant allies it to a universal human nature – which we might cavil with – but the perception that a change of scale may reveal supervening patterns where close observation reveals only unfettered individual choice remains applicable:

> we know that history, simply by taking its station at a distance and contemplating the agency of the human will upon a large scale, aims at unfolding

---

[65] Ian Hacking, *The Taming of Chance* (Cambridge University Press, 1990), 41.

to our view a regular stream of tendency in the great succession of events;
so that the very same course of incidents, which taken separately and individually would have seemed perplexed, incoherent, and lawless, yet viewed
in their connexion and as the actions of the human *species* and not of independent beings, never fail to discover a steady and continuous though slow
development of certain great predispositions in our nature. Thus for instance
deaths, births, and marriages, considering how much they are separately
dependent on the freedom of the human will, should seem to be subject
to no law according to which any calculation could be made beforehand
of their amount: and yet the yearly registers of these events in great countries prove that they go on with as much conformity to the laws of nature
as the oscillations of the weather: these again are events which in detail are
so far irregular that we cannot predict them individually; and yet taken as a
whole series we find that they never fail to support the growth of plants –
the currents of rivers – and other arrangements of nature in a uniform and
uninterrupted course.[66]

Here the large-scale flow of history makes a neat parallel with Puttenham's
vision of style as a quality only apparent over the full sweep of a literary
work. Probability emerged as the key concept in the unfolding of this principle of apparently freely fluctuating local events and larger regularities in
the decades following Kant's observation, and came to dominate physics as
well as sociology by the first half of the twentieth century. Newton's laws
of motion, articulated in the late seventeenth century, were strictly causal
and had no need of probability: action determined reaction and could be
predicted by an equation. By contrast, James Clerk Maxwell's nineteenth-
century observations on the motion of molecules depended on patterns and
accumulations: no individual movement is predictable, but the combined
effect is (within a limited range of fluctuation).

It was not until well into the nineteenth century that measurement was
embraced as a core aspect of the natural sciences, and this paved the way for
the view that in the natural and human worlds 'laws of chance' provided a
better explanation for events than 'strictly causal laws' – that is, 'equations
with constant numbers in them'.[67] The fundamental discovery of computational stylistics as developed by John Burrows is that literary language,
too, is stochastic.[68]

---

[66] Immanuel Kant, 'Idee zu einer allgemeinen Geschichte in weltbürgerlicher Absicht', trans. Thomas
de Quincy, 'Idea of a Universal History on a Cosmo-Political Plan', *The London Magazine* Oct.
1824, 385–93 (385).
[67] Hacking, *Taming of Chance*, 5, 1, 63.
[68] Willard McCarty, 'Getting There from Here: Remembering the Future of Digital Humanities',
Literary and Linguistic Computing 29.3 (2014), 283–306, esp. 289.

Language is a creative human production, and from one perspective a corpus – such as a collection of the dialogue of early modern plays – is best seen as flux, wildly gyrating cross-currents, the competing, endlessly inventive voices of thousands of characters from tavern hostesses to duchesses and from base villains to stout heroes. Yet there are patterns that emerge from the flux, regularities in categories of plays and scenes and characters. Along with probabilistic thinking, philosophical pragmatism is one way to conceptualise this relationship of chaos and pattern. In Lars Engle's words, pragmatism suggests that 'strata of stable contingency underlie and shape the liquid flow of experience and the volatility of thought'.[69] Frank Lloyd Wright's Imperial Hotel in Tokyo was built on a subsoil of mud in an earthquake-prone location, but achieved stability by having the building rest on concrete rafts floating in the mud and allowing independent movement.[70] In the same way, numerical analysis allows us to see that in the flux of language there are continuities and predictable patterns, by no means absolute, but resiliently present nevertheless.

The statistical findings in this book are themselves a challenging mixture of certainty and ambiguity. At the level of numbers there is certainty, with some caveats. For example, in the first 1,000 running words of *Hamlet* there is an exact number of instances of the word *the*, provided we specify one particular version of the play and some rules, such as that 'th'end' contractions are regularised to 'the end' and 'th'art' contractions are regularised to 'thou art', so that one yields an instance of *the* and the other does not.

At a second level of processing we might compare the counts for *the* or some other word for 10 Shakespeare plays with counts in 100 plays we know are not by Shakespeare, in each case converting the counts to a figure for how many instances per 100 words. Perhaps the average Shakespeare score is higher than the average score for the others. We can say with certainty (as long as the caveats about text and modernisation are borne in mind) that this is so, but the question then follows, *is this difference significant?* Are the Shakespeare scores consistently higher than non-Shakespeare ones, or is it more a matter of the occasional extreme raising the average? Do scores fluctuate wildly as a result of local variation in theme or style, so that we cannot rely much on differences across a canon, or are they relatively steady, so that a consistent high or low score demands interpretation? Here statistics can help with measures of difference between two groups of scores, taking into account the degree of difference and the degree of scatter.

---

[69] Lars Engle, *Shakespearean Pragmatism: Market of His Time* (University of Chicago Press, 1993), 37.
[70] Engle, *Shakespearean Pragmatism*, 233 n.27.

Nevertheless, at this point we are well and truly in the domain of relativity and judgement. The statistics can only give a probabilistic finding by telling us that in the universe of similar patterns, this difference will only rarely come about as a chance effect rather than a true underlying contrast. We get an estimate along a spectrum rather than an absolute 'yes' or 'no'. Then, even when there is a very large difference with a small chance that this is simply random variation, there are more questions: this may be statistically highly significant, but would it mean anything to readers, and how could we explain it in terms of the writer? What about other Shakespeare plays, and other plays by other writers? If we wish to think of this as an immutable Shakespeare characteristic, what about his published poems, and what about the plays and poems he wrote which did not survive, and what about the works he was capable of writing but did not?

This Book

In this book, we offer a series of largely independent treatments of some specific literary-historical questions. After detailing our methods in Chapter 1, we assess how far the medium of verse itself governs style, both in all-verse plays and in plays that mix verse and prose in Chapter 2. Chapter 3 analyses the plays by character, highlighting characters from plays by different authors whose dialogue styles are very similar, suggesting that they occupy the same dramatic niche. In Chapter 4, we move away from dialogue to look at the distribution of props in plays staged in professional theatres between 1590 and 1609. Do authorship and genre have an effect on the use of props? Chapter 5 focuses on chronology and highlights collective change in dramatic dialogue from the 1580s to the 1630s. Chapter 6, like Chapter 2, examines a long-standing belief about broad patterns in style in early modern drama – the claim that repertory companies cultivated a distinctive style, analogous to an authorial style. The final chapter, Chapter 7, moves beyond the immediate period to examine how comedies and tragicomedies of the 1660s compare stylistically with their pre-Restoration counterparts. As a coda, we consider the implications of the findings as a group and sketch promising avenues for future work, and appendices detail the plays, characters, prop-lists, and function words we have used.

CHAPTER I

Methods

In this chapter, we outline our principles of text selection and preparation and then describe the statistical and computational methods we employ throughout this book. Each description includes a working example to demonstrate the method.

Text Selection and Preparation

Appendix A lists the full-text corpus of plays we use throughout this book, along with their authors (where known), dates of first performance, the source text we use, its date of publication, and its genre. We depart from our main bibliographical source, the second edition of the *Annals of English Drama, 975–1700* (hereafter '*Annals*'), only where new research is persuasive and sound, as with the attribution of *Soliman and Perseda* to Thomas Kyd.[1]

To construct our corpus of machine-readable (that is, electronic) texts, we have relied upon base transcriptions from *Literature Online*, checked and corrected against facsimiles from *Early English Books Online*. Since our analysis concerns word frequency and distribution, and not orthography, spelling was regularised and modernised. For the sub-set of plays used in Chapter 6, this was done using VARD, a software tool developed by Alistair Baron for regularising variant spelling in historical corpora.[2] Spelling was

---

[1] Alfred Harbage and Samuel Schoenbaum, *Annals of English Drama, 975–1700*, 2nd edn (Philadelphia: University of Pennsylvania Press, 1964). The authors also consulted available volumes of Martin Wiggins's (in association with Catherine Richardson) *British Drama, 1533–1642: A Catalogue*, 10 vols. (Oxford University Press, 2011–), and Alan B. Farmer and Zachary Lesser (eds.), *DEEP: Database of Early English Playbooks* (2007–). On Kyd's authorship of *Soliman and Perseda*, see Lukas Erne, *Beyond 'The Spanish Tragedy': A Study of the Works of Thomas Kyd* (Manchester University Press, 2001), 157–67, as well as his Introduction to the Malone Society Reprints edition of the play (Thomas Kyd, *Soliman and Perseda*, ed. Lukas Erne (Manchester University Press, 2014)).

[2] See Alistair Baron, Paul Rayson, and Dawn Archer, 'Word Frequency and Key Word Statistics in Historical Corpus Linguistics', *Anglistik* 20.1 (2009), 41–67. While *VARD* can be trained to regularise words algorithmically (i.e., when a given certainty threshold is met) with little to no human supervision or intervention, we instead used *VARD* as a tool to generate a list of variant word types

modernised, but early modern English word forms with present tense *-eth* and *-est* verb-endings (e.g. *liveth* and *farest*) were retained. For the larger sets of plays utilised in Chapters 2 and 7, we regularised spelling using a function in the Intelligent Archive software to combine variant forms with their headwords.[3] In all texts used, function words with homograph forms – such as the noun and verb form of *will* – were tagged to enable distinct counts for each. Appendix E lists the function words used in our analysis. Contractions were also expanded, such that where appropriate 'Ile' was expanded as an instance of *I* and one of *will*$_{verb}$, 'thats' as an instance of *that*$_{demonstrative}$ and one of *is*, and so on.

Unless otherwise specified, texts are segmented into non-overlapping blocks of words – typically 2,000 words – with the last block, if incomplete, discarded to ensure consistent proportions. Proper names, passages in foreign languages, and stage directions are also discarded.[4] It is standard practice in authorship attribution testing to exclude proper names and foreign-language words from the analysis, because these are more closely related to local, play-specific contexts rather than indicative of any consistent stylistic pattern. As for stage directions, Paul Werstine has demonstrated that their status as authorial or non-authorial cannot be assumed, but varies from text to text.[5] We deemed it safer to exclude stage directions as a general rule rather than attempt to assess every instance.

Principal Components Analysis

Principal Components Analysis, or PCA, is a statistical procedure used to explain as much of the total variation in a dataset with as few variables as possible. This is accomplished by condensing multiple variables that are correlated with one another,[6] but largely independent of others, into a

and provide a list of possible modern equivalents. We chose equivalents on a case-by-case basis in light of the context in which the variant spelling forms appeared.

[3] For a fuller discussion of this functionality, see Hugh Craig and R. Whipp, 'Old Spellings, New Methods: Automated Procedures for Indeterminate Linguistic Data', *Literary and Linguistic Computing* 25.1 (2010), 37–52.

[4] That is, single words in languages other than English are included, but passages with two or more consecutive words in a foreign language are excluded.

[5] Paul Werstine, *Early Modern Playhouse Manuscripts and the Editing of Shakespeare* (Cambridge University Press, 2013), esp. 123–30, 157–84.

[6] As mentioned in the previous chapter, the term 'correlation' is used in statistics to describe and measure the strength (low to high) and direction (positive or negative) of the association between two sets of counts. Counts increasing or decreasing in parallel with one another are said to have a positive correlation; by contrast, a negative correlation arises where one count increases while the other decreases (and *vice versa*).

smaller number of composite 'factors'.[7] The strongest factor or 'principal component' is the one that accounts for the largest proportion of the total variance in the data. PCA produces the strongest factor (the 'first principal component'), and then the factor that accounts for the greatest proportion of the remaining variance while also satisfying the condition that it is uncorrelated with the first principal component – a property which we can visualise in a two-dimensional example as being at right-angles to it. Since each principal component only ever represents a proportion of the underlying relationships between the variables, PCA is a data reduction method. The method is also considered 'unsupervised', because it does not rely upon any human pre-processing of the data – the algorithm treats all of the samples equally and indifferently.[8]

A classic example of how PCA is used to reduce the dimensions of multivariate data involves taking a table of the heights and weights of a group of people from which a new composite factor – which we might call 'size' – is generated as the sum of the two variables.[9] 'Size' will represent the patterns of variation within the two original variables with a high proportion of accuracy – shorter people will tend to be lighter, and taller people heavier – but it will not account for all the possible variations in height and weight, since some short people will be heavy and some taller people light. As a principal component, 'size' still captures a basic fact about the relationship between height and weight, one that, in a sense, is the most important. If we add two variables, say, waist size and muscle mass, a new first principal component may be calculated to account for the strongest correlation between all four variables, on the same principle of accounting for most of the variation by weighing the best-coordinated variables similarly. In this scenario, waist size and weight together may represent a proxy for 'obesity', and muscle mass and weight together may represent a proxy for 'muscularity', and so on.

---

[7] Christopher Chatfield and Alexander J. Collins, *Introduction to Multivariate Analysis* (New York: Chapman & Hall, 1980), 57–79; and I. T. Jolliffe, *Principal Component Analysis* (New York: Springer, 1986). For a gentler introduction to the procedure, see Mick Alt, *Exploring Hyperspace: A Non-Mathematical Explanation of Multivariate Analysis* (Maidenhead: McGraw-Hill, 1990), 48–80.

[8] This is not to conflate 'unsupervised' with 'objective', as James E. Dobson rightly cautions in 'Can an Algorithm Be Disturbed?: Machine Learning, Intrinsic Criticism, and the Digital Humanities', *College Literature* 42.4 (2015), 543–64. However principled they may be, the processes of selecting and preparing the underlying corpus (outlined earlier in this chapter) are not free of subjectivity, just as all so-called 'unsupervised' methods contain human elements.

[9] As the name suggests, 'multivariate' data involves two or more variables, as opposed to 'univariate' data, which involves only a single variable.

Table 1.1 *A select corpus of plays*

Author	Play	Date
Lyly, John	*Campaspe*	1583
Lyly, John	*Endymion*	1588
Lyly, John	*Galatea*	1585
Lyly, John	*Mother Bombie*	1591
Marlowe, Christopher	*1 Tamburlaine the Great*	1587
Marlowe, Christopher	*2 Tamburlaine the Great*	1587
Marlowe, Christopher	*Edward the Second*	1592
Marlowe, Christopher; others (?)	*The Jew of Malta*	1589
Middleton, Thomas	*A Chaste Maid in Cheapside*	1613
Middleton, Thomas	*A Mad World, My Masters*	1605
Middleton, Thomas	*A Trick to Catch the Old One*	1605
Middleton, Thomas	*Your Five Gallants*	1607
Shakespeare, William	*The Comedy of Errors*	1594
Shakespeare, William	*Richard the Third*	1592
Shakespeare, William	*The Taming of the Shrew*	1591
Shakespeare, William	*The Two Gentlemen of Verona*	1590

As noted in the Introduction, PCA has been widely adopted as a method for stylistic investigation.[10] Its use in authorship attribution relies on the fact that, when analysing word-frequency counts across a mixed corpus of texts known to be of different authorship, the strongest factor that emerges in the relationship between the texts is generally authorial in nature. Other stylistic signals may also be present, such as the effect of genre, period of composition, gender of the author, and so on, but these are usually demonstrably weaker. For example, Table 1.1 lists a selection of plays by John Lyly, Christopher Marlowe, Thomas Middleton, and William Shakespeare, representing a range of genres and dates of first performance.[11]

With this corpus of machine-readable texts, prepared as outlined above, we use Intelligent Archive, a software tool developed by the Centre for Literary and Linguistic Computing at the University of Newcastle, to generate word-frequency counts for the 500 most frequent words across the corpus, segmented into 2,000-word non-overlapping blocks and discarding any smaller blocks that remain. Proper nouns, foreign-language

[10] See José Nilo G. Binongo and M. W. A. Smith, 'The Application of Principal Component Analysis to Stylometry', *Literary and Linguistic Computing* 14.4 (1999), 445–65.

[11] Appendix A provides further bibliographical details for these plays, including the source texts used and date of publication. The text of *The Jew of Malta* we used excludes the prologues and epilogues attributed to Thomas Heywood. On the possibility of further non-Marlovian revision, see D. J. Lake, 'Three Seventeenth-Century Revisions: *Thomas of Woodstock*, *The Jew of Malta*, and *Faustus B* ', *Notes & Queries* 30.2 (1983), 133–43.

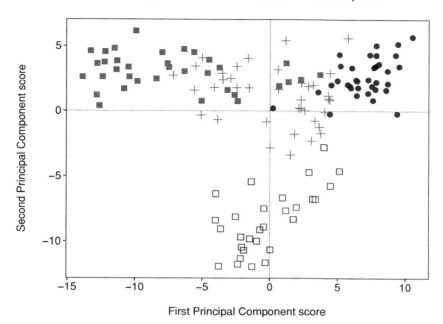

Figure 1.1 PCA scatterplot of 2,000-word non-overlapping segments of plays listed in Table 1.1, using the 500 most frequent words.

words, and stage directions are excluded from the procedure. The result is a large table, with 138 rows (one for each 2,000-word block) and 500 columns (one each for the total of each block's occurrences of each word counted). As one might expect, words such as *the, and, I, to,* and *a* – that is, function words – are among the most frequent.

If it were possible to visualise, and effectively comprehend, every 2,000-word segment could be plotted as a point on a graph along 500 separate axes or dimensions in space. With PCA, we can reduce the dimensionality of the data while preserving as much of the variance as possible. If we use PCA to reduce the data to the two strongest factors, we can then project each 2,000-word segment into a two-dimensional space as a data-point, treating the scores for each segment on the first and second principal components as Cartesian coordinates (Figure 1.1).[12]

---

[12] Coordinates are a set of numbers that define position in space relative to an origin. In the Cartesian coordinate system, the origin is a fixed point from which two or more axes or 'dimensions' are

The first principal component (the *x*-axis) is the most important latent factor in the various correlations between the word-variables in the segments, and the second principal component (the *y*-axis) is the second most important (independent) latent factor. The relative distances between the points or 'observations' within this space represent degrees of affinity, so that segments of similar stylistic traits – specifically, similar rates of occurrence of our 500 words – cluster tightly together, whereas dissimilar segments are plotted further apart.

To make it easier to read the scatterplot, we use different symbols to label segments belonging to different authors. Although the separation between them is not perfect, segments belonging to the same author tend to cluster together, with Marlowe's segments (plotted as grey squares) typically scoring low on the first principal component and high on the second principal component. The PCA algorithm determines a weighting for each word, negative or positive, to give the best single combination to express the collective variability of all 138 segments' word uses. Marlowe's low score for the first principal component means that the Marlowe segments relatively rarely use the words with a high positive weighting on this component and relatively frequently use the words with a high negative weighting. The algorithm then identifies a second set of weightings for the words, to best account for the remaining collective variability of the 138 segments' word uses after the first principal component has accounted for its fraction of the collective variability. The Marlowe segments use the words with high positive weightings on this second principal component relatively often and the words with high negative ratings relatively rarely. We could, in theory, go on to calculate further principal components (a third, a fourth, and so on) until we run out of variance in the data – which must in any case happen for this experiment when we calculate the 500th principal component and so exhaust our 500 variables' capacity to differ from one another. The most important consideration here is that this method demonstrably captures the affinity of segments by single authors, with Middleton's segments (plotted as black circles) typically scoring high on both axes. Lyly's segments cluster away from the others, scoring comparatively low on the second principal component, whereas Shakespeare's segments gravitate towards the centre of the scatterplot, forming a stylistic 'bridge' between the other authors.

We have plotted the first and second principal components – those which account for the greatest and second greatest proportion of the

defined, with each axis perpendicular to the other. Readers may recall charting plots on graph paper in school mathematics in this same way. We use a Cartesian coordinate system throughout this book to generate scatterplots along two axes – the horizontal or *x* axis, and the vertical or *y* axis.

variance – and what emerge there are separations by author. This is evidence that authorship is a more important factor in stylistic differentiation than other groupings, such as genre or date, as we show below. However, there may be times when we may not be interested in the most important factors, whatever they may be. Since PCA can create as many components as there are variables, it is possible to target a particular factor. If we were interested in date, for example, we could work through the other components to find one which differentiates the sample by date – that is, which single set of weightings given to the 500 words will separate those favoured early in the period from those favoured late in the period – and then either use that component to classify a sample of unknown date, or explore the stylistics of the date-based groupings by examining the patterns of word-variables that create the component.

A different pattern in the data of the first two principal components emerges if we simply re-label the points on the scatterplot according to genre (Figure 1.2). The underlying data has not changed, only the labels of the points. Along the first principal component, segments appear to cluster in generic groups from 'heroical romance' (plotted as black circles) through to 'history' (grey plus symbols), 'tragedy' (unfilled triangles), and 'comedy' (unfilled squares). This perhaps explains some of the internal variation evident within the authorial clusters identified in Figure 1.1. For example, segments from Marlowe's 'heroical romance' plays, *1* and *2 Tamburlaine the Great*, cluster tightly together, whereas segments from his *Edward the Second* are plotted closer to – sharing stylistic traits with – segments from Shakespeare's play of the same genre, *Richard the Third*. Similarly, Lyly's 'comedy' *Mother Bombie* is plotted higher on the second principal component than segments from his other 'classical legend' comedies.[13]

PCA works by finding weightings for the variables to establish new composite variables – the components. We can examine these weightings to find out which variables contribute the most to a given component. To visualise the weightings, we can plot them in a separate biaxial chart, show them as a column or bar chart, or display them on the same chart as the segments in the form of a 'biplot'. The biplot allows us to visualise the contributions of each word-variable in the same two-dimensional space as the play segments (Figure 1.3).[14] It shows the segment scores (as in Figures 1.1

---

[13] We also re-labelled the data-points by decade of first production. There were some clusters, but a far less clear-cut division than by author or genre. Plays of the 1590s occupied the middle part of the first principal component, but 1580s plays overlapped them substantially, and 1610s plays were all within the range of the 1600s plays. Plays of the 1580s were spread over almost the full range of the second principal component.

[14] Michael Greenacre, *Biplots in Practice* (Bilbao: Fundación BBVA, 2010), 15–24, 59–68; Alt, *Exploring Hyperspace*, 92–7.

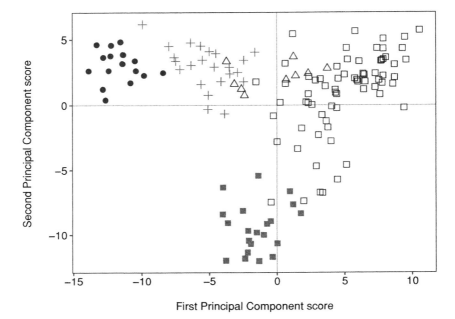

Figure 1.2 PCA scatterplot of 2,000-word non-overlapping segments of plays listed in Table 1.1, labelled by genre, using the 500 most frequent words.

and 1.2), but also overlays on these the weightings for the word-variables. In a biplot, the word-variables are generally represented by an arrow or 'vector' drawn from the origin – the point where the *x* and *y* axes intersect, i.e., 0,0 – rather than as points. This is a reminder that each variable is an axis, and the length and direction of the vector is also a convenient indication of the importance of that variable for a given component.

The positions of the ends of the vectors in the biplot are determined by the weightings of the variables for the two components, re-scaled to fit into the chart space.[15] Since the vectors are scaled to fit the biplot, the distance between the end or 'head' of a vector and a play segment is unimportant; what matter are the directions and relative lengths of the vectors.

[15] The biplots in this book were produced with the R statistical computing package, using the default scaling factors.

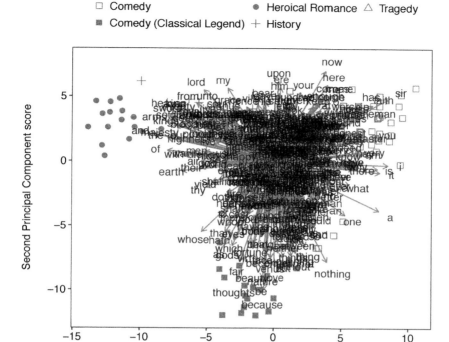

Figure 1.3 PCA biplot of 2,000-word non-overlapping segments of plays listed in Table 1.1, labelled by genre, using the 500 most frequent words.

The direction of a vector indicates how a word-variable contributes to each of the principal components. A segment with many instances of the word-variables strongly positively weighted in one of the principal components will have been 'driven' in that direction, whereas a segment dominated by word-variables weak in both components will be plotted towards the origin.[16] The relative length of a vector corresponds to the magnitude of the contribution. In Figure 1.3, a long vector extending in an easterly direction shows that the corresponding word-variable has a heavy positive

---

[16] To increase legibility, PCA biplots often omit the vectors and plot only the word-variable labels, projected as points. The result is the same: the word-variables are plotted by their weightings on the two principal components, so that word-variables appearing to the extremes of the axes are those that make the most difference in the scatter of the segments along the axes. In our book, we have sometimes created a separate chart of the variables or a selection of variables for increased legibility.

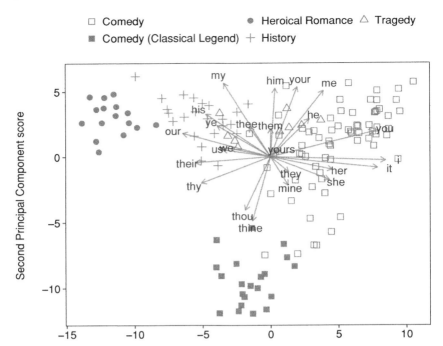

Figure 1.4 PCA biplot of 2,000-word non-overlapping segments of plays listed in Table 1.1,
labelled by genre, using the 500 most frequent words and highlighting personal pronouns.

weighting on the first principal component, while a short vector extending
in a southerly direction shows that the corresponding word-variable has a
weak negative weighting on the second principal component.

If, as in Figure 1.3, all 500 of the word-variable vectors are drawn, the
biplot becomes too difficult to analyse. Instead, we can redraw the biplot
highlighting only word-variables of thematic interest or those belonging
to a particular grammatical class. For example, Figure 1.4 gives the same
biplot with only vectors for word-variables of personal pronouns drawn.

Inspection of the biplot reveals that 'comedy' segments plotted to the east
of the origin are dominated by singular personal pronouns, such as the first-
person *I*, *me*, and *mine*, the second-person formal *you*, *your*, and *yours*, and
the third-person *he*, *she*, *it*, *him*, and *her*. By contrast, the 'heroical romance'
and 'history' segments plotted west of the origin are dominated by plural
personal nouns, such as the first-person *we*, *us*, and *our*, the second-person

ye, and the third-person *their*, while 'classical legend' comedy segments, plotted south-west of the origin, favour the second-person informal singular *thou* and *thine* forms. Speeches in heroical romances, tragedies, and history plays are evidently cast more in terms of collectives, as we might expect with a focus on armies in battle and political factions. Comedies, on the other hand, tend to include more one-on-one interpersonal exchanges, so that the singular pronouns figure more strongly in their dialogue.

Random Forests

The decision-making process is often characterised as a series of questions: answers to one question may lead to a decision being reached, or prompt a further question – or series of questions – until a decision is made. For example, a doctor asks a patient to describe their symptoms and they respond that they have a runny nose. Among other conditions, rhinorrhea – the technical term for a runny nose – is a symptom common to both allergy (e.g. hayfever) and certain infections (e.g. the common cold). To reach a diagnosis, the doctor may ask further questions of the patient: how long have the symptoms persisted? Is the nasal discharge clear or coloured? Does the patient suffer from itchy eyes, aches, or fever?

While the common cold often causes a runny nose and may sometimes occasion aches, it rarely results in fever or itchy eyes and typically does not last longer than a fortnight. By contrast, rhinorrhea and itchy eyes are frequent allergic reactions and may last as long as the patient is in contact with the allergy trigger – minutes, hours, days, weeks, even months and seasons. (The term 'hayfever' is somewhat misleading, because fever and aches are not typical allergic responses.) Our hypothetical doctor's decision-making process may be visualised as a decision tree (Figure 1.5).

Of course, this is a simplified example (and correspondingly simple visualisation) of a complex consideration of multiple variables, some of which are 'weighted' – or more important to the decision-making process than others.

Random Forests is a supervised machine-learning procedure for classifying data using a large number of decision trees.[17] Whereas our hypothetical doctor relied upon centuries of accumulated knowledge to identify

[17] Leo Breiman, 'Random Forests', *Machine Learning* 45.1 (2001), 5–32. Much of the description that follows appeared in an earlier form as part of Jack Elliott and Brett Greatley-Hirsch, ''Arden of Faversham*, Shakespeare, and "the print of many"', in Gary Taylor and Gabriel Egan (eds.), *The New Oxford Shakespeare: Authorship Companion* (Oxford University Press, 2017), 139–81. We thank the editors for their permission to reproduce and adapt those passages here.

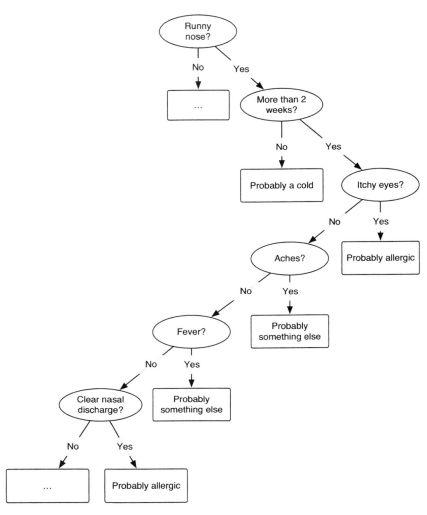

Figure 1.5 Binary decision tree diagram.

attributes or features distinguishing one medical condition from another, decision tree algorithms instead begin by testing variables in a set of data with a known shared attribute (a so-called 'training set') to derive a rule – like the series of questions posed by the doctor – that best performs the task of splitting the data into desired categories or classes. At each succeeding level of the tree, the sub-sets created by the splits are themselves split according to another rule, and the tree continues to grow in this fashion until all of the data has been classified. Once a decision tree is 'trained' to classify the data of the training set, it can then be employed to classify new, unseen data.[18]

Random Forests combines the predictive power of hundreds of such decision trees (hence 'forests'). Each tree is derived using a different and random sub-set of the training dataset and variables. To enable validation of the technique and to avoid the problem of 'over-fitting',[19] randomly selected segments of the training set are withheld from the algorithm so that they do not inform the construction of the decision trees (and thus allowing us to determine how accurate the trees' predictions are in classifying these withheld segments). By default, one-third of all training-set segments are withheld for this purpose. This testing, using segments of a known class or category, treated as if this was unknown, gives us an expected error rate for when the decision trees are used to classify new data. The higher the classification error rate, the weaker the relationship between the variables and the classes, and *vice versa*. Hundreds of such trees are constructed, and for each classification to be made each tree contributes one vote to the outcome. This aggregation of decision trees evens out any errors made by individual trees that may arise from the construction of apparently reliable – but in fact false – rules based on anomalous data.[20]

By way of example, we use Intelligent Archive to generate word-frequency counts for the 500 most frequent words across the selection of plays listed in Table 1.1, segmented into 2,000-word non-overlapping blocks and discarding any smaller blocks that remain. As before, proper nouns, foreign-language passages, and stage directions are excluded from the procedure. This produces a large table of 138 rows and 500 columns, which we split into two separate tables: one to serve as our training dataset

[18] As such, the procedure is 'supervised' because the algorithm relies upon human pre-processing of the training-set data to ensure that it is characterised by a shared attribute, such as particular medical conditions, or, for our purposes, play-texts of common authorship, genre, period, or repertory company.

[19] 'Over-fitting' occurs when a machine-learning algorithm or statistical model performs well on the training data, but generalises poorly to any new data. To classify training data on a two-dimensional chart, for example, we may use a highly complex equation to generate a wavy line snaking around each data-point to serve as a boundary between groups. While this equation might perfectly separate the data-points into groups, it may also 'fit' or reflect the exact contours of the training data too closely. A simpler equation, producing a line with a looser fit to the training data, may better serve as a boundary when we wish to classify newly introduced data.

[20] For example, a decision tree derived from analysis of a patient suffering from a runny nose caused by an unusually resilient and long-lasting cold might generate the rule 'If symptoms persist for longer than two weeks, then it is a cold'. While accurate in the case of this particular, local anomaly, this rule does not perform well as a predictor for the majority of cases.

(109 rows, 500 columns), and another containing all of the segments from each author's first-listed play to serve as a test dataset (29 rows, 500 columns). After a randomly selected one-third of segments in the training dataset are withheld by the algorithm to be tested later, 500 decision trees are populated using the remaining two-thirds of the training dataset, trying 22 random word-variables at each 'split' in the decision tree.[21] A diagram of one of the decision trees populated in this experiment is given in Figure 1.6, in which the rules are expressed as the rates of occurrence of a word-variable per 2,000 words. Thus, according to its rules, if a 2,000-word segment contains 1 or fewer instances of the word *hath* and 61 or fewer instances of the word *and*, then this decision tree predicts it is a Middleton segment.[22] Of course, as the outcome of a single decision tree, this prediction would count as one out of 500 votes cast by the 'forest' of trees.

The algorithm then uses the decision trees to classify the training dataset as a whole, with the randomly withheld one-third of segments reintroduced. This produces an expected error rate for when the unseen test dataset will be classified later. Table 1.2 gives the confusion matrix for the 109 segments of the entire training dataset, tabling four misclassifications made by the decision trees: three segments of *The Jew of Malta* assigned to Shakespeare, and one segment of *Richard the Third* assigned to Marlowe. This produces a promisingly low expected error rate of 3.67 per cent ($= 4 \div 109 \times 100$).

The decision trees are then used to classify all of the data – i.e., the whole training dataset, including the previously withheld segments, as well as the newly introduced segments of the test dataset. Table 1.3 gives the resulting confusion matrix. The decision trees classify all of the segments in the test dataset correctly, resulting in a classification error rate of 2.89 per cent for all of the segments in both the training and test datasets – that is, 4 misclassified segments out of the total 138.

---

[21] A function built into the Random Forests algorithm compares estimated error rates when different values for the number of variables are tried at each split and selects the optimal value (i.e., the value resulting in the lowest expected error rate). By default, the first number of variables tried is the square root of the total number of variables, rounded down to the nearest whole number – in our case 22 (the approximate square root of 500). The algorithm then generates other values to try by multiplying or dividing the first number by a factor – by default, this factor is 2. New values are continuously tried so long as the expected error rate improves beyond a given threshold (by default, 5 per cent). Here and elsewhere in this book, we use the default settings of the Random Forests algorithm. Thus, in this example, the algorithm first tries 22 variables at each split, and then compares the estimated error rates when 6 (or $22 \div 2 \div 2$), 11 (or $22 \div 2$), 44 (or 22×2), 88 ($22 \times 2 \times 2$), and 176 (or $22 \times 2 \times 2 \times 2$) variables are tried. Of these, 22 is determined the optimal value.

[22] Although the actual split for *hath*, as per the diagram, is a rate of ≥ 1.5 instances per 2,000 words, our word-frequency counts are given only in whole, discrete numbers. Since we cannot have 1.5 instances of *hath*, in practice the rule applies to ≥ 1 instances in a 2,000-word segment.

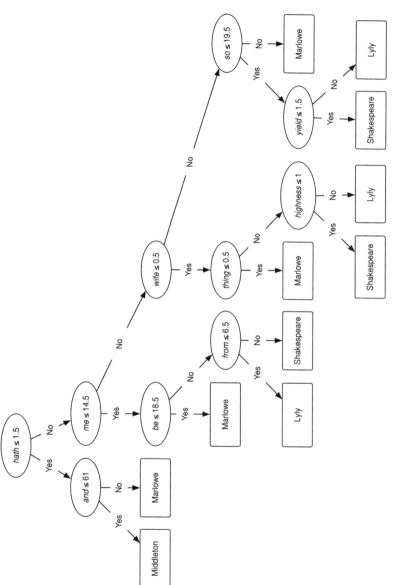

Figure 1.6 Diagram of a single binary decision tree populated for Random Forests classification of 2,000-word non-overlapping segments in a training dataset of 109 segments drawn from plays listed in Table 1.1, using the 500 most frequent words.

Table 1.2 *Confusion matrix for Random Forests classification of 2,000-word non-overlapping segments in a training dataset of 109 segments drawn from plays listed in Table 1.1, using the 500 most frequent words*

	Lyly, John	Marlowe, Christopher	Middleton, Thomas	Shakespeare, William	Misclassification (%)
Lyly, John	23	0	0	0	0
Marlowe, Christopher	0	24	0	3	11
Middleton, Thomas	0	0	28	0	0
Shakespeare, William	0	1	0	30	3

Delta

Delta is a supervised method introduced by John Burrows to establish the stylistic difference between two or more texts by comparing the relative frequencies of very common words.[23] Although well established as a tool for authorship attribution study, Delta is also used more broadly as a means to describe 'the relation between a text and other texts in the context of the entire group of texts'.[24]

In its usual deployment, the procedure establishes a series of distances between a single text of interest and a comparison set typically comprising a series of authorial sub-sets of texts. The author with the lowest distance score is judged to be the 'least unlikely' author of the mystery text.[25] There are two main steps. The procedure begins by generating counts of

[23] John Burrows, 'Delta: A Measure of Stylistic Difference and a Guide to Likely Authorship', *Literary and Linguistic Computing* 17.3 (2002), 267–86, and 'Questions of Authorship: Attribution and Beyond', *Computers and the Humanities* 37.1 (2003), 5–32. For assessments of the method, see David L. Hoover, 'Testing Burrows's Delta', *Literary and Linguistic Computing* 19.4 (2004), 453–75, and Shlomo Argamon, 'Interpreting Burrows's Delta: Geometric and Probabilistic Foundations', *Literary and Linguistic Computing* 23.2 (2008), 131–47. A number of refinements of Delta have been proposed for the purpose of authorship attribution; see, for example, Peter W. H. Smith and W. Aldridge, 'Improving Authorship Attribution: Optimizing Burrows' Delta Method', *Journal of Quantitative Linguistics* 18.1 (2011), 63–88. However, for simplicity, we here describe the original version as proposed by Burrows.

[24] Fotis Jannidis and Gerhard Lauer, 'Burrows's Delta and Its Use in German Literary History', in Matt Erlin and Lynne Tatlock (eds.), *Distant Readings* (Rochester: Camden House, 2014), 32.

[25] Sections of the description that follows appeared in an earlier form as part of Jack Elliott and Greatley-Hirsch, '*Arden of Faversham*'. We thank the editors for their permission to reproduce and adapt those passages here.

Table 1.3 *Confusion matrix for Random Forests classification of 109 training and 29 test segments of plays listed in Table 1.1, segmented into 2,000-word non-overlapping blocks, using the 500 most frequent words*

	Lyly, John	Marlowe, Christopher	Middleton, Thomas	Shakespeare, William	Misclassification (%)
Lyly, John	29	0	0	0	0
Marlowe, Christopher	0	32	0	3	8
Middleton, Thomas	0	0	36	0	0
Shakespeare, William	0	1	0	37	2

high-frequency words in the 'test' text and comparison set. Counts for individual texts in the comparison set are retained, allowing Delta to derive both a mean figure for the set as a whole, and a standard deviation – a measure of the variation from that mean – for each variable.[26] The counts on the chosen variables – usually very common words – are transformed into percentages to account for differing sizes of text and then into z-scores by taking the difference between the word counts and the mean of the overall set and dividing that by the standard deviation for the variable. Using z-scores has the advantage that low-scoring variables are given equal weight with high-scoring ones, since a z-score is the number of standard deviations of an observation from the mean, unrelated to the size of the original units. The z-score also takes into account the amplitude of fluctuations within the counts. Wide fluctuations result in a high standard deviation and thus a lower z-score.

The differences between z-scores for the test text and each authorial subset are then found for each variable, adding up the absolute differences – that is, ignoring whether the figures are positive or negative – to form a

[26] The four-figure sets {6, 7, 2, 9} and {8, 1, 3, 12} both have a mean of 6, since this is one-fourth of $6 + 7 + 2 + 9$ (= 24) also one-fourth of $8 + 1 + 3 + 12$ (= 24). However, the figures in the second set differ more widely from their mean than those in the first set. To express this, the standard deviation for each set is derived by squaring each data-point's difference from its set's mean, dividing the resulting squares by $(N - 1)$, i.e., the number of samples less one, and then finding the square root of that number. For the first set, this is the square root of one-third of $(6 - 6)^2 + (7 - 6)^2 + (2 - 6)^2 + (9 - 6)^2$, which comes to about 2.9. For the second set, this is the square root of one-third of $(8 - 6)^2 + (1 - 6)^2 + (3 - 6)^2 + (12 - 6)^2$, or roughly 5. These are 'sample standard deviations' – i.e., the standard deviations of samples understood to be representing larger populations. This is the version of the metric we use in the studies in this book.

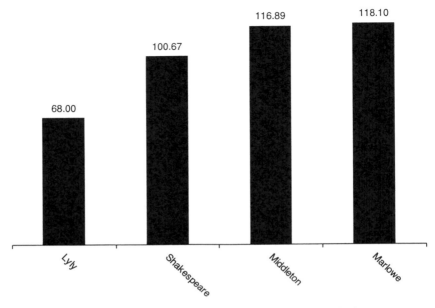

Figure 1.7 Delta distances between *Galatea* and four authorial sub-sets.

composite measure of difference (or 'Delta' distance). The procedure is complete at this point, with a measure for the overall difference between the test text and each of the authorial sub-sets within the comparison set.

To illustrate the method, consider an example using the set of sixteen plays listed in Table 1.1, with four plays each by Lyly, Marlowe, Middleton, and Shakespeare. We first generate frequency counts for the 100 most common function words in all 16 plays and transform these into percentages. We then choose one Lyly play at random to serve as a test text – in this case, *Galatea* – and withdraw this play from the Lyly authorial sub-set. We transform the word-frequency scores for *Galatea* into z-scores, using the means and standard deviations for the whole set of sixteen plays. We do the same for the mean scores for the Lyly, Marlowe, Middleton, and Shakespeare plays – the Lyly set consisting of the three remaining plays, the others retaining their full sub-set of four plays each. To arrive at a composite distance measure, we add up the absolute differences between the *Galatea* z-scores and each of the authorial sub-set z-scores for the 100 word-variables. Figure 1.7 shows the resulting Delta distances as a column chart.

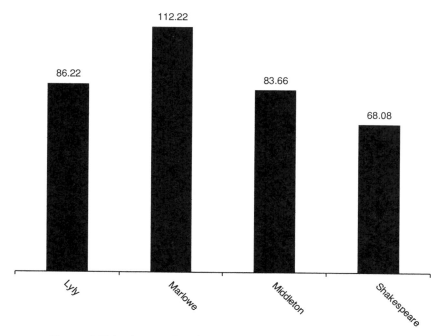

Figure 1.8 Delta distances for *The Jew of Malta* and four authorial sub-sets.

When treated as a mystery text, *Galatea* finds its closest match in a Lyly sub-set based on the three remaining Lyly plays, with a Delta distance of 68. Shakespeare, with a Delta distance of 100.67, is the next nearest author, followed by Middleton (116.89) and Marlowe (118.10). We can then do the same for the other three Lyly plays, withdrawing each in turn and testing the resemblance between that play and each of the four authorial sub-sets. As it turns out, and as we would expect (but could not guarantee), each Lyly play matched the sub-set of remaining Lyly plays most closely.

We repeat the procedure for the other authors along the same lines, holding out and testing each play in turn. In every case, the known author was the closest match, with the exception of *The Jew of Malta* (Figure 1.8), which matched Shakespeare most closely (with a Delta distance of 68.08), then Middleton (at 83.65), then Lyly (at 86.22) – with Marlowe the most distant at 112.22.[27]

---

[27] It is worth noting that the Random Forests algorithm, outlined above, also classified segments of *The Jew of Malta* as Shakespeare's.

Evidently, this play represents a radical departure from Marlowe's typical practice in the use of very common function words (established on the basis of the three other plays in the sub-set). As the only (potentially) incorrect attribution out of sixteen Delta tests, this anomalous result is certainly worthy of further investigation. However, for the purposes of demonstration, it is enough to note that, overall, Delta is a good – but perhaps not infallible – guide to authorship and stylistic difference, even when using small sub-sets to represent an author.

Shannon Entropy

Shannon entropy is a measure of the repetitiveness of a set of data, and is the key concept in information theory as developed by Claude Shannon in the 1940s.[28] Shannon entropy calculates the greatest possible compression of the information provided by a set of items considered as members of distinct classes. A large entropy value indicates that the items fall into a large number of classes, and thus must be represented by listing the counts of a large number of these classes. In an ecosystem, this would correspond to the presence of a large number of species each with relatively few members. The maximum entropy value occurs where each item represents a distinct class. Minimum entropy occurs where all items belong to a single class. In terms of language, word tokens are the items and word types the classes.[29] A high-entropy text contains a large number of word types, many with a single token. A good example would be a technical manual for a complex machine which specifies numerous distinct small parts. A low-entropy text contains few word types, each with many occurrences, such as a legal document where terms are repeated in each clause to avoid ambiguity. Entropy is a measure of a sparse and diverse distribution versus a dense and concentrated one. High-entropy texts are demanding of the reader and dense in information – they constantly move to new mental territories; they are taxing and impressive. Low-entropy texts are reassuring and familiar – they are implicit in their signification, assuming common

---

[28] C. E. Shannon, 'A Mathematical Theory of Communication', *Bell System Technical Journal* 27 (1948), 379–423, and 'Prediction and Entropy of Printed English', *Bell System Technical Journal* 30 (1951), 50–64. For a more accessible overview of entropy and information theory, see Luciano Floridi, *Information: A Very Short Introduction* (Oxford University Press, 2010), 37–47; and James Gleick, *The Information: A History, a Theory, a Flood* (New York: Pantheon, 2011), 204–32.

[29] On the application of Shannon entropy and other measures to literary study, see Osvaldo A. Rosso, Hugh Craig, and Pablo Moscato, 'Shakespeare and Other English Renaissance Authors as Characterized by Information Theory Complexity Quantifiers', *Physica A* 388 (2009), 916–26.

knowledge, while high-entropy texts specify and create contexts for themselves. High-entropy texts contain more description and narrative, while low-entropy texts contain more dialogue.

Shannon entropy is defined as the negative of the sum of the proportional counts of the variables in a dataset each multiplied by its logarithm.[30] A line consisting of a single word-type repeated five times (e.g. 'Never, never, never, never, never!' *King Lear* 5.3.307) has a single variable with a proportion of $\frac{5}{5}$ (or 1). The log of 1 is 0. The Shannon entropy of the line is therefore:

$$-\left(\frac{5}{5}\log\frac{5}{5}\right) = 0$$

The line 'Tomorrow, and tomorrow, and tomorrow' from *Macbeth* (5.5.18) has three instances of *tomorrow* and two of *and*. The proportional count for *tomorrow* is $\frac{3}{5}$ (or 0.6) and for *and* is $\frac{2}{5}$ (or 0.4), thus the Shannon entropy for the line is

$$-\left[\left(\frac{3}{5}\log\frac{3}{5}\right) + \left(\frac{2}{5}\log\frac{2}{5}\right)\right] \approx 0.673$$

For a final comparison, consider the line: 'If music be the food of love, play on' (*Twelfth Night* 1.1.1). This time, each of the nine words making up the line occurs only once. Since each word-variable has a proportional score of $\frac{1}{9}$ (or $\approx$ 0.111), the Shannon entropy for this line is:

$$-\left[\begin{array}{l}\left(\frac{1}{9}\log\frac{1}{9}\right) + \left(\frac{1}{9}\log\frac{1}{9}\right) + \left(\frac{1}{9}\log\frac{1}{9}\right) + \left(\frac{1}{9}\log\frac{1}{9}\right) + \left(\frac{1}{9}\log\frac{1}{9}\right) \\ + \left(\frac{1}{9}\log\frac{1}{9}\right) + \left(\frac{1}{9}\log\frac{1}{9}\right) + \left(\frac{1}{9}\log\frac{1}{9}\right) + \left(\frac{1}{9}\log\frac{1}{9}\right)\end{array}\right] \approx 2.197$$

– a higher score than for our two previous examples, reflecting comparatively greater variability in word use.[31]

---

[30] The formula to derive the Shannon entropy (*H*) for *X* is:

$$H(X) = -\sum_{x_i \in X} x_i \log x_i$$

A logarithm represents the power to which a fixed number or base must be raised to produce a given number. In all of our Shannon entropy calculations, we use natural logarithms, where the base is *e*, approximately 2.718. Because the logarithm of a fraction (as all proportions are) is always negative, the Shannon entropy formula calls for the negative of the sum ($-\Sigma$) of these proportional counts multiplied by their logarithms ($x_i \log x_i$) to ensure that the result is positive.

[31] Shannon entropy is sensitive to text length – the maximum possible entropy increases as text length increases. To account for this, we work with samples of the same length when we go beyond the illustrative examples given here.

t-tests

Consider the following experiment. We compile a set of Shakespeare's comedies (*All's Well That Ends Well, As You Like It, The Merchant of Venice, A Midsummer Night's Dream, Much Ado About Nothing*, and *Twelfth Night*) and a set of Shakespeare's tragedies (*Antony and Cleopatra, Hamlet, King Lear, Othello, Romeo and Juliet*, and *Troilus and Cressida*). Are there more instances, on average, of the word *death* in the tragedies compared with the comedies? If there is a difference in these averages, how consistent is it, in the sense that any large group of tragedies will have more occurrences of *death* overall? Our experiment calls for us to find a way to see past mere averages to the varying counts that lie behind them.

The occurrence of *death* in each of these plays, expressed as a percentage of the total number of words, is 0.08, 0.03, 0.05, 0.08, 0.08, and 0.05 respectively for the comedies, and 0.14, 0.13, 0.08, 0.06, 0.29, and 0.06 for the tragedies. The mean for the comedies is 0.062, and for the tragedies it is 0.127 – more than twice as large. But how can we take the fluctuations within the groups into account?

One way to do this is to use a *t*-test, a common statistical procedure to determine whether the 'mean' or average of a 'population' – that is, all members of a defined group or dataset from which a selection or 'sample' is drawn – differs significantly from a hypothetical mean or the mean of another population. The test was first proposed in 1908 by W. S. Gosset, writing under the pseudonym 'Student' while working in quality control for the Guinness brewery in Ireland.[32] Student's *t*-test, as it has come to be known, generates a simple metric called the *t*-value, calculated as the difference in means between two sets divided by the combination of their standard deviations. A high *t*-test score means that the average use in one set is much higher or lower than the use in a second set, and the word overall does not fluctuate much.

Student's *t*-test assumes that the two populations under investigation follow a 'normal distribution' and have an equal variance (i.e., the data in both populations is 'spread' or 'scattered' equally).[33] In 1947 B. L. Welch adapted Student's *t*-test to accommodate populations of unequal variance,[34] and we

---

[32] 'Student' [= W. S. Gosset], 'The Probable Error of a Mean', *Biometrika* 6.1 (1908), 1–25.

[33] If plotted on a graph, data with a 'normal distribution' would resemble a symmetrical, bell-shaped curve, with the density of the curve centred about its mean. With an equal 'variance', the data in both populations is 'spread' or 'scattered' equally. (Standard deviation is the square root of the variance.)

[34] B. L. Welch, 'The Generalization of "Student's" Problem When Several Different Population Variances Are Involved', *Biometrika* 34.1–2 (1947), 28–35. We use the two-tailed heteroscedastic version.

use this variation in the present experiment and generally throughout this book. For Welch's *t*-test, the one we have used in this book, the formula is:

$$t = \frac{\bar{x}_1 - \bar{x}_2}{\sqrt{\frac{s_1^2}{n_1} + \frac{s_2^2}{n_2}}}$$

Here $\bar{x}_1$ and $\bar{x}_2$ are the means of the first and second samples, s_1^2 and s_2^2 the squared standard deviations of the first and second samples, and n_1 and n_2 the number of items in each respective sample. For our experiment, we already have the means (as above, 0.062 and 0.127), and the standard deviations are 0.021 and 0.087 for the comedies and tragedies respectively. The sample size is 6 for both sets. Using these figures, the formula produces a *t*-value of −1.778.

The other necessary piece of information is the number of degrees of freedom in the analysis. The more degrees of freedom, the more information the result is based on and the more confident we can be that the result reflects an underlying truth. Degrees of freedom in the *t*-test depend on the number of samples, but with Welch's *t*-test we are allowing for the possibility of different variances for the two groups, and estimating the true number of degrees of freedom requires taking into account the distribution of the data using the Welch-Satterthwaite formula.[35]

The result in this case is 5.6. Given this number, we can find a *t*-test probability by consulting a table or using a *t*-test probability calculator.[36] This *t*-test probability (or '*p*-value') indicates how often a difference like this would come about merely by chance, even when the two sets in fact belong to the same overall population, given the sample size. For this experiment, using a figure of 5.6 for the relevant degrees of freedom results in a *p*-value of 0.129. This is the probability (given that the data is normally distributed) that the two samples come from the same parent population – that the difference is a matter of local variation rather than something underlying and consistent. That is, 13 per cent of the time (one time in seven or

See George W. Snedecor and William G. Cochran, *Statistical Methods*, 8th edn (Ames: Iowa State College Press, 1989), 53–8.

[35] This is a complicated formula, and researchers normally use a statistics package to find the degrees of freedom in a particular case. Here we use *SPSS*. For the background, see Welch, 'The Generalization', and F. E. Satterthwaite, 'An Approximate Distribution of Estimates of Variance Components', *Biometric Bulletin* 2.6 (1946), 110–14. See also Les Kirkup and Bob Frenkel, 'The *t*-distribution and Welch-Satterthwaite Formula', in *An Introduction to Uncertainty and Measurement* (Cambridge University Press, 2006), 162–90.

[36] Here and elsewhere in this book, we use the TTEST function in Microsoft Excel. Figures will vary when using different *t*-test calculators as a result of how values are rounded.

eight) we should expect to see this apparent difference between the comedies and tragedies purely by chance alone, even if comedies and tragedies have no underlying preference for or against using the word *death*. This suggests that although the tragedies in our sample on average have twice the instances of the word, the fluctuations within the sets and the small number of samples mean that we should not base any broad conclusions on this result.

Glancing at the proportional scores for *death* in these texts might have indicated the same thing. There is one aberrant high score, for *Romeo and Juliet*, which accounts for a great deal of the high average for the set of tragedies overall, and there are three comedies at 0.8, which are all higher than the two lowest-scoring tragedies at 0.6. The *t*-test offers a way to treat these fluctuations systematically, a summary statistic which can be carried over from one comparison to another, and a broad indication about the inferences we can safely make about wider populations (such as about Shakespeare comedy and tragedy in general) from the current sample.

PCA, Random Forests, Delta, Shannon entropy, and the *t*-test are all well-established tools that we have found useful in making sense of the abundant, multi-layered data which can be retrieved from literary texts. They take us beyond what we can readily see with the naked eye, as it were – a count that stands out as high or low, or an obvious pattern of association between variables or samples – to larger-scale, more precise summaries that have some in-built protections from bias. PCA is a data reduction method; Random Forests a classification tool; Delta a distance measure; Shannon entropy a density metric; and the *t*-test takes us back to single variables and the question of whether two sets of counts have an underlying difference, or only an apparent one. They are just five of the numerous methods available, and by no means the most complex, but they are all tried and tested and offer a useful range. They come from different eras and were developed for different purposes – only Delta was devised specifically for computational stylistics. All five can be used both to test a hypothesis and to explore data more inductively, as we demonstrate in the chapters that follow.

CHAPTER 2

Prose and Verse

Sometimes 'transparent', Sometimes Meeting with 'a jolt'

In the first scene of John Marston's comedy *The Dutch Courtesan* (1605), Freevill, a free-thinking law student, announces to his Puritan friend Malheureux that he is planning to visit a brothel. Malheureux is shocked and tries to talk him out of it:

> FREEVILL. [. . .] not to disguise with my friend, I am now going the way
>   of all flesh.
> MALHEUREUX. Not to a courtesan.
> FREEVILL. A courteous one.
> MALHEUREUX. What, to a sinner?
> FREEVILL. A very publican.
> MALHEUREUX. Dear my loved friend, let me be full with you.
>   Know, sir, the strongest argument that speaks
>   Against the soul's eternity is lust,
>   That wise man's folly and the fool's wisdom.
>   But to grow wild in loose lasciviousness,
>   Given up to heat and sensual appetite,
>   Nay, to expose your health and strength and name,
>   Your precious time, and with that time the hope
>   Of due preferment, advantageous means
>   Of any worthy end, to the stale use,
>   The common bosom, of a money-creature,
>   One that sells human flesh, a mangonist!
>
> (1.1.80–97)¹

Freevill speaks in prose, Malheureux in verse. Unconstrained prose seems right for Freevill and formal verse right for Malheureux. But things get more complicated. At the end of his next long irreverent prose speech – a

---

¹ References are to David Crane's New Mermaids edition of John Marston, *The Dutch Courtesan* (London: A&C Black, 1997).

mock peroration in defence of prostitutes, punning on laying up and laying down, falling and rising – Freevill changes to rhymed verse:

> FREEVILL. [...] Why do men scrape, why heap to full heaps join?
>   But for his mistress, who would care for coin?
>   For this I hold to be denied of no man:
>   All things are made for man, and man for woman.
>   Give me my fee!
>
> (1.1.130–4)

Malheureux responds in verse, before both return to speaking in prose. Malheureux sounds very different in prose – more like the slangy, if still indignant, law student that he is:

> MALHEUREUX. Of ill you merit well. My heart's good friend,
>   Leave yet at length, at length; for know this ever:
>   'Tis no such sin to err, but to persever.
> FREEVILL. Beauty is woman's virtue, love the life's music, and woman the dainties or second course of heaven's curious workmanship. Since, then, beauty, love, and woman are good, how can the love of woman's beauty be bad? And *bonum, quo communius, eo melius.* Wilt, then, go with me?
> MALHEUREUX. Whither?
> FREEVILL. To a house of salvation.
> MALHEUREUX. Salvation?
> FREEVILL. Yes, 'twill make thee repent. Wilt go to the Family of Love? I will show thee my creature: a pretty, nimble-eyed Dutch Tanakin; an honest, soft-hearted impropriation; a soft, plump, round-cheeked frow, that has beauty enough for her virtue, virtue enough for a woman, and woman enough for any reasonable man in my knowledge. Wilt pass along with me?
> MALHEUREUX. What, to a brothel? to behold an impudent prostitution? Fie on't! I shall hate the whole sex to see her. The most odious spectacle the earth can present is an immodest, vulgar woman.
>
> (1.1.135–56)[2]

Marston is alternating prose and verse in a very flexible and skilful way, seemingly well aware of the expressive possibilities of the different forms and confident that an audience will recognise the change from one mode to another and make the appropriate inferences, even if subliminally.

---

[2] Malheureux does go with Freevill to visit Tanakin and indeed falls for her. Both men, incidentally, end up rejecting her, and in the harsh dénouement she is led off to prison.

Scholars have proposed a number of motivating factors in the choice of prose or verse in early modern English drama. Verse is 'high' style, prose is 'low'.[3] Comedy and comedic scenes are suited to prose.[4] Kings, dukes, and nobles tend to speak in verse, while the middling sort (city merchants and tradesmen) and the lower orders speak in prose.[5] Matters of romantic love are dealt with in verse – characters otherwise speaking in prose often switch to verse within a speech when talking of love – while clowns and fools generally speak in prose.[6] Both patterns are evident in the exchanges between Bottom and Titania in *A Midsummer Night's Dream*, for example, where the infatuated fairy speaks verse and her 'rude mechanical' lover answers in prose.[7] Children, madmen, and characters for whom English is a second language typically speak in prose.[8] In *King Lear* Gloucester 'as a nervous and rather ludicrous old man is given prose', but when 'blind' or 'tending Lear' is given verse; Lear in his madness responds in prose.[9] Even in otherwise purely verse plays, proclamations and letters read aloud are in prose.[10] Choruses are always in verse; soliloquies often so, though not invariably – George Chapman has soliloquies in both mediums.[11] Reasoned argument is often in prose.[12] Jonas Barish singled out 'rank, realism, and . . . risibility' – lower rank, greater realism, and increased risibility – as the key factors in the choice to move to prose within a verse play in the period.[13] Douglas Bruster suggests that Marlowe develops a practice of using prose in mainly verse plays for passages of 'resentment', 'reckoning', and 'ritual'.[14]

In characterising the styles of prose as against verse, commentators then as now offer a range of epithets and general features. George Puttenham in *The Art of English Poesy* (1589) contrasts the musicality and intensity of verse with the plainness and prolixity of prose. In the hierarchy of modes, verse

[3] David Crystal, *'Think on My Words': Exploring Shakespeare's Language* (Cambridge University Press, 2008), 208.

[4] Jonas A. Barish, *Ben Jonson and the Language of Prose Comedy* (Cambridge, MA: Harvard University Press, 1960), 273.

[5] G. L. Brook, *The Language of Shakespeare* (London: André Deutsch, 1976), 160.

[6] Crystal, *'Think'*, 209; see also Akihiro Yamada's introduction to the Revels Plays edition of George Chapman, *The Widow's Tears* (London: Methuen, 1975), esp. lxxiii. Further references to the play are from this edition.

[7] Brook, *Language*, 160–1.   [8] Busse, *Linguistic*, 64–5.

[9] Brian Vickers, *The Artistry of Shakespeare's Prose* (London: Methuen, 1968), 351; see also Brook, *Language*, 5.

[10] Vickers, *Artistry*, 5.   [11] Yamada, 'Introduction' to Chapman, *The Widow's Tears*, lxxiii–iv.

[12] Brook, *Language*, 160.

[13] Jonas A. Barish, 'Hal, Falstaff, Henry V, and Prose', *Connotations* 2.3 (1992), 268.

[14] Douglas Bruster, 'Christopher Marlowe and the Verse/Prose Bilingual System', *Marlowe Studies* 1 (2011), 152.

was clearly the higher. Puttenham writes that verse 'is a manner of utterance more eloquent and rhetorical' than 'ordinary prose'.[15] Modern commentators note the 'ordinariness', 'simplicity', and 'flat[ness]' of prose.[16]

The indications are that audiences in early modern English theatres could easily distinguish prose from verse in spoken dialogue. Some scholars argue that actors emphasised the difference by declaiming verse passages.[17] Characters sometimes remark on the change from prose to verse in another's dialogue. After a prose exchange in *As You Like It* between Rosalind and Jacques, Orlando enters and speaks a single iambic pentameter, 'Good day and happiness, dear Rosalind' to which Jacques retorts, 'Nay, then, God b'wi'you, an you talk in blank verse' before he exits (4.1.28–30). Just before the previously cited passage in *The Dutch Courtesan*, Freevill is asked what happened in a tavern brawl that evening, and starts his reply: 'In most sincere prose, thus' (1.1.11). In Chapman's comedy *The Widow's Tears*, Tharsalio brings the loquacious Lycus down to earth after the latter has offered a long-winded verse account of his own sorrow with the rejoinder: 'In prose, thou wept'st' (4.1.48).

Printed texts retained the familiar manuscript conventions of lineation and capitalisation for verse, although modern editors sometimes feel the need to vary from a particular compositor's arrangement. For instance, Mercutio's 'Queen Mab' speech in *Romeo and Juliet* is set as prose in the 1623 Folio text (TLN 510–44),[18] evidently to save space, but modern editors invariably render the passage as verse. Hal's speech at the end of Act 2, Scene 2 in *1 Henry the Fourth* – beginning 'Got with much ease' – is set out as prose in the 1598 Quartos and in the Folio (TLN 841–6).[19] Alexander Pope, who remarks in the preface to his 1725 Shakespeare edition that 'Prose from verse [the Folio editors] did not know, and they accordingly printed one for the other throughout the volume', prints the speech as verse.[20] This is followed in many, but not all, modern editions.[21]

---

[15] Puttenham, *Art*, 1.4 (98).

[16] Russ McDonald, *Shakespeare and the Arts of Language* (Oxford University Press, 2001), 129, 127, 134.

[17] See, for example, McDonald, *Shakespeare*, 108.

[18] References to the 1623 First Folio are by Through-Line Number (TLN) from William Shakespeare, *The First Folio of Shakespeare: The Norton Facsimile*, ed. Charlton Hinman (New York: W. W. Norton, 1968).

[19] Since the editors add an additional scene division, the passage appears at 2.3.12–18 in the Oxford *Complete Works*; in other editions, it typically appears in 2.2.

[20] Alexander Pope, 'The Preface of the Editor', in William Shakespeare, *The Works of Shakespear in Six Volumes*, ed. Alexander Pope, 6 vols. (London, 1723–5), I: xix. Hal's speech appears at 3:215.

[21] Recent examples rendering the passage in verse include David Bevington's Oxford Shakespeare edition (Oxford University Press, 1994; 2.2.98–104); Herbert and Judith Weil's New Cambridge Shakespeare edition (Cambridge University Press, 1997, rev. edn 2007; 2.2.86–92); David Scott Kastan's Arden edition (London: Arden Shakespeare, 2002; 2.2.101–7); and Jonathan Bate and Eric

Shakespeare's practice in prose and verse dialogue has been studied inten-
sively. Books on Shakespeare's language usually have a section on verse and
prose, and there are numerous specialised studies.[22] Work on other dramatists is less developed, with the exception of Barish's magisterial book on
Jonson's prose, but a number of intriguing instances of the alternation
between prose and verse have been noted, such as the case from *The Dutch
Courtesan* discussed above. For example, Akihiro Yamada discusses Chapman's practice in *The Widow's Tears*, in which the playwright reserves verse
for sections drawing directly on his classical source, and prose for passages
composed independently. Douglas Bruster considers the case of an early
anonymous play, (*The Rare Triumphs of*) *Love and Fortune* (1582), which
uses prose exclusively and consistently for the more dignified of the gods,
with doggerel for the more comical Vulcan, the lame god of fire married to
the unfaithful Aphrodite.[23]

Bruster identifies four phases in the use of verse and prose in English
plays through to *c.*1600. According to Bruster, medieval plays were composed exclusively in verse, but humanist playwrights in the mid sixteenth
century began to write prose plays as well, reserving this mode mostly for
comedies. In the late 1570s and 1580s, individual plays began to include a
'sporadic mingling' of the two modes, often by including proclamations
and letters in prose in a play otherwise in verse. Finally, alternating prose
and verse emerged as an important part of the 'world-picturing system' of
the plays. This development is 'inaugurate[d]' by Christopher Marlowe's
Tamburlaine plays and taken to new heights of expressivity in Shakespeare's
plays.[24]

The full system as Bruster describes it goes beyond the association of
'low' comic scenes with prose and 'high' aristocratic scenes with verse, and
allows some characters the capacity to move between the modes, 'depend-
ing upon context and situation'. Characters such as Hal and Hamlet cross
between prose and verse as part of a display of the 'flexibility of the self'
which seems to be characteristic of early modern writing.[25] Bruster suggests

Rasmussen's RSC edition (Basingstoke: Palgrave Macmillan, 2009; 2.2.100–6). Rosemary Gaby's
edition for Internet Shakespeare Editions sets the passage as prose (Peterborough: Broadview Press,
2013; 2.2.87–91).
[22] Representative examples include Elizabeth Tschopp, *The Distribution of Verse and Prose in Shakespeare's Dramas* (Bern: Francke Verlag, 1956); Vickers, *Artistry*; Busse, *Linguistic*; and Douglas
Bruster, 'The Politics of Shakespeare's Prose', in Bryan Reynolds and William N. West (eds.), *Rematerializing Shakespeare: Authority and Representation on the Early Modern English Stage* (New York:
Palgrave Macmillan, 2005), 95–114.
[23] Bruster, 'Politics', 98.   [24] Bruster, 'Politics', 97–9.
[25] Bruster, 'Politics', 99, quoting Thomas Greene, 'The Flexibility of the Self in Renaissance Literature', in Peter Demetz, Thomas Greene, and Lowry Nelson, Jr. (eds.), *The Disciplines of Criticism*
(New Haven: Yale University Press, 1968), 241–64.

this may reflect the convergence of playwright and the planning, arranging main character, both of whom need to make skilful transitions from one mode to the other.[26] The alternation of prose and verse is thus one of the key elements in creating the three-dimensionality of the Shakespearean stage world: meaning along a number of different axes is created by the powerful short-hand of prose contrasted with verse, and *vice versa.*

Bruster ends his account with the close of the sixteenth century and Shakespeare's accomplished handling of alternating prose and verse within a play, but in the next century playwrights such as Ben Jonson abandoned the mixture and reverted to all-prose and all-verse drama.[27] After 1614 Thomas Middleton abandoned prose comedy, and the next generation of comedy writers – among them Philip Massinger, John Fletcher, and James Shirley – avoid prose almost entirely.[28] Barish argues that 'the triumph of prose as the language of comedy, and its convergence with realism, seem by hindsight an almost inevitable outcome of the history of the genre',[29] but this broader historical trend is not necessarily apparent everywhere in early modern English drama. A tally of early modern comedies suggests that the association of comedy and prose does not mean that prose is the normal medium for a comedy. There are at least as many all-verse comedies in the period as all-prose ones. There are more comedies with a mixture of the two modes than either. Prose and verse are obviously different, on stage and on the page, but it is hard to generalise about them and get a sense of how much they matter and how they are used in any systematic way.

Seven Shakespearean Characters

As already noted, it is common for individual characters to move between verse and prose in the drama. Shakespeare in particular exploited this possibility in his plays of the late 1590s and early 1600s. Bruster names Hal in the two *Henry the Fourth* plays, Hamlet, Iago, King Lear, Duke Vincentio in *Measure for Measure*, and Portia in *The Merchant of Venice* as the most important examples.[30] How different is the prose part from the verse one in each case, and is there a consistent difference? We begin by assembling texts of their speeches, sorted into prose and verse parts. Table 2.1 gives the total words spoken in prose and verse for each character.

---

[26] Bruster, 'Politics', 108.   [27] Barish, *Ben Jonson*, 142.   [28] Barish, *Ben Jonson*, 280.

[29] Barish, *Ben Jonson*, 273.

[30] Bruster, 'Politics', 108. We accept that the text of *Measure for Measure* may be a posthumous adaptation by Middleton; for a recent editorial attempt to distinguish the shares of Middleton and Shakespeare, see John Jowett's edition, in Thomas Middleton, *Thomas Middleton: The Collected Works*, Gary Taylor and John Lavagnino (gen. eds.) (Oxford University Press, 2007), 1542–85.

Table 2.1 *Prose and verse parts for seven Shakespearean characters*

Character	Play	Total words (prose)	Total words (verse)
Prince Henry	*1 Henry the Fourth*	2,776	1,672
Prince Henry	*2 Henry the Fourth*	877	1,463
Hamlet	*Hamlet*	5,165	6,367
King Lear	*King Lear*	2,082	3,399
Duke Vincentio	*Measure for Measure*	1,761	4,831
Portia	*The Merchant of Venice*	762	3,869
Iago	*Othello*	2,335	6,007

We generate word-frequency counts for the top 100 most frequent function words across all of the dialogue samples.[31] To account for the difference in sample size, proportions for each word in every sample are derived from the word-frequency counts. We then project these proportions for each sample into a two-dimensional space using Principal Components Analysis (PCA), treating the scores on the first and second principal components as Cartesian coordinates defining each segment as a point on a scatterplot (Figure 2.1).

Evidently, Portia's prose part is very different in word use from all the other dialogue samples, and the first principal component (PC1) singles out this difference as the most important factor in the data: the prose marker for Portia is plotted far to the lower end of PC1. PCA provides a figure for the fraction of the total variance accounted for by each of the components: PC1 in this case accounts for approximately 32 per cent, and the second principal component (PC2) roughly 21 per cent, together accounting for ~53 per cent. The strong PC1 effect can be explained by the fact that Portia has only a small portion of dialogue in prose (at 762 words; see Table 2.1), confined to her exchanges with Nerissa discussing the merits or otherwise of her suitors in 'light-hearted banter'.[32] This small and specialised sample stands out among the fourteen verse and prose parts, and if we examine the biplot of the PCA data to visualise the word-variable loadings (Figure 2.2), we see that *he, his, him,* and *them* are among the heavily weighted words to the lower end of PC1. This is where the prose part of Portia's dialogue is plotted, reflecting the unusually high incidence of these words in Portia's prose speeches to Nerissa as she contemplates the series of eligible males who visit

[31] To recapitulate, 'function words' are very common words that mostly have a purely grammatical function, such as *a, at, on,* and *the*. See Appendix E for a list.
[32] Brook, *Language*, 160–1.

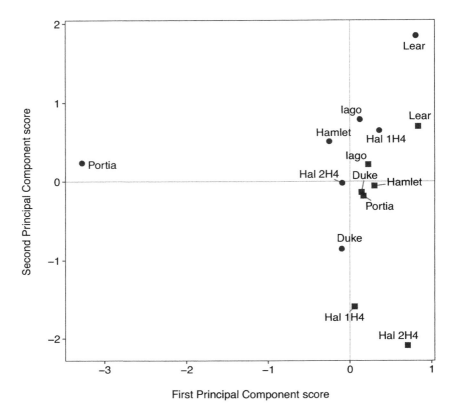

Figure 2.1 PCA scatterplot of prose and verse parts for 7 Shakespearean characters using the 100 most frequent function words.

Belmont to try their hand at the casket test devised by her father. For example, Portia dismisses the Neapolitan prince as 'a colt indeed, for *he* doth nothing but talk of *his* horse, and *he* makes it a great appropriation to *his* own good parts that *he* can shoe *him* himself' (1.3.39–41, emphasis added).

Plural forms dominate the highly weighted word-variables on PC2 in Figure 2.2, the *y*-axis – words such as *are, we* as a true plural (as opposed to a royal plural), *them, these,* and *their.* The dialogue samples plotted to the high end of PC2 are distinguished by considering groups rather than individuals. In these passages, characters generalise and make observations on behaviour – often satirical ones. T. S. Eliot's term 'sardonic comment'

● Prose ■ Verse

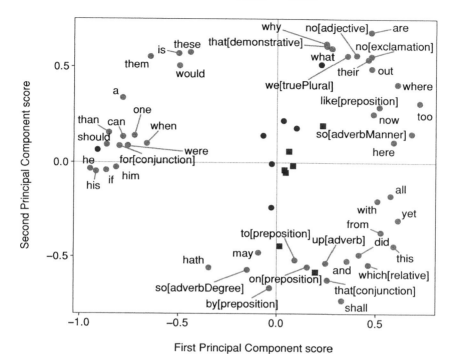

Figure 2.2 PCA biplot of prose and verse samples from 7 Shakespearean characters, using the 100 most frequent function words, highlighting the 48 most weighted word-variables.

for Hamlet's prose speeches is apt.[33] Plotted highest of all is Lear's prose part, which includes his speeches deploring human frailty and corruption: 'When *we are* born, *we* cry that *we are* come to this stage of fools' (4.5.171–2, emphasis added).

To the low end of PC2 are two old-fashioned words: *that* as a conjunction, which is often used in earlier texts and omitted in later ones, and *hath*. The lowest-weighted of all is *shall*, used in orders and discussion of the future. There are also three prepositions – *by*, *on*, and *to* – associated with specificity and detail. In these dialogue samples, characters give orders and concern themselves with detailed reports and actions. The dialogue sample with the lowest PC2 score is Hal's verse part in *2 Henry the Fourth*, in

[33] T. S. Eliot, *Poetry and Drama* (London: Faber and Faber, 1951), 14.

which he meditates (in verse) on his father's crown, and then rehearses the soliloquy to his father once the latter wakes – all passages of serious meditation, well-articulated, and logical. He addresses the Lord Chief Justice and others in the court, and Falstaff, once King, in archaic verse, poised and formal:

> [. . .] Yet be sad, good brothers,
> For, *by* my faith, it very well becomes you.
> Sorrow so royally in you appears
> *That* I will deeply put the fashion on,
> And wear it in my heart. Why then, be sad;
> But entertain no more of it, good brothers,
> Than a joint burden laid upon us all.
> For me, *by* heaven, I bid you be assured
> I'll be your father and your brother too.
> Let me but bear your love, I'll bear your cares.
> Yet weep *that* Harry's dead, and so will I;
> But Harry lives that *shall* convert those tears
> *By* number into hours of happiness.
> (5.2.49–61, emphasis added)

Along the *y*-axis, from Lear's prose part at the top and the verse part of Hal from *2 Henry the Fourth* at the bottom, the prose and verse parts of individual characters generally have very different scores. In these cases, the differences between prose and verse prove stronger than the similarities of the same character in the same play. The prose parts of six of the seven characters – Portia, Hamlet, Iago, Lear, and Hal in the two parts of *Henry the Fourth* – are plotted higher on PC2 than their corresponding verse parts. Nevertheless, overall the prose parts are not plotted higher than the verse parts. For example, Lear's verse part is on much the same level as the prose parts for Hamlet, Iago, and Hal from *1 Henry the Fourth*, even though Lear's verse part is plotted lower than his prose on the PC2 axis.

The stylistic profiles of these characters do vary as between the parts of their dialogue in verse and those in prose. In the prose parts, they adopt the stance of commentators and observers; in verse, they are involved in the action, and they offer detailed descriptions and instructions. One exception to this generalisation is the Duke in *Measure for Measure*, who is a direct participant in the action in his prose dialogue and is more like a commentator in his verse, reversing the pattern for the other characters. His prose is spoken when he is in disguise as the Friar, and acting to direct the course of events; in his role as Duke, out of disguise, he dispenses observations on the actions of his subjects, and his dialogue conforms better to the commentator pattern. He is an exception to the rule that prose for these characters is the medium for commentary, for 'criticism', to use Frank Kermode's term.[34] For prose to be adopted when a noble character is in disguise,[35] a contradictory pressure has reversed the usual polarity.

Generally, though, when one of the seven characters in this experiment moves to prose, his or her dialogue will be generalising and observing, a step away from close involvement in the action and from direct engagement with others on stage. In the terminology of Robert Weimann, he or she will take up a *platea Figurenposition* rather than a *locus* one and will, metaphorically at least, move to the edge of the stage, relate more directly to the audience, and leave the urgently forward-moving time scheme of the action for a speaking position sharing the audience's separate – more Olympian – temporality.[36]

Fourteen All-Verse and Fourteen All-Prose Comedies

Some patterns in the PCA scatterplot (Figure 2.1) relate readily to the familiar understanding of how verse and prose are used in plays, but nevertheless the difference between the two is not overwhelming. There are a number of cross-cutting factors. For instance, it is Portia's particular dramaturgic orientation in her prose speeches, rather than any general prose–verse distinction, that emerges as the most powerful factor overall. Among the dialogues of seven Shakespearean characters, there is no consistent and marked style that goes with verse as opposed to prose.

In order to explore the possibility of a 'verse' style distinct from a 'prose' one, we consider the helpfully clear-cut case of all-verse and all-prose plays belonging to the same genre. If the medium does impose a constraint, this should appear with regularity in the patterns of word use in one group as against the other. We begin by assembling two text sets for comparison: one with fourteen 'all-verse' comedies, and another with fourteen 'all-prose' comedies. A number of plays from the period are entirely verse or prose, but the majority contain a mixture of both forms in varying proportions. To account for this, we removed demonstrably prose passages (e.g. letters and brief exchanges involving servants) from predominantly verse comedies included in the 'all-verse' set, and demonstrably verse passages

---

[34] Frank Kermode, *Shakespeare's Language* (London: Penguin, 2000), 81.
[35] Bruster, 'Politics', 100.
[36] Bruster, 'Politics', 105. On the *locus* and *platea* schema, see Robert Weimann, *Shakespeare and the Popular Tradition in the Theater: Studies in the Social Dimension of Dramatic Form and Function*, ed. Robert Schwartz (Baltimore: Johns Hopkins University Press, 1978).

Table 2.2 *Fourteen more or less 'all-prose' and fourteen more or less 'all-verse'*
comedies. An obelisk indicates plays from which verse or prose
passages were excised

'All-prose' comedies	'All-verse' comedies
Chapman, *An Humorous Day's Mirth*	Fletcher, *Monsieur Thomas*
Chapman, *May Day*	Fletcher, *The Pilgrim*
Fletcher & Shirley (?), *Wit Without Money*	Fletcher, *The Wild-Goose Chase*
Greene & Lodge, *A Looking Glass for London*	Greene, *Orlando Furioso*†
Jonson, *Bartholomew Fair*†	Jonson, *The Alchemist*
Jonson, *Epicene*	Jonson, *The Devil is an Ass*
Lyly, *Campaspe*	Jonson, *The Tale of a Tub*
Lyly, *Midas*	Lyly, *The Woman in the Moon*†
Lyly, *Mother Bombie*	Middleton & Fletcher (?), *The Nice Valour*
Middleton, *The Puritan*†	Middleton, *The Widow*†
Middleton, *A Trick to Catch the Old One*†	Middleton, *The Witch*†
Shakespeare, *The Merry Wives of Windsor*†	Rowley, *A New Wonder, a Woman Never Vexed*
Sharpham, *Cupid's Whirligig*	Uncertain, *George-a-Greene*†
Sharpham, *The Fleer*	Uncertain, *A Knack to Know a Knave*†

(e.g. choruses and songs) from the 'all-prose' set.[37] Table 2.2 lists the plays
in the resulting 'more or less' all-prose and all-verse sets, indicating those
requiring prose or verse passages to be excised.[38]

We compare the frequencies of the top 100 most frequent function words
in both sets, using Welch's t-test as a measure of difference. To recall, the
t-test is a simple metric – the difference in means in the two sets divided
by a combination of the standard deviations of the two sets. A high t-test
score means that the average use in one set is much higher or lower than
the use in a second set, and the word overall does not fluctuate much. The
t–test generates a p-value estimating how often this level of difference in
this trial would come about if the two sets belonged to the same parent
population. The usual thresholds for this probability are $p < 0.05$, or one
in twenty, taken to be a 'significant' difference, and $p < 0.01$, or one in
a hundred, taken to be 'highly significant'. We use this second threshold

---

[37] The difficulty – and, in some cases, impossibility – of distinguishing verse set as prose in early
modern printed playbooks and *vice versa* also renders the task of compiling sets of *nearly* 'all-verse'
and 'all-prose' plays in statistically significant numbers a practical, if not theoretical, necessity.

[38] For this and subsequent tables of plays, see Appendix A for fuller bibliographical details.

here. The understanding is that in random data this degree of difference between two groups of samples for a given variable would appear around once in a hundred similar trials.

To provide a further calibration, we assemble several additional sets of twenty-eight plays: fourteen comedies and fourteen tragedies, all with mixed prose and verse dialogue; fourteen plays by Jonson and fourteen by Shakespeare; fourteen plays from 1600–4 and fourteen from 1610–14; and five randomly assembled comparison sets, each containing two groups of fourteen plays (Tables 2.3 and 2.4). Our question is, how does the prose–verse difference compare with those three other kinds of difference?

We take the top 100 most frequent function words, apply the *t*-test to each in the comparisons, and then count how many of the results exceeded a probability of 1 in a 100 of occurring by chance. In 100 such applications of the test – 100 different words – we expect one word-variable to exceed this probability threshold merely by chance. Figure 2.3 gives the results as a column chart.

The theoretical expectation for random data is that there would be 1 variable in a 100 over the 0.01 threshold, as represented by the grey column. The randomly assembled sets do indeed fit this expectation pretty well. One word-variable was below the threshold – that is, significantly different – in three of the tests, and in two tests there were none. There were seven word-variables with significant differences between the comedies and the tragedies,[39] ten between the two half-decades,[40] and twenty-three between the Shakespeare and Jonson plays.[41] It is unexpected that comedies are less different stylistically from tragedies than plays from two different half-decades with just a half-decade between them, but not surprising that Shakespeare is more different from Jonson than either, since that is the sort of result that is very common in studies of overall likenesses between plays and is the basis for authorship attribution.[42] The 'all-verse'

---

[39] The *t*-test *p*-value scores for these seven word-variables are: *well* (0.0003), *from* (0.0009), *a* (0.0011), *was* (0.0014), *that*$_{relative}$ (0.0043), *why* (0.0049), and *which*$_{relative}$ (0.0064).

[40] The *t*-test *p*-value scores for these ten word-variables are: *are* (0.0044), *hath* (0.0083), *have* (0.0013), *O* (0.0015), *how* (0.0026), *it* (0.003), *one* (0.0047), *upon*$_{preposition}$ (0.0058), *they* (0.0072), and *them* (0.0072).

[41] The *t*-test *p*-value scores for these twenty-three word-variables are: *for*$_{conjunction}$ (0.000000067), *that*$_{conjunction}$ (0.000002), *or* (0.000015), *can* (0.000019), *to*$_{preposition}$ (0.000057), *them* (0.000083), *all* (0.00032), *any* (0.00038), *so*$_{adverbManner}$ (0.00062), *thou* (0.00089), *hath* (0.0013), *thee* (0.002), *from* (0.0021), *are* (0.0028), *me* (0.0033), *they* (0.0038), *now* (0.0047), *did* (0.0055), *my* (0.0057), *that*$_{relative}$ (0.0059), *would* (0.0062), *too* (0.0066), and *thy* (0.0071).

[42] See, for example, Hugh Craig, 'Is the Author Really Dead? An Empirical Study of Authorship in English Renaissance Drama', *Empirical Studies in the Arts* 18.2 (2000), 119–34, where authorship emerges as the strongest factor creating resemblances between plays, followed by genre and then date.

Table 2.3 *Paired sets of fourteen mixed prose–verse plays: comedies and tragedies, plays by Jonson and Shakespeare, and plays dated 1600–4 and 1610–14*

Comedies	Tragedies	Jonson	Shakespeare	1600–4	1610–14
Brome, *A Jovial Crew*	Chapman, *Bussy D'Ambois*	*The Alchemist*	*2 Henry the Fourth*	Chapman, *Bussy D'Ambois*	Beaumont & Fletcher, *A King and No King*
Cooke (?), *Greene's Tu Quoque*	Chapman, *Byron's Conspiracy*	*Bartholomew Fair*	*All's Well That Ends Well*	Chapman, *May Day*	Cooke (?), *Greene's Tu Quoque*
Day, *The Isle of Gulls*	Chettle, *Hoffman*	*The Case is Altered*	*As You Like It*	Heywood, *1 If You Know Not Me*	Daborne, *A Christian Turned Turk*
Dekker, *The Shoemaker's Holiday*	Ford, *'Tis Pity She's a Whore*	*Catiline His Conspiracy*	*The Comedy of Errors*	Heywood, *The Wise Woman of Hoxton*	Dekker, *If It Be Not Good*
Greene, *Friar Bacon and Friar Bungay*	Kyd, *The Spanish Tragedy*	*Cynthia's Revels*	*Hamlet*	Heywood, *A Woman Killed with Kindness*	Field, Fletcher & Massinger, *The Honest Man's Fortune*
Heywood, *The Wise Woman of Hoxton*	Marlowe & others, *Doctor Faustus*	*Epicene*	*Henry the Fifth*	Jonson, *Cynthia's Revels*	Fletcher, *Bonduca*
Marston, *Jack Drum's Entertainment*	Marston, *Antonio's Revenge*	*Every Man Out of His Humour*	*Julius Caesar*	Jonson, *Poetaster*	Fletcher & Beaumont (?), *The Captain*
Marston, *Parasitaster*	Marston, *Sophonisba*	*The Magnetic Lady*	*King John*	Marston, *Antonio's Revenge*	Fletcher & Shakespeare, *Henry the Eighth*
Marston, *What You Will*	Middleton, *The Revenger's Tragedy*	*The New Inn*	*Love's Labour's Lost*	Marston, *Jack Drum's Entertainment*	Jonson, *The Alchemist*
Middleton, *A Mad World, My Masters*	Middleton, *The Second Maiden's Tragedy*	*Poetaster*	*The Merry Wives of Windsor*	Marston, *Parasitaster*	Jonson, *Bartholomew Fair*
Middleton, *Michaelmas Term*	Shakespeare & others (?), *Arden of Faversham*	*The Sad Shepherd*	*Richard the Second*	Marston, *What You Will*	Middleton, *More Dissemblers Besides Women*
Middleton, *Your Five Gallants*	Suckling, *Aglaura*	*Sejanus His Fall*	*Romeo and Juliet*	Shakespeare, *Othello*	Middleton, *The Second Maiden's Tragedy*
Uncertain, *The Taming of a Shrew*	Webster, *The Duchess of Malfi*	*The Staple of News*	*The Taming of the Shrew*	Shakespeare, *Troilus and Cressida*	Shakespeare, *The Tempest*
Wilson, *The Cobbler's Prophecy*	Webster, *The White Devil*	*The Tale of a Tub*	*The Winter's Tale*	Uncertain, *1 Hieronimo*	Webster, *The White Devil*

Table 2.4 *Five randomly paired comparison sets of fourteen mixed prose–verse plays*

Set A1	Set A2	Set B1	Set B2	Set C1
Dekker & Webster, *Sir Thomas Wyatt*	Beaumont & Fletcher, *A King and No King*	Fletcher, *The Island Princess*	Fletcher, *The Faithful Shepherdess*	Barkstead, Machin & Marston, *The Insatiate Countess*
Fletcher, *The Chances*	Dekker, *If It Be Not Good*	Jonson, *Catiline His Conspiracy*	Ford, *The Lover's Melancholy*	Chapman, *Bussy D'Ambois*
Fletcher, *A Wife for a Month*	Dekker, *The Shoemaker's Holiday*	Jonson, *Poetaster*	Lyly, *Galatea*	Dekker, *The Whore of Babylon*
Heywood, *2 The Fair Maid of the West*	Fletcher & Shakespeare, *The Two Noble Kinsmen*	Kyd, *The Spanish Tragedy*	Marston, *Antonio and Mellida*	Fletcher, *The Wild-Goose Chase*
Lyly, *Midas*	Greville, *Mustapha*	Markham & Sampson, *Herod and Antipater*	Shakespeare, *1 Henry the Fourth*	Greene & Lodge, *A Looking Glass for London*
Marlowe, *1 Tamburlaine the Great*	Greene, *James the Fourth*	Marlowe & Nashe (?), *Dido, Queen of Carthage*	Shakespeare & others, *2 Henry the Sixth*	Jonson, *The Case is Altered*
Massinger, *The Roman Actor*	Marston, *Sophonisba*	Marmion, *The Antiquary*	Shakespeare & Middleton, *Measure for Measure*	Lyly, *Mother Bombie*
Middleton, *A Mad World, My Masters*	Middleton, *No Wit, No Help Like a Woman's*	Marston, *The Dutch Courtesan*	Shakespeare & Middleton, *Timon of Athens*	Marlowe, *The Massacre at Paris*
Nashe, *Summer's Last Will and Testament*	Shakespeare, *Julius Caesar*	Middleton, *The Widow*	Sharpham, *Cupid's Whirligig*	Marlowe & others (?), *The Jew of Malta*
Shakespeare, *2 Henry the Fourth*	Shakespeare, *King Lear*	Phillip, *Patient and Meek Grissel*	Shirley, *Love's Cruelty*	Middleton, *A Chaste Maid in Cheapside*
Shirley, *The Cardinal*	Shakespeare, *Love's Labour's Lost*	Shakespeare & others (?), *Arden of Faversham*	Uncertain, *Appius and Virginia*	Middleton, *The Second Maiden's Tragedy*
Uncertain, *Edmond Ironside*	Shakespeare, *Romeo and Juliet*	Shakespeare & Wilkins, *Pericles, Prince of Tyre*	Uncertain, *The True Tragedy of Richard the Third*	Middleton, *The Witch*
Uncertain, *Fair Em*	Uncertain, *John of Bordeaux*	Shirley, *The Traitor*	Uncertain, *The Valiant Welshman*	Wilmot & others, *Tancred and Gismund*

(*cont.*)

Table 2.4 (cont.)

Set C2	Set D1	Set D2	Set E1	Set E2
Uncertain, *The Famous Victories of Henry the Fifth*	Uncertain, *The Wars of Cyrus*	Uncertain, *George-a-Greene*	Webster, *The Devil's Law-Case*	Wilson, *The Three Lords and Three Ladies of London*
Cooke (?), *Greene's Tu Quoque*	Chapman, *1 The Blind Beggar of Alexandria*	Chapman, *Caesar and Pompey*	Brandon, *The Virtuous Octavia*	Beaumont & Fletcher, *The Maid's Tragedy*
Ford, *The Broken Heart*	Chettle, *Hoffman*	Chapman, *An Humorous Day's Mirth*	Chapman, *Byron's Conspiracy*	Cary, *The Tragedy of Mariam*
Heywood, *The Wise Woman of Hoxton*	Fletcher, *Women Pleased*	Chapman, *Monsieur D'Olive*	Dekker, *1 Old Fortunatus*	Davenant, *The Unfortunate Lovers*
Jonson, *Cynthia's Revels*	Ford, *'Tis Pity She's a Whore*	Chapman, *Sir Giles Goosecap*	Fletcher, *The Loyal Subject*	Fletcher, *Valentinian*
Marston, *Jack Drum's Entertainment*	Jonson, *Bartholomew Fair*	Daniel, *Cleopatra*	Fletcher & Beaumont (?), *The Captain*	Haughton, *The Devil and His Dame*
Marston, *The Malcontent*	Jonson, *Every Man Out of His Humour*	Fletcher & Massinger, *The Double Marriage*	Goffe, *The Courageous Turk*	Jonson, *The Devil is an Ass*
Middleton, *A Game at Chess*	Jonson, *The Sad Shepherd*	Ford, *Love's Sacrifice*	Heywood, *The Four Prentices of London*	Jonson, *Epicene*
Middleton, *The Phoenix*	Lodge, *The Wounds of Civil War*	Jonson, *Every Man in His Humour*	Heywood, *A Woman Killed with Kindness*	Jonson, *The New Inn*
Munday & others, *Sir Thomas More*	Middleton, *Hengist, King of Kent*	Lyly, *Endymion*	Jonson, *The Staple of News*	Lyly, *The Woman in the Moon*
Peele, *Edward the First*	Porter, *1 The Two Angry Women of Abingdon*	Marston, *What You Will*	Lyly, *Campaspe*	Shakespeare, *Henry the Fifth*
Peele, *The Old Wife's Tale*	Shakespeare, *Othello*	Middleton, *The Puritan*	Marlowe, *1 Tamburlaine the Great*	Shakespeare, *King John*
Shakespeare & others, *1 Henry the Sixth*	Suckling, *Aglaura*	Shakespeare, *Cymbeline*	Marston, *Antonio's Revenge*	Shakespeare, *A Midsummer Night's Dream*
Uncertain, *1 Hieronimo*	Uncertain, *1 Selimus*	Shakespeare & others, *3 Henry the Sixth*	Rowley, *A New Wonder, a Woman Never Vexed*	Shakespeare, *Twelfth Night*
Uncertain, *John a Kent and John a Cumber*	Uncertain, *A Warning for Fair Women*	Uncertain, *The Hector of Germany*	Shakespeare, *Much Ado About Nothing*	Shakespeare, *The Two Gentlemen of Verona*

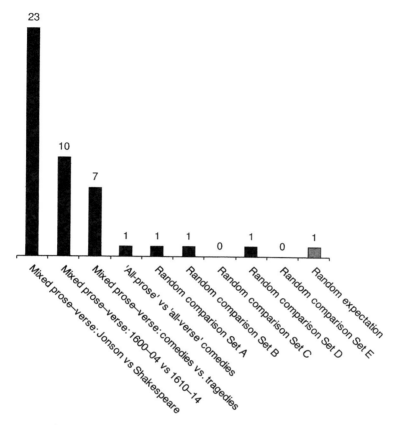

Figure 2.3 Column chart of word-variables exceeding the 0.01 probability threshold in the groups plays detailed in Tables 2.2–2.4

and 'all-prose' comedies show only the sort of difference we expect in any assemblage of plays (the grey column). There was only one word-variable with a significant difference – *an*, with a *p*-value of 0.004.

In early modern English drama, it would seem that comedies in prose are not immediately distinguishable stylistically from comedies in verse. There is evidently nothing about writing in verse as against prose that requires a particular profile of use of very common words – nothing so powerful, at least, that it emerges whenever verse plays are compared directly with prose plays. When tackling a comedy with dialogue entirely in prose, it seems that playwrights were able to vary their style even within that mode to achieve effects of rich elaboration and conscious artificiality. Equally, if writing a

verse comedy, playwrights were seemingly able to present domestic business and exchanges on everyday topics within the constraints of metre and
within the language conventions that come with verse, in a way that is not
distinguishable from prose drama.

There may, of course, be other ways in which the styles of 'all-prose'
and 'all-verse' comedies differ. We have only taken function words into
account, and then only the summary whole-play incidence of these words,
with no regard, for instance, for the placement of the words in the order of
sentences. On the other hand, whatever its limitations, the common-words
data does evidently bear traces of difference in contrasts by genre, author,
and date, so any inherent prose–verse stylistic distinction is fainter than
these, or different in kind from them.

In another study, Ulrich Busse examined word use in prose and verse
comedies – this time confined to Shakespeare. Busse finds a correlation
between prose passages and *you* pronoun forms, and between verse passages and *thou* forms in Shakespeare.[43] In fifteen out of eighteen Shakespeare comedies, where there is a significant difference, *thou* forms are
over-represented in verse sections.[44] Yet these correlations do not appear
in the all-prose and all-verse plays. None of the *thou* and *you* forms – *thou*,
thy, *thine*, *thee*, *ye*, *you*, *your*, and *yours* – are higher or lower in the prose
plays compared with the verse plays, at least not markedly and consistently
higher.

It seems we have to rethink the prose–verse contrast on every level. If
there is indeed little difference between the style of 'all-prose' and 'all-verse'
comedies, then why would readers and writers – then and now – have paid
such heed to the distinction? Why did John Lyly feel the need to forsake his
career-long practice of writing comedies in prose to write *The Woman in
the Moon* in verse? The most obvious explanation is the enduring prestige
of verse, and one small benefit of casting doubt on the idea of a necessary
stylistic difference with prose is to throw attitudes towards verse into a new
light.

Mixed Prose–Verse Comedies

The 'all-verse' and 'all-prose' comedies do not show any marked and consistent differences in their use of very common words. But, as we saw
earlier, there were some significant differences in characters within one
play who mix verse and prose. What about comedies which contain mix-
tures, looked at overall? To explore this, we selected fourteen comedies with

---

[43] Busse, *Linguistic*, 63–76.   [44] Busse, *Linguistic*, 69.

Table 2.5 *Set of fourteen comedies with prose-to-verse ratios between 1:1 and 3:17*

Play	Percentage prose	Words (prose)	Percentage verse	Words (verse)
Brome, *A Jovial Crew*	31.9	7,725	68.1	16,465
Chapman, *Sir Giles Goosecap*	26.1	5,337	73.9	15,096
Cooke (?), *Greene's Tu Quoque*	38.4	8,986	61.6	14,393
Day, *The Isle of Gulls*	14.7	3,129	85.3	18,219
Dekker, *The Shoemaker's Holiday*	42.7	8,189	57.3	10,981
Field, *Amends for Ladies*	53.4	9,503	46.6	8,278
Jonson, *Every Man in His Humour*	79.7	20,520	20.3	5,228
Jonson, *Poetaster*	35.8	9,011	64.2	16,150
Marston, *The Dutch Courtesan*	25.5	4,623	74.5	13,471
Middleton, *A Mad World, My Masters*	24.2	4,449	75.8	13,915
Middleton, *The Phoenix*	34.4	6,910	65.6	13,181
Shakespeare, *As You Like It*	42.6	9,146	57.4	12,311
Shakespeare, *Twelfth Night*	42	8,283	58	11,437
Wilson, *The Cobbler's Prophecy*	71.8	9,074	28.2	3,572

prose-to-verse ratios somewhere between 1:1 (or 50% to 50%) and 3:17 (or 15% to 85%). Table 2.5 lists these plays.[45]

We repeat the procedure as before, only this time pitting the fourteen verse and prose portions listed in Table 2.5 against each other. How many of the 100 very common words are significantly more or less common between the two groups, prose versus verse? Figure 2.4 introduces the results from the new test (in the striped column) to those from the previous test.

There are seventeen word-variables with significant scores, much more than we expect in a pairing of randomly chosen plays, and somewhere between the chronology and author comparisons. Evidently, playwrights do pursue consistently different styles in verse and prose when they are deployed within a play. This time, also, some of the words Busse discussed are significantly different – *thy* is much higher in the verse portions and *you* is much higher in the prose portions.[46]

Another aspect which may well differ between mixed prose–verse and 'all-verse' plays is the amount of rhymed verse included. While our texts

---

[45] John Day's *The Isle of Gulls* only just satisfies the criterion, with 15 per cent prose if we round up to whole numbers. Thomas Dekker's *The Shoemaker's Holiday*, as well as Shakespeare's *As You Like It* and *Twelfth Night*, are closer to an even split, with roughly 57 per cent verse to 43 per cent prose.

[46] The *t*-test *p*-value scores for these word-variables, with whole plays first, rumps second, are as follows: *thou* 0.865, 0.773; *thee* 0.095, 0.507; *thy* 0.940, 0.000; *you* 0.281, 0.001; and *your* 0.646, 0.058. *Thine* and *yours* do not appear in the list of the 100 most common words used in this experiment.

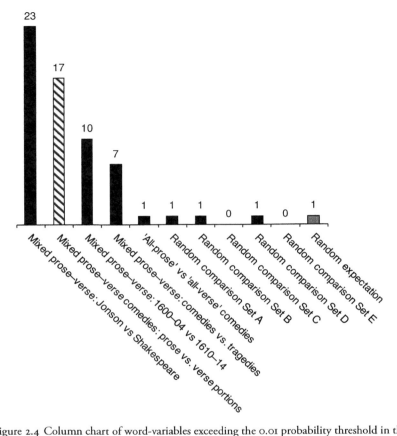

Figure 2.4 Column chart of word-variables exceeding the 0.01 probability threshold in the groups plays detailed in Tables 2.2–2.5.

were not marked up to identify rhymed lines, which meant we could not pursue this systematically, examination of the plays suggested that the mixed-form plays had more rhymed verse. We did not find any rhymed verse in *Monsieur Thomas*, *The Wild-Goose Chase*, or *The Woman in the Moon*, for example, and while other plays listed in Table 2.2 certainly include songs and interior masque speeches in verse, and numerous couplets to end speeches, as well as rhyming prologues and epilogues, the overall proportion seems low. By contrast, all the mixed-form plays listed in Table 2.5 have significant amounts of rhymed verse, going beyond isolated couplets and the familiar specialised forms. *The Isle of Gulls*, for example, is almost entirely in rhyme, whereas just under 20 per cent of the verse

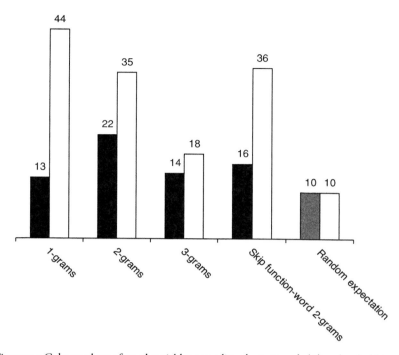

■ All-verse vs all-prose comedies □ Verse vs prose portions of comedies

Figure 2.5 Column chart of word-variables exceeding the 0.01 probability threshold in the groups of plays detailed in Tables 2.2 and 2.5.

lines are rhymed in the two mixed-form Shakespeare plays examined, *As You Like It* and *Twelfth Night*.[47]

This relatively high proportion of rhymed to blank verse could be regarded as part of the specialisation of forms in the mixed-mode plays: perhaps playwrights are more inclined to draw attention to the fact that lines are in verse by using rhyme? It may also help explain the differentiation between prose and verse if we posit that rhymed verse brings with it more constraints on sentence construction than blank verse. This is mere speculation, however, until a suitable corpus is marked up to separate rhymed verse from the rest.

We were able to test prose–verse differentiation in the plays as already marked up with a longer list of word-types and some other kinds of variable. Figure 2.5 gives the test results as a column graph, indicating the

---

[47] E. K. Chambers, *William Shakespeare: A Study of Facts and Problems* (Oxford: Clarendon Press, 1930), II: 397–408.

Table 2.6 *Shannon entropies of 'all-prose' versus 'all-verse' comedies and prose portions versus verse portions of mixed-mode comedies*

Comparison	t-test p-value	Mean Shannon entropy	
		Prose	Verse
'All-prose' versus 'all-verse' comedies	0.63	5.62	5.63
Prose portions versus verse portions of mixed-mode comedies	0. 00000000002	5.60	5.80

number of significant differences among the 1,000 most frequent words (or '1-grams'), rather than the 100 most frequent function words as before, the 1,000 most frequent word-pairs (or '2-grams'), the 1,000 most frequent word-triplets (or '3-grams'), and the 1,000 most frequent function-word 'skip' word-pairs.[48] The 'all-prose' and 'all-verse' comparison groups in Table 2.2 are represented by black columns and the mixed-plays comparison group in Table 2.5 by unfilled columns.

While the 'all-prose' versus 'all-verse' comparison picks up some more significant word-variables, above random expectation (represented by the grey column), the comparison between the prose and verse portions in mixed-mode plays picks up even more.

Finally, we examined the Shannon entropies of the various texts. To recall, Shannon entropy is a measure of the repetitiveness of a set of data; when applied to linguistic data, it scores each text along a spectrum of word use from the highly repetitive (with a correspondingly low entropy score) to the constantly varied (with a high entropy score). For this test, all the vocabulary – from the most common function word to the rarest exotic term – was included.[49] The texts were segmented into non-overlapping 3,000 word blocks, with the smaller blocks at the ends of the segments discarded. Table 2.6 gives the t-test p-value scores for the two comparisons, as

---

[48] Consider the following eleven-word sentence: 'As such, he would only count the words he could read.' If we counted individual function words, our total would be seven – that is, everything except *only, count, words,* and *read.* If we counted function-word word-pairs (that is, pairs of function words found directly adjacent to one another), our total would be four: *as such, such he, he would,* and *he could.* If we ignored the lexical words that fall between the function words and counted the resulting word-pairs (so-called 'skip' function-word word-pairs), our total would be six: *as such, such he, he would, would the, the he, he could.* On 'skip' n-grams and their use in authorship attribution, see Alexis Antonia, Hugh Craig, and Jack Elliott, 'Language Chunking, Data Sparseness, and the Value of a Long Marker List', *Literary and Linguistic Computing* 29.2 (2014), 147–63.

[49] Proper names, however, were excluded from the analysis.

an estimate of how different they are on this measure, as well as the mean Shannon entropies for verse and prose respectively in the two pairings.

The 'all-prose' and 'all-verse' comedies score much the same on this measure, with their mean Shannon entropies suggesting that verse drama is not necessarily richer in vocabulary than prose drama. This confirms an intuition that poetic diction does not of itself bring a greater diversity in vocabulary, and neither does the informality or unboundedness of prose. By contrast, the prose and verse portions of mixed-mode plays produce significantly different entropy scores, with the verse portions incorporating a more varied vocabulary.

Conclusion

There is, it seems, no necessary stylistic adaptation for prose comedy as against verse comedy. However, the contrast between prose and verse was laden with meaning in the theatrical and literary world of early modern England, and authors exploited these associations in their work. If we move from plays exclusively in prose or verse to plays employing a mixture of both, systematic contrasts appear in terms of character groups, register, and tone. Prose and verse drama do not necessarily have to be different, but they often are. If they set out to write a play entirely in one mode, playwrights were perfectly capable of representing the same kaleidoscope of styles using prose or verse alone. Often, though, they mixed the two modes within the same play, as Shakespeare does in many cases. In these instances, we observe a sharp divergence in styles.

T. S. Eliot's lectures on *Poetry and Drama* offer a helpful framework for this odd-seeming situation. 'Whether we use prose or verse on the stage,' he remarks, 'they are both but means to an end.' 'The difference', for Eliot, 'is not as great as one might think': prose, like verse, 'has been written, and rewritten', such that 'prose, on the stage, is as artificial as verse' and 'verse can be as natural as prose'.[50] In the same vein, Frank Kermode notes that Hamlet's prose speech on human nobility – beginning 'What a piece of work is man' (2.2.305–12) – is so well crafted that it 'might have been designed to show that prose can double poetry'.[51] On the opposite side of the question, the capacity of verse to approach prose, Eliot demonstrates that Shakespeare for one was capable of a wide range of styles within verse, evident in the first scene of *Hamlet*, all in verse, where we find lines of

---

[50] Eliot, *Poetry and Drama*, 12–13.   [51] Kermode, *Shakespeare's Language*, 111.

simple speech which might be either prose or verse. Lines 1–22 of the opening scene of *Hamlet* are 'built of the simplest words in the most homely
idiom', such that 'we are unconscious of the medium of its expression'. Eliot
characterises Horatio's comment, 'So have I heard and do in part believe
it' (1.1.146), as 'a line of the simplest speech which might be either prose
or verse'. Here, as elsewhere in the scene, the verse is '*transparent*', and the
audience is not likely to be aware that the medium is verse.[52] Nevertheless,
there are lines in the same scene that demand a different sort of attention:
Eliot offers Horatio's 'the morn in russet mantle clad' (1.1.147), which follows hard on the line quoted before, in which we can see 'a deliberate brief
emergence of the poetic into consciousness'.[53]

   Other scholars have made similar points about the potential of dramatic
verse and dramatic prose to converge and even overlap in the characteristics
for which each is noted. N. F. Blake comments that although it is sometimes claimed that the language of Shakespeare's prose is 'more colloquial
and less artificial than that found in the verse', many prose passages, such as
the speech of Shylock's servant Lancelot Gobbo Blake analyses, are in fact
'literary in [their] affiliation[s]' – in them, 'little or nothing' is 'inserted
as a marker of informal language'.[54] Shakespeare is capable of writing a
highly decorative prose, as with Osric and Falstaff.[55] On the 'absence of
cant, slang and dialect in Shakespearian plays', Blake offers the example of
1 Henry the Fourth, which, despite having 'low-life' characters, contains no
'low-life language'.[56] All this suggests for the purposes of the present study
that Shakespeare's prose – and, by extension, early modern dramatic prose
generally – might not be as far apart from verse stylistically as the numerous
contrasts of the two would suggest. On similar lines, Brian Vickers urges
modern readers to 'read Renaissance prose as if it were poetry', not to treat
it as an 'antithetical' medium to verse.[57]

   The *Hamlet* scene Eliot singles out is entirely in verse, and that is
what he recommends for the modern playwright – to remain in a single
medium. However, Eliot acknowledges that it was common for early modern playwrights to mix verse and prose. The *transparency* of verse which

---

[52] Eliot, *Poetry and Drama*, 16, 18, 16. Crystal's reminder that 'in a "verse play", like *Richard II*, even
      the gardeners talk verse' is apposite ('*Think*', 208). Barish notes that in Molière's celebrated prose
      comedy *L'Avare*, his prose 'displays much the same neutral clarity as his verse' (*Ben Jonson*, 292).
[53] Eliot, *Poetry and Drama*, 18.
[54] N. F. Blake, *Shakespeare's Language: An Introduction* (London: Macmillan, 1983), 29–30.
[55] Blake, *Shakespeare's Language*, 28–9.   [56] Blake, *Shakespeare's Language*, 30.
[57] Brian Vickers (ed.), 'Introduction', *Seventeenth-Century Prose* (London: Longmans, Green & Co.,
      1969), 3.

he has identified as an ideal disappears abruptly when prose and verse are mixed: 'each transition makes the auditor aware, with a jolt, of the medium'. Such transitions, however risky for the modern playwright, were 'easily acceptable to an Elizabethan audience, to whose ears both prose and verse came naturally; who liked highfalutin and low comedy in the same play'.[58] Here Eliot anticipates the contrast between verse and prose used as the entire mode for a play as against verse or prose used side by side within the same play which emerges from the quantitative results we have been discussing.

Eliot's main interest in his lectures is in establishing the requirements for an *ideal* modern verse drama. His advice to the playwrights of his own time is that they should avoid including prose in these plays. He also regards prose drama as foregoing a 'peculiar range of sensibility [which] can be expressed by dramatic poetry, at its moments of greatest intensity'.[59] These concerns take him in a different direction from the present focus on the *actual* performance of early modern playwrights. Yet the ideas in the Eliot lectures of a possible 'transparency' for verse, and of the opposite, the 'jolt' when the two modes are juxtaposed, forcing the audience to an awareness of the medium, help to conceptualise a system where prose or verse could be neutral, and brought with them no automatic consequences in style at the level of common word use frequency, and yet could also be polarised for local expressive purposes.

We can conclude that verse in these comedies does not require any variation in the overall use of words compared with prose, despite the obvious and often remarked-on differences between these two mediums for drama.[60] The interchangeability of prose and verse puts another clear fact about these two mediums – that the availability of a contrast is a powerful expressive means in plays, with no simple rules for local effects, but all the more effective for that – into the spotlight. Verse and prose can be transparent, but in juxtaposition they can become suddenly visible and bring

---

[58] Eliot, *Poetry and Drama*, 13–14.   [59] Eliot, *Poetry and Drama*, 34.

[60] This finding is significant for attribution studies, since practitioners often assume *a priori* and as a matter of common sense that the prose–verse difference is a confounding variable in authorship. They therefore limit themselves to samples in one or other mode, for example, to dramatic and non-dramatic verse – such as Ward E. Y. Elliott and Robert J. Valenza, 'Oxford by the Numbers: What Are the Odds that the Earl of Oxford Could Have Written Shakespeare's Poems and Plays?' *The Tennessee Law Review* 72.1 (2004), 323–453 – or even to dramatic verse in one metre – such as John Nance, 'From Shakespeare "To ye Q"', *Shakespeare Quarterly* 67.2 (2016), 204–31. The work above suggests the possibility that the prose–verse difference within dramatic dialogue is less important than the difference between dramatic verse and non-dramatic verse, and offers a promising area for further quantitative study.

audiences to an intense awareness of different orders of being, from sanity and madness to close engagement and sharp disaffection. The prose–verse contrast does not, apparently, bring with it stylistic constraints. That may free us to see it more clearly as a carrier of dramatic meaning, as when Freevill switches to verse, or Malheureux abruptly reverts to prose.

CHAPTER 3

Sisters under the Skin
Character and Style

If we extract the speeches of each of the individual speakers in the plays and combine them into a single document, we are then able to compare these composite 'character' texts with one another, within the same play or across a larger corpus. This allows us to view 'characters' in a shared, neutral space, independently of their local contexts in plays and of the larger structures of the plays from which they are extracted, such as authorial canon and genre.

In some ways, this returns us to the realities of the early modern theatre, since for actors 'character' was almost certainly a more important conceptual unit than 'play'. Actors learning their parts, as Simon Palfrey and Tiffany Stern remind us, were supplied with a paper roll containing only their characters' lines and necessary cues, and not the entire playbook. In this sense, as they note, 'the part has a physical as well as an institutional reality', and this physical aspect 'facilitates not only intra-play, but inter-play references'.[1] Audiences and readers may similarly privilege 'character' in their appreciation of drama, as when characters like Tamburlaine or Faustus seem to loom larger than the plays in which they appear. Some characters, such as Shakespeare's Falstaff, may reappear in sequels or in entirely different plays. King Charles I famously replaced the titles of three of the plays in his copy of the Shakespeare Second Folio with the names of their main characters, Malvolio, Falstaff, and Paroles, apparently as substitute titles.[2] In 2016 Rebecca McCutcheon premiered a 'new' play 'by' Shakespeare, *Margaret of Anjou*, fashioned by Elizabeth Schafer and Philippa Kelly from Margaret's appearances in *Richard the Third* and the three *Henry the Sixth* plays.[3]

---

[1] Simon Palfrey and Tiffany Stern, *Shakespeare in Parts* (Oxford University Press, 2007), 7.

[2] Michael Burns, 'Why No *Henry VII*? (With a Postscript on Malvolio's Revenge)', in B. A. W. Jackson (ed.), *Manner and Meaning in Shakespeare: Stratford Papers 1965–67* (Hamilton: McMaster University Library Press, 1969), 231.

[3] *Margaret of Anjou: A New Play by Shakespeare*, dir. Rebecca McCutcheon (Caryl Churchill Theatre, Egham, 8 Mar. 2016).

We might expect the closest resemblances to be between characters created by the same authors, but there are reasons for similarities to appear
across authorial canons as well. Impressive characters may well inspire
derivatives and imitations. Recognisable stock characters are an important
resource for playwrights, since they help audiences see lines of action and
bring with them ready-made expectations, which can be fulfilled or frus-
trated. Since the repertoire of plots and settings will always be limited,
shared structures will create dramatic niches to be filled by the same 'sort'
of character, just as ecological niches in different parts of the globe may give
rise to very similar evolutionary outcomes in species. Thus characters have
their own identities and functions within particular plots, but they also
fall into recognisable categories. When John Marston's boy actors confer
on their roles in the Induction to *Antonio and Mellida*, with their '*parts in
their hands*', they speak in terms of such stock character types: a 'proud'
duke who 'strut[s]' with his hair 'stroke up', a penurious lover, a fool, a
parasite, a cross-dressing male lover, a *braggadocio*, a Stoic, and a mercurial
duke's son – each describing how to 'dispose [his] speech to the habit of
[his] part'.[4]

The methods of computational stylistics give us the opportunity to
explore these resemblances across plays and to relate patterns in characters' language use to broader structures in the drama. The quantitative part
of our analysis is confined to the characters' spoken dialogue, and then to
what profiles of frequency among the commoner words can tell us. With
these figures and profiles, we then return to the richer, more comprehensive
matrix which embraces action, costume, casting, and dramatic meaning –
literary history in the broadest sense – for context. The observations we
make below – that Richard III is the quintessential mainstream character,
Bosola and Flamineo are closer than most sequel characters, Queen Margaret and the Duke of Anjou are exact matches along the most important stylistic axes, and that *Julius Caesar* is a standout in its immediate
theatrical context – enshrine truths of a sort, since we can trace each of
them back to an empirical base. Yet in a larger sense they are best thought
of as challenges to interpretation, each dependent on a particular frame
of reference. It is a tribute to the complex codes in language and their
robust underlying structures that we get even these occasional tantalising
glimpses of deeper dramatic realities from a simple calculus of percentage
counts.

---

4 John Marston, *Antonio and Mellida*, ed. W. Reavley Gair (Manchester University Press, 1991), Ind.
  0 sd., 14, 45.

This is an exercise in the empirical sociology of character. We start by looking at characters in the mass, rather than as individuals, on the basis of a literal-minded approach to language as a series of word tokens. This analysis shares the double-edged quality typical of most quantitative generalisations in the humanities and social sciences. Two people live in the same area, earn $1,000 a week (plus or minus $100), and are both vegetarian. This series of alignments is immediately suggestive, but when we interview the individuals concerned we may or may not sense some parallels in the dimensions which were our primary interest, such as world-view and personality. Even so, at least we shall have the comfort of a rigorous, explicit beginning to the search for the subtler differentiations and parallels.

Proximities between Characters

As the long history of character criticism in Shakespeare studies has shown,[5] it is tempting to treat each character in early modern English drama as one-of-a-kind, with motivations and life histories peculiar to themselves. In a sense, this is true: all characters reflect aspects of the individuality of their authors and actors, while characters based on recognisable figures, from famous rulers to infamous renegades, rely upon – and contribute towards – the shared histories of their namesakes. However, characters are also creations in a specific cultural context, products of imitation as well as invention, brought into being to figure within the particular structures of a constrained dramatic world. If we focus on the resemblances between characters rather than their differences, we can then bring out this patterned effect.

With this aim in mind, we extracted 666 characters with more than 2,000 words of dialogue from a corpus of 243 plays performed by professional companies between 1580 and 1642 (Appendix B). Confining the analysis to characters with larger speaking roles such as these narrows the overall range in size, and reduces size as a factor in comparisons. It also allows more of the 'law of large numbers' to come into play, so that local aberrations are evened out in a more extended to and fro of situations and motivations. We found the 100 most common function words in the plays overall and compiled a table of percentage counts for these words for each character. We then calculated a distance between each character and every

---

[5] Representative examples include Maurice Morgann, *An Essay on the Dramatic Character of Sir John Falstaff* (London: T. Davies, 1777), and A. C. Bradley, *Shakespearean Tragedy* (London: Macmillan, 1904). See also Christy Desmet, *Reading Shakespeare's Characters: Rhetoric, Ethics, and Identity* (Amherst: University of Massachusetts Press, 1992).

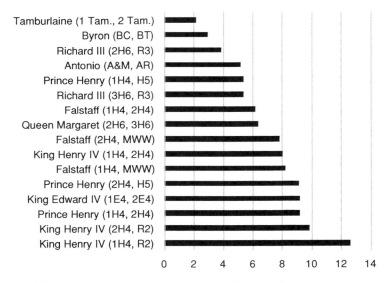

Figure 3.1 Distances between characters in plays and their sequels, using percentage counts
of the 100 most common function words combined by Squared Euclidean Distance.

other character based on a simple geometric relationship between their
various word counts.[6] Our interest was to see which pairs of matching
characters emerged, and to identify any wider patterns in these pairings.

Comparing each of the 666 characters with every other results in a total
of 221,445 pairings. Of these, the closest was Tamburlaine from *1 Tamburlaine the Great* and Tamburlaine from *2 Tamburlaine the Great*. Figure
3.1 shows the distance between these two characters in relation to the other
pairings in the set which involve a character reappearing in a sequel or
sequels – the shorter the bar for a pairing, the closer are the two characters
concerned.

Eight of the sixteen pairings have distances over 7.5 and fall into a
crowded part of the overall distribution of distance scores. They are only a
little closer as pairings than we would expect in a pair of characters taken
at random from the full set (Figure 3.2).

---

[6] There are two distance metrics typically used in such experiments: Manhattan and Squared
Euclidean. The Manhattan distance is the sum of absolute differences, so-named because city blocks
in Manhattan cannot be cut across by travellers, who must instead navigate around them. Between
two characters, the Manhattan distance is calculated by finding the absolute difference in frequency-
counts for each word, and then adding these together. Squared Euclidean distance, by contrast, takes
the square root of these absolute differences, thus corresponding to distance 'as the crow flies'. In this
chapter, we adopt Squared Euclidean distance as our standard method for estimating proximities
between characters.

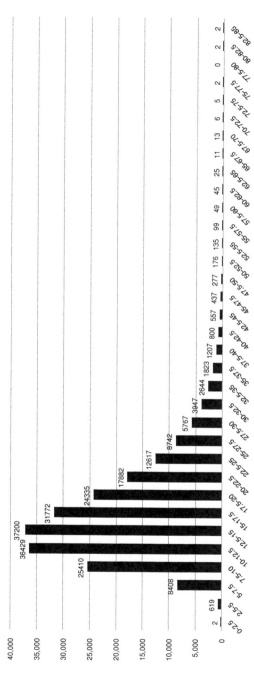

Figure 3.2 Histogram of distances between 666 characters based on percentage counts of the 100 most common function words (221,445 pairings in total).

All the distances are represented in Figure 3.2, grouped in 34 cells covering the span from 0 to 85. This is a skewed normal distribution with a high
peak: there is a long tail of distance scores to the high end, and the most
populous cell – the range between 12.5 and 15 – contains 37,200 values, or
16.8 per cent of the whole. There are just two values under 2.5, and two
over 82.5. The lowest value – that is, the shortest distance – is between the
two Tamburlaine characters.

Reverting to Figure 3.1, we see that next closest pairing of a character
appearing in a play and its sequel involves Byron from George Chapman's
Byron's Conspiracy and the same character from *Byron's Tragedy*. In between
(and not shown in Figure 3.1) are eight other pairings. In ascending order
of distance, they are: Shakespeare's Richard III and Hoffman from Henry
Chettle's eponymous play; Ithocles and Orgilus from John Ford's *The Broken Heart*; Herod and Antipater from the collaborative play named for
them by Gervase Markham and William Sampson; two characters from
different plays by John Webster – Bosola from *The Duchess of Malfi* and
Flamineo from *The White Devil* – nihilistic, philosophical characters, both
villainous yet not unambiguously evil; the eponymous Richard III and
Volpone; Sejanus from Ben Jonson's play of that name and Cicero from
Jonson's *Catiline*; two Thomas Middleton characters from different plays,
both schemers in city comedies – Witgood, penniless nephew of a rich
uncle in *A Trick to Catch the Old One*, and Quomodo, the rich conniving
merchant from *Michaelmas Term*; and two characters from different plays
by Christopher Marlowe – Faustus from *Doctor Faustus* and Barabas from
The Jew of Malta.

This is a group of the very tightest pairings. The distances between
them are very low indeed, belonging in the two extreme left-hand columns
of Figure 3.2. Some of the characteristics of this group are as one might
have predicted: all but the two involving Richard III share an author, for
instance. It is a surprise, though, that two of the pairings bring together
characters from the same play, since character differentiation is often
regarded as an inherent characteristic of theatre: Hubert C. Heffner, for
example, defined character as 'the differentiation of one agent from another
agent in the action', and drama as 'the art purely of character in action'.[7]

Equally unexpected is the result that sequel characters, such as Falstaff
in both parts of *Henry the Fourth* and King Edward in Thomas Heywood's
two-part *Edward the Fourth*, have higher distances than this group. One
would have thought that the conjunction of so many factors in sequel

---

[7] Hubert C. Heffner, 'Pirandello and the Nature of Man', *Tulane Drama Review* 1.3 (1957), 24.

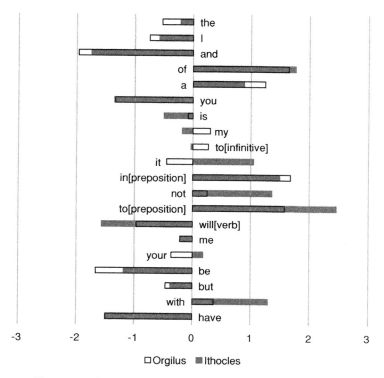

Figure 3.3 The *z*-scores for the 20 most common function words for Orgilus and Ithocles in John Ford's *The Broken Heart,* using averages and standard deviations from the full set of 666 characters with ≥ 2,000 words of dialogue.

characters – the same author, genre, and dramatic niche and setting, as well as the same or similar plot dynamic – would guarantee a near perfect match, but they are exceeded in the event by quite unrelated characters. Of the face of it, this analysis suggests we should regard likeness between characters less as a matter of identity – a function of the dramatist's aim to represent a unique on-stage personality – and more as a matter of functional role, closer to the types Marston describes – proud dukes, penurious lovers, fools, parasites, and so on. Ithocles and Orgilus are cases in point. They are bitter enemies. Ithocles is determined to prevent the marriage of his sister to Orgilus, and finally murders him. Yet when viewed in the context of a vast mass of dramatic characters, they are close to indistinguishable, and resemble each other more than the Hal of the two parts of *Henry the Fourth* or indeed the Falstaffs from those two plays. Figure 3.3

shows how the percentages for the twenty most common function words in the set varies from the overall average for these two characters.

The measure we use in this instance is the z-score, which is the difference between the observed count and the mean, divided by the standard deviation for that variable. The closer a word score is to the axis, the better the character's dialogue conforms to the overall average of the 243 plays. The negative scores to the left indicate that the character's count is lower than the average, and the positive scores to the right that it is higher. *Me* is an example of a word which is only just below the average for both characters. The general pattern, though, is that the words have high z-scores, meaning a marked variation from the average. Most vary from the average in the same direction – sixteen of the total twenty – and there are some very close matches: *and, of, you, in*$_{\text{preposition}}$, and *have*, for example. These characters are unusual, but unusual in the same way.

After the two Tamburlaine characters in the array of characters with a very close pairing come Richard III and Hoffman. This is another reciprocal pair, since Richard III is Hoffman's closest match also. Unlike the others mentioned so far, Richard III and Hoffman are paired as a result of their shared closeness to the common patterns in the set overall. Figure 3.4 shows the ten closest matches for Richard III and for the nine other characters with very low-scoring closest matches, the ten lowest overall in the set of 666.

Richard III's closest match is second to the Tamburlaine pair, but his second closest match, third closest, and so on, are lower than the corresponding matches for any of the others. The Tamburlaine of *2 Tamburlaine the Great* is an example of the opposite pattern: a very low score for the closest match, with the Tamburlaine of *1 Tamburlaine the Great*, is followed by a jump in distance to the next closest – Friar Bacon in Robert Greene's *Friar Bacon and Friar Bungay*. This Tamburlaine character's closeness to his counterpart from the other Tamburlaine play is an exception – in general, he shows no great affinity with other characters. Richard III, on the other hand, is close to a range of other characters in a way that makes him the 'odd man out' in this group of ten. Richard's other matches, in order of closeness, are with Volpone, Faustus, Barabas, the eponymous Sir Thomas More, Pericles, Cardinal Wolsey (from *Henry the Eighth*), Antony (from *Antony and Cleopatra*), Arden (from *Arden of Faversham*), Young Geraldine (from Heywood's *The English Traveller*), and Elinor of Castile (from George Peele's *Edward the First*).

Although the plays from which they are drawn differ in authorship and date, these characters have some broad features in common. All are main

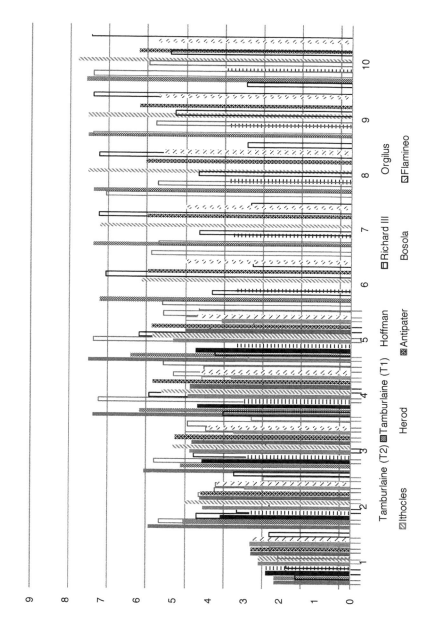

Tamburlaine (T2) ▨ Tamburlaine (T1) ▨ Hoffman ▨ Antipater
Ithocles ▨ Herod ▨ Orgilus ▨ Flamineo
Richard III ▨ Bosola

characters. All but Elinor and Wolsey are signalled as the protagonist by their plays' titles, and the exceptions both have large speaking parts and important roles in the main action. Volpone, feigning illness to gull his clients, Barabas, secretly planning evil on all around him, and Elinor, contriving to increase foreign influence at court and guilty of a jealous murder, could be described as scheming deceivers, and More and Wolsey as politicians, but in the group there are also character types less obviously related to Richard's role: Hoffman – revenger; Antony, Faustus, and Arden – tragic heroes in different styles; Geraldine – a wronged lover; and Pericles – hero of romance and adventure. We have to go beyond the idea of the Machiavellian or Vice-like villain to summarise the pattern of resemblance. The negatives are instructive: none of these characters are outlandish or mannered. If we examine the characters with the greatest distance from Richard, we find a tendency to extravagance and the exaggeration of some characteristic. Seven of the ten most distant are 'humours' characters, for instance, in the loose sense of comic characters with a marked obsession: Fluellen from *Henry the Fifth*, Belleur from John Fletcher's *The Wild-Goose Chase*, Wasp from Jonson's *Bartholomew Fair*, the Humorous Lieutenant from Fletcher's play of that name, Mistress Barnes from Henry Porter's *1 The Two Angry Women of Abingdon*, Zuccone from Marston's *Parasitaster*, and Lantern Leatherhead from *Bartholomew Fair*.[8]

Richard III has a large, mixed part which brings him close to the overall average score on the 100 most common function words. If we add up all the differences from the mean for the 100 most common function words for the 666 characters, Richard III has the lowest total – and Fluellen from *Henry the Fifth* the highest. Richard III has a profile unusually close to the overall pattern of the set. This comes about partly because he has a large speaking part – 8,368 words – one of only 11 characters out of 666 with more than 8,000 words of dialogue. Larger parts come closer to the mean by dint of their greater opportunities to balance departures in one direction with departures in others.

Yet this is only part of the explanation. Figure 3.5 shows that Richard III is remarkable for consistent low scores for his pairings with other characters, even among the characters with the largest parts.

Richard III is the model serious main character: his profile fits snugly with those of a number of others. While other characters may have a closer best match, he accumulates more close matches than they do moving along

---

[8] The remaining three are the Duchess from James Shirley's *The Opportunity*, Lylia-Bianca from *The Wild-Goose Chase*, and Alicia Saleware from Richard Brome's *A Mad Couple Well Matched*.

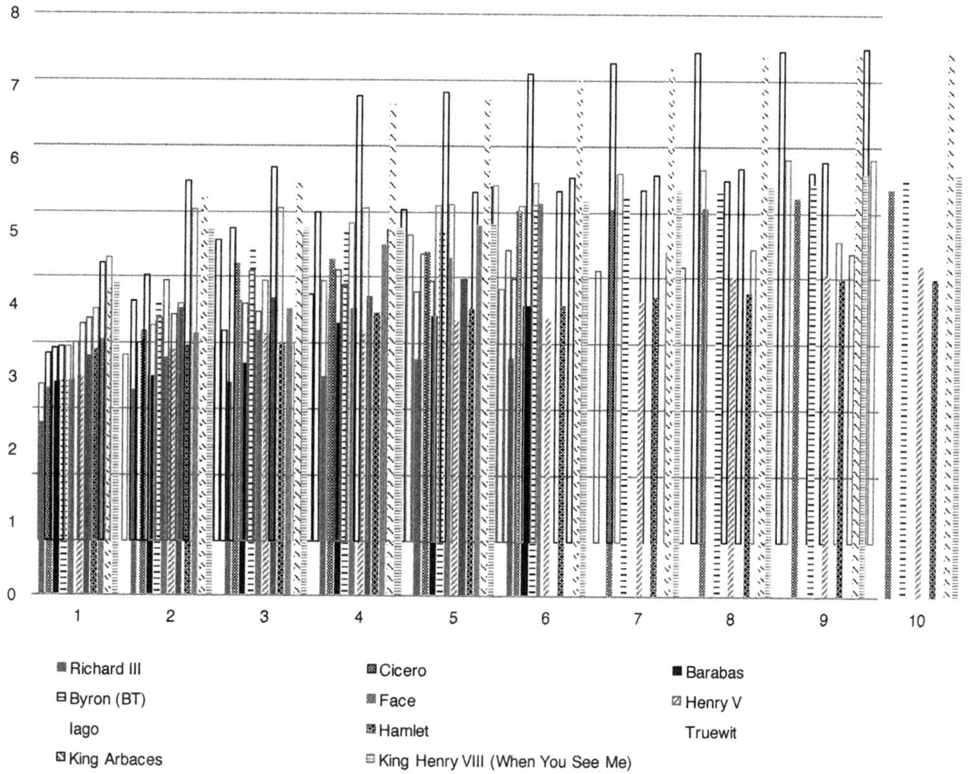

8
7
6
5
4
3
2
1
0
1
2
3
4
5
6
7
8
9
10
Richard III
Byron (BT)
Iago
King Arbaces
Cicero
Face
Hamlet
King Henry VIII (When You See Me)
Barabas
Henry V
Truewit

the succession of next closest pairings (Figure 3.4), and this is true for other characters with large speaking parts, as well as for the generality of other characters (Figure 3.5). The analysis helps us see Richard in the wider perspective as a standard all-round active protagonist, with a role balancing commentary and direct interaction with others.

Richard's full, rounded part brings him to the centre of the professional drama of the period under investigation, closer than any other character to the typical practice in speechmaking of the larger characters. His is the lowest average distance from other characters in the full table. Hunchbacked he may be, and extreme in the difference between his private thoughts and public declarations, but, taken all together, he is balanced and orthodox in terms of the style of his speeches. He has much to say that is orotund and periphrastic, but he is also sometimes savagely direct: 'I wish the bastards dead' (4.2.19). He gives orders, ponders situations, confers with associates, wheedles, and sometimes abuses enemies. He has what is surely an unusual amount of his part in soliloquies, but they are framed in observations, addresses to absent others and to himself in such a way that they do not tip his part overall away from the centre. He woos twice at length, as well as directing political and military strategy. He traverses the full range from intimate thoughts and dreams through private exchanges to public utterances. He is colloquial and also poetical – 'Into the blind cave of eternal night' (5.5.15). He is supremely confident and also self-hating and doubtful. The framework of style summarises his speeches as fitting the balance that is struck by the longer characters as a set, and overlooks the idiosyncrasies of his character which are so plain to audiences focusing on plot, the content of what he says, and his actions. It helps us see the roundedness of this part in more schematic, dramaturgical terms. His virtuosity in different situations gives him a style which conforms very closely to a standard main character in a serious play, so that in these terms he appears just as much as the brother, lover, king, and warrior of his preferred public image as the murderous Machiavel he privately confesses himself to be.

Fluellen from *Henry the Fifth* is the character sharing least with his closest fellow-characters. His nearest match is Compass from Jonson's *The Magnetic Lady*, but their proximity score is 22.9, which is on the high side for matches in general, let alone for closest matches (see Figure 3.2). Fluellen's is a very unusual part – an extended study in a limited repertoire, varying little from the narrow role of a comic *aficionado* of military tactics and ethos imbued with exaggerated national characteristics, with a restricted range of interactions which includes no casual or intimate relationships.

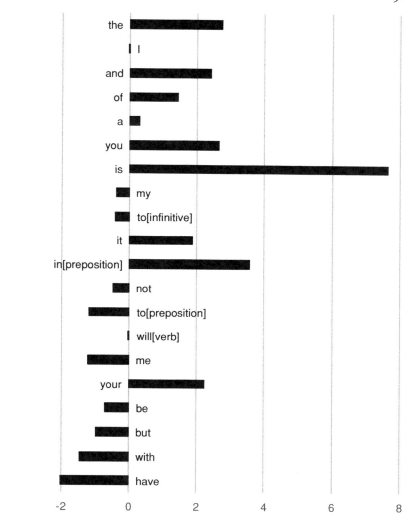

Figure 3.6 The *z*-scores for 20 most common function words for Fluellen (*Henry the Fifth*), using averages and standard deviations from the full set of 666 characters with ≥ 2,000 words of dialogue.

Figure 3.6 shows the *z*-scores for Fluellen for the twenty most common function words, as in Figure 3.3.

Fluellen is highly unusual in his recourse to *is*, and also an outlier in using *the, and, you, in*preposition, and *your* very freely. These reflect his insistent, repetitive speaking style among other things as a pioneer version of 'stage Welsh':

> I think it *is* e'en Macedon where Alexander *is* porn. I tell *you*, captain, if *you* look *in*_{preposition} *the* maps of *the* world I warrant *you* sall find, *in*_{preposition} *the* comparisons between Macedon *and* Monmouth, that *the* situations, look *you*, *is* both alike. There *is* a river *in*_{preposition} Macedon, and there *is* also moreover a river at Monmouth. It *is* called Wye at Monmouth, but it *is* out of my prains what *is the* name of the other river – but 'tis [= it *is*] all one, 'tis [= it *is*] alike as my fingers *is* to my fingers, and there *is* salmons *in*_{preposition} both. (4.6.21–30; emphasis added)

Figure 3.7 shows the scores for Fluellen's ten closest matches in the set, in the context of the ten closest matches for the next nine characters with the most distant closest matches. Fluellen is exceptional even in this company of idiosyncratic one-offs. His tenth closest match is as unusually remote as his closest. This group of ten (including Fluellen) is a collection of *sui generis* characters, not necessarily like each other, but rather brought together because they have narrowly focused, atypical speaking parts. We find in them not individuality so much as hypertrophied aspects of one kind or another. The Humorous Lieutenant, Humphrey Wasp, Mistress Barnes, Belleur, and Zuccone all have monomanias of various sorts – respectively, hypochondria, impatience, anger, bashfulness, and jealousy. Cardinal Como and King David, like Fluellen, have lop-sided, specialist roles, as intriguer and rhapsodising monarch respectively, to match Fluellen's narrow focus on the arts of war. Ricardo is a confessional, expostulating, scheming rogue, and Syphax is a portrait of unbridled lechery and ruthless cruelty, described by A. H. Bullen as 'so prodigiously brutal as to appear perfectly grotesque'.[9]

When considered separately from their home plays and matched with each other in this way, some characters emerge as worthy of scrutiny in new ways. Richard III appears as a balanced all-rounder rather than an egregious villain. The two Tamburlaines are truly one, in a way no other sequel characters are. Bosola and Flamineo, although from different plays, share a profile, as do Ithocles and Orgilus, who share a stage. Fluellen is an experiment in writing a major but flat character, more bounded in range than any of his rivals in fixedness in our sample, whether they be humours characters, termagants, extravagant rogues, or dyed-in-the-wool villains.

---

[9] In John Marston, *The Works of John Marston*, ed. A. H. Bullen, 3 vols. (London: Nimmo, 1887), 1: xlv.

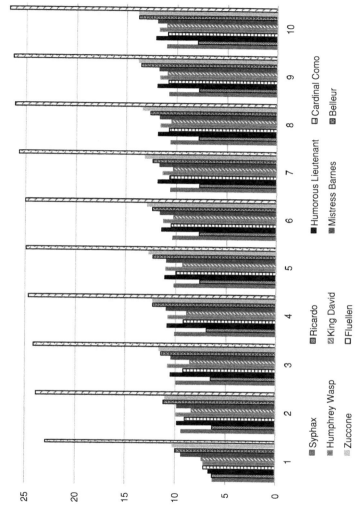

Figure 3.7 The *z*-scores for the ten closest matches for ten characters with very distant closest matches, ordered by distance to the closest match.

Newly Created Characters of 1599

Including as full a sweep as possible, as with the 666 larger characters, has its advantages. The numbers involved help show what is genuinely unusual, and the range gives more opportunity for the unexpected to emerge. However, we can also narrow the range to get a more local perspective, restricting ourselves for instance to a set of plays which one playgoer could have readily have seen, and close enough in time for memory to allow close comparison. One year's worth of new plays provides a basis for a set like this.

1599, the last year of the old century, is an attractive starting point. This is the year singled out by James Shapiro in his historical micro-study, and he makes a good argument that the two 1599 seasons show a new generation of playwrights – Ben Jonson, Thomas Dekker, and Thomas Heywood – starting to hit their straps and providing stimulating competition for Shakespeare, to replace the challenge offered by John Lyly, Thomas Kyd, Christopher Marlowe, George Peele, and Robert Greene, who had left the scene by 1597.[10] In 1599 the Globe was built on Bankside, and Thomas Kempe left the Chamberlain's Men. Numerous studies have commented that the most obvious difference across the sweep of early modern English drama occurs around 1600. D. J. Lake observes that 'there was a fairly sudden revolution in the linguistic practices' of several dramatists around 1599–1600, as they began to use contracted and colloquial forms at a much higher rate.'[11]

What new plays might a dedicated London playgoer have seen in 1599? To be conservative, we compile a set containing the eleven extant plays which three standard bibliographical sources (i.e., *DEEP: Database of Early English Playbooks*, the *Annals of English Drama*, and the Wiggins *Catalogue*) agree belong to 1599[12] – Dekker's *1 Old Fortunatus* and *The Shoemaker's Holiday*; both parts of Heywood's *Edward the Fourth*; Jonson's *Every Man Out of His Humour*; Marston's *Antonio and Mellida*; Shakespeare's *Henry the Fifth* and *Julius Caesar*; the collaboratively authored *1 Sir John Oldcastle*; and two anonymous plays, *A Larum for London* and *Look About*

[10] See James Shapiro, *1599: A Year in the Life of William Shakespeare* (London: Faber and Faber, 2005), esp. 9.
[11] D. J. Lake, 'Three Seventeenth-Century Revisions: *Thomas of Woodstock, The Jew of Malta*, and *Faustus* B', *Notes & Queries* 30.2 (1983), 134.
[12] The Wiggins *Catalogue* disputes the dates for four plays dated 1599 by both the *Annals* and *DEEP: Database of Early English Playbooks* – *Histriomastix* (1602), *As You Like It* (1600), *A Warning for Fair Women* (1597), and *The Wisdom of Doctor Dodypoll* (1600). A single source champions 1599 as the date for two more plays: *The Trial of Chivalry* is dated 1599 by the *Catalogue* (otherwise dated 1601), and *The Weakest Goeth to the Wall*, dated 1599 by the *Annals* (otherwise dated 1600).

You.[13] Beyond this, there are thirty professional plays for which we have titles but no more, and there may have been others of which all trace has been lost.[14]

This one-year set presents us with a manageable sample of closely related larger characters to put in a pool for comparison. As before, we chose the larger characters to focus on – namely, those with 2,000 words or more of dialogue – so that we avoid the idiosyncrasies of smaller parts. Figure 3.8 shows how long each play is in terms of dialogue, as well as the number of characters with larger speaking parts, and the combined total words of these parts.

Every Man Out of His Humour is by far the longest play, with 37,000 words and seven larger characters who together constitute 70 per cent of the dialogue of the play. *A Larum for London* is the shortest, with 12,000 words. *Antonio and Mellida* has just one character with 2,000 words or more of dialogue – Antonio – and his part constitutes about 20 per cent of the play's dialogue. Thus the dialogue of these plays can be contributed mainly by large characters, or mainly by multiple small characters, and so on. For the purposes of this chapter, we leave this potentially fruitful topic of 'concentrated' or 'dispersed' dialogue and focus instead on the similarities or otherwise of the spoken styles of these thirty-five characters from 1599.

As before, we take the 100 most common function words as the basis for comparisons. These words are the skeleton of language, and a remarkably good guide to styles of discourse, narrative, persuasion, banter, direct or indirect address – intimate, distant, eloquent, blunt, and so on. Used together as a profile, they provide a flexible and revealing index of style. Instances of these 100 words make up almost half the words spoken in the plays, and they appear regularly in any play regardless of topic or genre. They form a framework for comparison of all or any segments of dialogue.[15]

We have as our starting point the dialogue for 35 characters and their counts for the 100 most common function words. We can go back to the complete table of distances already created – that is, the data behind Figure 3.2 – and extract those scores for these characters. The lowest distance, and thus the closest pair, is Brutus and Cassius from *Julius Caesar.*

---

[13] Eleven surviving plays is something of a high-water mark for this immediate period. According to *DEEP: Database of Early English Playbooks*, only five new plays which are extant were published in 1597, with six more printed in 1598, ten in 1600, and eight in 1601, if closet plays and moral interludes are excluded.

[14] The *Lost Plays Database* contains thirty-one entries for 1599, one of which is a university play.

[15] See the Introduction for a more detailed discussion of function words and style.

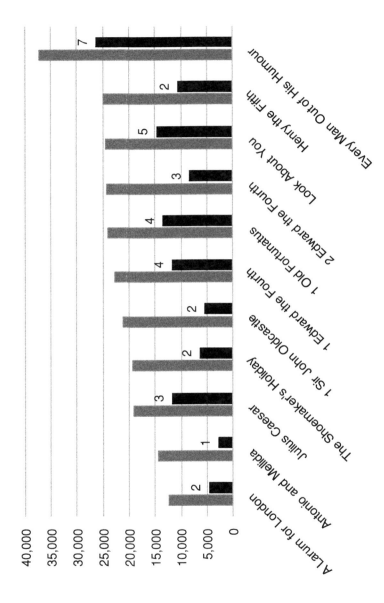

Figure 3.8 Total words spoken, number of and combined total words spoken by characters with ≥2,000 words of dialogue in 11 plays performed in 1599 by professional companies.

■ Total words of dialogue   ■ Total words for characters with ≥ 2,000 words

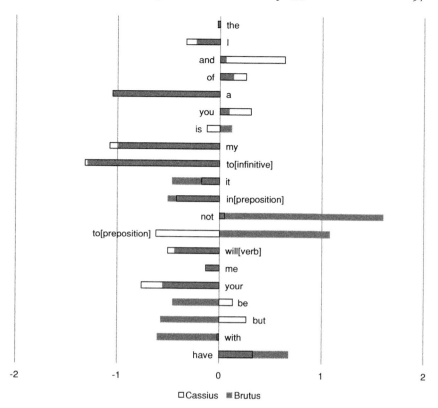

Figure 3.9 The *z*-scores for the 20 most common function words for Brutus and Cassius in Shakespeare's *Julius Caesar*, using averages and standard deviations from the set of 666 characters with ≥2,000 words of dialogue.

Their proximity score is 3.18, very low in a general sense. A closer look at the *z*-scores for the twenty most common function words in their dialogue (Figure 3.9) reveals just how closely Brutus and Cassius match in profile.

None of the *z*-scores for these words vary greatly from the mean for the whole set of 666 characters, but *I*, *a*, *my*, and *to*$_{infinitive}$ are low for both characters. For example, consider Brutus's and Cassius's speeches immediately following the assassination of Caesar:

> BRUTUS. Fates, *we* will know your pleasures.
>   That *we* shall die, *we* know; 'tis but the time
>   And drawing days out that men stand upon.
>   . . . .

Grant that, and then is death a benefit.
So are *we* Caesar's friends, that have abridged
His time of fearing death. Stoop, Romans, stoop,
And let *us* bathe our hands in Caesar's blood
Up to the elbows, and besmear our swords;
Then walk *we* forth even to the market-place,
And, waving our red weapons o'er our heads,
Let's all cry 'peace, freedom, and liberty!'
CASSIUS. Stoop, then, and wash. [...] How many ages hence
     Shall this our lofty scene be acted over,
     In states unborn and accents yet unknown!
BRUTUS. How many times shall Caesar bleed in sport,
     That now on Pompey's basis lies along,
     No worthier than the dust!
CASSIUS.   So oft as that shall be,
     So often shall the knot of *us* be called
     The men that gave their country liberty.
DECIUS. What, shall we forth?
CASSIUS.   Ay, every man away.
     Brutus shall lead, and *we* will grace his heels
     With the most boldest and best hearts of Rome.
                              (3.1.99–101, 104–22, emphasis added)

Brutus and Cassius sound very similar, and for good reason. At this
point, they are fellow conspirators striving to create a common interpretation of this historical moment, perfectly in tune. They speak on behalf of
the group – preferring *we* and *us* to the singular *I* and *my* – and develop
each other's points. It would be difficult to ascribe a speech to one or other
of them if presented without a speaker prefix. Earlier in the play, a convergence of the two characters is crystallised in an image when Cassius offers
himself as a mirror for Brutus, so the latter can discover his own merits,
and perhaps his destiny: 'I, your glass, | Will modestly discover to yourself
| That of yourself which you yet know not of' (1.2.70–72).[16]

However, this is not always the case: overall, Brutus is distinctly more
philosophical, and Cassius more pragmatic, and they become estranged as
the action continues, leading to the quarrel scene, the 'half-sword parley'
which was singled out already in the seventeenth century as a touchstone
of Shakespeare's power over audiences.[17] Nevertheless, the function-word
data suggests that they share a style to a remarkable degree and might have

---

[16] We are grateful to Claire Hansen for this reference.
[17] Leonard Digges, 'Upon Master William Shakespeare', in William Shakespeare, *Poems* (London,
1640), *3v.

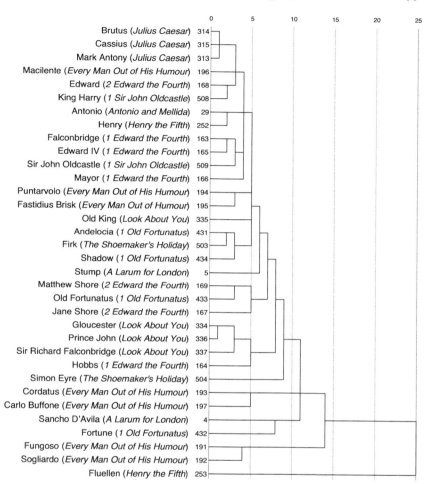

Figure 3.10 Hierarchical cluster analysis of 35 character parts, using Ward's Linkage and Squared Euclidean Distance, based on counts of the 100 most common function words.

seemed more distinctive as part of a play-wide, *Julius Caesar* style than contrasting with each other.

Cluster analysis is a simple way of combining the various distances between characters in a single chart. It works by joining the two closest items, then treating the combination as a single entity, and joining the next two closest individual items or combinations, and so on until finally the two most remote items or combinations are added. Figure 3.10 is a cluster analysis of the 35 characters speaking more than 2,000 words of dialogue in the 11 plays from 1599. This is a local ecosystem, on a scale that allows closer examination of each character and the assurance that a single spectator might have heard all these parts performed in the latter part of the 1598–9 season and the first part of the 1599–1600 season.

The first sub-groups formed have vertical bars closest to the left-hand border. Brutus, Cassius, and Mark Antony – the three characters from *Julius Caesar* large enough to be included – join first. The three *Julius Caesar* characters are judged to be more like each other than like any other character in the set. There are seven other plays with more than one character large enough to qualify, but in each case characters fall into two different groups in the cluster or into one group and then a wider collection of ungrouped characters. Gloucester and Prince John from *Look About You*, a knockabout romance of multifarious disguises set in the reign of Henry II, are at a similar level of closeness to the *Julius Caesar* characters, but Sir Richard Falconbridge from the same play is more remote, and the Old King (that is, Henry II) is in another part of the cluster altogether.

The *Julius Caesar* characters are remarkable for their consistency. If we can extrapolate from this to an audience reaction, this play might have seemed different in texture from the others, with main characters similar rather than markedly different in style. In his discussion of the dramatic output of 1599, James Shapiro argues that in crafting *Julius Caesar* Shakespeare was working his way to a new kind of dramaturgic texture, a departure from the (by then) well-established patterns of the history play and the romantic comedy, towards a more 'symphonic' form.[18] The cluster analysis supports this idea, at least to the extent that the play's characters are revealed as unusually close to each other in linguistic profile when compared with the rest of the 1599 sample. Recalling the 1599 plays the next year, our thoughtful playgoer might think in terms of an innovative play with a consistent texture, a new kind of Roman play, historical and philosophical at the same time, with some characters with a common *romanitas*, a collective and public-minded outlook.

Every Man Out of His Humour contributes seven characters to the collection. Macilente joins the *Julius Caesar* group and two kings, Edward from *2 Edward the Fourth* and King Harry from *Sir John Oldcastle*; Puntarvolo and Fastidius Briske form their own group; Cordatus and Carlo Buffone form another, closest to each other, but still not very close; and Sogliardo and Fungoso still another. In this perspective, *Every Man Out* characters look diverse, in contrast to the unity of their counterparts in *Julius Caesar*.

---

[18] Shapiro, *1599*, 151–3, 182.

The character which is last to join any other is Fluellen, whom we have already discussed as an extreme odd-man-out in the larger collection of 666 characters. It is hard to imagine that the two Shakespeare plays would have seemed as exceptional as they now appear to us – and it is worth noting that, according to the analysis, King Henry from *Henry the Fifth* is in a mixed grouping of characters in the middle of the cluster – but it is plausible that elements of the two plays might stand out.

This is a view of new plays from the professional drama of 1599 in terms of character type, from serious all-round main protagonists who form the large group at the top of Figure 3.8, to highly specialised humours or alle-gorical characters. It is not really a view by 'play', since the consistency of *Julius Caesar* is a remarkable exception rather than the rule. It is not really a view by 'author' or by 'genre' either: sub-clusters of characters come from plays by four different authors (Heywood, Jonson, Marston, and Shakespeare) and four different genres (Roman tragedy, humours com-edy, romantic comedy, and English history). Divisions within genres, and within sequences, are apparent. The Edward of *1 Edward the Fourth* joins with a more domestic-drama group, while his character from the sequel joins with a group of other rulers and statesmen.

The characters of professional plays from 1599 might be roughly divided into the *centripetal*, which find matches in their own or other plays rea-sonably soon in the process, and the *centrifugal* – oddities and one-offs to various degrees, which take a while to be paired up, 'characters' in the full sense, like Simon Eyre from *The Shoemaker's Holiday* and Hobbs and the Mayor from *1 Edward the Fourth*, unclubbable types like the quartet of *Every Man Out* characters and the goddess Fortune from *1 Old Fortunatus* – and the greatest oddity of all, Fluellen.

Neighbours on Principal Components

The proximities we have been examining take the chosen variables (in our case, the 100 most common function words) and treat them all equally, offering a neutral, open framework in which to place the individual items – that is, the characters. For a third view of the relations between characters in early modern drama, we return to Principal Components Analysis (PCA) and isolate the most important underlying vectors of the characters' lan-guage. This is a particular, weighted, selective view of the data, emphasising two factors in particular rather than taking the word counts as they come. We continue to use the 100 most common function words as our variables, but modify our sample to contain only those characters with speaking parts of 2,000 words or more from plays performed between 1580 and 1619. This results in a reduced sample of 531 characters from 197 plays. Although the larger 1580–1642 set (with 666 characters parts across 243 plays) provides a more comprehensive overview and the 1599 set (with 35 character parts across 11 plays) a tighter focus, this reduced four-decade sample presents something of a 'middle ground' while also keeping the analysis within the range of a notional single writing career.[19]

The most important of the components which emerges from the analysis is a contrast between stately kings and choric figures on the one hand and fussy busy-bodies on the other (PC1). The first group makes considered, authoritative, finished pronouncements, while the second acts on others, reacts to others, and obsesses about themselves. In parts of speech, this is a contrast between prepositions, which are used in locutions which render the detail of a depicted world, and auxiliary verbs, which are the vehicle for close interaction and personal reflection. The extreme at one end is King David from Peele's *David and Bethsabe*. His speeches are well-turned, replete with stately, elaborate poetic illustration. Even when addressing a single interlocutor, the style is formal and spells out well-rounded connections:

> Welcome fair Bethsabe, King David's darling.
> Thy bones' fair covering, erst discovered fair,
> And all mine eyes with all thy beauties pierced,
> As heaven's bright eye burns most when most he climbs
> The crooked zodiac with his fiery sphere,
> And shineth furthest from this earthly globe;
> So, since thy beauty scorched my conquered soul,
> I called thee nearer for my nearer cure.[20]

The 'Humorous Lieutenant', from Fletcher's play of the same name, is at the opposite extreme. He is a valiant soldier, but also a hypochondriac. His 'humour' is an exaggerated preoccupation with his health and his immediate sensations. He is entirely caught up in the moment:

> Away! How should I know that then? [*Aside*] I'll knock softly.
> Pray heaven he speak in a low voice now to comfort me;
> I feel I have no heart to't. – Is't well, gentlemen?[21]

[19] As noted in Chapter 5, a handful of early modern playwrights had their first and last plays performed thirty or forty years apart – a span that might be considered a single unit of the dramatic tradition.
[20] George Peele, *David and Bethsabe*, in Russell A. Fraser and Norman Rabkin, eds., *Drama of the English Renaissance*, 2 vols. (New York: Macmillan, 1976), 1: 1.105–12.
[21] John Fletcher, *The Humorous Lieutenant*, in Francis Beaumont and John Fletcher, *Comedies and Tragedies* (London, 1647; Wing B1581), 3S2r.

The second axis of differentiation uncovered by PCA (PC2) is a contrast between lovers – or, more generally, those caught up in an action and focused on personal relations (domestic or intimate) – and characters whose role is to dissect some aspect of the play-world. One style is dramatic, in the sense of here-and-now engagement between characters; the other is more descriptive, with characters creating conceptual worlds through discourse. It is a rival version of the contrast of the first principal component – a second refraction of an underlying division in the dialogue of plays – between speeches which assume the world as given and present, and those which create a world by description and narrative. This time, the important word-variables are *thou*, *thee*, and *thy*, and *I*, *me*, and *my* – more common in the dialogue of the lovers and intriguers – and the articles *a*, *and*, and *the*, some prepositions, and *most* and *own* – all used freely by the commentators and analysts.

Mistress Barnes, from Porter's *1 The Two Angry Women of Abingdon*, has one of the lowest scores on the second principal component. She has a long quarrel with Mistress Goursey, and her spoken part is mainly an assertion of her antagonism, with few ventures into anything approaching analysis or commentary. Aside from Mistress Goursey, she also engages fiercely with her husband, her daughter, and her son, all of whom she addresses as *thou* at times. At the other extreme of this axis are Cardinal Como from Dekker's *The Whore of Babylon*, Ariosto from Webster's *The Devil's Law-Case*, Fluellen from *Henry the Fifth*, and Savoy from Chapman's *Byron's Conspiracy*. Each of these comment on situations to their peers, and so do not use *thou*, *thee*, or *thy*. They are pundits offering analysis of military arrangements, or of legal, political, and religious affairs, and so tend not to call attention to their own subjectivity through the use of *I*, *me*, or *my*. Their concrete and well-illustrated commentary leads to a high incidence of the articles and of the prepositions *of* and *in*. In the following example, this language profile has the effect of making it unclear whether Savoy is summarising the ambassador's aims or expressing his own:

> To note *the* state and chief sway *of the* court
> To which they are employed, to penetrate
> *The* heart, and marrow *of the* king's designs,
> And to observe *the* countenances and spirits
> *Of* such as are impatient of rest,
> And wring beneath some private discontent.[22]

[22] George Chapman, *Byron's Conspiracy*, in his *The Conspiracy and Tragedy of Byron*, ed. John Margeson (Manchester University Press, 1988), 1.1.6–11 (emphasis added).

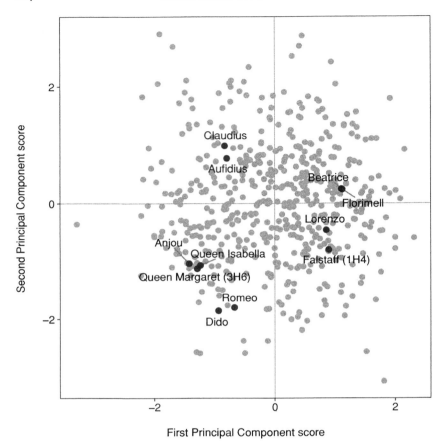

Figure 3.11 PCA scatterplot of 531 character parts from 197 plays performed between 1580 and 1619, using the 100 most common function words.

The principal components are summaries of a great deal of information. They are principled abstractions from the use of 100 words in speeches of 531 characters from 197 plays. Characters from different plays, authors, genres, and eras are mapped together. Some of the groupings are instructive, offering a categorisation of characters which gives a fresh perspective on their place in their own plays and within the discourse of late sixteenth- and early seventeenth-century English drama sampled here. Figure 3.11 highlights some of the pairings that emerge.

Claudius from *Hamlet* and Tullius Aufidius from *Coriolanus* are placed close together and in the top left of Figure 3.11, best described as a combination of disquisitory and detached in the orientation of its characters. Claudius and Aufidius are each an antagonist to the formidable protagonist after whom their plays are named. Their fates are entangled with this powerful, dramatically charismatic other, a fact on which they both ruefully reflect. They both occupy worlds of great affairs – one political, the other military – with some formal set-pieces, kingly addresses for Claudius and the impassioned welcome to Coriolanus for Aufidius. Both focus their speeches on a single male other, whether the latter is present or absent.

We may think of Claudius as a villainous intriguer, but viewed in structural terms his dialogue places him more as someone who amplifies or explains, a commentator as opposed to someone intimately involved with others. If we read through his speeches we realise that he does not enter into any sort of quipping immediate interchanges, nor into direct participation in the action. He almost always maintains a rounded, deliberate, detached tone. Aufidius is a warrior, but his dialogue does not reflect direct action but a measured consideration of Coriolanus's impact on his city's destiny and his own.

Florimell in John Day's comedy *Humour Out of Breath* appears close to Beatrice from *Much Ado About Nothing* in the detached and interlocutory (and modern-sounding) area of Figure 3.11. Florimell is an outspoken young woman, not exactly in the way Beatrice is – Florimell goes beyond wittiness to something more akin to lewdness – but, like Beatrice, Florimell is an uncomfortable fit with the conventional gender roles of the time. Beatrice risks her marriageability should her challenge to Benedick tip her from 'wit' to 'shrewishness', and Florimell likewise if her bawdiness should define her as 'unchaste', though both end their respective plays with advantageous marriages.[23]

Lorenzo is a garrulous, amorous old man in Chapman's comedy *May Day*, and in the PCA he is placed close to the Falstaff of *1 Henry the Fourth*, in the lower-right, interlocutory-involved area of the graph. In pursuit of his misdirected *amour*, Lorenzo disguises himself as a chimney sweep. He might well be modelled on this Falstaff, or the Falstaff of *The Merry Wives of Windsor*. J. M. Robertson noted parallels between the language of Lorenzo

---

[23] In *Queer Virgins and Virgin Queans on the Early Modern Stage* (Oxford University Press, 2000), Mary Bly describes Florimell as 'essentially unmarriageable, in the context of early modern morality' (10).

and Falstaff in *Merry Wives*, which suggested to him that Chapman might have collaborated in the play.[24]

Dido and Romeo, two lovers from early plays, Marlowe's *Dido, Queen of Carthage* and Shakespeare's *Romeo and Juliet*, are placed close together in the lower-left, or disquisitory-involved area of Figure 3.11. Dido's dialogue rarely strays from a focus on Aeneas whom she addresses as *thou* from the beginning, and on her own feelings and situation. Romeo gives Mercutio, the Nurse, and the Friar *thou*, as well as Juliet. His focus is on his situation, his feelings, and – of course – on Juliet. Romeo's 'concern with self-perception' and 'autonomous, self-doubting subjectivity' have led Lynette Hunter and Peter Lichtenfels to treat his character-part as 'a first take on Hamlet'.[25] Unlike Hamlet, however, neither Dido nor Romeo is a notable speechmaker, or notable for staccato interchanges, and both are involved in the action rather than detached.

Queen Margaret from *3 Henry the Sixth*, Queen Isabella from Marlowe's *Edward the Second*, and the Duke of Anjou (later Henry III of France) from the same playwright's *Massacre at Paris* are brought together in the same disquisitory-involved section of Figure 3.11 as Dido and Romeo, though further in the disquisitory direction and not as far in the involved direction. These characters are all from history plays performed in the early 1590s: two dealing with English history of the fourteenth and fifteenth centuries respectively, and the other treating events in France twenty years or so prior. Margaret, Isabella, and Anjou all rule countries and direct armies at various times, but they also have moments of impotent rage or lament at betrayals by spouses and allies or defeats by enemies. Although she is Queen, Margaret is repeatedly forced to plead with, berate, and exhort her hearers. Anjou (or rather Henry) later becomes King of France, but threats from the Guise faction and from his brother-in-law, the King of Navarre, render his rule insecure. Like Margaret, he is often reduced to mocking and then cursing his enemies and plotting revenge on them. He is in a contestatory role, even after his coronation.

All three of these characters are shrewd politicians, and yet they remain prey to emotion. For example, Mortimer tells Isabella she is 'too passionate in speeches' for a 'warrior' (4.4.14–15).[26] At times, these emotions beget

---

[24] J. M. Robertson, *The Problem of 'The Merry Wives of Windsor'* (London: Chatto and Windus [for The Shakespeare Association], 1917), 14, 24.

[25] Lynette Hunter and Peter Lichtenfels, *Negotiating Shakespeare's Language in 'Romeo and Juliet': Reading Strategies from Criticism, Editing and the Theatre* (Farnham: Ashgate, 2009), 168.

[26] All references to *Edward the Second* are taken from Charles R. Forker's Revels edition of the play (Manchester University Press, 1994).

physical violence: Margaret stabs York (1.4.177 sd.), Isabella facilitates the capture of Gaveston and wishes him slain (2.4.37–9, 68–9), and Anjou has the Guise murdered (Scene 21).[27] Charles R. Forker argues that Margaret's murderous and warlike actions may have 'prompted' aspects of Isabella.[28] The dialogue of this trio is entirely public, comprising well-fashioned, purposeful pronouncements, with no asides or domestic interludes. They have little time for witty analysis, courtly prevarication, or subtle distinctions.

Margaret, Isabella, and Anjou are traditional speech-makers, not fussy busy-bodies, with low scores on PC1. They are involved in intense personal relations, rather than reflective and analytical, and so score low on PC2. The long chain of arithmetic analysis, from spoken part to counts of particular words to principal components, seems to have uncovered a genuine likeness. In small fragments, Margaret and Anjou in particular are difficult to tell apart:

> Warwick, these words have turned my hate to love,
> *And* I forgive and quite forget old faults,
> *And* joy that thou becom'st King Henry's friend.
>> (Margaret, *3 Henry the Sixth* 3.3.199–201;
>> emphasis added)

> . . . I here do swear
> To ruinate that wicked Church of Rome
> That hatcheth up such wicked practices,
> *And* here protest eternal love to thee,
> *And* to the Queen of England specially,
> Whom God hath bless'd for hating papistry.
>> (Anjou, *Massacre at Paris* 5.64–9; emphasis added)

There are two instances of *and* in each of these short quotations. This is a heavily weighted word-variable to the low end of PC1. Both Margaret and Anjou use this word very freely: Margaret's z-score for this word-variable is 1.74; Anjou's is 1.70.

Late in *3 Henry the Sixth*, Margaret is left to rally her son and their supporters, who are dismayed by their defeat at Barnet and need to gather their strength before returning to the fray at Tewkesbury. She begins: 'Great lords, wise men ne'er sit and wail their loss, | But cheerly seek how to redress

---

[27] All references to *The Massacre at Paris* are taken from H. J. Oliver's Revels edition of the play (London: Methuen, 1968).

[28] Charles R. Forker, 'Marlowe's *Edward II* and Its Shakespearean Relatives: The Emergence of a Genre', in John W. Velz (ed.), *Shakespeare's English Histories: A Quest for Form and Genre* (Binghamton: Medieval and Renaissance Texts and Studies, 1996), 71–2.

their harms' (5.4.1–2). The Duke of Anjou urges unrelenting pursuit of the Huguenots with the same recourse to popular wisdom: 'Yet will the wisest note their proper griefs, | And rather seek to scourge their enemies | Than be themselves base subjects to the whip' (4.14–16). Margaret and Anjou are 'sisters under the skin' – created by different playwrights, placed in different geographic settings and in different fictional centuries, one a queen and one a king, but with an underlying common orientation to the dramatic worlds in which they are situated.

Conclusion

As this chapter has shown, statistical analysis of language provides a new way to model characters' interactions in early modern drama. It winnows the myriad connections and contrasts between characters' language styles and highlights particular examples, which are then a challenge to interpretation. The conjunctions and disparities can be traced back to individual instances of words in phrases, sentences, and speeches, though accumulated into totals. It is possible to define exactly how the numbers which go into the analysis came about. Given this text, and this way of counting, the number has to be exactly so. Familiar canonical texts and forgotten plays by unknown or obscure authors are treated alike, with an effect which from one perspective is a distortion – Hamlet is just a character like any other and may be lost from sight altogether in the middle of a cloud of datapoints – and from another point of view is a way of glimpsing a different terrain, wider and flatter than the one we are used to. In this analysis, the motivation of characters and the twists and turns of plot are obscured, while discourse types and patterns of dramatic interaction are brought to the fore.

When given the chance to escape from their plays, characters do often group by author, in the obvious way by sequel, but also by category (e.g. protagonist, antagonist) or character type. Pairings across authorial canons also appear, and take us back to traditional stock character types (e.g. garrulous old men, wily schemers). Pairings within plays are unexpected, but their occurrence reminds us that a generic play style may prevail over local differentiation when seen in wider frames.

The representative, balanced, internally various character is an unfamiliar concept which the analysis offers, along with its complement – the specialised, hypertrophied character, an eccentric bit part magnified. This is what the characters of early modern English drama would look like to Martians who had no earthly language and could only interpret the plays through patterns of word use. Their response, however primitive and schematic, would have its own logic and might prompt an interesting conversation with those who can read the plays, explore the historical record, and see them performed, and thus have a different understanding of these precious traces of a crowded, noisy, competitive, corporate activity now more than four centuries in the past.

CHAPTER 4

Stage Properties
Bed, Blood, and Beyond

Some things are best to act, others to tell;
Those by the ear conveyed, do not so well,
Nor half so movingly affect the mind,
As what we to our eyes presented find.
Yet there are many things, which should not come
In view, nor pass beyond the tiring-room:
Which, after in expressive language told,
Shall please the audience more, than to behold.[1]

(John Oldham)

Our study of early modern drama has focused thus far on the frequency and distribution of words in spoken dialogue. As noted in the Introduction, other aspects of literary language are similarly tractable to quantification and analysis, including patterns in vocabulary, grammar, rhetorical devices, sentence length, and versification. None of these linguistic features is unique to drama, which, like poetry and prose fiction, relies upon 'the written or spoken word' as a means of expression. Drama, however, 'combine[s] the verbal with a number of non-verbal or optical-visual means'.[2] In this chapter, we turn to one of the non-verbal features that distinguishes drama from other literary genres: the use of stage properties or 'props'.

Materialist critics have debunked the long-held belief in the 'bare' Shakespearean stage,[3] citing evidence from the eyewitness accounts of contemporary theatregoers, tiring-house inventories, anti-theatrical polemics, revels account-books, and the play-scripts themselves to demonstrate that the early modern theatre 'was as concerned with the effective combination and display of costumes and other stage properties ... as it was with poetic

---

[1] John Oldham, 'Horace His Art of Poetry, Imitated in English', in *The Works* (London, 1684; Wing O225), ii: Biv.

[2] Mario Klarer, *An Introduction to Literary Studies*, 3rd edn (New York: Routledge, 1999), 44.

[3] Representative recent studies include Andrew Sofer, *The Stage Life of Props* (Ann Arbor: University of Michigan Press, 2003), Catherine Richardson, *Shakespeare and Material Culture* (Oxford University Press, 2011), and essays in Jonathan Gil Harris and Natasha Korda (eds.), *Staged Properties in Early Modern English Drama* (Cambridge University Press, 2002).

language'.⁴ For example, the playwright-turned-Puritan Stephen Gosson mocked the contemporary drama for its reliance on props:

> Sometime you shall see nothing but the adventures of an amorous knight passing from country to country for the love of his lady, encountering many a terrible monster made of brown paper, and at his return is so wonderfully changed that he cannot be known but by some posy in his tablet, or by a broken ring, or a handkercher, or a piece of a cockle-shell.⁵

Gosson's characterisation of the theatre as a meaningless pageant of trifles and unconvincing devices may be an exaggeration, but the early modern commercial stage was understood to be 'a theatre of easily held things'.⁶ Studies of early modern props, Douglas Bruster observes, typically adopt one of three critical modes: the 'iconographic' (e.g. explaining the use of skulls on stage in relation to the *memento mori* emblem tradition), the 'semiotic' (e.g. a psychoanalytic reading of Othello's spotted handkerchief as signifying the blood-stained sheets of the marriage-bed), or the 'cultural materialist' (e.g. treating the viol as an index of gender in Jacobean city comedies).⁷ As illuminating as these studies may be, a tendency to focus on 'specific objects in specific plays' restricts whatever insights they offer 'to the prop in question' and risks 'unnecessarily limit[ing] our understanding of such props' significance'.⁸ For this reason, Bruster advocates a quantitative approach – 'a thin description' – to provide 'a general account of such objects, an account in relation to which more specific claims [can] be measured', and principled generalisations about 'the number, kinds, and roles of hand props in early modern plays'.⁹

Only two quantitative studies of early modern stage props have appeared to date. In *Shakespeare's Speaking Properties*, Frances Teague traces 'patterns of presentational imagery' by counting and categorising props appearing in Shakespeare's dramatic canon, excluding *The Two Noble Kinsmen*.¹⁰ Analysis of prop-lists and counts for each play, provided in the appendices, enable Teague to make a variety of generalisations about Shakespeare's stage practice and development as a playwright. For example, even though

---

⁴ Justin Kolb, '"To me comes a creature": Recognition, Agency, and the Properties of Character in Shakespeare's *The Winter's Tale*', in Wendy Beth Hyman (ed.), *The Automaton in English Renaissance Literature* (Farnham: Ashgate, 2011), 49.
⁵ Stephen Gosson, *Plays Confuted in Five Actions* (London, 1582; STC 12095), C6r. For an engaging reading of this passage, see Kolb, '"To me comes a creature"', 50.
⁶ Douglas Bruster, *Shakespeare and the Question of Culture: Early Modern Literature and the Cultural Turn* (New York: Palgrave, 2003), 95.
⁷ Bruster, *Shakespeare*, 96.   ⁸ Bruster, *Shakespeare*, 96–7.   ⁹ Bruster, *Shakespeare*, 97.
¹⁰ Frances Teague, *Shakespeare's Speaking Properties* (Cranbury: Associated University Presses, 1991), 10.

Shakespeare used fewer props in his later history plays 'than he did when he started writing histories', histories as a genre still 'need more properties than the comedies' by virtue of their 'subject matter and structure'.[11]

The second and most recent quantitative study of props is 'The Dramatic Life of Objects in the Early Modern Theater',[12] in which Bruster extends beyond Shakespeare to analyse twenty non-Shakespearean plays performed between 1587 and 1636.[13] Bruster not only tallies the total number of props per play, but also averages out the frequencies of props per every 1,000 lines to account for variable play-length.[14] Like Teague, whose figures he uses for Shakespeare's plays, Bruster observes chronological and generic patterns in prop-use across the Shakespeare corpus. 'If we were to graph the frequency of properties in Shakespeare's plays', Bruster suggests, 'we would see something like a shallow V over the course of his career' – a 'gradual diminishing' in prop-use after the prop-heavy histories of the early 1590s, followed by 'a significant increase beginning about 1605'.[15] He finds that Shakespeare's tragedies 'tend to have the most props, histories the second greatest number, and comedies the least', averaging 11.48, 10.6, and 8.42 props per 1,000 lines respectively.[16] Bruster concludes that genre 'affects not only the number but the kinds of props appearing on stage', such that 'certain kinds of properties serve as generic signals' in Shakespeare – 'a lute or hobby-horse' for comedy, 'a skull or a dagger' for tragedy.[17]

Bruster's analysis of twenty non-Shakespearean plays allows him to contextualise his Shakespeare findings and to offer generalisations about the early modern theatre more broadly. For example, Bruster notes that Shakespeare's contemporaries not only 'approximate his practice' in relation to the frequency of 'hand props' used, but 'are also equivalent to one another'.[18] Bruster also detects 'a general decline in the number of hand

[11] Teague, *Shakespeare's Speaking Properties*, 40, 55.
[12] Bruster, *Shakespeare*, 95–118; an earlier version, with the same title, appears in Harris and Korda (eds.), *Staged Properties*, 67–96.
[13] The non-Shakespearean plays included are Francis Beaumont and John Fletcher's *A King and No King*; William Cartwright's *The Royal Slave*; Elizabeth Cary's *The Tragedy of Mariam*; George Chapman's *All Fools*; Daniel's *Philotas*; John Ford's *Perkin Warbeck*; Ben Jonson's *Catiline, The Devil is an Ass, Every Man in His Humour*, and *Sejanus*; Thomas Kyd's *The Spanish Tragedy*; Christopher Marlowe's *The Jew of Malta*; Philip Massinger's *The Roman Actor* and *The Picture*; Thomas Middleton's *The Revenger's Tragedy, A Trick to Catch the Old One*, and *Women Beware Women*; George Peele's *The Battle of Alcazar*; and, the anonymous *Edmond Ironside* and *Thomas of Woodstock*.
[14] By contrast, Teague gives the distribution of props in Shakespeare's plays as the number of lines per single property, in whole numbers – thus, '1 property per 102 lines' for *Othello*, '1 property per 98 lines' for *Hamlet*, and so on.
[15] Bruster, *Shakespeare*, 109–10.   [16] Bruster, *Shakespeare*, 107.
[17] Bruster, *Shakespeare*, 108.   [18] Bruster, *Shakespeare*, 112–13.

props used' between 1587 and 1636, regardless of genre, possibly reflecting a 'reduction in the numbers of actors and roles' over time and, concomitantly, 'a diminished need to differentiate characters from one another' as playwrights incorporate 'fewer "group" scenes' into their plays.[19]

This chapter offers a fresh interpretation of early modern stage props, departing from Teague and Bruster in both scope and method. Our sample is not Teague's corpus of Shakespeare plays (excluding *The Two Noble Kinsmen*), or Bruster's extension of Teague's corpus by an additional selection of twenty non-Shakespearean plays, professional and non-professional,[20] from the period 1587 to 1636. Instead, our sample comprises 160 plays first appearing on the commercial stage between 1590 and 1609. Appendix B provides bibliographical details for the plays used in this chapter. In addition to a substantially larger sample, our analysis extends beyond simple prop-frequency and distribution statistics to incorporate findings gleaned from Principal Components Analysis (PCA).

Sourcing and Counting Props

As mentioned above, information about early modern stage props comes from a number of sources. Each of these sources varies in utility. Antitheatrical tracts are inherently biased and often do not name the plays they target – it is unclear, for example, whether Gosson's 'monster made of brown paper', 'posy', 'broken ring', 'handkercher', and 'piece of cockleshell' in fact belong to a specific play or plays, or whether his list is intended as hyperbole. Few eyewitness accounts of early modern drama survive, and those that do record only those particular aspects of the plays that caught the authors' attention – even modern theatre critics fail to provide their readers with comprehensive prop-lists, presumably much to the irritation of future performance historians. So too, surviving tiring-house inventories offer only a partial snapshot of the stage properties available to a particular company at a given point in time. For example, the inventory of properties rented from Philip Henslowe by the Admiral's Men at the Rose, dated 10 March 1598, lists some (e.g. a 'sign for Mother Redcap') but not all of the props, generic and specific, required to stage *1 Robin Hood*, a play licensed for performance later that month.[21] Perhaps because they were easily procured as required, the Admiral's Men's inventory does not record

[19] Bruster, *Shakespeare*, 113–14.
[20] Bruster includes Cary's *Tragedy of Mariam*, which is a closet drama.
[21] The inventory is transcribed in W. W. Greg (ed.), *Henslowe Papers* (London: A. H. Bullen, 1907), 116–18. For an insightful discussion of these documents, see Lena Cowen Orlin, 'Things with Little Social Life (Henslowe's Properties and Elizabethan Household Fittings)', in Harris and Korda (eds.),

many common prop items such as papers (standing for a variety of documents, e.g. commissions, letters, patents, and supplications), generic small
portable objects (e.g. bags, money, napkins, and rings), and weapons necessary to stage *1 Robin Hood* and other plays.[22] Perishable items, such as food-
stuffs and other organic materials, are similarly absent.[23] Revels account-
books, where extant, present similar challenges.

For our purposes, play-scripts represent the most comprehensive source
about props – but they are far from ideal. A considerable number of play-
scripts simply do not survive,[24] and those that do vary in their treatment of
props. Although *dramatis personae* are often present, play-scripts from the
period typically do not include a prop-list. Instead, information about the
props needed to perform a play must be gleaned from explicit references
in the stage directions, and from references and implied directions in the
dialogue. Even when explicit mention of a prop is made, the reference is
often ambiguous. In *A Larum for London*, for example, Sancho D'Avila
carries a weapon referred to variously as a 'rapier' and a 'scimitar', although
the distinctiveness of the design and difference in cultural valence means
that this sword must be one or the other.[25] Elsewhere, the ambiguity is of
number, not kind: for instance, it is unclear how many asps Cleopatra uses
to kill herself in Act 5, Scene 2 of *Antony and Cleopatra* – are two or more
required, or is one industrious serpent sufficient? Most frustrating of all
are ambiguities of both number and kind: for example, when Fustigo is
beaten by apprentices in Thomas Dekker and Thomas Middleton's *1 The
Honest Whore* (TLN 1353), there is no direction as to how many 'fellow
prentices' rush in to take part (TLN 1294) and with what they 'cudgel' him

Staged Properties, 99–128. While the play was not licensed for performance until 28 March 1598, the inclusion of props named for characters in the play suggests that it was 'in preparation for performance' at the time the inventory was made: Wiggins and Richardson, *British Drama*, IV: 12.

[22] For example, stage directions in the playbook for *1 Robin Hood* (London, 1601; STC 18271) call for a purse (A2v, A3r), a napkin (A4v), a fardel (F2v), and a basket (H4v, said to carry eggs, but actually carrying a seal in some hay). The stage directions also refer to halberds (D3r), which are either excluded from the inventory or are perhaps listed erroneously as 'lances' (116). Similarly, the inventory mentions 'Cupid's bow and quiver' (117), but not the many bows and arrows carried by Robin Hood and his men (E4r).

[23] For example, stage directions in *1 Robin Hood* call for wine (F4r), meat (F4r, I4v), and flowers (F4v). It is possible that the 'black dog' listed in the inventory (118) is the same that appears when the Jailer of Nottingham enters 'leading a dog' (I3r), but the dialogue makes no mention of its colour.

[24] The *Lost Plays Database* lists over 300 plays attributed to professional companies for the years 1590–1609. This figure represents a mere fraction of the total, since it includes only those plays for which we have a title.

[25] *A Larum for London* (London, 1602; STC 16754), D1v, D3v. This is not an isolated case: in *Edmond Ironside*, for example, Edricus's sword is also variously called a 'rapier', 'falchion', and 'cutlass'. On the types of sword and their function as a social index, see Tomoko Wakasa, 'Swords in Early Modern English Plays', M.Phil. thesis (University of Birmingham, 2011).

(TLN 1297).[26] Likewise, a surprising number of play-scripts are entirely indifferent to the sum, currency, and form of money meant to appear on stage, perhaps reflecting a degree of professional flexibility on the part of repertory companies.[27]

As one might expect, modern editors approach such ambiguities differently: for some, Cleopatra uses multiple asps, others only one. Textual variation presents an added complication when using play-scripts, as the explicit and implicit references to props can vary markedly from one version to another. The 1616 B-text of Marlowe's *Doctor Faustus*, for instance, requires a false head and dismembered limbs, where the 1604 A-text calls only for a false leg. Thus, the choice of text and edition will have an effect on which, and how many, props are counted.[28]

Once a source has been selected, one consideration when quantifying early modern stage props is *what* to count. There is little consensus on what constitutes a 'stage property' as opposed to other accoutrements of the theatre – costuming, furniture, scenery, machinery, pyrotechnics and special effects, and so on. For David Bevington and Felix Bosonnet, portability is the key criterion: Bevington defines stage properties as 'appurtenances worn or carried by actors',[29] and Bosonnet, 'any portable article of costume or furniture, used in acting a play'.[30] By contrast, Brownell Salomon distinguishes between costume and prop on the basis of function:

> Unanchored physical objects, light enough for a person to carry on stage for manual use there, define hand properties for semiological purposes. Elements usually thought of as part of the decor, or clothing accessories like jewelry or handkerchiefs which are normally considered articles of costume, become hand properties when they assume this independent function.[31]

This emphasis on functional fluidity echoes in the later distinction made between 'object' and 'thing' in 'Thing Theory', as developed by Bill Brown.

---

[26] All references to *1 The Honest Whore* are to Joost Daalder's text for Digital Renaissance Editions (2015–), cited by Through-Line Number (TLN).

[27] On the relationship between flexibility and notions of distinct repertory company styles, see Chapter 6.

[28] For her counts of props in Shakespeare, Teague uses print facsimiles of the First Folio and early quartos (*Shakespeare's Speaking Properties*, 157); for his counts of props in twenty non-Shakespearean plays, Bruster uses eleven different editions (*Shakespeare*, 250 n.42). This does not invalidate either critics' counts or findings, of course, but it does raise questions about editorial consistency.

[29] David Bevington, *Action is Eloquence: Shakespeare's Language of Gesture* (Cambridge, MA: Harvard University Press, 1984), 35.

[30] Felix Bosonnet, *The Function of Stage Properties in Christopher Marlowe's Plays* (Bern: Francke, 1978), 10.

[31] Brownell Salomon, 'Visual and Aural Signs in the Performed English Renaissance Play', *Renaissance Drama* 5 (1972), 160–1.

For Brown, 'things' are 'what is excessive in objects, as what exceeds their mere materialization as objects or their mere utilization', and 'the magic by which objects become values, fetishes, idols, and totems'.[32] Pamela Bickley and Jenny Stevens have recently proposed an application of 'Thing Theory' to the question of props in early modern drama:

> [W]hile every visible 'object' in stage performance is not necessarily a 'thing' (actors may well wear boots, drink from goblets, sit on chairs that have limited significance beyond their utility), when an object is named in the text itself, it is surely destined for 'thing' status.[33]

If, as Nathalie Rivere de Carles remarks, 'performance turns objects into props', then perhaps 'it is only when an object is actively part of the performance that it gains a real theatrical value'.[34]

After a definition has been agreed upon, the next consideration when quantifying props is *how* to count them – as tokens or types, as discrete objects or classes of objects. In her study of Shakespeare, Teague constructs six composite categories and classes every prop as either 'light' (e.g. candles, tapers, lanterns), 'weapon or war gear' (e.g. helmets, shields, swords), 'document' (e.g. letters, warrants), 'riches or gift' (e.g. coins, jewels, rings), 'token of a character' (e.g. costumes, crowns, military colours), or 'other' (e.g. cups, keys, musical instruments).[35] While the use of composite categories may facilitate the discovery of broader patterns in classes of props, it is – as Teague admits – a 'highly subjective' exercise,[36] and one that will frame the terms of the analysis. For example, Bruster remarks that Shakespeare's tragedies 'heavily use lights, a fact that reminds us how many of these plays unfold mainly at night', compared with the history plays, which 'take place largely during the day and have the fewest lights of any genre'.[37] This may be a valid observation, but it is one that assumes that every instance of a prop Teague classes as 'light' in fact functions to signify that the action takes place at night. This may not necessarily always be the case.[38] It is also an observation enabled (or constrained) by the classification system itself: had Teague created a category for 'consumables' instead of 'light', which

---

[32] Bill Brown, 'Thing Theory', *Critical Inquiry* 28.1 (2001), 5.

[33] Pamela Bickley and Jenny Stevens, *Shakespeare and Early Modern Drama: Text and Performance* (London: Bloomsbury Arden Shakespeare, 2016), 192.

[34] Nathalie Rivere de Carles, 'Performing Materiality: Curtains on the Early Modern Stage', in Farah Karim-Cooper and Tiffany Stern (eds.), *Shakespeare's Theatres and the Effects of Performance* (London: Bloomsbury Arden Shakespeare, 2013), 64.

[35] Teague, *Shakespeare's Speaking Properties*, 157.

[36] Teague, *Shakespeare's Speaking Properties*, 157.   [37] Bruster, *Shakespeare*, 109.

[38] A further example is Starveling's lantern, representing the moon in the rude mechanicals' play in *A Midsummer Night's Dream*, which is classified by Teague as a 'token of a character', not a 'light'.

presumably would separate lanterns and lamps from candles and tapers, could Bruster have readily made the same generalisations about day and night? The use of such composite categories becomes further complicated when membership of a class is exclusive and a prop can belong to only a single category. Portia's ring in *The Merchant of Venice*, for example, is counted by Teague (and therefore also Bruster) as an instance of 'riches or gift' alone, but not also as a 'token of a character', even though the resolution of the play rests upon this identification.

For the present study, we compile prop-lists for every play first appearing on the early modern commercial stage between 1590 and 1609 using the relevant volumes of Martin Wiggins's *British Drama, 1533–1642: A Catalogue* as our source.[39] Every entry in the *Catalogue* distinguishes the 'costumes' of a play from its 'props', dividing the latter into sub-categories: 'lighting', 'pyrotechnics', 'weapons', 'musical instruments', 'clothing', 'money', 'small portable objects', 'large portable objects', 'scenery', and 'miscellaneous'. In each sub-category, props are listed along with a citation locating the scenes in which they appear and whether the references are explicit or implicit. The 'props' section of the catalogue entry for *A Larum for London*, for example, is presented as follows:

Pyrotechnics: cannon shot off (sc. 2, s.d.)

Weapons: pikes (sc. 2, s.d.); Stump's sword (sc. 4, dialogue; sc. 6, s.d.); Havré's sword (sc. 4, s.d.; sc. 5, dialogue); D'Avila's rapier (sc. 5, 8, 15, dialogue; sc. 7, s.d.; also referred to as a scimitar); Egmont's weapons (sc. 5, s.d.); van End's rapier (sc. 7, s.d.; sc. 12, dialogue); three rapiers (sc. 7, s.d.; belonging to Alva, Romero, and Verdugo); strappado equipment (sc. 8, dialogue); probably muskets (sc. 8, dialogue); a pistol (sc. 8, s.d.); a blade weapon (sc. 8, implicit); two Spaniards' swords (sc. 10, s.d.); a rope with a halter (sc. 11, dialogue); a sword (sc. 14, dialogue)

Musical Instruments: a drum (sc. 2, 15, s.d.)

Money: a bag containing 500 dollars (sc. 8, dialogue)

Small Portable Objects: six stones (sc. 12, s.d.); a cord (sc. 14, s.d.); a letter (sc. 15, s.d.)

Large Portable Objects: mourning pennons (sc. 2, s.d.); a hearse covered with black (sc. 2, s.d.); military colours (s.c. 15, s.d.)

Scenery: a gibbet (sc. 11, dialogue; sc. 14, s.d.)[40]

---

[39] Wiggins and Richardson, *British Drama*. We use volumes III (1590–7), IV (1598–1602), V (1603–8), and VI (1609–16).

[40] Wiggins and Richardson, *British Drama*, IV: 121.

Our use of a single external source ensures a level of consistency and expedites the process of generating prop-lists, but it also means our analysis inherits any biases, errors, and inconsistencies already present in the data. For example, are 'writing implements' (as listed in the *Catalogue* entry for *Love's Metamorphosis*) the same as, or different from, 'writing instruments' (as listed for *John of Bordeaux*) or 'writing materials' (as in *Cymbeline*)? For an additional layer of consistency, we also exclude a number of plays from our analysis on the basis of the chronology and performance histories provided by Wiggins rather than from our usual source, the *Annals*.[41] Appendix C lists the resulting sample of 160 plays.

To avoid ambiguities of number, we decide to analyse the plays in our sample on the basis of whether a particular prop archetype (or 'prop-type') is absent from, or present in, a given play's prop-list. We are not concerned with multiples of given props (e.g. how many asps Cleopatra may have handled), or whether the same prop reappears at different points of a play (e.g. whether the same prop letter in Scene 2 is used again in Scenes 3, 4, and 26), but only whether or not the *Antony and Cleopatra* prop-list includes the 'asp' and 'letter' prop-types. We manipulate the *Catalogue* data accordingly, so references to specific props become generic prop-types and duplicate entries are removed. Thus, an entry for 'Stump's sword' becomes 'sword' (and all other sword entries are discarded), and money is recorded simply as 'money', regardless of the sum, currency, and form (if stated). While it is impossible to perfectly resolve ambiguities of kind, we attempt to minimise the effects by standardising equivalent references (e.g. instances of 'writing instruments' and 'writing implements' become 'writing materials') but retain references to unspecified prop-types (e.g. 'unspecified weapon' and 'unspecific musical instrument'). The prop-list for *A Larum for London* previously cited, for example, is transformed into:

> cannon-shot, pike, sword, rapier, weapon-unspecified, torture-device, musket, pistol, weapon-blade, halter, musical-drum, money, money-bag, stone, cord, letter, pennon, hearse, military-colours, gallows

In this example, the 'strappado equipment' cited in the *Catalogue* entry becomes the generic 'torture-device'; the 'bag containing 500 dollars' separates into instances of 'money' and 'money-bag' (hyphenated to distinguish

---

[41] We exclude *Summer's Last Will and Testament* (no evidence of public performance); *The Taming of a Shrew* (Wiggins thinks the performance history is conflated with *The Shrew*); *Two Lamentable Tragedies* (no evidence of performance, public or otherwise); all of William Percy's plays (no evidence they were ever staged, publically or otherwise); *Histriomastix* (uncertainty whether it was staged anywhere other than the Middle Temple); *Wily Beguiled* (uncertainty whether its auspices are professional or academic); and *Four Plays in One* (anthology of four different genres).

between other types of bag, just as 'drum' becomes 'musical-drum'); and 'gibbet' is equated with 'gallows'. Thus the tally of prop-types for *A Larum for London* is twenty.

Frequency and Distribution of Prop-Types

Appendix C lists the tallies of prop-types for all 160 plays in our sample, along with their authorship, date of first performance, genre, and total lines of spoken dialogue. With the prop-lists compiled, we begin by counting the number of plays in which each prop-type is present (see Appendix D). In total, there are 691 different prop-types, but the majority appear in very few plays: 596 are called for in fewer than 10 plays, and of these 596, 321 prop-types are unique, appearing in only a single play. This suggests that dramatists perhaps did not feel overly constrained in their writing practice by the availability of a given prop-type – that playwrights assumed repertory companies could source materials as required, no matter how exotic or mundane, regardless of the likelihood for later re-use in another play.[42]

The figures in Appendix D also allow us to distinguish between common and uncommon prop-types. The generic 'sword' is the most common, present in 119 plays, followed closely by 'money' (116) and 'letter' (102). It is perhaps unsurprising that these prop-types are the most common, given how they encapsulate many of the thematic concerns and motivations that propel much of the period's drama: conflict and violence, wealth and status, language and communication. After these top three, there is a sharp drop in the number of plays in which each prop-type appears. The remainder of the top ten most common prop-types, in descending order, are 'paper' at seventy-one plays, followed by 'seating' (sixty-seven), 'wine' (sixty-two), 'table' (fifty-five), 'blood' and 'document' (both fifty-four), 'purse' (fifty), and 'musical-drum' (forty-eight).

Returning to the prop-list data in Appendix C, we calculate statistics about the distribution of prop-types in the sample, broken down by period, genre, playwright, and mode of authorship. These are summarised in Table 4.1.

Our analysis reveals a statistically significant positive correlation between the number of prop-types and total lines spoken in each play – in other words, lengthier plays tend to employ more prop-types.[43] Perhaps this is simply a matter of opportunity: more dialogue means greater opportunities

---

[42] On the question of 'company' styles, see also Chapter 6.

[43] This finding confirms Teague's and Bruster's assumption that play-length and prop-use are related, as reflected by their counting of props in terms of per-line frequency.

Table 4.1 *Distribution of props in 160 plays from the professional theatre,*
1590–1609

Set	Mean prop-types	Median prop-types	Standard deviation	Total plays	Mean lines spoken
All plays	23.27	21.5	10.84	160	2330.07
1590–1599	23.65	22	10.36	63	2322.44
1600–1609	23.03	21	11.18	97	2335.02
Comedy	22.46	20.5	10.14	74	2354.88
Tragedy	26.94	25	13.84	35	2445.29
History	23.87	22.5	9.17	30	2422.83
Romance	19.69	18	8.11	13	1901.46
Tragicomedy	17.20	14	9.88	5	2190.60
Moral	20.33	18	7.77	3	1536.00
Chapman, George	17.67	17.5	5.87	12	2262.08
Dekker, Thomas	31.17	30	6.21	6	2452.83
Heywood, Thomas	27.00	25	5.20	7	2267.00
Jonson, Ben	30.29	30	8.85	7	3130.71
Marston, John	29.43	28	7.23	8	2005.75
Middleton, Thomas	21.25	19	7.59	8	2089.75
Shakespeare, William	19.32	17	7.68	25	2776.64
Sole-author	23.84	22.5	10.71	102	2415.32
Collaborative	26.26	24	11.59	27	2527.04

for new props to be introduced. The play with the most prop-types in our sample is Barnabe Barnes's tragedy, *The Devil's Charter*, which uses eighty-one prop-types. It is also one of the lengthier plays, with 2,986 spoken lines. At 4,210 spoken lines, Jonson's *Every Man Out of His Humour* is the longest play in our sample, with 43 prop-types – tied sixth out of the top 10 plays with the most prop-types.[44] Samuel Daniel's *Philotas*, with 2,131 spoken lines, has the fewest prop-types (4), followed closely by the anonymous *Fair Em* (5) at 1,474 lines. At 913 spoken lines, the shortest play in our sample is the anonymous *Jack Straw*, which uses only 10 prop-types – tied seventh out of the 10 plays with the fewest prop-types.[45]

[44] In descending order, the top ten plays with the most prop-types are: *The Devil's Charter* (eighty-one); *Look About You* (forty-nine); *1 The Honest Whore* and *Macbeth* (both forty-eight); *1 Robin Hood* (forty-six); *Titus Andronicus* (forty-five); *2 Edward the Fourth* and *Every Man Out of His Humour* (both forty-three); *Antonio's Revenge* (forty-two); *Satiromastix*, *1 Sir John Oldcastle*, and *Edward the First* (all forty-one); *The Knight of the Burning Pestle* (forty); and *Your Five Gallants* and *A Warning for Fair Women* (both thirty-eight).

[45] In ascending order, the ten plays with the fewest prop-types are: *Philotas* (four); *Fair Em* (five); *The Merry Devil of Edmonton* and *Mucedorus* (both six); *As You Like It*, *Byron's Conspiracy*, and *Measure for Measure* (all seven); *The Turk* (eight); *Troilus and Cressida* (nine); *All's Well That Ends Well, The*

Although the sample spans only two decades, our analysis nonetheless confirms Bruster's observation that, on average, the use of props decreases over time,[46] from a mean and median of 23.65 and 22 prop-types per play in the 1590s to 23.03 and 21 prop-types in the first decade of the seventeenth century. If these differences are only slight, it is still a curious result, given the increase – not decrease – in average total lines spoken from 2,322.44 lines per play for 1590–9 to 2,335.02 lines per play for 1600–9.

The results in Table 4.1 confirm a genre effect on the number of prop-types, but also qualify the assumption that 'the genre that is most reliant on props is romance'.[47] In our sample of plays from 1590 to 1609, tragedies call for the highest number of prop-types, with an average of 26.94, followed by histories (23.87) and comedies (22.46). On average, romances employ only 19.69 prop-types, followed by tragicomedies (17.20). Table 4.1 also gives the standard deviations for these distributions, which temper the results somewhat: while tragedies use the most prop-types on average, they also have the highest standard deviation (13.84) of any genre. Since these figures relate only to the number of prop-types and not the quantities of individual props, it may still be possible that romances require a greater quantity of props than plays of other genres. That is, perhaps romances used fewer types of prop but in greater numbers. However, for the reasons outlined above, the uncertain quantities of the same prop-type used in any given play make this a difficult – if not impossible – claim to support or challenge.

Authors vary in the number of prop-types they use. With averages of 31.17 and 30.29 respectively, Dekker and Jonson typically use more prop-types than any other playwright with 6 or more sole-authored plays in our sample – almost twice as many as Chapman, with a mean of 17.5 prop-types per play, just below Shakespeare, with a mean of 19.32. However, as we might expect, individual authors also vary in prop-type use when writing in different genres. Shakespeare uses 23.63 prop-types on average between his 8 sole-authored tragedies, for example, but only 21 and 15.27 prop-types on average between his 6 and 11 sole-authored histories and comedies respectively. Chapman's practice is the opposite of Shakespeare's, using more prop-types on average between his 7 comedies (19.57) than his 3 tragedies (17.33). With only 2 sole-authored plays in each of 3 genres

---

Comedy of Errors, The Fair Maid of Bristol, The Maid's Metamorphosis, and *Jack Straw* (all ten); *The Fleer, 2 Henry the Sixth, Monsieur D'Olive,* and *1 The Two Angry Women of Abingdon* (all eleven); *The Fair Maid of the Exchange, John of Bordeaux,* and *The Two Gentlemen of Verona* (all twelve); and *The Isle of Gulls, John a Kent and John a Cumber, A Midsummer Night's Dream,* and *The Woman Hater* (all thirteen).

[46] Bruster, *Shakespeare,* 113–14.
[47] Laurie Maguire and Emma Smith, *30 Great Myths about Shakespeare* (Oxford: Blackwell, 2013), 180.

to compare, on average Heywood uses more prop-types when writing tragedies (31) than histories (29) and romances (22). These results also suggest that individual authors remain distinctive in the numbers of prop-types used, even when genre is taken into account: Shakespeare and Chapman, for example, use fewer prop-types than most of their peers, regardless of genre. Curiously, whether a play is sole- or collaboratively authored also appears to affect the number of prop-types used. If we exclude the 31 plays of uncertain authorial status from our sample, of the 129 plays that remain those that are sole-authored tend to require fewer prop-types than plays with multiple authors, with averages of 23.84 and 26.26 respectively.

Genre and Patterns of Prop-Type Use

To investigate further the genre effect apparent from the summary statistics, and to reveal any latent patterns in the distribution of prop-types, we conduct a Principal Components Analysis (PCA) on the data. We begin by generating a large table with 691 columns (one for each prop-type) and 160 rows (one for each play). When a prop-type is present in a given play, a '1' is recorded in the corresponding cell; when absent, it is marked with a '0'.

While it is unusual to conduct PCA using a binary matrix such as this, the method will work so long as the data is not too sparse. To reduce the sparsity of the data, we remove the least common variables – that is, we exclude prop-types present in fewer than 10 plays – leaving us with a smaller, but denser, table of 160 rows and 95 columns. We then use PCA to find the strongest un-correlated factors, projecting each play into a two-dimensional space as a data-point (Figure 4.1), treating the scores for each play as Cartesian coordinates on the two Principal Components which account for most of the differences in prop-type use between genres: the second principal component (PC2) on the horizontal axis, and the fourth principal component (PC4) on the vertical axis.[48]

Of the seventy-four comedies in our sample, sixty score low on the second principal component (PC2), plotted as filled squares to the left-hand side of the chart. By contrast, histories and tragedies typically score highly

---

[48] In choosing which of the principal components to focus on for discussion, we looked for those in the top four which related most directly to genre differences. PC1 captured the contrast between plays with abundant prop-types and those with few prop-types, so does not add much to what we already know. Of the other three, PC2 and PC4 were most correlated with genre, as discussed below. From PC1 to PC4, the percentages of variance accounted for by each component were 4.906%, 4.152%, 3.446%, and 3.299% respectively.

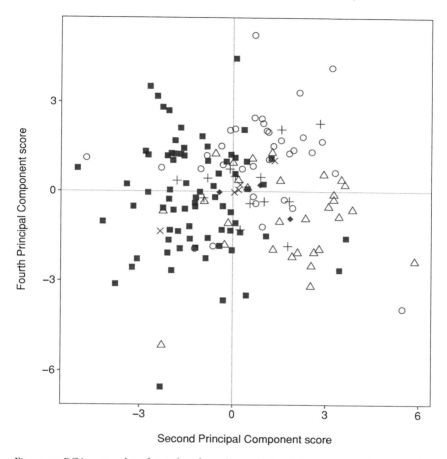

Figure 4.1 PCA scatterplot of 160 plays from the professional theatre, 1590–1609, using the 95 most common prop-types.

on PC2 and are plotted to the right of the origin. Histories and tragedies (plotted as unfilled triangles and circles respectively) are distinguished, albeit imperfectly, along the fourth principal component (PC4): twenty-seven of the thirty-five tragedies score positively on PC4 and are plotted above the origin, whereas twenty of the thirty histories score negatively and are plotted below it. Different types of comedy are also discernible

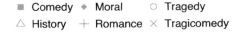

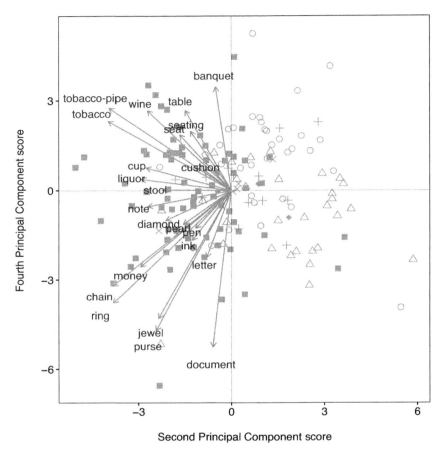

Figure 4.2 PCA biplot of 160 plays from the professional theatre, 1590–1609, using the 95 most common prop-types, highlighting selected 'comedic' prop-types.

along PC4. As shown in Figure 4.2, comedies populated with prop-types that Teague classifies as 'riches or gift' and 'document' ('chain', 'diamond', 'jewel', 'money', 'pearl', 'purse', and 'ring', as well as 'document', 'ink', 'letter', 'note', and 'pen') score low on PC4, whereas comedies scoring highly on PC4 are those in which characters sit down to eat, drink, and smoke together, requiring prop-types such as 'cushion', 'seat', 'seating', 'stool', and 'table', as well as 'banquet', 'cup', 'liquor', 'tobacco', 'tobacco-pipe', and 'wine'.

Inspection of the PCA biplot also reveals a number of generic and thematic patterns in the distribution of prop-types. If 'Jonson's defining interest in trust and exchange, honesty and deceit, credit and coining' is typical in the comedies of this period,[49] we may expect, and indeed find, 'money' to be a staple comedic prop-type (Figure 4.3). However, genre appears also to have an effect on *how* prop-money is stored and/or carried in our sample of 160 plays. The PCA reveals that 'purse' is strongly associated with comedy, plotted to the bottom-left of the chart with a low score on PC2. By contrast, 'money-bag' (as opposed to the generic 'bag') is associated with history plays, plotted to the bottom right of the chart, with high scores on PC2 and low scores on PC4.

Of course, this is not an absolute rule – purses can and do appear as prop-types in histories and tragedies, just as money-bags are also found in comedies. However, there is a generic logic to the distinction: a purse is more intimate and personal, capable of holding only moderate sums at best – in other words, it is a prop one expects to find in the day-to-day world of changing fortunes characteristic of comedy, and city comedy in particular. Too big to offer the intimacy of a purse and too flimsy to share the grandeur of a chest, money-bags often serve a negative or satirical purpose. In comedies, money-bags are the trappings of avaricious misers and usurers, such as Volpone and Shylock, or the ironic accoutrement of beggars.[50] Shakespeare cleverly combines both of these associations in *The Winter's Tale*, when Autolycus peddles a ballad, 'one to a very doleful tune, how a usurer's wife was brought to bed of twenty money-bags at a burden' (4.4.260–2). In histories and tragedies, money-bags often suggest something underhanded and unjust – ransoms, bribes, thefts, and spoils of war. In the Induction to *The Devil's Charter*, for example, 'a table is furnished with divers *bags* of money' as a display of papal corruption,[51] while Sir Francis tempts Susan to whoredom with 'a *bag* of gold' in the sub-plot of Thomas Heywood's *A Woman Killed with Kindness*.[52]

Taking our cue from Bruster's observation about the effect of genre on Shakespeare's use of 'light' props, we next inspect the biplot for prop-types

---

[49] Christopher Burlinson, 'Money and Consumerism', in Julie Sanders (ed.), *Ben Jonson in Context* (Cambridge University Press, 2010), 281.
[50] Tom Nichols, *The Art of Poverty: Irony and Ideal in Sixteenth-Century Beggar Imagery* (Manchester University Press, 2007), 46 n.33, 59.
[51] Barnabe Barnes, *The Devil's Charter* (London, 1607; STC 1466), A2r (emphasis added).
[52] Thomas Heywood, *A Woman Killed with Kindness*, ed. R. W. van Fossen (London: Methuen, 1961), 9.46 (emphasis added).

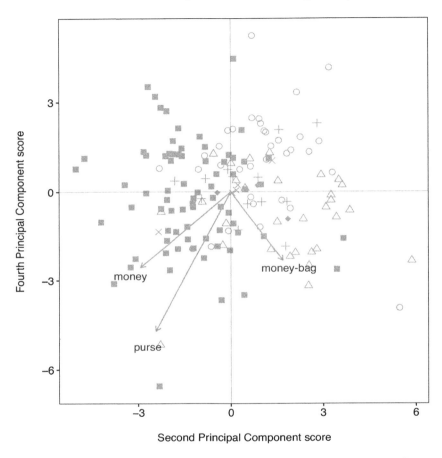

Figure 4.3 PCA biplot of 160 plays from the professional theatre, 1590–1609, using the 95 most common prop-types, highlighting money-related prop-types.

that would fall into that category: 'candle', 'fire', 'lantern', 'light', 'light-ning', 'taper', and 'torch' (Figure 4.4). The existence of a generic 'light' prop-type draws our attention to the peculiar problem of distinguishing between different forms of artificial light on the early modern commercial stage, and to the fundamental issue of ambiguity in quantification. According to R. B. Graves, the 'major obstacle in attempting to reconstruct the

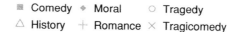

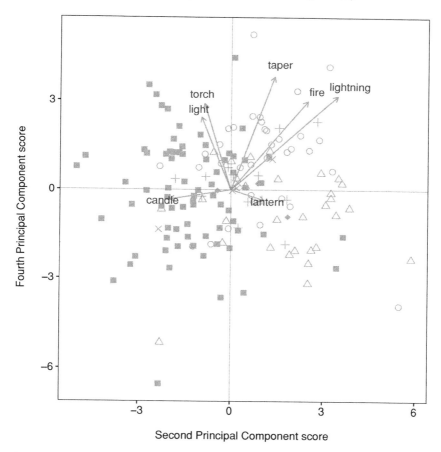

Figure 4.4 PCA biplot of 160 plays from the professional theatre, 1590–1609, using the 95 most common prop-types, highlighting prop-types associated with artificial light.

artificial illumination of the early drama is that nearly every light could be and was confused with others' – that 'torches and tapers were some-times called candles, large candles were called torches', and 'even tapers were called lanterns' – with all variously and 'frequently identified simply by the general term "light"'.[53] We could ignore all instances of the generic

[53] R. B. Graves, *Lighting the Shakespearean Stage, 1567–1642* (Carbondale: Southern Illinois University Press, 1999), 23.

'light' prop-type on the grounds that it is ambiguous, but this would be to discount a significant proportion of the prop-list data. Alternatively, following Teague and Bruster, we could count all of the distinct prop-types as instances of a composite 'light' category instead; however, this would render potential patterns in the use of particular 'light' prop-types invisible to our analysis. In the end, we chose to retain the *Catalogue* data, cognisant that the ambiguity may introduce a measure of noise to the analysis, but hopeful that any patterns in the use of specific artificial light prop-types would remain discernible.

As shown in Figure 4.4, the PCA reveals that 'taper', 'fire', and 'lightning' are strongly associated with tragedies, scoring high on both PC2 and PC4. As destructive elements and otherworldly signs, fire and lightning are at home in tragedy. Henry Chettle's *Hoffman*, for example, clumsily opens with the titular character interpreting thunder and lightning – 'the powers of heaven in apparition | And frightful aspects as intended' – as divine assent for his father's revenge.[54] Tapers, as Alan Dessen and Leslie Thomson suggest, are typically found in 'mourning, devotional, and penitential scenes', or 'the setting of tables for banquets, the study, reading and writing'.[55] Candles, by contrast, are mundane, domestic, everyday, and thus more characteristic of comedies in our sample, scoring low on both PC2 and PC4.[56] Only lanterns appear to be more commonly associated with histories in our sample, perhaps reflecting (as Bruster suggests) a higher proportion of outdoor night-time scenes, or an increased number of associated character-types, such as guards and watchmen. An unexpected result is the low PC2 score for both 'torch' and the generic 'light', since we might assume these prop-types to be plotted with the tragedies in our sample. Instead, they are plotted just to the comedy end of the divide between comedy and tragedy.

In the 1953 Broadway hit *The Solid Gold Cadillac*, sometime actress-turned-stockholder Laura Partridge explains that she 'never cared much for Shakespeare' because 'He's so tiring. You never get a chance to sit down unless you're a king.'[57] This is not the case, of course, but a genre effect is observable in the distribution of furniture prop-types. As the biplot shows in Figure 4.5, the PCA strongly associates thrones with histories in the

---

[54] Henry Chettle, *Hoffman* (London, 1631), B1r.

[55] Alan Dessen and Leslie Thomson, *A Dictionary of Stage Directions in English Drama, 1580–1642* (Cambridge University Press, 1999), 226.

[56] Candles were made from wax, tallow, or other solid fat formed around a wick. A taper is properly a slender form of wax candle – i.e., a long wick coated in wax.

[57] Howard Teichmann and George S. Kaufman, *The Solid Gold Cadillac: A Comedy* (New York: Random House, 1954), 79.

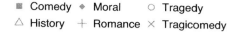

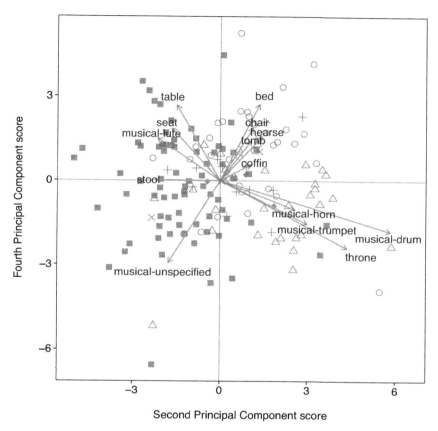

Figure 4.5 PCA biplot of 160 plays from the professional theatre, 1590–1609, using the 95 most common prop-types, highlighting furniture and musical prop-types.

sample, scoring high on PC2 and low on PC4. Along with the domestic 'table', 'seat', and 'stools' – seating options more appropriate for the commoner sort – are aligned with comedy, all scoring low on PC2. As we might expect from prop-types so strongly linked with death, coffins, tombs, and hearses are plotted with the tragedies, scoring high on both PC2 and PC4. So too the PCA strongly associates 'bed' with tragedy, aligning with Sasha Roberts's characterisation of beds as 'an especially rich source of image-making, particularly around sex, marriage, sickness and death'.[58] Writing with Shakespeare's practice in mind, Roberts argues that although bed imagery is frequent in the dialogue of plays in all genres, there is little call for beds as stage properties outside of tragedy. Beds 'may be a site of marital conflict in the middle acts of comedies', but their physical presence on-stage is unnecessary to play out 'the comic resolutions of the final act', in which the bed becomes 'the pleasurable, chaste domain of marital consummation'. In histories, beds may function as important indices of 'marital conflict or union', but 'the only occasions on which a bed is required as a stage property in the histories is in the context of sickness and death'.[59]

The biplot in Figure 4.5 also shows the PCA weightings for prop musical instruments along PC2 and PC4 (all prefixed with 'musical-'). 'Horn', 'trumpet', and 'drum' are all strongly connected with the history plays, scoring high on PC2 and low on PC4. The 'penetrating' sound of these instruments was associated primarily with 'military might', and, according to Christopher Marsh, 'such instruments were regularly spoken of as weapons' – as '"clamorous", "repercussive", "lofty", "rattling" and "warlike"'. The 'approach of pre-eminent individuals' was also signalled with trumpet calls, which simultaneously evoked 'the glitz of aristocracy while alluding to the intimidating power that lay behind it'.[60] If the drum, horn, and trumpet belong to the public arena of war and aristocratic display characteristic of the histories, then the proper domain of the lute is the private sphere of the comedies. As we might expect, the 'lute' is indeed plotted with the comedies in our sample, reflecting its association with the female body (on account of its shape), and with sexuality and whoredom (on account of the Italian courtesans famed for playing it) – apposite themes for humorous and satirical treatment.

Like musical instruments, certain weapons are better suited to particular genres because they also function as social indices. For this reason, many of the weapon prop-type weightings shown in Figure 4.6 are unsurprising. The 'dagger', a perennial favourite of the murderer, along with the 'sword' of the revenger, is plotted with the tragedies, scoring high on both PC2 and PC4. As an instrument of judicial punishment, the 'halter' understandably straddles the divide between tragedy and history, scoring high on PC2 with

[58] Sasha Roberts, '"Let me the curtains draw": The Dramatic and Symbolic Properties of the Bed in Shakespearean Tragedy', in Harris and Korda (eds.), *Staged Properties*, 153.

[59] Roberts, '"Let me the curtains draw"', 166.

[60] Christopher Marsh, *Music and Society in Early Modern England* (Cambridge University Press, 2010), 14.

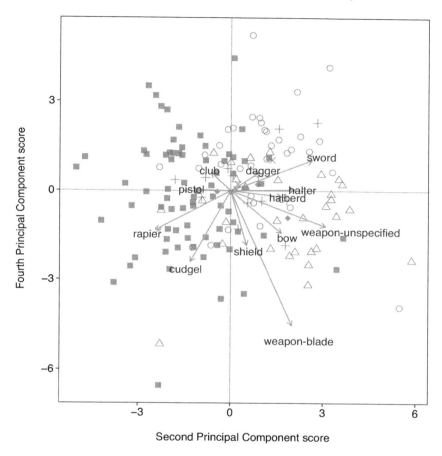

Figure 4.6 PCA biplot of 160 plays from the professional theatre, 1590–1609, using the 95 most common prop-types, highlighting weapon prop-types.

just a fraction of a negative score on PC4. The 'cudgel' and 'club', weapons of the lowly apprentice, score low on PC2, to commingle with the 'rapier' and 'pistol' of the city gallant in the comedies, while the 'halberd' brandished by those guarding the aristocracy – along with the 'bow' of the archer, and the generic 'blade', 'weapon', and 'shield' of the soldier – is plotted with the histories.

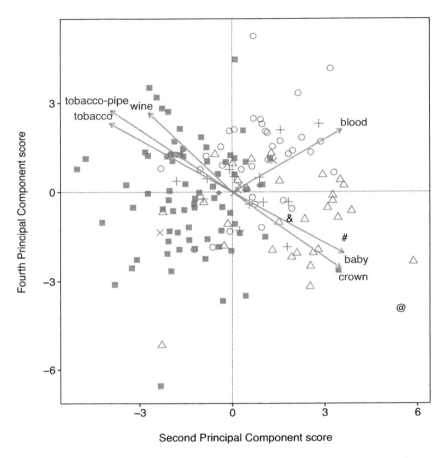

Figure 4.7 PCA biplot of 160 plays from the professional theatre, 1590–1609, using the 95 most common prop-types, highlighting selected prop-types.

Of the ninety-five most common prop-types used in the PCA, one in particular stands out as unusual – 'baby'.[61] As the biplot in Figure 4.7 shows, the PCA plots 'baby' squarely in the 'history' region, with a high

[61] For an insightful discussion of the theatrical challenges of using live and fake babies, see Andrew Sofer, "'Take up the Bodies": Shakespeare's Body Parts, Babies, and Corpses', *Theatre Symposium* 18 (2010), 137–9.

score on PC2 and a corresponding low score on PC4. Since only three of
the ten plays in our sample that list 'baby' as a prop-type are classified by
the *Catalogue* as histories,[62] this is an unexpected result.

If the weighting of 'baby' on PC2 and PC4 is a surprise, it is also a
welcome one because it serves as a timely reminder that PCA is an unsupervised method. The procedure does not rely upon any human pre-
processing of the data – it does not 'know' what genre each of the plays
belong to and treats all of the variables equally and indifferently. PCA clusters some plays together and distances others because they have similar and
dissimilar traits – in this case, the relative absence and presence of prop-
types. Because of these shared traits, the PCA gives three more plays scores
that place them in the same region of the chart as the histories: a comedy (*The Weakest Goeth to the Wall*), a moral (*The Cobbler's Prophecy*), and
a tragedy (*Titus Andronicus*). These are marked in Figure 4.7 with a hash
symbol ('#'), an ampersand ('&'), and an at symbol ('@') respectively.

Inspection of the relevant prop-lists confirms these plays' affinity with
those formally classified as histories. *The Weakest Goeth to the Wall* contains a number of prop-types heavily weighted towards history – that
is, high on PC2 and low on PC4 – such as 'crown', 'drum', 'money-
bag', and 'throne'. Similarly, *The Cobbler's Prophecy* counts 'drum', 'trumpet', and 'unspecified weapon' among its prop-types, while *Titus Andronicus* includes all three history-heavy musical instruments ('drum', 'horn',
'trumpet'), three history-heavy weapons ('bow', 'weapon-blade', 'weapon-
unspecified'), 'money-bag', and 'crown'. These plays also lack prop-types
more common in plays of their genre classifications: for example, the 'wine',
'tobacco', and 'tobacco-pipe' typical of city comedies – and plotted in dia-
metric opposition to 'baby' in Figure 4.6 – are absent from *The Weakest
Goeth to the Wall*'s prop-list, while *Titus Andronicus* lacks the 'fire', 'light-
ning', and 'taper' prop-types regularly found in tragedies.

Conclusion

When we focus simply on the number of prop-types used in plays appearing on the commercial stage between 1590 and 1609, our analysis suggests that genre has a significant effect. The number of prop-types used
also varies from author to author, and within authorial canons according
to genre. When we shift focus to consider the distribution of prop-types

---

[62] These plays are *Edward the First*, *The Travels of the Three English Brothers*, and *When You See Me You Know Me*.

according to genre, we find a number of readily explicable associations – purses with comedy, drums and trumpets with history, beds with tragedy, and so on.

Approaching genre through the lens of prop-type use, rather than the other way round, we observe, for instance, that there are some comedies which look more like histories than other comedies in terms of their prop-list profile. This leads to the odd case of 'baby' as a prop-type: according to the PCA, it is a prop-type associated with history plays, but this is partly because some plays in which it is present are comedies that have general affinities in prop-type use with histories. The seeming anomaly of the 'baby' prop-type is a reminder of the fluidity of the relationship between props and genres – we observe tendencies and conventions rather than strict laws in genre, while prop-types elicit their own patterns which sometimes, but not always, correspond with genre.

It seems fair to say that there is a 'language of props'[63] that must have been familiar to audiences in the early modern professional theatres, even if it was never formally or fully articulated. Comedies are populated with chairs, tobacco pipes, and purses, for instance, and their presence on stage must surely have steadily reinforced a consciousness that the action was set within a 'comedy' world. Language, however, is never static, and changing cultural resonances must have affected the relationship between prop-types and genres. If 'a cigar is sometimes just a cigar', as the apocryphal aphorism ascribed to Sigmund Freud suggests, then it is also sometimes not 'just a cigar' – the exigencies of culture dynamically fill the interpretive space between signifier and signified at any given moment. The indiscretions of Bill Clinton and Monica Lewinsky, for example, rendered the cigar a topically comic prop during the late 1990s. If we were to analyse prop-types over a longer period, would the same generic patterns emerge? By the same token, awareness of these temporally and culturally bound associations between prop-types and genres must certainly have allowed playwrights to manipulate audience expectations. Of course, these and other tantalising questions take us beyond the present data. What does it mean to be a playwright who, like Dekker and Jonson, habitually introduces an abundance of props into his plays, or to be one who is more sparing, like Chapman or Shakespeare? Do differences in the dialogue styles of these dramatists reflect the contrasts of stage-worlds thickly or thinly populated by things?

---

[63] Alan S. Downer, 'The Life of Our Design: The Function of Imagery in the Poetic Drama', *The Hudson Review* 2.2 (1949), 243. See also Bruster, *Shakespeare*, 245 n.3.

We hope this schematic outline of the patterning of prop-type distribution in these two decades opens the way for further exploration. But whatever future work may show, it is already possible to glimpse a system which gives a context for each prop-type as it appears on stage – as connected to or contrasting with other neighbouring prop-types, as part of a sparse or crowded deployment of prop-types in this play, and as expected (or otherwise) given this genre, author, or period. It is pleasing to think that the quantitative approach may give a new prominence to 'trumpet', 'taper', 'purse', and 'baby', in the same way that it brings lowly pronouns and prepositions to critical attention.

CHAPTER 5

'Novelty carries it away'
Cultural Drift

After purpose-built playhouses were established in London during the 1570s and 1580s, early modern English drama made remarkable progress artistically and commercially up until the early 1640s when the theatres were closed as the Civil War was looming. This busy, innovative group of enterprises attracted celebrated individual talents like Thomas Kyd, Christopher Marlowe, Ben Jonson, Thomas Middleton, and of course William Shakespeare, but it also achieved a collective momentum. Theatrical successes such as Kyd's *The Spanish Tragedy* (1587), Marlowe's two *Tamburlaine* plays (1587–8), or Jonson's *Humour* plays (1598–9) had both an immediate and lasting impact on the drama.[1] Playwrights copied each other and competed and collaborated to meet the demands of an increasingly discerning audience. Genres flourished and decayed, just as companies adapted to changing personnel and resources over time. The early modern theatre formed an interconnected and evolving culture.

Changes in the world outside the theatre also had an effect. The steady increase in the number of printed books available changed the balance towards a more 'literate' kind of dialogue, at the same time as London was growing in population and importance, with a money economy replacing more traditional systems of obligation. New places came into the collective consciousness through exploration, trade, and travel. There were specific historical developments in the language as it was spoken outside the theatre: in vocabulary, an unprecedented influx of new words; and in syntax,

---

[1] Representative recent studies of the impact of these plays on the drama include Erne, *Beyond 'The Spanish Tragedy'*, esp. ch. 4; Robert A. Logan, *Shakespeare's Marlowe: The Influence of Christopher Marlowe on Shakespeare's Artistry* (Aldershot: Ashgate, 2007), esp. ch. 6; W. David Kay, 'The Shaping of Ben Jonson's Career: A Reexamination of Facts and Problems', *Modern Philology* 67.3 (1970), 224–37; and Randall Martin (ed.), *Every Man Out of His Humour*, in Ben Jonson, *The Cambridge Edition of the Works of Ben Jonson*, David Bevington, Martin Butler, and Ian Donaldson (gen. eds.), (Cambridge University Press, 2012), 1: 235–9.

you replacing *thou*, the use of auxiliary *do* taking the modern pattern, and so on.[2]

Playwrights were acutely aware of change and especially attuned to the fact that audience tastes determined the success or failure of their latest offerings. Occasionally, playwrights commented on fashion, novelty, and obsolescence in the plays. Thomas Nashe noted a contemporary vogue for Senecan tragedy in 1589, but warned it would not last long.[3] John Marston promised his audience in a prologue that he would not 'torment your listening ears | With mouldy fopperies of stale poetry, | Unpossible dry musty fictions'.[4] In the Induction to *Cynthia's Revels* (1601), Jonson has a child actor remark on the unpopularity of old plays:

> Oh, I had almost forgot it, too, they say the *umbrae* or ghosts of some three or four plays departed a dozen years since have been seen walking on your stage here. Take heed, boy, if your house be haunted with such hobgoblins, 'twill fright away all your spectators quickly.[5]

A few years later, in 1606, the author of *The Woman Hater* signals that the satirical fashion is in retreat when 'he that made this play' disowns 'the ordinary and over-worn trade of jesting at lords and courtiers and citizens' in the prologue.[6] In the 1603 First Quarto version of Shakespeare's *Hamlet*, Gilderstone reports that adult players have recently been supplanted by boys' companies:

> I'faith, my lord, novelty carries it away. For the principal public audience that came to them are turned to private plays, and to the humour of children.[7]

Modern critics of early modern drama have also noted broad changes in style over time. It is sometimes suggested, for instance, that from the beginning of the seventeenth century the drama moves towards a more inward and personal focus. G. K. Hunter remarks that history plays generally drift from the political to the personal, from the public to the private, from

[2] Representative studies include Charles Barber, *Early Modern English* (Edinburgh University Press, 1997); and Terttu Nevalainen and Helena Raumolin-Brunberg, *Historical Sociolinguistics: Language Change in Tudor and Stuart England* (London: Longman, 2003), esp. ch. 4.

[3] Thomas Nashe, 'To the Gentleman Students of both Universities', in Robert Greene, *Menaphon* (London, 1599; STC 12272), 2*1r–A3r.

[4] John Marston, *Jack Drum's Entertainment* (London, 1601; STC 7243), A2v.

[5] Ben Jonson, *Cynthia's Revels*, ed. Eric Rasmussen and Matthew Steggle, *Cambridge Edition of the Works of Ben Jonson* (Cambridge University Press, 2012), Praeludium 154–7.

[6] Francis Beaumont and John Fletcher (?), *The Woman Hater* (London, 1607; STC 1692), A2r–v.

[7] William Shakespeare, *Hamlet: The Texts of 1603 and 1623*, ed. Ann Thompson and Neil Taylor (London: Arden Shakespeare, 2006), Q1: 7.271–3.

the military-political to the political-erotic, and that this change is 'urged on . . . by the same current as produced Fletcherian tragicomedy'.[8]

The arrival of machine-readable texts of the plays and of computational tools offers new ways to write a systematic literary history. Quantification brings myriad problems of specification and interpretation, but it does provide scale, which is needed for a broad literary history. If we are asking the computer to count instances of a feature, or multiple features, then a corpus of 50 or 500 plays, once it is prepared, is hardly more of a challenge than a single play. It also has the advantage that attention is paid evenly to every item in the corpus, and effects can be precisely judged.

Our focus in this chapter is on the dialogue of plays specifically. Although dialogue is but one dimension of the dramatic experience, alongside setting, plot, and action, not to mention *mise-en-scène*, casting, and dramaturgy, it is the bulk of what survives as unequivocal evidence from a distant historical period like the sixteenth and seventeenth centuries. Our definition of 'dialogue' is the words likely to have been spoken on stage, so we include prologues but not dedications, addresses to the reader, or any other prefatory matter. Our corpus for this chapter comprises 243 plays listed in Appendix A as first performed between 1580 and 1644, covering a tradition of productions – mainly in London – with no major interruptions, from shortly after the opening of the professional theatres to their closing by edict in the Civil War period.

Thirteen Half-Decades

We begin by arranging the plays in the corpus into half-decade sets, starting with 1580–4 and ending with 1640–4, thirteen in all. We then select the fifty most frequent function words, and find the averages for these words in each of the thirteen half-decades treated as a group.[9] We then perform a Principal Components Analysis (PCA) to find the most important patterns in the way these function words are used in the groupings. In this experiment, each half-decade grouping of plays has a single score for each variable – an average of the counts for the plays that are included. We thus

---

[8] G. K. Hunter, *English Drama, 1586–1642: The Age of Shakespeare* (Oxford University Press, 1997), 264, 278, 473, 278.

[9] The sheer weight of numbers in the very common words at the top of the list means that these words offer more steady and balanced data. On the other hand, a longer list brings in wider dimensions of style. As a compromise between these two competing motivations, we use the fifty most frequent function words in this experiment (out of the total 221 function words listed in Appendix E). It is also desirable for technical reasons to reduce the excess of variables over samples, so 50 words are preferable here to our more usual 100.

work with a table of fifty columns (one for each of the words) and thirteen rows (one for each half-decade group of plays).

Our interest is in whether the first principal component arranges the half-decades in exact chronological order, since this implies a consistent factor related to progressive change running through the set. A set of half-decades where this has happened we label a 'sequence'. The logic here is that if there is a strong sequential current, PCA will find it, given that the mix of genres and authors within the averages for the half-decades mutes the competing influences of genre and author. Conversely, if there is no strong sequential pattern, the first principal component is very likely to put half-decades out of order, given that the number of different ways of ordering a set of items is the factorial of the number of items. With 8 items, for instance, as in the longest sequence we found, this number is $8 \times 7 \times 6 \times 5 \times 4 \times 3 \times 2 \times 1 = 40{,}320$.

There are thirteen half-decades, so a sequence of thirteen is the longest possible. At the other end, we decided on a lower limit of five half-decades. Shorter than this, such as four half-decades, means a span which fails to cover the careers of the more long-lived authors, such as Thomas Heywood (who wrote over nine half-decades), Jonson (who wrote over eight), and Fletcher, Middleton, and Shakespeare (who all wrote over five).

There are nine different possible sequences starting with the first half-decade, one of each length from thirteen down to five. Then there are eight starting with the second half-decade, starting with the longest possible, twelve, and so on, seven starting with the third decade, down to one starting with the ninth decade. This makes for forty-five possible sequences in all. For each of these sets we ran a separate PCA and inspected the resulting scores for the half-decades to check whether they were arranged in exact chronological order or not. Figure 5.1 identifies the thirteen sequences where the half-decades were arranged in perfect chronological order along the principal component. All of the sets are arranged in Figure 5.1 in order of vertical window – that is, starting with those including the first row – and within that by order of size. Light grey shading indicates a set which did not yield a chronological array; dark grey shading indicates a sequence – i.e., a set placed in exact chronological order.

The dark grey chronological sequences are clustered in the upper part of the chart. None of them include a half-decade beyond 1620–4. This suggests that there are strong currents of collective change early in the set, but a more mixed pattern later. For instance, the five decades 1620–4 to 1640–4 did not form their own sequence. In this case, the first principal component is not associated with a progressive change in style. There may well

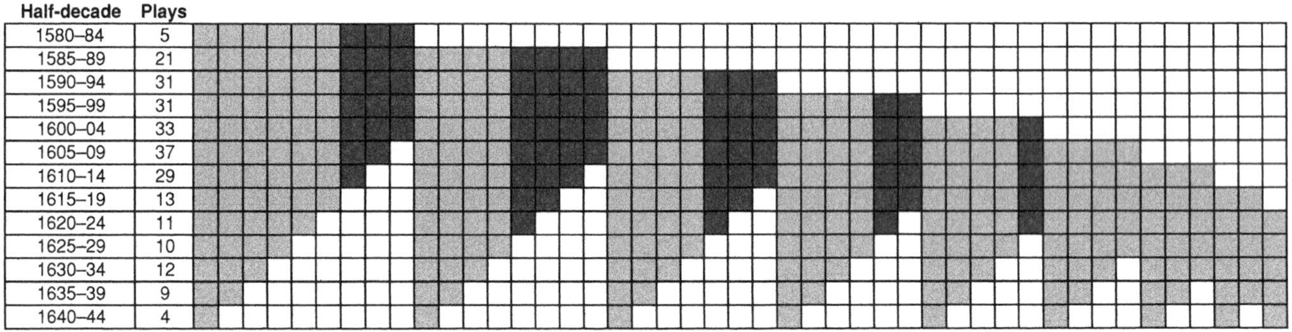

Half-decade	Plays
1580–84	5
1585–89	21
1590–94	31
1595–99	31
1600–04	33
1605–09	37
1610–14	29
1615–19	13
1620–24	11
1625–29	10
1630–34	12
1635–39	9
1640–44	4

Figure 5.1 Vertical chronological sequences arising from PC1 of a PCA using the 50 most frequent function words in 243 plays from the professional theatre grouped into 13 half-decades between 1580 and 1644.

be some elements of such a change, but if there are, they are not prominent enough to emerge in the competition against cross-cutting alternative clusterings of half-decades.

The longest sequence is eight half-decades, 1585–9 to 1620–4, and there is only one of this length. There are 40,320 ways to arrange eight half-decades, as already mentioned, so this result is highly unlikely to have come about by chance. All the other sequences to the right of this in Figure 5.1 are sub-sequences of this one: it seems that whatever the fluctuations there are within shorter sequences, they are not strong enough to disturb the arrays. There is a complete set of sequences within the sequences starting with the first half-decade as well, indicating that they are reasonably stable affairs.

With powerful statistical techniques there is always the danger of eliciting an artificially created pattern. In this case, though, we make no choices in the variables to predispose the system to a chronologically ordered result – they are simply the *commonest* words – and allow the method to make a set of weightings for them based entirely on what emerges from the algorithm. The procedure knows nothing of chronology and is simply presented with thirteen unlabelled sets of counts for the words. The analysis of the word frequencies is open-ended, seeking only the most powerful underlying pattern, whatever it may turn out to be. The requirement of a perfect sequence is a high threshold, given the number of possible combinations.

All in all, we can be confident that where such a sequence emerges, a strong current of language change has been uncovered. It is certainly not the *only* possible factor which is associated with chronology. We could, of course, go deeper into the list of words which appear in the plays, or be more selective, use a different statistical procedure, or treat the plays as individual items rather than in half-decades, and so on, and come up with more candidates for underlying trends in the language use of the plays. However, the mixture of word weightings which creates the sequence of eight half-decades is certainly a consistent, powerful stylistic force.

Magnitude and Variability, 1585–1624

As it represents the longest chronological sequence, we examine the 203 plays from the eight half-decades from 1585–90 to 1620–4 in further detail. For this PCA, with eight samples and fifty word-variables, PC1 accounted for 60 per cent of the variance. The weightings of the word-variables are shown in Figure 5.2.

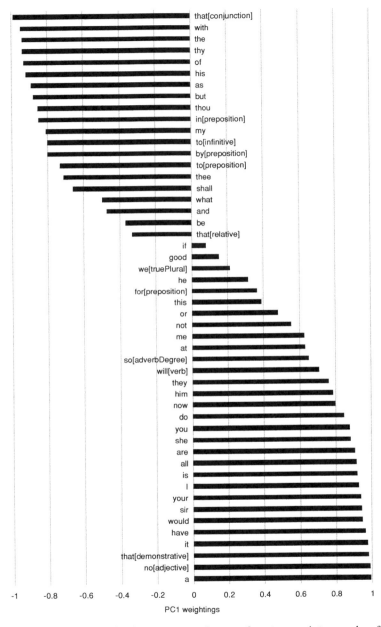

Figure 5.2 PC1 weightings for the top 50 most frequent function words in 203 plays from the professional theatre grouped into eight half-decades between 1585 and 1624.

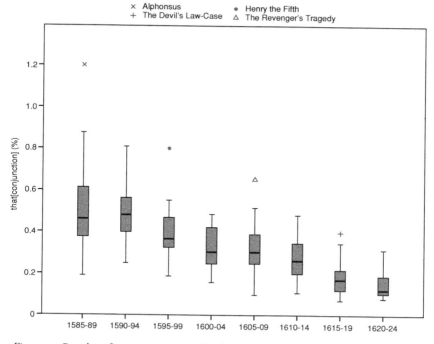

Figure 5.3 Boxplot of percentage counts for *that*_{conjunction} in plays between 1585 and 1624, grouped in half-decades.

Counts for the words with very low weightings on the component, those shown at the top of Figure 5.2, tend to start high in the plays and then decline, whereas counts for words with high weightings, at the lower end of Figure 5.2, are lower in the early plays and increase over time.

The changes in the counts for the most heavily weighted words can be considerable, although there are also wide variations in individual plays. Figure 5.3 is a boxplot of counts for *that* as a conjunction – the most heavily weighted word in the negative direction in the component, and appearing at the top of Figure 5.2. Here we get a sense of how much the counts fluctuate in individual plays, and of how large the overall change in frequency is.

The boxes show the middle half of the counts; the median is indicated by the internal line; the whiskers show the full range; and outliers are marked with symbols as per the legend.

That as a conjunction makes up somewhere between 0.4 per cent and 0.5 per cent of the total words spoken for the median play of the late 1580s,

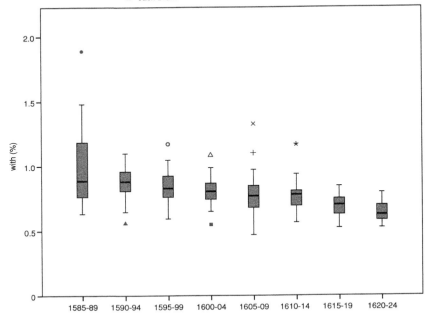

Figure 5.4 Boxplot of percentage counts for *with* in plays between 1585 and 1624, grouped in half-decades.

and closer to 0.1 per cent for the median play of the early 1620s. That means we expect ninety or so instances in an early 1580s play and more like twenty in one from the early 1620s. Among the outliers are *Alphonsus* (1587), with a count very high (even for an early play) at 1.2 per cent, and *The Devil's Law-Case* (1617), which still has a count of over 0.4 per cent though coming from the 1615–19 half-decade. There is variation within the pattern of decline. All sorts of local circumstances and preferences dictated a relative dearth in the odd early play, and a sudden profusion in one or other late play, but the overall drift downwards is unmistakable, and the effect is large.

The preposition *with* has the second lowest weighting in this component (Figure 5.2). Figure 5.4 again shows how the proportional counts change from half-decade to half-decade in this case.

The boxes and whiskers outline the steady decline overall. The outliers and extreme outlier (marked by a star) show that some plays stand outside the trend. The median for late 1580s plays is around 0.8 per cent, declining

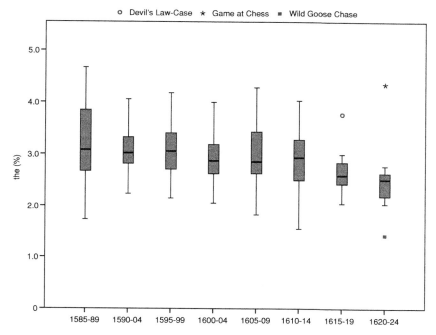

Figure 5.5 Boxplot of percentage counts for *the* in plays between 1585 and 1624, grouped in half-decades.

to 0.6 per cent in the early 1620s. The percentage in *David and Bethsabe* is close to 2 per cent. It is still possible for later plays, such as *Byron's Conspiracy* (1608), *Byron's Tragedy* (also 1608), and *The Valiant Welshman* (1612) to have high counts, against the broader trend.

The decline in use of *the*, the third most heavily weighted word in the negative direction (Figure 5.2), is less even.[10] As shown in Figure 5.5, the last half-decade is distinctly lower than the first, 3 per cent compared with 2.5 per cent, but the changes are in steps rather than on a steady slope. The first three half-decades show little change, and the 1610–14 half-decade has a higher median frequency than its predecessor. The median for 1620–4 is low, but there is one extreme outlier on the high side, *A Game at Chess* (1624) at 4.4 per cent, and an outlier on the low side, *The Wild-Goose Chase* (1621) at 1.4 per cent. Nevertheless, this is a very common word indeed, and the drop in proportional counts from 1584–9 to 1620–4 means that

[10] An earlier study with a slightly smaller corpus found no significant correlation of date with frequencies of *the* over the period 1580–1639; see Craig, '*A* and *an*', 277.

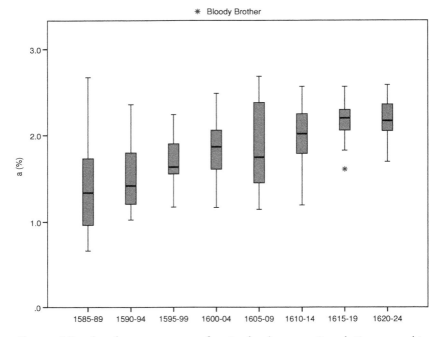

Figure 5.6 Boxplot of percentage counts for *a* in plays between 1585 and 1624, grouped in half-decades.

the expectation for a 20,000-word play goes from around 600 to around 500 instances.

We can also inspect the scores for some of the words that are heavily weighted in the positive direction in Figure 5.2. Figure 5.6 presents a box-plot of the frequencies of *a* in the plays. The change over the period is marked, from medians of 1.25 per cent in 1585–9 to 2.1 per cent in 1620–4, or from 250 in a 20,000-word play to 420. There are two phases: a steady climb over the first three half-decades, then a drop, then a steady climb from 1605–9 onwards peaking in 1615–19, and a plateauing to 1620–4.

The word with the second largest positive weighting in the component is *no* as an adjective[11]. Figure 5.7 presents a boxplot of the counts of this word form by half-decade.

The median frequency increases half-decade by half-decade, with one very slight backward step between 1600–4 and 1605–9. The median for

---

[11] In the texts, instances which modify nouns and adjectives ('*no* time', '*no* more') are marked as adjectival, and instances where this word stands alone are marked as adverbial ('willing or *no*').

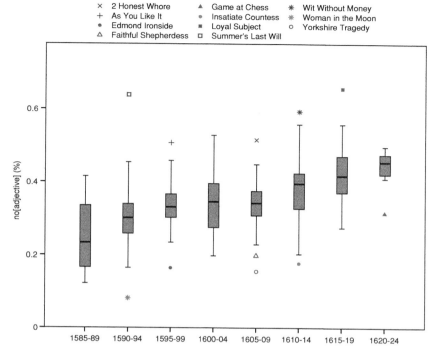

Figure 5.7 Boxplot of percentage counts for *no*~adjective~ in plays between 1585 and 1624, grouped in half-decades.

the 1585–9 plays is 0.25 per cent of all words (or 50 instances in 20,000 words) and 0.44 per cent (or 88 instances) for the 1620–4 plays. Thomas Middleton's *A Game at Chess* is a late play, but notably low in the frequency of the adjectival *no* – an outlier once again. It has sober, pragmatic dialogue, with little room for hypothesis, generalisation, or abstraction.

The third most heavily weighted word in the positive direction is *that* as a demonstrative (Figure 5.2). The boxplot in Figure 5.8 shows how the counts are distributed by half-decade.

Percentage counts increase from a median of about 0.3 per cent in 1585–9 to 0.5 per cent in 1620–4, from an expectation of 60 in 20,000 words to one of 100. Six of the seven outliers on the high side are Middleton plays: *The Phoenix* (1604), *Your Five Gallants* (1605), *A Mad World, My Masters* (1606), *The Revenger's Tragedy* (also 1606), *The Second Maiden's Tragedy* (1611), and *The Widow* (1616).

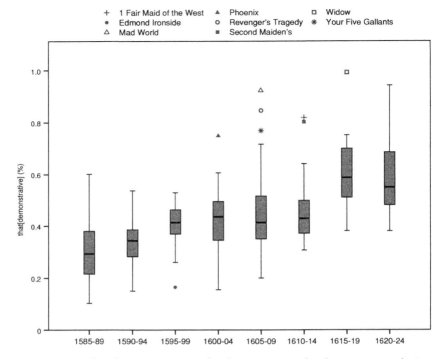

Figure 5.8 Boxplot of percentage counts for *that*_{demonstrative} in plays between 1585 and 1624, grouped in half-decades.

Words in Context

Figure 5.2 is a mathematical way of defining a chronological trend in language use in the plays. Figures 5.3–8 indicate how large the changes are in some individual words forming the trend, and how variable. To understand what this means in terms of style, we need to explore the patterns that go with the declining and increasing use of the different words.

We begin with *that*_{conjunction}, which shows a broad pattern in decline over the eight decades (Figures 5.2–3). An instance reflects a complex construction, dependent rather than coordinated, and also the fact that this conjunction has not been omitted (inclusion and omission being equally idiomatic in many constructions). 'Go fetch my son, *that* he may live with me', says the titular David in George Peele's *David and Bethsabe* (1587).[12] On the other hand, Panura in John Fletcher's *The Island Princess* (1621)

---

[12] George Peele, *David and Bethsabe*, in Fraser and Rabkin (eds.), *Drama*, I: 7.65.

says, 'Would I were so provided, too',[13] rather than 'Would *that* I were so provided, too.' Passages with an unusually high proportion of instances of this word will be strong in argument, and will make the patterning of sentences explicit, rather than casual. There are evidently more such passages in the early plays than in the late ones.

The second most heavily weighted word in the negative direction in Figure 5.2 is *with*, and changes of this word by half-decade are shown in Figure 5.4. High counts of *with* go with dense description, and in particular with a wealth of attributes. The highest-scoring play in the set as a whole is *David and Bethsabe*, with 280 instances in 14,808 words (or 1.9 per cent). For example, there are five instances in the following seven-line passage:

> Up to the lofty mounts of Lebanon,
> Where Cedars, stirred *with* anger of the winds
> Sounding in storms the tale of thy disgrace,
> Tremble *with* fury and *with* murmur shake
> Earth *with* their feet, and *with* their heads the heavens,
> Beating the clouds into their swiftest rack,
> To bear this wonder round about the world.
>
> (3.56–62, emphasis added)

The lowest-scoring play in the full corpus is Middleton's *Michaelmas Term* (1606), which has just 94 instances of *with* in almost 20,000 words – less than half a percent of the dialogue.

To explore the styles associated with high or low counts of a particular word further, we divide the plays into 500-word segments and examine those at the high and low ends, as a kind of extended concordance. There are five 500-word segments in *Michaelmas Term* with no instances of *with*, for example.[14] These segments contain colourful, vigorous, colloquial dialogue, but in short, additive phrases and clauses. There is plenty of detail in canting talk, sharp exchanges, worldly-wise commentary, and collections of sayings and observations, but it is suggestive more of fragmentation than integration. The world presented is centrifugal.

Shakespeare's highest-scoring play is a collaboration, *Titus Andronicus* (1594), where instances of *with* go with specificity and lingering description:

> Alas, a crimson river of warm blood,
> Like to a bubbling fountain stirred *with* wind,
> Doth rise and fall between thy rosèd lips,
> Coming and going *with* thy honey breath.
>
> (2.4.22–5, emphasis added)

---

[13] John Fletcher, *The Island Princess*, ed. Clare McManus (London: Arden Shakespeare, 2013), 3.2.79.
[14] These include the 10th, 19th, 22nd, 28th, and 36th 500-word segments.

With is used thickly in passages of circumstantial entanglements. Among Shakespeare's comedies, the highest frequency proportionally is in *A Midsummer Night's Dream* (1595). Egeus offers a cluster of instances in his accusation of Lysander:

> Thou, thou Lysander, thou hast given her rhymes,
> And interchanged love tokens *with* my child.
> Thou hast by moonlight at her window sung
> *With* feigning voice verses of feigning love,
> And stol'n the impression of her fantasy
> *With* bracelets of thy hair, rings, gauds, conceits,
> Knacks, trifles, nosegays, sweetmeats – messengers
> Of strong prevailment in unhardened youth.
> *With* cunning hast thou filched my daughter's heart,
> Turned her obedience which is due to me
> To stubborn harshness.
>
> (1.1.28–38, emphasis added)

A style low in *with* tends to be one that is bare of elaborate description, focused on interpersonal action; or, if descriptive, moves lightly forward rather than pauses to add attributes. Overall, in the English drama of the period, flow and forward progress become more important, it seems, than knotty rhetoric.

The definite article *the* is also very heavily weighted in the negative direction in PC1, and its use declines over time (Figures 5.2 and 5.5). An abundance of *the* implies spelling out and specifying unfamiliar objects of discourse. The highest-scoring segment of all is from segment 17 of Thomas Heywood's *The Rape of Lucrece* (1607), with 57 instances. Many of these occur within a song, 'The Gentry to the King's Head', in which classes of patrons are matched up with appropriately named taverns: 'To *the* Drum, *the* man of war', '*The* shepherd to *the* Star', '*The* huntsman to *the* White Hart', and so on.[15] The Shakespeare segment with the highest count is segment 41 of *As You Like It* (1599), containing Touchstone's explanation of the 'degrees' of quarrelling:

> *The* first, *the* Retort Courteous; *the* second, *the* Quip Modest; *the* third, *the* Reply Churlish; *the* fourth, *the* Reproof Valiant; *the* fifth, *the* Countercheck Quarrelsome; *the* sixth, *the* Lie with Circumstance; *the* seventh, *the* Lie Direct. (5.4.90–4, emphasis added)

15 Thomas Heywood, *The Rape of Lucrece* (London, 1638; STC 13363), E1v–E2r (emphasis added). The precise circumstances of the song's composition and auspices remain unclear; see John P. Cutts, 'Thomas Heywood's "The Gentry to the King's Head" in *The Rape of Lucrece* and John Wilson's Setting', *Notes & Queries* 8.10 (1961), 384–7.

Defining terms and establishing a taxonomy brings a concentration of instances of *the*. By contrast, dialogue focusing on people familiar to the speakers and on common actions and feelings will have very low counts of *the*. The fifteenth 500-word segment of George Chapman's *The Gentleman Usher* (1602), for example, contains no occurrences of the word *the*. Prince Vincentio wins over the usher Bassiolo, who runs the household of the father of Margaret, Vincentio's beloved. They refer to each other, Vincentio's father, and Margaret, and express friendship for each other in a light, simple, direct discourse. For example:

> BASSIOLO. I perceive your lordship.
> VINCENTIO. 'Your lordship'? Talk you now like a friend?
>   Is this plain kindness?
> BASSIOLO.   Is it not, my lord?
> VINCENTIO. A palpable flattering figure for men common:
> O' my word I should think, if 'twere another,
> He meant to gull me.
> BASSIOLO.   Why, 'tis but your due.
> VINCENTIO. 'Tis but my due if you be still a stranger.[16]

The article *a* is the most heavily weighted word in the positive direction (Figure 5.2), indicating that this word increases in frequency over the period in the plays and is one of the most important in creating the principal component.[17] An earlier study has charted the advance of *a* and *an* in the plays over a slightly longer span, 1580–1639, and its implications for style, concluding that this change reflects a shift in dialogue towards seeing 'the world more as a series of multiples than as concrete, particular people, concepts, and objects'.[18] Characters who have above-average rates of use of *a* and *an* belong either to a tradition of 'disruptive, disenchanting clowning' or share an analytic perspective which can be associated with humanist ideals and with philosophers such as Montaigne and Descartes.[19] Shakespeare characters with low frequencies are those most closely involved in the action, while those with high frequencies are commentators and clowns. The choice of *a* or *an* is one of the 'markers of perspective' within the 'precise and rich structure of reference' in the language.[20] The increase in incidence in the plays can best be associated with an increasingly detached point of view in characters. Comedies, with their characteristic focus on

---

[16] George Chapman, *The Gentleman Usher* (London, 1606; STC 4978), D3r. The 500-word segment occurs in 3.2, from Vincentio's 'But I cannot flatter' (D3r) through to Bassiolo's line, 'But who saw ever summer mixed with winter?' (D3v).
[17] *An* is not common enough to be included in the fifty most frequent function words tested.
[18] Craig, '*A* and *an*', 287.   [19] Craig, '*A* and *an*', 285–6.   [20] Craig, '*A* and *an*', 273, 275.

'the replaceable and the interchangeable' tend to have higher frequencies than histories and tragedies, which focus on more 'concrete and specific' elements, such as 'personal dilemmas, or the specificity of a particular chain of events'.[21]

Demonstrative *that* is the second most heavily weighted in the positive direction and thus likely to be more frequent in the later plays (Figures 5.2 and 5.6). It functions either as an adjective, as in '*That* face will get money'[22] or '*that* fellow handles his bow like a crow-keeper',[23] or as a pronoun, as in 'fear not *that*, sir'[24]. In both cases, the word implies a shared world, either present or absent but known by all, and a familiarity of reference. The referents are tied to speakers rather than belonging to a free-standing depicted world. High scores of the word imply frequent pointing, as in '*that* reverend Vice, *that* grey Iniquity, *that* father Ruffian, *that* Vanity in Years',[25] use of anaphora, or both. Rather than render a world or a discourse, assuming little common knowledge and spelling out the links and the details, passages with higher frequencies of this variety of *that* are more schematic, with place-holders rather than objects, and a reference tied directly to the speakers, vectored, as in Pandarus's speech in *Troilus and Cressida*:

> *That*'s true, make no question of *that*. 'Two-and-fifty hairs', quoth he, 'and one white? *That* white hair is my father, and all the rest are his sons'. (1.2.156–8, emphasis added)

The adjective *no* is the third most heavily weighted in the positive direction in the principal component, and the plays show a steady increase in its use over time (Figures 5.2 and 5.7). This word brings one degree of remove to a statement. Instead of presenting a simple state of affairs, it offers an idea and at the same time negates it. Olivia in *Twelfth Night* defends Feste thus:

> There is *no* slander in an allowed fool, though he do nothing but rail; nor *no* railing, in a known discreet man, though he do nothing but reprove. (1.5.89–92, emphasis added)

The two instances of *no* in Olivia's speech are part of an assertion made by negation, one that is inherently a step more abstract than a straightforward proposition.

---

[21] Craig, '*A* and *an*', 285, 288.
[22] Thomas Middleton, *Your Five Gallants*, ed. Ralph Alan Cohen with John Jowett, in Thomas Middleton, *The Complete Works*, 1.1.215 (emphasis added).
[23] Shakespeare, *King Lear*, Quarto Text, 20.87 (emphasis added).
[24] Middleton, *Your Five Gallants*, 1.1.252 (emphasis added).
[25] Shakespeare, *1 Henry the Fourth*, 2.5.458–9 (emphasis added).

Fletcher stands out for his regular recourse to the adjectival *no*. Some of the high counts are explained by the anodyne expression 'no more', but other instances belong with Fletcher's courtly, florid style. In *The Loyal Subject* (1618), for example, Theodore remarks, 'I carry *no* tales, nor flatteries: In my tongue, sir, | I carry *no* forked stings.'[26] Likewise, Leontes in *The Winter's Tale* (1610) has his own flourish worked around the word. Hermione is gone, and she was matchless, so he will remain single: '*No* more such wives, therefore *no* wife.'[27] *No* here brings with it emphasis, authority, and an abstract frame of reference.

Shakespeare does not necessarily increase his use of the word markedly over time – no more do Chapman, Fletcher, or Middleton, to single out the four largest authorial sets[28] – but a comparison of Shakespeare characters within the same play who use adjectival *no* at different rates is illustrative. In *Julius Caesar* (1599), for example, Brutus is high (0.6 per cent) and Cassius low (0.2 per cent). This follows Brutus's more contemplative and philosophical dialogue, compared with the more pragmatic and practical Cassius. In *Hamlet*, Claudius is high (0.4 per cent) and Ophelia low (0.2 per cent), reflecting a dialogue of authoritative pronouncements versus a more concrete and literal focus. Among clown characters, Feste in *Twelfth Night* is high (0.8 per cent), with a whimsical style of humour, and Gobbo in *The Merchant of Venice* (1596) is low (0.1 per cent), with a more literal style, hardly venturing out from his immediate situation. Among characters with the largest speaking parts (of 4,000 words or more), Rosalind, Brutus, Lear, and Cleopatra are notably high, and Falstaff from *1 Henry the Fourth*, Falconbridge, Cassius, Iago, and Proteus are low. The speculative, reflective characters use the word freely, the intriguers less so.

Wider Patterns

Figure 5.2 suggests that the stylistic change in the plays over eight half-decades is from more explicit, more formally patterned dialogue to more detached commentary and more anaphoric exchanges focusing on shared material.

If we look beyond the extremes in Figure 5.2, we find other clusters among the parts of speech which also suggest some trends in style. More

---

[26] John Fletcher, *The Loyal Subject*, in Francis Beaumont and John Fletcher, *Comedies and Tragedies* (London, 1647; Wing B1581), 3D3r (emphasis added).

[27] Shakespeare, *The Winter's Tale*, 5.1.56 (emphasis added).

[28] All these have positive correlations between the dates of their plays and proportions of *no*$_{adjective}$, but all above the 0.01 'highly significant' threshold – that is, not especially consistent in the association between date and frequency.

of the auxiliary verbs are in the positively weighted lower section of the chart, suggesting an increased focus on speakers' intentions and attitudes in the later plays. *Have, would, is, are, do* (as already mentioned), and *will* are positively weighted, and *shall* and *be* negatively.

Against this predominance of verbs in the words characterising later plays is a concentration of prepositions in the top part of the chart, suggesting the earlier dialogue is heavy on nouns. Of the prepositions included, *with, of, in, by*, and *to* are in the negatively weighted group. The auxiliary verbs in the lower section of Figure 5.2 are all present or future tense, or conditional, and in dialogue are associated with declarations of states, preferences, or future actions. Overall, dialogue with an abundance of these auxiliary verbs – and with a scarcity of prepositions – will have a focus on immediate interactions, with characters referring familiarly to themselves and to those on stage and in their immediate circle.

The forty-seventh 500-word segment of *A Larum for London* (1599) has the highest concentration of the six auxiliary verbs in the full 1580–1624 set. The scene in which the segment falls is focused on action, on the present, and on motivation and brief exchanges. Stump, a one-legged soldier, has just rescued the governor's wife from the sexual depredations of a pair of Spanish soldiers:

> LADY. Good soldier, here's one jewel that they *have* not
>   That I *do* value at a thousand crowns;
>   I pray thee take it.
> STUMP.   What should I *do* w'it,
>   Can you tell? To *have* my throat cut for't, ha!
>   No, no, your Sister Mincepie's groat
>   *Will do* me no pleasure now.
> LADY.   For God's love,
>   As you ever did respect a woman,
>   Help to convey me to some place of safety.
> STUMP. Where *is* it? Not in Antwerp.
>   Your closet *will* not serve your turn,
>   You cannot walk to your garden-house.
> LADY. For God's sake help me, as you *are* a man.
> STUMP. Well, follow me. I'll [I *will*] *do* the best I can.[29]

By contrast, consider the following pair of speeches from the sixth 500-word segment of *The Battle of Alcazar* (1589), which has a high

---

[29] *A Larum for London* (London, 1602; STC 16754), D1r–v (emphasis added).

concentration of the prepositions in the upper half of Figure 5.2. In this first example, the widow Rubin Alchis addresses Calsepius Bashaw:

> Rubin, that breathes but *for* revenge,
> Bashaw, *by* this commends herself *to* thee . . .
> . . . . . .
> Resigns the token *of* her thankfulness.
> *To* Amurath, the god *of* earthly kings,
> Doth Rubin give and sacrifice her son,
> Not *with* sweet smoke *of* fire or sweet perfume,
> But *with* his father's sword his mother's thanks
> Doth Rubin give her son *to* Amurath.[30]

In this second example, the Irish Bishop addresses Diego Lopes, the governor of Lisbon:

> These welcomes, worthy governor *of* Lisbon,
> Argue an honorable mind *in* thee,
> But treat *of* our misfortune therewithal.
> *To* Ireland *by* Pope Gregory's command,
> Were we all bound, and therefore thus embarked
> To land our forces there *at* unawares,
> Conquering the land *for* his Holiness,
> And so restore it *to* the Roman faith.
> This was the cause *of* our expedition,
> And Ireland long ere this had been subdued
> Had not foul weather brought us *to* this bay.
> (2.2.9–18, emphasis added)

The speakers in both examples are not concerned with moment-to-moment motives and impulses, nor with the regular, low-key business of questioning and influencing others. Rather, they spell out connections and directions between people, places, and objects, and thus call on the prepositions with great regularity.

It and *is* are both weighted in the positive direction in Figure 5.2. *Othello* (1604) has one of the higher counts for both of these words. Some of the highest counts for it in the play are in Act 3, Scene 4, primarily as a result of the dialogue's focus on the lost handkerchief. This item is so much uppermost in characters' minds that it can be referred to as *it*

---

[30] George Peele, *The Battle of Alcazar*, in Charles Edelman (ed.), *The Stukeley Plays* (Manchester University Press, 2005), 2.1.28–35 (emphasis added; ellipses Edelman).

without any ambiguity over a long stretch of dialogue. Consider the following example:

> OTHELLO. Is't [*is it*] lost? Is't [*is it*] gone? Speak, is't [*is it*] out o'th'way?
> DESDEMONA. Heaven bless us!
> OTHELLO. Say you?
> DESDEMONA. *It is* not lost, but what an if *it* were?
> OTHELLO. How?
> DESDEMONA. I say *it is* not lost.
> OTHELLO. Fetch't [fetch *it*], let me see't [see *it*].

> (3.4.80–5, emphasis added)

The characters share knowledge about the topics under discussion. Reference is repeated and immediate. By contrast, in passages with very low counts of *it* and *is*, the reference is to offstage entities and various, constantly changing abstractions. The first 500-word segment of Robert Greene's *Orlando Furioso* (1591), for example, contains only two instances of *is* and no instances of *it*. In this opening scene, princely suitors to the daughter of Emperor Marsilius declare their worth and praise her charms in language fit for an epic:

> MARSILIUS. Victorious princes, summoned to appear
>   Within the continent of Africa,
>   From seven-fold Nilus to Taprobany
>   Where fair Apollo darting forth his light
>   Plays on the seas . . .
> . . . . .
> SULTAN. The fairest flower that glories Africa,
>   Whose beauty Phoebus dares not dash with showers,
>   Over whose climate never hung a cloud,
>   But smiling Titan lights the horizon.
>   Egypt *is* mine and there I hold my State
> . . . . .
> RODAMANT. Cuba my seat, a region so enriched
>   With favours sparkling from the smiling heavens,
>   As those that seek for traffic to my coast
>   Accounted like that wealthy Paradise
>   From whence floweth Gibon, and swift Euphrates.[31]

Words which were retreating in the English language also play a role – *thy* and *thou* are in the top ten words weighted in the negative and

---

[31] Robert Greene, *Orlando Furioso* (London, 1594; STC 12265), A3r–A4r (emphasis added). The first 500-word segment runs from Marsilius's opening line ('Victorious princes') through to Mandricard's 'There I did act as many'.

Table 5.1 *Correlations between date of first performance and PC1 score for 203 plays between 1585 and 1624, grouped by genre*

Set	Total plays	Correlation	*p*-value
All plays, 1585–1624	206	0.64	<0.0001
Comedy	89	0.69	<0.0001
Tragedy	49	0.63	<0.0001
History	40	0.53	0.0004
Other	28	0.82	<0.0001

associated with early half-decades, for instance – but they by no means dominate. As would be expected, *thy*, *thou*, and *thee* are among the words with negative principal component weightings towards the top of Figure 5.2, generally declining in the successive half-decades, whereas *your* and *you* appear in the lower part of the chart, with positive weightings, indicating that they are becoming more common over time. *Do* also is positively weighted, and we might associate that increase with progressively established *do* regulation in the modern form, where *do* supports questions – as in, 'do you mind if I stay?' – while other forms of this verb have less of a role in simple declaratives.

Authors and Genres

So far we have followed the broad stylistic drift identified by the first principal component across a corpus of 203 plays in half-decades from 1585–9 to 1620–4 taken as a whole. However, the same stylistic drift is also evident within genres. We use the genres listed in the *Annals of English Drama* to separate the plays into broad generic 'comedy', 'tragedy', 'history', and 'other' sets.[32] For each set, we calculate the correlation between the date of first performance and the PC1 score, and the *p*-value or probability that the correlation value might have come about by chance, given the number of samples. These results, along with the total number of plays in each set, are listed in Table 5.1. Values for *p* of less than 0.05 are conventionally described as 'significant', and values of less than 0.01 as 'highly significant'. The *p*-values of <0.001 and 0.0004 suggest that all the play dates in each of the genre sets are very strongly correlated with the PC1 score.

[32] 'Comedy' also includes plays listed as 'Classical Legend (Comedy)', 'Domestic Comedy', and 'Romantic Comedy' in *Annals*; 'History' includes 'Allegorical History', 'Biblical History', 'Classical History', 'Foreign History', and 'Pseudo-History'; and 'Other' comprises 'Biblical Moral', 'Burlesque Romance', 'Heroical Romance', 'Political Satire', and 'Tragicomedy'.

Table 5.2 *Correlations between date of first performance and PC1 score for 203 plays between 1585 and 1624, grouped by author*

Set	Total Plays	Correlation	*p*-value
Chapman, George	12	−0.66	0.02
Fletcher, John	16	0.48	0.06
Heywood, Thomas	9	0.32	0.40
Jonson, Ben	12	0.26	0.41
Lyly, John	6	−0.32	0.54
Marlowe, Christopher	7	0.44	0.32
Marston, John	9	0.23	0.55
Middleton, Thomas	18	−0.06	0.81
Shakespeare, William	28	0.12	0.54

By contrast, authors appear not to have changed markedly or consistently along these lines within their writing careers. Table 5.2 lists the calculated correlations between the date of first performance and the PC1 score across nine authorial canons,[33] alongside the *p*-value or probability that the correlation values might have come about by chance, given the number of samples.

There are no 'highly significant' *p*-values in Table 5.2, and only one 'significant' one – for George Chapman, whose correlation is negative, indicating that scores for his plays decline over time. Treated as a collective whole, the drama between 1585 and 1624 unmistakably changes consistently in the period, as we have seen. On the other hand, as Table 5.2 shows, playwrights themselves do not change their styles in the same way over the course of their writing careers. Figure 5.9 plots the PC1 scores against the dates for the Marlowe, Shakespeare, and Fletcher canons against the backdrop of the corpus of 1585–1624 plays.

Marlowe composes plays that generally score low on PC1. Shakespeare begins writing (or at least his plays are performed) a little later and writes plays with generally higher PC1 scores. Fletcher's sole-authored plays cover the final part of the period and are mostly higher than Shakespeare's, with the exception of his pastoral, *The Faithful Shepherdess*, which is in the negative range for PC1. The linear trend-line for all three authorial sets moves upwards, but the pattern in all three cases is very mixed and could not be called a steady increase, as Table 5.2 confirms.

---

[33] For the sake of brevity, we limit Table 5.2 to authors with six or more sole-authored plays dated between 1585 and 1624.

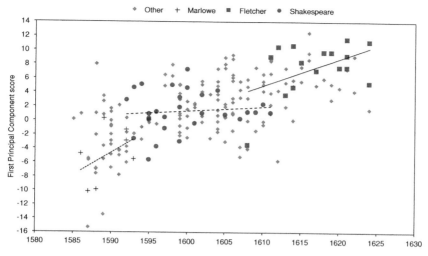

Figure 5.9 PCA scatterplot of PC1 scores for Fletcher, Marlowe, and Shakespeare plays by date, 1585–1624.

We observe a near-perfect correlation of 0.95 if we take the 9 authors with 6 or more plays in the set of 203 plays between 1585 and 1624 and compare their average score on PC1 with the average date of the plays. The match with the playwright's date of birth is not as close, with a correlation of 0.69.[34] Thus date of composition, or at least date of first performance, is a better predictor of PC1 score than a playwright's year of birth. While this is what we might expect, since we know PC1 arranges the plays in perfect half-decade order, it does establish that year of birth is not a factor that necessarily trumps others. The straightforward conclusion is that dramatists conformed to a pattern in the playwriting of their time, rather than inheriting language characteristics from their generation.[35]

If we concentrate on Shakespeare and distinguish plays according to genre, we find that PC1 scores within his canon are more influenced by genre than by chronology (Figure 5.10). Shakespeare's comedies score higher than his history plays, with tragedies falling in between. None of the genres shows a marked increase with time – *The Tempest*, for

[34] Dates of birth, sourced from the *Oxford Dictionary of Biography*, are as follows: Lyly (1554), Chapman (1559/60; correlated as 1559.5), Marlowe (1564), Shakespeare (1564), Jonson (1572), Heywood (*c*.1573; correlated as 1573), Marston (1576), Fletcher (1579), and Middleton (1580).

[35] For a discussion of the influences of date and region of birth in the language characteristics of Shakespeare and Fletcher, see Jonathon Hope, *The Authorship of Shakespeare's Plays: A Socio-Linguistic Study* (Cambridge University Press, 1994).

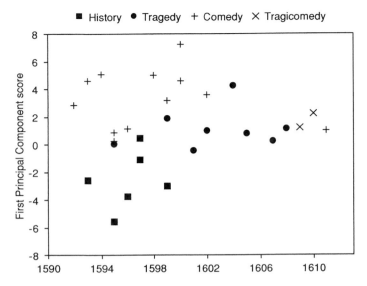

Figure 5.10 PCA scatterplot of PC1 scores for Shakespeare's plays by date.

example, is the last sole-authored play and among the lowest-scoring of the comedies.

This is a tale without a hero. None of the playwrights we studied is responsible for the evident change in the style of dialogue over this period. If a writer had shown a marked increase in the adoption of this style, then it might have been possible to credit them with introducing or accelerating the changes, but this is not what we see.

Analogies

One aspect of the first principal component (PC1) axis is a contrast between *nominal* and *verbal*, as already mentioned. The early plays have more of the prepositions that are included in the list of 50 function words, and the later plays more of the auxiliary verbs. As the plays move along the PC1 axis, instances of the fifty function words tend to represent a greater proportion of all the words used, with lexical items like nouns correspondingly reduced.[36]

[36] For this calculation, we used only the first 5,000 words of each play to ensure consistent sample size and found the total number of instances of the 50 most common function words as a measure of the compactness or otherwise of vocabulary. We then correlated this total number of instances with the scores of the same 5,000-word segments for each of the 203 plays on PC1. The correlation was 0.61, two-tailed $p < 0.0001$.

PC1 is calculated specifically for this set of texts, but it is also related to a very widespread contrast in language between *specifying* and *assuming* context. The best-known version of this contrast is Douglas Biber's axis between what he calls the *informational* (comparable to the left-hand end of PC1, where context is specified) and the *involved* (comparable to the right-hand end, where context is assumed). In Biber's study of speech and writing, this axis emerged as the most important factor, a contrast between 'a high informational focus and a careful integration of information in a text', and passages with 'an involved, non-informational focus, due to a primarily interactive or affective purpose and/or to highly constrained productive circumstances'.[37]

Although Biber's study employed a factor analysis using a wide range of complex linguistic features rather than words, there is a clear relationship in the features that loaded on his first factor and the highly weighted variables of our PC1: he finds prepositional phrases to the informational end, first- and second-person pronouns and *it* to the interactive end, and so on. PC1 correlates with vocabulary density, as we have seen, and Biber's first factor correlates with type-token ratio, a closely related measure.[38]

A similar factor appears as the first principal component in Jonathan Hope and Michael Witmore's study of Shakespeare play sections.[39] This analysis is derived not from function words directly but from 'bundles' of features – single words and combinations of words – or 'Language Action Types' (LATs) as defined in *DocuScope*, the software program they employ for this analysis. At one end of their first principal component are the bundles labelled 'Motions', 'SenseProperty', and 'SenseObject', related to objects in motion, the sensory experience of properties of objects, and mention of the objects themselves. At the other end are the bundles 'SelfDisclosure', 'DirectAddress', and 'FirstPer', containing words associated with self-reference allied with verbs and prepositions, address to an interlocutor, and first-person pronouns.[40] Here, physical description is opposed to a focus on persons and interactions – a contrast compatible with the one in our PC1.

The broader pattern we observe in PC1 is thus not peculiar to our dataset. Rather, it is a fundamental opposition in language styles, one

---

[37] Douglas Biber, *Variation across Speech and Writing* (Cambridge University Press, 1988), 104, 105.
[38] Biber, *Variation*, 104–5.
[39] Hope and Witmore, 'The Hundredth Psalm', 357–90.
[40] For an account of *DocuScope*, see David Kaufer, Suguru Ishizaki, Brian Butler, and Jeff Collins, *The Power of Words: Unveiling the Speaker and Writer's Hidden Craft* (Mahwah: Lawrence Erlbaum Associates, 2004), which contains descriptions of these variables at 59–61, 144–7, 185–7, and 191.

of what Biber calls the 'basic discourse dichotomies'.[41] This opposition emerges in the plays as two different understandings of what drama can be, two different kinds of appeal to audiences. The 'informational' aspect is drama with high-born characters, remote in time or place or both, making claims on other potentates, tyrannising subjects and enemies, describing past feats, or threatening new ones. Characters declaim, boast, persuade, and report. The other, 'involved', tendency has characters familiar with each other engaged in an immediate local exchange, a private struggle for advantage or self-defence, a more staccato and interactive conversation.[42]

Conclusion

There is a combination of weighted very common words which captures a marked and consistent change in play dialogue over forty years between 1585 and 1624. Its claim on our attention derives from the statistical robustness of the pattern and from the amplitude of the changes in word frequency, suggesting that they are significant stylistically as well as statistically. The words in the analysis are at the structural level of language, and changes in their use reflect changes in syntax, which in turn follow underlying shifts in orientations of discourse.

The quantitative results suggest that, over a forty-year span, early modern English tragedy becomes steadily more comic, and comedy more farcical. Generally, elaboration and picture-painting in speeches give way to categorical thinking, and more attention is paid to attitudes and interactions. Audiences are offered fewer lectures and more banter. Successive authors from Marlowe to Fletcher adopt more of the 'new' style, but none of them changes markedly in the common direction in the course of a career. This particular trend peters out in the late 1620s.

The change from elaborate, entrammeled dialogue to more direct and casual speech fits a thesis that, as time went on, dramatists took more interest in reflecting the language of everyday exchanges in the world outside the theatre, and collectively developed methods for achieving this sort of verisimilitude. Peter Holbrook, for example, suggests that English

---

[41] Biber, *Variation*, 108.
[42] Within the span of early modern English drama, the declamatory form develops early, and the more intimate form dominates later, as we have seen. However, neither form is generally tied to any particular time frame. In late eighteenth- and early nineteenth-century attempts to imitate Shakespearean drama, for instance, the focus is on the bold bombastic speeches, to the neglect of the more private and deictic exchanges. See John Burrows and D. H. Craig, 'Lyrical Drama and the "Turbid Mountebanks": Styles of Dialogue in Romantic and Restoration Tragedy', *Computers and the Humanities* 28 (1994), 63–86.

dramatists in this period became 'progressively better at representing how people actually think, talk and feel', and achieved 'a technical advance in the means of representation', an 'improved mimetic quality'.[43]

The shifts we have been following also parallel the ascension of Humanist-inspired detachment in characters.[44] G. K. Hunter places Flamineo and Bosola, from John Webster's *The White Devil* (1612) and *The Duchess of Malfi* (1614) respectively, in a generation of impoverished offspring of profligate landowners, graduates who worked their way through university and 'now relish with Montaignian detachment the immorality of the world in which they make their living'.[45] Similarly, Hunter finds Middleton's *A Game at Chess* (1624) to be more 'detached' than an earlier exercise in politico-religious allegory, Thomas Dekker's *The Whore of Babylon* (1606): 'The difference between the two plays conforms closely to that ... between the providential history of the chronicles and the pragmatic history of Bacon and Macchiavelli; one might guess that both instances point to a larger change in cultural sensibility.'[46]

This broad stylistic change transcends authorship. A writer like Shakespeare takes his place in the progression from one style to another, but the changes begin before he was writing and continue afterwards. The shifts are so deeply embedded in the language of dialogue and so long in their sweep that they may well be more a matter of 'cultural drift' than of 'literary history'. Either way, they provide us with a new way to think of playwrights like Shakespeare, as well as of Marlowe before and Fletcher afterwards, as sharers in broader movements as well as individual creators. In creating their characters and scenes, these playwrights were exercising particular sets of skills and a personal vision. They were also, probably without being conscious of it, writing the dialogue of their day and taking their place at a given moment in the evolution of dramatic language from elaborate exposition to detached commentary and fast-moving exchange.

---

[43] Peter Holbrook, *English Renaissance Tragedy: Ideas of Freedom* (London: Arden Shakespeare, 2015), 55–6.

[44] A third parallel is with the *locus–platea* contrast proposed by Robert Weimann in *Shakespeare and the Popular Tradition*. For analogies and divergences between Weimann's scheme and the patterns revealed by a common-words analysis, see Craig, '*A* and *an*'.

[45] G. K. Hunter, *English Drama*, 476. We discuss this pair in Chapter 3.

[46] G. K. Hunter, *English Drama*, 492.

CHAPTER 6

Authorship, Company Style, and horror vacui

A number of studies published over the past thirty years mark a shift in scholarship away from individual dramatists and plays towards the playing companies for whom they wrote and were written, considered alongside 'other contributors to a company's dramatic output, such as actors, sharers, playhouse owners (and the buildings themselves), audiences, and patrons'.[1] These include monographs and collections of essays attending to particular companies, such as the Children of Paul's, the Chamberlain's/King's Men, Queen Elizabeth's Men, the Children of the King's Revels, the Children of the Queen's Revels, the Admiral's Men, Queen Anne's Men, and Strange's Men,[2] as well as general surveys[3] and a dedicated *Oxford Handbook* on the subject.[4] The 'repertory approach', as it has come to be known, has

---

[1] Tom Rutter, 'Repertory Studies: A Survey', *Shakespeare* 4.3 (2008), 336.

[2] These include: Bly, *Queer Virgins*; Reavley Gair, *The Children of Paul's: The Story of a Theatre Company, 1553–1608* (Cambridge University Press, 1982); Eva Griffith, *A Jacobean Company and Its Playhouse: The Queen's Servants at the Red Bull Theatre (c. 1605–1619)* (Cambridge University Press, 2013); Andrew Gurr, *The Shakespeare Company, 1594–1642* (Cambridge University Press, 2004) and *Shakespeare's Opposites: The Admiral's Company, 1594–1625* (Cambridge University Press, 2012); Roslyn L. Knutson, *The Repertory of Shakespeare's Company, 1594–1613* (Fayetteville: University of Arkansas Press, 1991) and 'The Start of Something Big', in Helen Ostovich, Holger Schott Syme, and Andrew Griffin (eds.), *Locating the Queen's Men, 1583–1603: Material Practices and Conditions of Playing* (Farnham: Ashgate, 2009), 99–108; Lawrence Manley and Sally-Beth MacLean, *Lord Strange's Men and Their Plays* (New Haven: Yale University Press, 2014); Scott McMillin and Sally-Beth MacLean, *The Queen's Men and Their Plays* (Cambridge University Press, 1998); Lucy Munro, *Children of the Queen's Revels: A Jacobean Theatre Repertory* (Cambridge University Press, 2005); and Tom Rutter, *Shakespeare and the Admiral's Men: Reading across Repertories on the London Stage, 1594–1600* (Cambridge University Press, 2017).

[3] For example: John H. Astington, *Actors and Acting in Shakespeare's Time: The Art of Stage Playing* (Cambridge University Press, 2010); Andrew Gurr, *The Shakespearian Playing Companies* (Oxford University Press, 1996); Siobhan Keenan, *Acting Companies and Their Plays in Shakespeare's London* (London: Arden Shakespeare, 2014); Roslyn L. Knutson, *Playing Companies and Commerce in Shakespeare's Time* (Cambridge University Press, 2001); and Terence G. Schoone-Jongen, *Shakespeare's Companies: William Shakespeare's Early Career and the Acting Companies, 1577–1594* (Farnham: Ashgate, 2008).

[4] Richard Dutton (ed.), *The Oxford Handbook of Early Modern Theatre* (Oxford University Press, 2008).

proved fertile ground, enriching studies of early modern English drama by provoking scholars to move beyond canon- and author-centric analyses to address anonymous and collaborative plays, to reconstruct company repertoires and historical trajectories, and to situate the drama within complex networks of professional competition and rivalry, patronage and politics, actors, audiences, and performance spaces.

If it is now a critical commonplace to recognise the production of early modern plays in both the theatre and the print-shop as collaborative enterprises, for some it has become evidence of the impossibility of 'authorship' as individual labour: as David Scott Kastan remarks, 'authorial intentions are almost never solely determinative' and 'inevitably get transformed by the intentions of others in performance and in print', because 'the specific qualities of drama . . . inevitably dissolve authorial intentions into the collaborative demands of performance'.[5] Jeffrey Masten has gone so far as to insist on the futility of determining the discrete shares of collaborating playwrights, given that 'the collaborative project in the theatre was predicated on *erasing* the perception of any differences that might have existed, for whatever reason, between collaborated parts'.[6]

Recent theatre historiography and textual criticism has not only sought to disperse the authority of the 'author', but also – perhaps owing to a kind of *horror vacui* – to promote the playing companies to that privileged 'authorial' space newly vacated by the playwrights. 'The author', Lucy Munro reminds us, 'is a useful organising principle, but it is not the only one available.' Citing Foucault's claim that 'since the eighteenth century, the author has played the role of the regulator of the fictive', Munro argues that 'to a large extent, the main "regulator of the fictive" in the early modern playhouse was the playing company, not the author'.[7]

Those engaged in repertory study of early modern drama frequently assert that individual companies cultivated a 'house style', setting them apart from one another. In their influential study, Scott McMillin and Sally-Beth MacLean argue that 'each company would have had its own style, its own textual procedures, its own sense of purpose, and its own impact on audiences and other acting companies', before proceeding to identify the 'special characteristics' which gave Queen Elizabeth's Men 'its identity – its acting style, its staging methods, its kinds of versification, its

[5] David Scott Kastan, 'The Body of the Text', *ELH* 81.2 (2014), 444, 446.
[6] Jeffrey Masten, *Textual Intercourse: Collaboration, Authorship, and Sexualities in Renaissance Drama* (Cambridge University Press, 1997), 17.
[7] Munro, *Children of the Queen's Revels*, 4.

sense of what constituted a worthwhile repertory of plays'.[8] In the same vein, Mary Bly and Charles Cathcart note how 'a company preference for plural authorship coexists with the collective adherence to a consistent repertory style' in the case of the Children of the King's Revels, revealing 'a distinctive *company* imprint',[9] a 'constraining authority governing the tenor of the plays' and imposing 'managerial control of a theatrical product written by more than one person'.[10] Munro similarly maintains that the repertory of the Children of the Queen's Revels 'was predicated not only on authorial whim, but also on commercial exigency and on the relationship between individuals within companies', whose plays 'were created not only by the dramatists, but also through the ideas and desires of the company's shareholders, licenser, patrons, actors and audience'.[11]

The assumption that playing companies developed distinctive and recognisable styles – relocating the Foucauldian 'author function' from the playwright to the company and its agents – is not limited to the specialised discourse of repertory studies, but has become axiomatic in criticism of early modern drama more broadly. For example, in the course of dispelling thirty 'great myths' about Shakespeare, Laurie Maguire and Emma Smith liken the 'duopoly between the Admiral's Men and the Lord Chamberlain's Men during the 1590s', both with a 'contrasting personnel and house style', to the modern phenomenon of 'rival studios' associated with 'particular stars and a particular style of film'.[12] In his study of Shakespeare's late style, Gordon McMullan similarly equates the 'formation of an acting company' with 'an institutionalisation of the collaborative process', and argues that 'the nature of the early modern company repertory militates in several ways against the idea of individual style', giving rise instead to 'a *company style*'.[13]

As Gabriel Egan observes, set against this critical trend to 'emphasize the collaborative, socialized labours of the players, the scribes and compositors' to the extent that their 'effects upon the surviving script are treated as though they are nearly as important as the author's labour' are the 'extraordinary successes' in computational stylistics in 'distinguish[ing] quantitatively between the stints of different writers in one script', demonstrating the importance of authorship 'in the teeth of postmodernism's denial of

---

8 McMillin and MacLean, *The Queen's Men*, xii.
9 Charles Cathcart, 'Authorship, Indebtedness, and the Children of the King's Revels', *SEL: Studies in English Literature, 1500–1900* 45.2 (2005), 359.
10 Bly, *Queer Virgins*, 3, 33.   11 Munro, *Children of the Queen's Revels*, 164–5.
12 Laurie Maguire and Emma Smith, *30 Great Myths about Shakespeare* (Oxford: Blackwell, 2013), 126.
13 Gordon McMullan, *Shakespeare and the Idea of Late Writing: Authorship in the Proximity of Death* (Cambridge University Press, 2007), 239.

it'.[14] Such statistical studies 'might have revealed – were free to reveal – that authorship is insignificant in comparison to other factors like genre or period' and 'secondary to other forces in textual patterning'; instead, quantitative studies have consistently established authorship 'as a much stronger force in the affinities between texts'.[15]

This chapter considers the extent to which early modern playing companies constrained the style of the playwrights engaged to provide scripts for them and promoted a distinct 'house style'. Throughout our study we use 'style' to refer to the consistent patterns in word usage. On the one hand, this may seem a very limited concept of style. It is based entirely on quantitative measures, and inevitably relies only on a selection of the possible candidates for measurement. On the other hand, as numerous previous studies have shown, similarities and contrasts according to word frequencies do reflect the common distinctions we look for as readers in literary works – by author, genre, and period. Patterns in word frequencies are also richly revealing from a more interpretive point of view about local and more extended factors in expressive language. Stylistics by word frequencies, in other words, can be checked against formal categories to show that there is a genuine correspondence and can also, through its objectivity and capacity to work at scale, help in the usual business of literary analysis. If a given category does not emerge in this sort of study, we cannot conclude that it is not there in some shape or form, but we can reasonably conclude that it is not a powerful factor – certainly not in the way authors, genres, and eras are.

To test how strong repertory company performs as such a factor, we employ the robust quantitative methods of computational stylistics described in Chapter 1 to search a corpus of plays (for which the auspices of first performance are known) for stylistic patterns with which to generate distinct profiles for each repertory company. Just as plays of uncertain authorship can be attributed to playwrights on the basis of their stylistic affinity, plays of uncertain auspices may then be compared with the stylistic profiles generated for each repertory to determine whether it is attributable to that playing company – a procedure that, until now, has relied upon a scholar's 'ear' and familiarity with repertory company practices, such as casting and dramaturgy. For example, 'as a means of identifying potential repertory members', Roslyn L. Knutson has proposed to 'apply the dramaturgical house style' of Queen Elizabeth's Men – as enunciated by McMillin and MacLean's examination of the nine plays forming the

---

[14] Egan, 'What is Not Collaborative', 27.   [15] Craig, 'Style, Statistics', 2.3.

Table 6.1 *Plays with well-attributed first companies, c.1581–94*

First Company	Author	Play	Date	Genre
Admiral's (Nottingham's) Men	Marlowe, Christopher	*1 Tamburlaine the Great*	1587	Heroical romance
Admiral's (Nottingham's) Men	Marlowe, Christopher	*2 Tamburlaine the Great*	1587	Heroical romance
Admiral's (Nottingham's) Men	Uncertain	*A Knack to Know an Honest Man*	1594	Tragicomedy
Admiral's (Nottingham's) Men	Peele, George	*The Battle of Alcazar*	1589	History
Admiral's (Nottingham's) Men	Marlowe, Christopher; others	*Doctor Faustus*	1592	Tragedy
Admiral's (Nottingham's) Men	Uncertain	*Edward the Third*	1590	History
Admiral's (Nottingham's) Men	Lodge, Thomas	*The Wounds of Civil War*	1588	History
Chamberlain's (Hunsdon's) Men	Shakespeare, William	*The Two Gentlemen of Verona*	1590	Comedy
Children of Paul's	Lyly, John	*Endymion*	1588	Classical legend
Children of Paul's	Lyly, John	*Galatea*	1585	Classical legend
Children of Paul's	Lyly, John	*Love's Metamorphosis*	1590	Pastoral
Children of Paul's	Lyly, John	*Midas*	1589	Comedy
Children of Paul's	Lyly, John	*Mother Bombie*	1591	Comedy
Children of the Chapel Royal	Peele, George	*The Arraignment of Paris*	1581	Classical legend
Children of the Chapel Royal	Marlowe, Christopher; Nashe, Thomas (?)	*Dido, Queen of Carthage*	1586	Tragedy
Children of the Chapel Royal	Uncertain	*The Wars of Cyrus*	1588	History
Derby's (Strange's) Men	Shakespeare, William; others	*1 Henry the Sixth*	1592	History
Derby's (Strange's) Men	Shakespeare, William	*The Comedy of Errors*	1594	Comedy
Derby's (Strange's) Men	Uncertain	*Fair Em*	1590	Comedy

First Company	Author	Play	Date	Genre
Derby's (Strange's) Men	Marlowe, Christopher; others (?)	*The Jew of Malta*	1589	Tragedy
Derby's (Strange's) Men	Uncertain	*A Knack to Know a Knave*	1592	Comedy
Derby's (Strange's) Men	Greene, Robert; Lodge, Thomas	*A Looking Glass for London and England*	1588	Moral
Derby's (Strange's) Men	Marlowe, Christopher	*The Massacre at Paris*	1593	History
Derby's (Strange's) Men	Uncertain	*(The Rare Triumphs of) Love and Fortune*	1582	Moral
Derby's (Strange's) Men	Kyd, Thomas	*The Spanish Tragedy*	1587	Tragedy
Oxford's Boys	Lyly, John	*Campaspe*	1583	Classical legend
Oxford's Boys	Lyly, John	*Sappho and Phao*	1583	Classical legend
Pembroke's Men	Shakespeare, William; others	*2 Henry the Sixth*	1591	History
Pembroke's Men	Shakespeare, William; others	*3 Henry the Sixth*	1591	History
Pembroke's Men	Marlowe, Christopher	*Edward the Second*	1592	History
Queen Elizabeth's Men	Uncertain	*The Troublesome Reign of King John*	1591	History
Queen Elizabeth's Men	Uncertain	*1 Selimus*	1592	Heroical romance
Queen Elizabeth's Men	Uncertain	*The Famous Victories of Henry the Fifth*	1586	History
Queen Elizabeth's Men	Greene, Robert	*Friar Bacon and Friar Bungay*	1589	Comedy
Queen Elizabeth's Men	Peele, George	*The Old Wife's Tale*	1590	Romance
Queen Elizabeth's Men	Wilson, Robert	*The Three Lords and Three Ladies of London*	1588	Moral
Queen Elizabeth's Men	Uncertain	*King Leir*	1590	History
Queen Elizabeth's Men	Uncertain	*The True Tragedy of Richard the Third*	1591	History
Sussex's Men	Uncertain	*George-a-Greene*	1590	Comedy

company's 'core' canon[16] – to 'plays contemporary with their first decade of playing'.[17]

We first construct a corpus containing only those plays with well-attributed first companies and first performed between 1581 and 1594 – a range that spans the formation and dissolution of Queen Elizabeth's Men. Table 6.1 lists the resulting corpus of thirty-nine plays, along with each associated first company, genre, and date of first performance; Appendix A provides fuller bibliographical details for each play.

We project the word-frequency counts for the 500 most frequent words across the corpus for each 2,000-word segment into a two-dimensional space using Principal Components Analysis (PCA), treating the scores on the first and second principal components as Cartesian coordinates defining each segment as a point in the scatterplot (Figure 6.1). The relative distances between points within this space represent degrees of affinity, such that segments of similar stylistic traits will cluster tightly together, whereas dissimilar segments will be plotted further apart. With three exceptions, there are no tight discrete groupings of points on the scatterplot in Figure 6.1 – rather, points belonging to almost every repertory company are interspersed with one another around the origin of the graph. This suggests that segments of plays belonging to different repertory companies share similar stylistic traits. The exceptions include the cluster of interwoven points belonging to the Children of Paul's and Oxford's Boys, plotted as black and grey circles respectively to the bottom right of the scatterplot, and the selection of points belonging to the Admiral's (Nottingham's) Men, plotted as 'x' symbols, forming a tight cluster to the left of the origin. These outliers warrant further investigation.

When the points are re-labelled according to authorship rather than repertory company (Figure 6.2), with segments of uncertain attribution plotted as '.' symbols, discrete clusters become more discernible. The two outlier groupings previously identified in Figure 6.1 as segments from the Children of Paul's and Oxford's Boys are now revealed to constitute a single Lyly cluster, plotted as black triangles. The third outlier grouping, constituting a selection of segments from the Admiral's (Nottingham's) Men, are shown to belong to Lodge, Marlowe, and Peele.

This group is made up of Marlowe's *Tamburlaine* plays, Peele's *Battle of Alcazar*, and Lodge's *Wounds of Civil War*. Although classified in

---

[16] McMillin and MacLean, *The Queen's Men*, 91–2.
[17] Knutson, 'The Start of Something Big', 99.

× Admiral's (Nottingham's) Men   ● Oxford's Boys
+ Chamberlain's (Hunsdon's) Men   ■ Pembroke's Men
● Children of Paul's   ■ Queen Elizabeth's Men
△ Children of the Chapel Royal   ✳ Sussex's Men
▲ Derby's (Strange's) Men

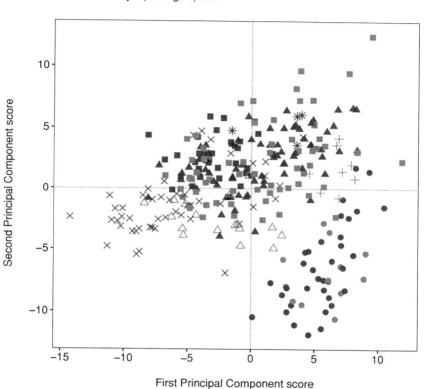

Figure 6.1 PCA scatterplot of 2,000-word non-overlapping segments of plays with well-attributed first companies, *c*.1581–94, using the 500 most frequent words, labelled by company.

Annals as 'history' plays, both *Alcazar* and *Wounds* share generic and stylistic traits with the 'heroical romance' of *Tamburlaine* and belong to a family of plays aptly described by G. K. Hunter as the 'sons of *Tamburlaine*'.[18] Critics have long recognised resemblances between *Wounds*

[18] G. K. Hunter, *English Drama*, 49ff.

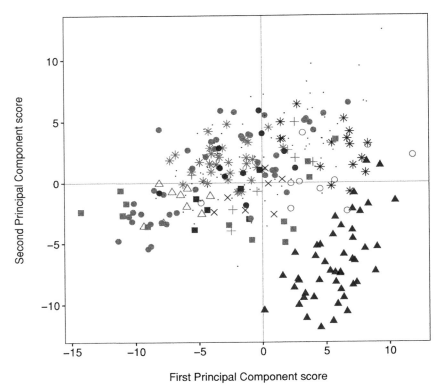

Figure 6.2 PCA scatterplot of 2,000-word non-overlapping segments of plays with well-attributed first companies, *c.*1581–94, using the 500 most frequent words, labelled by author.

and *Tamburlaine*, particularly in Lodge's portrayal of Sulla, although it is unclear which play came first.[19] Described as 'out-Tamburlaining

19 See, for example: Wolfgang Clemen, 'Imitations of Marlowe's *Tamburlaine: Selimus* and *The Wounds of Civil War*', in his *English Tragedy before Shakespeare* (London: Routledge, 1961), 130–40; Charles

Tamburlaine',[20] *Alcazar* is much indebted to Marlowe',[21] and Peele elsewhere links 'mighty Tamburlaine' with 'King Charlemagne' and 'Tom Stukeley' in *A Farewell*, a poem celebrating the departure of 'noble' John Norris and 'victorious' Francis Drake on their counter-Armada to the Iberian coast in 1589.[22] The similarities between the plays are demonstrated by the greater relative frequency of words associated with battle and conquest (*arms, bloody, fight, foes, soldiers, sword, war*) and the display of power (*honour, march, mighty, power, princely, proud, royal*) that they share (Figure 6.3).

The PCA uncovers further patterns in the use of personal and possessive pronouns (Figure 6.4), with this outlier grouping characterised by a greater relative frequency of the first-person plural genitive *our* and the second-person singular informal genitives *thy* and *thine*, as well as a corresponding relative infrequency of first-person singular pronouns (*I, me, my,* and *mine*) and second-person plural or formal singular pronouns (*ye, you,* and *your*). Many of these favoured pronouns occur in short succession within these plays; for example: 'That he hath given *our* foe into *our* hands', and '*Thy* love, *thy* loyalty and forwardness, | *Thy* service' in *Alcazar*;[23] 'I hope *our* lady's treasure and *our* own | May serve for ransom to *our* liberties: | Return *our* mules', and 'Go, stout Theridamas, *thy* words are swords, | And with *thy* looks thou conquerest all *thy* foes' in *1 Tamburlaine*;[24] and 'Forsake *our* friends, forestall *our* forward war | And leave *our* legions full of dalliance', and 'Draw forth *thy* legions and *thy* men at arms, | Rear up *thy* standard and *thy* steeled crest' in *Wounds*.[25]

In other words, the PCA reveals not only authorial patterns in the samples, but also patterns in genre, such as the clustering of segments with a higher relative proportion of words typical of heroical romances and their 'vast territorial scope', 'wandering hero[es]', 'great exploits of love and war', 'generation of emotions of sublime awe, wonder, [and] horror', 'gratification of wish-fulfilling fantasy', and 'providential design (however

---

W. Whitworth, '*The Wounds of Civil War* and *Tamburlaine*: Lodge's Alleged Imitation', *Notes & Queries* 22 (1975), 245–7; Clifford Ronan, '*Antike Roman': Power Symbology and the Roman Play in Early Modern England, 1585–1635* (Athens, GA: University of Georgia Press, 1995), 118; G. K. Hunter, *English Drama*, 56–9; and Andrew Hadfield, *Shakespeare and Republicanism* (Cambridge University Press, 2005), 66.

[20] G. K. Hunter, *Lyly and Peele* (London: Longman, 1968), 41.

[21] For a detailed discussion of the critical reception of *Alcazar*, see Charles Edelman in Peele, *The Battle of Alcazar*, 27–33.

[22] George Peele, *A Farewell* (London, 1589; STC 19537), A3r.

[23] Peele, *The Battle of Alcazar*, 5.1.235, 1.1.25–6 (emphasis added).

[24] Christopher Marlowe, *1 Tamburlaine the Great*, ed. J. S. Cunningham (Manchester University Press, 1981), 1.2.74–6, 1.1.74–5 (emphasis added).

[25] Thomas Lodge, *The Wounds of Civil War*, ed. Joseph W. Houppert (Lincoln, NE: University of Nebraska Press, 1969), 1.1.17–18, 1.1.231–2 (emphasis added).

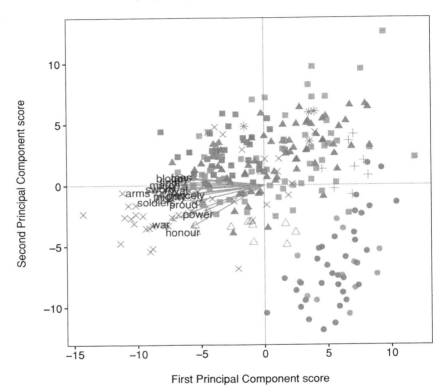

× Admiral's (Nottingham's) Men	● Oxford's Boys
+ Chamberlain's (Hunsdon's) Men	■ Pembroke's Men
● Children of Paul's	■ Queen Elizabeth's Men
△ Children of the Chapel Royal	✳ Sussex's Men
▲ Derby's (Strange's) Men	

Figure 6.3 PCA biplot of 2,000-word non-overlapping segments of plays with
well-attributed first companies, *c*.1581–94, using the 500 most frequent words,
highlighting selected generic markers.

qualified) . . . in tension with [their] chronicle-history basis'.[26] When the
points are re-labelled according to genre (Figure 6.5), segments categorised
as 'heroical romance' (plotted as black circles) all appear to the left of the
graph (the bottom left in particular), whereas 'classical legend', 'comedy',

[26] Brian Gibbons, 'Romance and the Heroic Play', in A. R. Braunmuller and Michael Hattaway (eds.),
The Cambridge Companion to English Renaissance Drama (Cambridge University Press, 1990), 218.

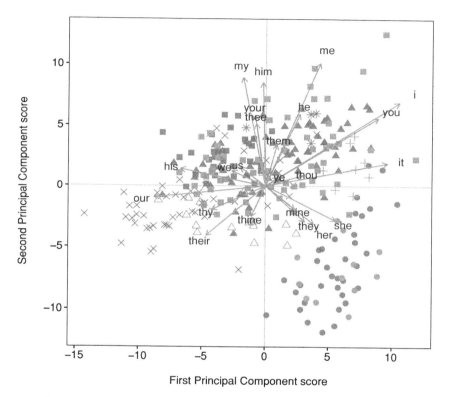

Figure 6.4 PCA biplot of 2,000-word non-overlapping segments of plays with well-attributed first companies, *c.*1581–94, using the 500 most frequent words, highlighting personal and possessive pronouns.

'moral', 'pastoral', and 'romance' segments are plotted to the right, with 'classical legend' occupying the bottom right almost exclusively.

Given the remarkable similarity between segments belonging to different repertory companies revealed by PCA (Figure 6.1), failure to classify segments by repertory company using Random Forests, a machine-learning technique outlined in Chapter 1, is unsurprising. After a randomly selected

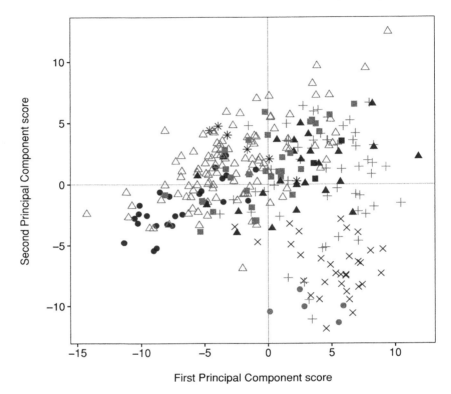

Figure 6.5 PCA scatterplot of 2,000-word non-overlapping segments of plays with well-attributed first companies, *c.*1581–94, using the 500 most frequent words, labelled by genre.

one-third of the segments are withheld by the algorithm to be tested later, 500 decision trees are populated using the remaining two-thirds of the training dataset, trying twenty-two random word-variables at each split in the decision trees. When the randomly withheld segments are reintroduced and classified using the decision trees, the resulting classification error rate is 38 per cent. The threshold for what constitutes an 'acceptable' classification error rate will depend upon the particular conditions of an experiment. The higher the error rate, the weaker the relationship between the variables and the classes. In the present experiment, 38 per cent is an unacceptable error rate for differentiating between nine classes. Table 6.2 gives the confusion matrix of the Random Forests classifications for each 2,000-word segment using the 500 most frequent words across the corpus. The only repertory company to have all of its segments correctly classified is the Children of Paul's (0 per cent error rate); however, this error rate ignores the fact that all eleven Oxford's Boys segments are incorrectly classified as belonging to Paul's (100 per cent error rate). The Chamberlain's (Hunsdon's) Men and Sussex's Men repertories are similarly misclassified in their entirety (eight and four segments respectively), with segments belonging to the three largest companies represented in the corpus – the Admiral's (Nottingham's) Men, Derby's (Strange's) Men, and Queen Elizabeth's Men – producing misclassification rates of 26 per cent, 23 per cent, and 32 per cent respectively. In other words, when trained on two-thirds of segments belonging to every repertory company from the period, the algorithm misclassifies almost one-third of all segments belonging to Queen Elizabeth's Men.

Mindful that Random Forests and similar machine-learning techniques fare better with classification problems where there are fewer classes, we repeat the tests on a sub-set of the corpus comprising only the Admiral's (Nottingham's) Men, Derby's (Strange's) Men, and Queen Elizabeth's Men. These are the three largest repertory groups in our sample, with fifty, sixty-nine, and sixty-five segments respectively. We project the word-frequency counts for the 500 most frequent words across this corpus sub-set for each 2,000-word segment into a two-dimensional space using PCA, treating the scores on the first and second principal components as Cartesian coordinates defining each segment as a point in the scatterplot (Figure 6.6).

As before, points belonging to all three repertory companies are interspersed with one another around the origin and are plotted all over the graph, suggesting a high degree of shared stylistic traits. Two outliers emerge: a selection of Admiral's (Nottingham's) Men segments similarly cluster in and around the bottom left – the same 'heroical romance' segments belonging to Lodge's *Wounds*, Marlowe's *Tamburlaine* plays, and Peele's *Alcazar* – and a loose series of three smaller clusters of Queen Elizabeth's Men segments towards the bottom-right edges of the scatterplot. When the points are re-labelled according to known authorship rather than repertory company (Figure 6.7), with segments of plays of uncertain provenance plotted with '.' symbols as before, the outlier clusters to the bottom right of graph are revealed to belong to Robert Wilson, plotted as unfilled grey circles.

Table 6.2 *Confusion matrix for Random Forests classification of 2,000-word non-overlapping segments of plays with well-attributed first companies, c.1581–94, using the 500 most frequent words*

	Admiral's (Nottingham's) Men	Chamberlain's (Hunsdon's) Men	Children of Paul's	Children of the Chapel Royal	Derby's (Strange's) Men	Oxford's Boys	Pembroke's Men	Queen Elizabeth's Men	Sussex's Men	Misclassification (%)
Admiral's (Nottingham's) Men	37	0	0	0	11	0	0	2	0	26
Chamberlain's (Hunsdon's) Men	0	0	0	0	7	0	0	1	0	100
Children of Paul's	0	0	35	0	0	0	0	0	0	0
Children of the Chapel Royal	7	0	0	1	6	0	0	3	0	94
Derby's (Strange's) Men	4	0	0	0	53	0	1	11	0	23
Oxford's Boys	0	0	11	0	1	0	0	0	0	100
Pembroke's Men	4	0	0	0	8	0	10	11	0	69
Queen Elizabeth's Men	4	0	0	0	17	0	0	44	0	32
Sussex's Men	0	0	0	0	2	0	0	2	0	100

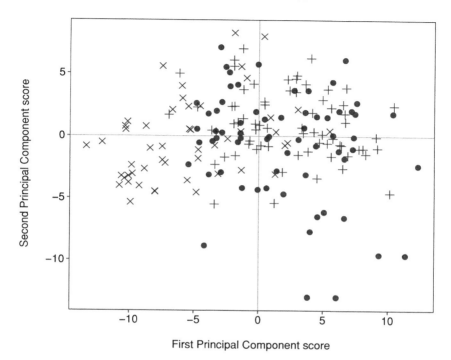

Figure 6.6 PCA scatterplot of 2,000-word non-overlapping segments of plays associated with the Admiral's (Nottingham's) Men, Derby's (Strange's) Men, and Queen Elizabeth's Men, c.1581–94, using the 500 most frequent words, labelled by company.

Contrary to our initial intuition, PCA of the smaller sub-set of the corpus reveals a higher degree of overlap between segments belonging to different repertory companies. Perhaps this is due to the absence of John Lyly's segments, which constituted a significant stylistic outlier and point of difference. As such, we anticipate similar – if not higher – error rates when using Random Forests to classify segments in the corpus sub-set by repertory company. As before, after a randomly selected one-third of the segments are withheld by the algorithm, 500 decision trees are populated using the remaining two-thirds of the data, trying twenty-two random word-variables at each split in the decision trees. This time, when the randomly

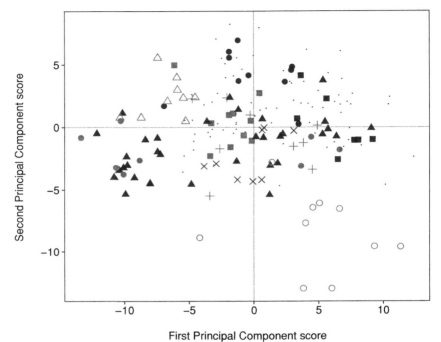

Figure 6.7 PCA scatterplot of 2,000-word non-overlapping segments of plays associated with the Admiral's (Nottingham's) Men, Derby's (Strange's) Men, and Queen Elizabeth's Men, *c.*1581–94, using the 500 most frequent words, labelled by author.

withheld segments are classified using the decision trees, the resulting classification error rate is 32 per cent, slightly lower than before. Table 6.3 gives the confusion matrix of the Random Forests classifications for each 2,000-word segment using the 500 most frequent words across the corpus sub-set. The algorithm misclassifies 32 per cent, 29 per cent, and 37 per cent of segments belonging to the Admiral's (Nottingham's) Men, Derby's (Strange's) Men, and Queen Elizabeth's Men respectively. This is an increase in error rate of 5–6 per cent when compared with the classifications made using

Table 6.3 *Confusion matrix for Random Forests classification of 2,000-word non-overlapping segments of plays associated with the Admiral's (Nottingham's) Men, Derby's (Strange's) Men, and Queen Elizabeth's Men, c.1581–94, using the 500 most frequent words*

	Admiral's (Nottingham's) Men	Derby's (Strange's) Men	Queen Elizabeth's Men	Misclassification (%)
Admiral's (Nottingham's) Men	34	15	1	32
Derby's (Strange's) Men	6	49	14	29
Queen Elizabeth's Men	6	18	41	37

the full corpus. In other words, when trained on two-thirds of segments belonging to all three companies with the largest surviving canon of plays from the period, the algorithm misclassifies approximately one-third of all segments.

These preliminary results suggest that repertory company is not a useful principle for stylistic discrimination, and that authorship and genre are stronger signals in the stylistic affinities between plays belonging to the same period of composition.

Internal Stylistic Cohesion: Queen Elizabeth's Men and the Children of the King's Revels

If we cannot accurately discriminate *between* plays of the same period of composition on the basis of company, is it still possible to measure adherence to a 'house style' *within* individual repertories analysed in isolation? This much has been argued for the repertories of Queen Elizabeth's Men and the Children of the King's Revels. When the 'plays are brought together as one textual group', McMillin and MacLean assert that 'sameness rather than variety is a leading characteristic' of Queen Elizabeth's Men's repertory, 'especially when it comes to such basic theatrical characteristics as casting, doubling, staging, and dramaturgy'.[27] In relation to the comedies associated with the Children of the King's Revels, Bly goes a step further to

---

[27] McMillin and MacLean, *The Queen's Men*, 98.

argue that 'while the plays are readily distinguishable from most early modern romantic comedies, they are barely distinguishable from each other'. For Bly, it is this 'homogeneity' in the Children of the King's Revels repertory – not just within the comedies – that suggests the existence of 'a cohesive decision-making body that directed the tenor of the plays'.[28]

PCA is an ideal computational method with which to test the internal variance within these individual repertories. If a company's output is stylistically cohesive – as has been claimed for both Queen Elizabeth's Men and the Children of the King's Revels – the greatest variance should be *within* the plays themselves. That is, we would expect PCA to differentiate between different segments of the same plays and split them apart. However, if a company's output is not stylistically coherent, the greatest variance should be *between* the plays. That is, we would expect PCA to cluster segments of the same plays together, and to differentiate between these play-clusters.

We project the word-frequency counts for the 500 most frequent words across the 8 plays known to have been written for and first performed by Queen Elizabeth's Men (listed in Table 6.1) for each 2,000-word segment into a two-dimensional space using PCA,[29] treating the scores on the first and second principal components as Cartesian coordinates defining each segment as a point in the scatterplot (Figure 6.8). The greatest variance is indeed between, and not within, the plays: segments of the same play cluster together with varying degrees of density, from a very tight cluster of *1 Selimus* segments, plotted as unfilled up-turned triangles, through to a sparser, but still clearly delineated, cluster of *The Famous Victories of Henry the Fifth* segments, plotted as unfilled black circles.

When the scatterplot is relabelled according to author, with segments of unknown authorship plotted with '.' symbols, it becomes clear that authorship is one of the factors explaining the variance between the plays, with well-defined clusters for each of the three known playwrights (Figure 6.9).

Another stylistic factor in the groupings of the play segments using PCA is genre, demonstrated when the scatterplot is relabelled accordingly (Figure 6.10). Segments classed as 'moral' cluster together in the north of the graph; 'comedy', 'heroical romance', and 'romance' segments cluster to

[28] Bly, *Queer Virgins*, 32, 35.
[29] Since its date remains unclear, we exclude *Clymon and Clamydes*. McMillin and MacLean argue that the play dates after 1583 and was written for Queen Elizabeth's Men (*The Queen's Men*, 91–2), but both the *Annals* and Wiggins date the play much earlier at 1570 (limits 1570–83) and 1578 (limits 1570–93) respectively, suggesting that the play was performed by – but not written for – the company.

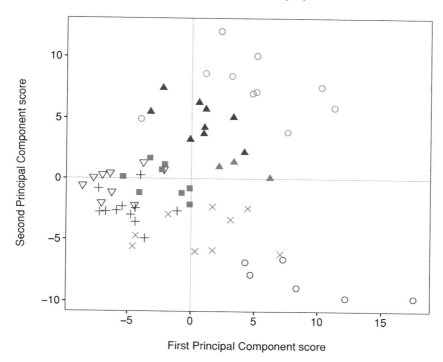

Figure 6.8 PCA scatterplot of 2,000-word non-overlapping segments of plays associated with Queen Elizabeth's Men, *c.*1581–94, using the 500 most frequent words, labelled by play.

the west and east of the origin; and 'history' segments group together in the southern region of the graph with one exception – segments belonging to *King Leir* – which may be distinguished from the others as a 'legendary history'.[30]

---

[30] This is the *Annals* designation. The precise generic category of *Leir* remains a matter of critical debate. For example, it is a 'prehistory, pseudo-history, [or] romance' (Janet Clare, *Shakespeare's Stage Traffic: Imitation, Borrowing and Competition in Renaissance Theatre* [Cambridge University Press, 2014], 212), a 'chronicle play that anticipates tragicomedy' (Tom MacFaul, *Problem Fathers in Shakespeare and Renaissance Drama* [Cambridge University Press, 2012], 145), a 'gentle, humorous,

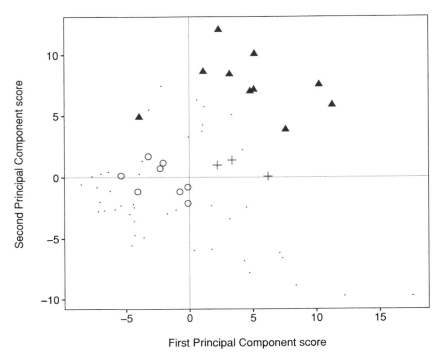

Figure 6.9 PCA scatterplot of 2,000-word non-overlapping segments of plays associated
with Queen Elizabeth's Men, *c.*1581–94, using the 500 most frequent words, labelled
by author.

In each of these graphs, an outlier segment of Robert Wilson's *The Three
Lords and Three Ladies of London* is plotted away from the rest of the play
and warrants further examination using a biplot (Figure 6.11). This segment
contains the climactic Armada scene, in which the titular lords of London
vanquish the Spanish enemy. At the 'centre of the contest' are shields on
both sides, and 'the battle is marked out by the advance and retreat of these
blazons'. McMillin and MacLean describe this scene as 'a ballet in which
England defeats Spain – virtually a dance of herald against herald, page

and unquestioningly Christian rendering' (Tiffany Stern in her edition of Ben Jonson, *King Leir*
[London: Nick Hern, 2003], ix), and a generic experiment with 'ample employment of the characteristics of the romance genre . . . cast in the framework of the chronicle play' (Donald M. Richie
in his edition of Jonson's *The True Chronicle History of King Leir* [New York: Garland, 1991], 37).

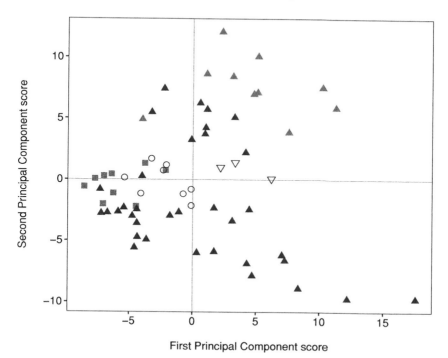

Figure 6.10 PCA scatterplot of 2,000-word non-overlapping segments of plays associated with Queen Elizabeth's Men, *c.*1581–94, using the 500 most frequent words, labelled by genre.

against page, lord against lord – which ends when the Spanish shields can be battered apart and the English held up in triumph'.[31] The verbal and physical sparring between these groups during this episode – particularly in reference to their shields – is reflected in the use of demonstrative (*that, those, this, these*) and relative (*which, whom, whose*) pronouns with greater relative frequency than in other segments of the play. For example: 'Then know, Castilian cavalieros, *this*: | The owners of *these* emblems are three lords, | *Those* three *that* now are viewing of your shields.'[32]

---

[31] McMillin and MacLean, *The Queen's Men*, 125.
[32] Robert Wilson, *The Three Lords and Three Ladies of London* (London, 1590; STC 25783), G2v (emphasis added).

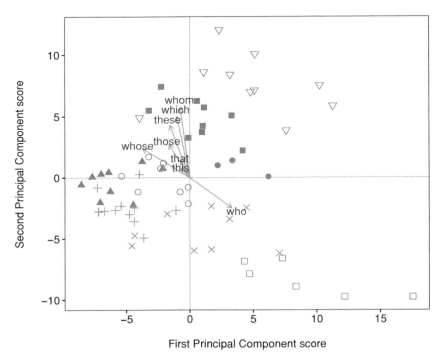

□ Famous Victories   ▲ Selimus
○ Friar Bacon   ▽ Three Lords and Three Ladies
▨ King Leir   + Troublesome Reign
● Old Wife's Tale   × True Tragedy

Figure 6.11 PCA biplot of 2,000-word non-overlapping segments of plays associated with Queen Elizabeth's Men, *c.* 1581–1594, using the 500 most frequent words, highlighting demonstrative and relative pronouns.

Perhaps it is unsurprising that the repertory of Queen Elizabeth's Men, with its range of authorial voices, genres, and dates of composition over a fourteen-year period, demonstrates a high degree of internal stylistic variance. Can the same be said for the four comedies written for and performed by the Children of the King's Revels, a company in existence for only a year (1607–8)? These include Edward Sharpham's *Cupid's Whirligig* (1607), Lewis Machin and Gervase Markham's *The Dumb Knight* (1608), John Day's *Humour Out of Breath* (1608), and Lording Barry's *Ram Alley* (1608). Bly's claim that these comedies are 'barely distinguishable from each other' incorporated a fifth play, John Day's *Law Tricks*, which we have excluded from our analysis because it properly belongs to another company and predates the formation of the Children of the King's Revels.[33]

We project the word-frequency counts for the 500 most frequent words across the four plays written for and first performed by the Children of the King's Revels for each 2,000-word segment into a two-dimensional space using PCA (Figure 6.12). With so many shared attributes – all the segments come from comedies written and performed within the space of a year for the same company by novice playwrights – one might expect PCA to discern a high degree of stylistic cohesion. In fact, this is not the case. As with Queen Elizabeth's Men, the greatest variance is in fact *between*, and not *within*, the plays, with segments associated with each comedy forming distinct clusters: *Ram Alley* to the north, *Humour Out of Breath* around the origin, *The Dumb Knight* to the east, and *Cupid's Whirligig* to the south.

When the points are relabelled according to author (Figure 6.13), the scatterplots look identical, for the simple reason that each of these four comedies is known to have been written by different hands – with one possible exception. In his epistle, Day refers to *Humour Out of Breath* as 'a poor friendless child . . . yet sufficiently featured too, had it been all of one man's getting (woe to the iniquity of Time the whilst)'.[34] Scholars have interpreted this remark as Day's acknowledgement of his unnamed collaborator, most probably Edward Sharpham, who, 'woe to the iniquity of Time', died in 1608 when the play was printed.[35] The plotting of the outlier first segment of *Humour Out of Breath* away from the rest of the play and closer to the *Cupid's Whirligig* cluster is perhaps suggestive of Sharpham's early involvement, but not conclusive.

Far from being 'barely distinguishable', this analysis suggests that authorship emerges as a stronger signal of the stylistic affinity even between segments of plays with a shared genre, repertory company, and date of composition.

---

[33] *Annals* dates the play to 1604 (1604–7) and assigns it to the Children of the King's Revels. Wiggins also dates the play to 1604 (1604–5) and assigns it to the Children of the Queen's Revels, as does Munro in her study of the repertory (*Children of the Queen's Revels*, Appendix A).

[34] John Day, *Humour Out of Breath* (London, 1608; STC 6411), A2r.

[35] M. E. Borish, 'John Day's *Humour Out of Breath*', *Harvard Studies and Notes in Philology and Literature* 16 (1934), 1–11; Robin Jeffs, 'Introduction', in Marston, *Works*, xx; Christopher Gordon Petter, 'Biographical Introduction', in Edward Sharpham, *A Critical Old Spelling Edition of the Works of Edward Sharpham*, ed. Christopher Gordon Petter (New York: Garland, 1986), 39–40; Charles Cathcart, *Marston, Rivalry, Rapprochement, and Jonson* (Aldershot: Aldgate, 2008), 52; Bly, *Queer Virgins*, 119.

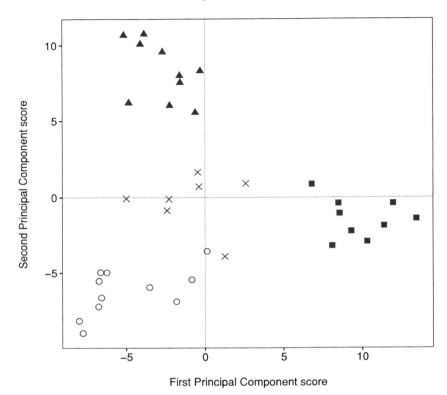

Figure 6.12 PCA scatterplot of 2,000-word non-overlapping segments of Children of the King's Revels comedies using the 500 most frequent words, labelled by play.

Authorial Constraint: Richard Brome, 1629–40

In order to look beyond any potential author, genre, and period effects, we construct a corpus of nine well-attributed, sole-authored plays belonging to the same period of composition (1629–40), genre (comedy), and author (Richard Brome), but associated with three different repertory companies (Beeston's Boys, the King's Men, and King's Revels Company). With such a corpus, we should be able to determine whether Brome adapted his authorial habits to suit different 'house styles' – that is, whether we can systematically distinguish Brome's comedies written for Beeston's Boys from those

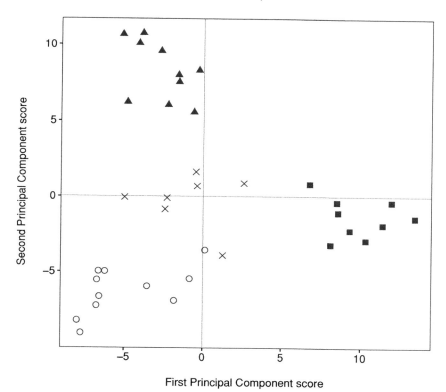

Figure 6.13 PCA scatterplot of 2,000-word non-overlapping segments of Children of the King's Revels comedies using the 500 most frequent words, labelled by author.

written for the King's Men or King's Revels Company. The plays in this corpus are *The Court Beggar* (1640), *The Damoiselle* (1638), and *A Mad Couple Well Matched* (1639) for Beeston's Boys; *Covent Garden Weeded* (1632), *The Northern Lass* (1629), and *The Novella* (1632) for the King's Men; and *The City Wit* (1630), *The New Academy* (1635), and *The Sparagus Garden* (1635) for the King's Revels Company.[36]

We project the word-frequency counts for the 500 most frequent words across the Brome corpus for each 2,000-word segment into a

---

[36] Appendix A provides fuller details for each of these plays and the source text used.

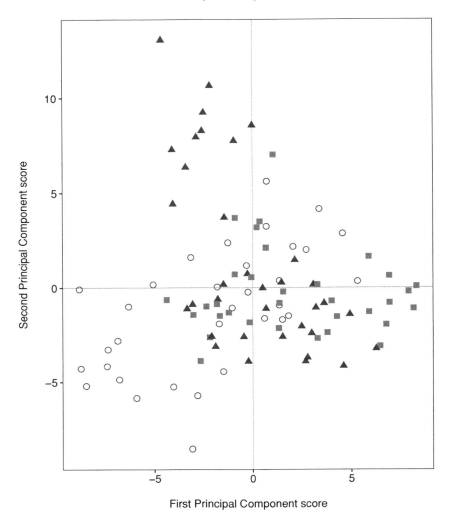

Figure 6.14 PCA scatterplot of 2,000-word non-overlapping segments of 9 comedies by
Richard Brome, 1629–40, using the 500 most frequent words.

two-dimensional space using PCA (Figure 6.14). With three exceptions,
there are no discrete groupings of points on the scatterplot – rather, points
belonging to all three repertory companies are plotted around the origin of
the graph and intermingle with one another. As before, this suggests that

segments of plays belonging to different repertory companies have common stylistic attributes. The exceptions include outlier clusters of Beeston's Boys segments to the bottom-left of the scatterplot, King's Revels segments to the top-left, and King's Men segments to the far right.

When the points are re-labelled according to play-title rather than repertory company (Figure 6.15), segments belonging to the same play are shown to cluster together in varying degrees, with segments from *The City Wit*, *Covent Garden Weeded*, and *A Mad Couple Well Matched* constituting the outliers identified in Figure 6.14.

With potential author-, genre-, and date-effects minimised – if not zeroed out – by the composition of the corpus, we may have expected adherence to a particular 'house style' to emerge as the strongest signal discernible by PCA. Examination of a series of biplots suggests that the PCA instead reveals underlying thematic and grammatical patterns in the comedies as more important stylistic factors, trumping any affinity there may be between plays of the same repertory company. In thematic terms, *The City Wit*, *Covent Garden Weeded*, and *A Mad Couple Well Matched* are not so much outliers as exemplars of three distinct comedic subjects which, in combination, characterise the plays in this corpus: wealth, wine, and women (Figure 6.16).

The City Wit, a city comedy following the tricks and travails of a London merchant as he recovers his fortune, exemplifies plays concerned with wealth and is characterised by a high relative frequency of words associated with financial prosperity and monetary exchange (e.g. *dear, fortune, given, poor, pound, purse, rich*, and *worth*). Wine, or rather the tavern community that renders 'conviviality and sociability as purchasable, at least in terms of the raw materials of food, drink, and entertainment',[37] is another thematic topic in these comedies, exemplified by *Covent Garden Weeded*, which features no fewer than two taverns, one of them playing host to the Brotherhood of the Blade, 'a fraternity of hooligans modelled on those known to have been active in Caroline London'.[38] Words associated with drinking and camaraderie (e.g. *civil, company, drink, gentlemen, men, together, welcome*, and *wine*) occur with relatively higher frequency in this play. As objects of sexual and financial desire, as well as significant characters within the plays themselves, women provide another thematic focus in this group

---

[37] Michael Leslie, 'Critical Introduction', *The Weeding of Covent Garden*, in Richard Brome, *Richard Brome Online*, Richard Allen Cave (gen. ed.) (Sheffield: HRI Online 2010), 55.
[38] Matthew Steggle, *Richard Brome: Place and Politics on the Caroline Stage* (Manchester University Press, 2004), 50.

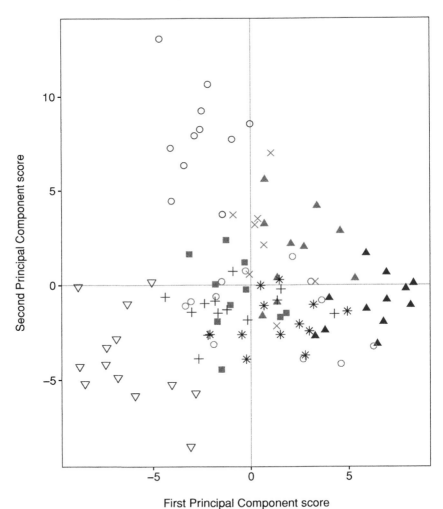

Figure 6.15 PCA scatterplot of 2,000-word non-overlapping segments of 9 comedies by Richard Brome, 1629–40, using the 500 most frequent words, labelled by play.

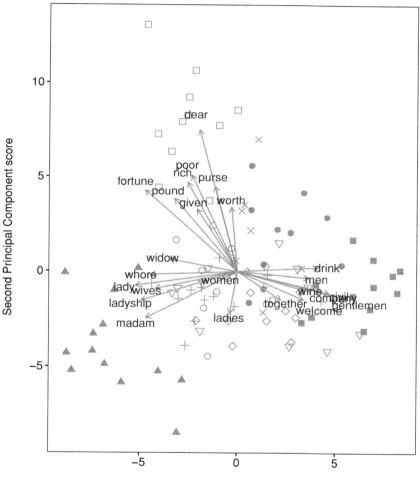

Figure 6.16 PCA biplot of 2,000-word non-overlapping segments of 9 comedies by Richard Brome, 1629–40, using the 500 most frequent words, highlighting thematic markers.

of Brome's comedies. *A Mad Couple Well Matched* offers a 'plentiful lady-feast', to quote Alicia, a 'light wife' who joins a *dramatis personae* that also includes a pregnant 'whore', a 'rich vintner's widow', an old crone, a steward who spends most of the play disguised as a woman, and a 'lady' who employs a bed-trick to evade the unwanted advances of her husband's nephew.[39] As the exemplar of this theme, *A Mad Couple Well Matched* contains a relatively high frequency of words associated with women (e.g. *ladies, lady, ladyship, madam, whore, wives, women,* and *widow*).

The PCA aligns segments of other plays in the Brome corpus in relation to these themes, and not by repertory company. *The Demoiselle*, for example, combines the wealth and wine themes in its portrayal of Dryground, a gentleman who mortgages his estate to Vermin, an old usurer, in order to establish a 'public ordinary, | For fashionable guests and curious stomachs, | The daintiest palates, with rich wine and cheer' with the funds.[40] The investment proves sound, and the food and fare on offer quickly become popular among the gallants of London. Dryground also raffles off the virginity of his 'daughter' – actually the cross-dressed son of Brookall, a gentleman brought to ruin by Vermin – recovering their collective fortunes in the process. In his study of Brome, R. J. Kaufmann concludes a chapter on 'Usury and Brotherhood' with a discussion of *The Demoiselle*, focusing on the play's treatment of usury as a practice that 'literally subverts the family and the hierarchy of loyalties which makes for the good community'.[41] The results of the PCA reflect this combination of the wealth and wine themes, such that *The Demoiselle* segments are plotted as 'bridging the gap' between *The City Wit* and *Covent Garden Weeded*.

The PCA of Brome's nine comedies also reveals grammatical patterns, such as in the relative frequency of personal pronouns (Figure 6.17). Second-person informal singular pronouns (*thee, thine, thou, thy*) form a group of vectors pushing the segments out to the north and north-east of the origin, diametrically opposed to the second-person plural or formal singular pronouns (*you, your, yours*) pushing south and south-west. *The Demoiselle*, plotted to the north and north-east of the origin, employs a relatively higher frequency of second-person informal singular pronouns in its exchanges between parents and children and between characters of

---

[39] Richard Brome, *A Mad Couple Well Matched*, in *Five New Plays* (London, 1653; Wing B4870), E5r, A5v.

[40] Richard Brome, *The Demoiselle*, ed. Lucy Munro, in Brome, *Richard Brome Online*, 2010, 2.1.speech179.

[41] R. J. Kaufmann, *Richard Brome, Caroline Playwright* (New York: Columbia University Press, 1961), 150.

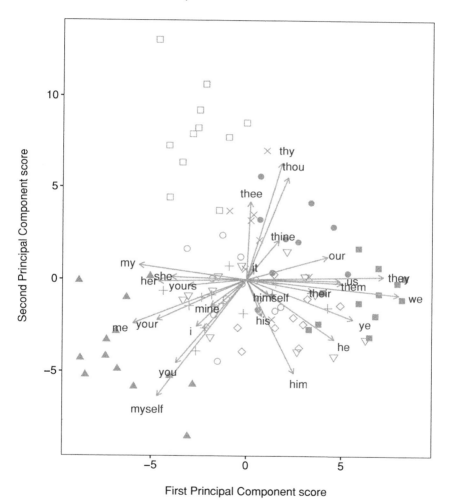

Figure 6.17 PCA biplot of 2,000-word non-overlapping segments of 9 comedies by Richard Brome, 1629–40, using the 500 most frequent words, highlighting personal pronouns.

differing social rank. As both a father and a ruined gentleman clinging to his former elevated status, Brookall's dialogue stands out for its informal register. Indeed, at one point he claims to 'speak more like a father than a beggar, | Although no beggar poorer'.[42] Plotted to the south-west of the origin in diametrical opposition to *The Demoiselle* is *A Mad Couple Well Matched*, which features a relatively higher proportion of first-person singular pronouns (*I, me, mine, my*), second-person plural or formal singular pronouns (*you, your, yours*), and third-person feminine pronouns (*her, she*), all registers appropriate to the elevated language of love and courtship associated with the theme of women. By contrast, in the opposite hemisphere first- and third-person plural pronouns (*our, their, them, they, us, we*), as well as masculine singular pronouns (*he, him, himself, his*), push out from the origin to the east and south-east respectively, in line with the language of tavern culture and the familiar register of camaraderie that populate the wine theme in that region of the plot.

In keeping with earlier experiments in this chapter, we also attempt to classify Brome's nine comedies into their respective repertory companies – thirty-three Beeston's Boys, thirty-three King's Men, and thirty-five King's Revels Company segments in total – using Random Forests. After a randomly selected one-third of all the segments are withheld by the algorithm, 500 decision trees are populated using the remaining two-thirds of the data, trying forty-four random word-variables at each split in the decision trees. When the decision trees are then used to classify the randomly withheld segments, the resulting classification error rate is 24 per cent. In earlier experiments, 38 per cent was considered an unacceptable error rate when differentiating between nine classes. Likewise, when differentiating between only three classes (as in the present experiment), an error rate above 12 per cent – or one-third of 38 per cent – is unacceptable. Table 6.4 gives the confusion matrix of the Random Forests classifications for each 2,000-word segment using the 500 most frequent words across the corpus sub-set. The algorithm misclassifies 36 per cent, 21 per cent, and 14 per cent of segments belonging to Beeston's Boys, the King's Men, and King's Revels Company respectively. In other words, when trained on two-thirds of segments belonging to all three companies – segments sharing the same author, genre, and period of composition – the algorithm misclassifies over one-third of all Beeston's Boys segments, over one-fifth of King's Men segments, and one-seventh of King's Revels Company segments.

---

[42] Brome, *Demoiselle*, 2.1.speech391.

Table 6.4 *Confusion matrix for Random Forests classification of 2,000-word non-overlapping segments of 9 comedies by Richard Brome associated with Beeston's Boys, the King's Men, and King's Revels Company, 1629–40, using the 500 most frequent words*

	Beeston's Boys	King's Men	King's Revels Company	Misclassification (%)
Beeston's Boys	21	2	10	36
King's Men	4	26	3	21
King's Revels Company	4	1	30	14

These results suggest that, even in the absence of competing authorial, genre, and period factors, repertory company is a weak – perhaps even insignificant – principle for stylistic discrimination and classification. In the case of Brome, unique archival materials provide additional external evidence and support for this conclusion. Brome signed a three-year contract with the King's Revels Company in 1635, committing to produce three plays annually for the exclusive enjoyment of the company at their Salisbury Court theatre. While the contract no longer exists, theatre historians have pieced its contents together through meticulous examination of the requests proceedings bill of complaint filed in 1640 against Brome by Queen Henrietta Maria's Men, the occupants of Salisbury Court at the time, and Brome's subsequent answer to the complaint.[43] Eleanor Collins, the most recent commentator on this convoluted and confusing legal narrative, summarises the proceedings as follows:

> [Richard] Heton and the [Salisbury Court] company claimed that Brome had broken the terms of his contract and was, by 1638, in arrears of the agreement by four plays. Furthermore, Brome had not observed the article of the contract that forbade him to 'write any playe or p[ar]t of a playe [for] anye other players or playe howse'. While Brome had been required to 'applie all his studdye and Endevours theerein for the Benefitte of the Salisbury Court company, he stood accused of delivering one of the company's promised plays to Christopher and William Beeston at the Cockpit theatre, where it would be performed by Beeston's Boys ... Despite this breach, Heton and Brome both renewed their contracts in 1638 ... [O]nce

[43] National Archives, PRO REQ2/622 pt. 1 and REQ2/723. A full transcription of the depositions is provided by Ann Haaker, 'The Plague, the Theater, and the Poet', *Renaissance Drama* 1 (1968), 283–306.

more, Brome agreed to supply the company with three plays each year, but this time for an extended term of seven years. This raised the total number of plays that Brome was expected to contribute to the Salisbury Court repertory from nine to twenty-one. In addition, the new contract required Brome to produce the plays that he owed from the prior agreement. Once more, the court case suggests that he failed to do so. By the end of the year he was in arrears by one new play, and the Heton complaint records that, by this time, Brome had 'wholly applie[d] himself unto the said Beeston and the Companie of players Acting at the playhouse of the Phoenix [or Cockpit] in Drury Lane'.[44]

The primary objective of the contract was to secure Brome's services as playwright 'to stock [the Salisbury Court] playhouse with current drama', thus enabling 'the consistent accumulation of a repertory' to supplement the company's existing corpus of old plays available for revival.[45] But this is not to suggest that Salisbury Court approached Brome because he was particularly industrious as a playwright. According to the contract, Brome's 'best art and industry' were valued equally.[46] Richard Gunnell, Heton's predecessor at Salisbury Court, 'saw how well Brome's plays were being received at the Red Bull', a rival theatre, 'and asked Brome to compose plays for their company' instead. Prompted by the success of Brome's plays for them, the Salisbury Court company 'sought to enhance its reputation and employed Brome exclusively as their poet'.[47]

Brome's 'art' – his craft, his *style* – was what attracted paying customers to the theatres; his 'industry' simply governed the rate at which his scripts became available. The contract's exclusivity clause attempted to exploit and maximise Brome's art and industry respectively by ensuring that his energies were focused on meeting the quota of scripts, and by associating his creative output with the theatre at Salisbury Court alone. If it were possible – or even desirable – for a playwright to adopt a company's distinctive 'house style' wholesale, and to radically constrain, subsume, or alter their authorial voice in the process, Salisbury Court might have sought a more industrious candidate than Brome, given his repeated failure to meet the stipulated quota. By the same token, if Brome had no distinctive 'art' of his own and was able to simply adopt and switch between recognisable

---

44 Eleanor Collins, 'Richard Brome and the Salisbury Court Contract', in Brome, *Richard Brome Online*, 2010, 3–6 (citing Haaker's transcript, 297–8, 299–300). See also Eleanor Collins, 'Richard Brome's Contract and the Relationship of Dramatist to Company in the Early Modern Period', *Early Theatre* 10.2 (2007), 116–28.

45 Collins, 'Richard Brome', 12–13.   46 Quoted in Haaker, 'The Plague', 297.

47 Haaker, 'The Plague', 285.

company styles, why should Salisbury Court deny him the opportunity to 'write, invent, or compose any play, tragedy or comedy, or any part thereof, for any other playhouse',[48] so long as he met their needs and made his quota?

Conclusion

What conclusions might be drawn from these experiments? If previous studies have demonstrated that authorship 'emerges as a much stronger force in the affinities between texts than genre or period',[49] our results suggest that 'repertory company' may be added to this list of secondary forces. As such, our results provide further support for Egan's argument that 'plays were relatively stable works': our continued ability to cluster and 'discriminate between writers', even when analysing plays written for the same repertory company in isolation, militates against the notion of the early modern theatre as 'a melting pot that blurred all boundaries'.[50]

Our results also provide much-needed quantitative support for the scepticism expressed by critics of repertory studies about the existence of, and pursuit to identify, distinct company styles. 'Just as author-centred criticism tends to assume a consistency of political or intellectual allegiance from one work to the next', Tom Rutter notes the danger of 'look[ing] for points of similarity between plays written by different dramatists for the same company', since in 'seeking to identify distinctive characteristics for the various playing companies repertory studies can end up hypostatizing them'.[51] Roslyn Knutson similarly inveighs against assuming that companies cultivated a 'house style', given the difficulties of distinguishing between evidence of 'company ownership and company influence' and gauging 'how much of a house style is the result of the dramatists' sense of identity rather than that of the company'.[52] Rutter has since published a study of the Admiral's Men repertory, in which he concludes that:

> while a repertory-based approach may encourage the identification of a company style, perhaps the best response to the varied, innovative and ideologically unfixed drama of the Admiral's Men between 1594 and 1600, open to the influence of Shakespeare while shaping his own dramatic development, is to refrain from doing so.[53]

[48] Quoted in Haaker, 'The Plague', 298.   [49] Craig, 'Style, Statistics', 2.3.
[50] Egan, 'What Is Not Collaborative', 28.   [51] Rutter, 'Repertory Studies', 346–7.
[52] Knutson, 'The Start of Something Big', 99–100.
[53] Rutter, *Shakespeare and the Admiral's Men*, 201.

Even if repertory company performs feebly as a principle for stylistic dis-crimination between plays, this does not in and of itself discount the possibility that individual companies cultivated a recognisable 'house style'. It does, however, suggest that recent theatre historiography and textual crit-icism has exaggerated the extent to which repertory companies constrained the authorial habits of the playwrights they employed. It also raises impor-tant questions about the nature of such 'house styles', since they are not evident in the places where we find authorial, genre, and period styles – that is, in the language of the plays themselves. If not in the language of the plays, evidence for company styles may well be found in performance – in the vocal, physical, and expressive qualities of different actors and types of acting, in the incorporation of dance, music, song, tumbling, 'wit', and other feats, and so on. However, performative elements such as these are ephemeral and, as G. K. Hunter observes, 'the evidence left in texts is much too sporadic for the point to be developed'.[54] 'The case for the development of consistent or long-lived "house" styles' is similarly undermined, as Siob-han Keenan remarks, by 'the fact that playwrights often wrote for several companies without necessarily changing their writing style and that plays (and players) moved between companies'. 'It might be more appropriate', Keenan adds, 'to speak of acting companies fostering occasional dramatic and staging specialities, rather than developing wholly distinctive company repertories and performance practices'.[55] For example, Derby's (Strange's) Men may have cultivated expertise in the use of pyrotechnics,[56] but this feature is not present in every play of their repertory,[57] nor is it absent from the repertories of rival companies.[58]

As Munro notes, to recognise that 'companies purchased plays from dramatists – sometimes buying a complete script, more often paying in instalments after discussions over an idea, a plot or a completed act', with 'near-complete control over those plays' progress to the stage', is not neces-sarily a question 'of denying the playwright's agency' but of 'acknowledging the compromises which writers make when they engage with institutions

---

[54] G. K. Hunter, *English Drama*, 6.   [55] Keenan, *Acting Companies*, 66.

[56] Lawrence Manley, 'Playing with Fire: Immolation in the Repertory of Strange's Men', *Early Theatre* 4 (2001), 115–21. Manley cites *A Knack to Know a Knave*, *A Looking-Glass for London and England*, and *The Jew of Malta* as examples.

[57] There are no pyrotechnics in *The Comedy of Errors*, *Fair Em*, or *(The Rare Triumphs of) Love and Fortune*, for example.

[58] Representative examples include: *The Battle of Alcazar*, *Doctor Faustus*, and the *Tamburlaine* plays for the Admiral's (Nottingham's) Men; *Dido, Queen of Carthage* for the Children of the Chapel Royal; and *Friar Bacon and Friar Bungay* and *The Old Wife's Tale* for Queen Elizabeth's Men.

such as the early modern theatre industry'.[59] Whatever these compromises were, however, our results suggest they were not enough for companies to constrain an author's habits or fashion a repertory with a style that was distinctive, internally cohesive, or even statistically detectable in the absence of other competing factors such as genre and period.

[59] Munro, *Children of the Queen's Revels*, 4.

CHAPTER 7

Restoration Plays and 'the Giant Race, before the Flood'

Repertory theatre began in London in 1576, when James Burbage and John Brayne opened The Theatre in Shoreditch, and continued with only minor interruptions up to the ban on performance imposed by Parliament in 1642. By 1610, seating for 10,000 spectators was available across the various London playhouses.[1] The London theatre became a considerable employer and creator of numerous fortunes, as playwrights built considerable public prestige – and, in some cases, notoriety – through print as well as performance. In previous chapters, we have presented some quantitative perspectives on the body of play-texts which survive from this endeavour.

Regular performances in the public playhouses came to an abrupt end in 1642, following the Parliamentary ban. There were only surreptitious public performances during the Civil War and the English Republic, when theatre companies were disbanded and some theatres themselves dismantled.[2] When the monarchy was restored in 1660, Charles II granted patents to two theatrical companies and performances resumed, dominated at first by surviving plays written before the Civil War. Those who wrote new plays did so conscious of a vastly talented and celebrated previous generation, divided from them by a civil war and a broken theatrical tradition, conscious also that they were writing in sharply different times and for changed tastes.

In 1667, John Dryden lamented the belatedness of his generation's playwrights. Ben Jonson, John Fletcher, and William Shakespeare 'are

---

[1] Ann Jennalie Cook, *The Privileged Playgoers of Shakespeare's London, 1576–1642* (Princeton University Press, 1981), 176–7.

[2] Dale B. J. Randall, *Winter Fruit: English Drama, 1642–1660* (Lexington: University of Kentucky Press, 1995). See also Martin Butler, *Theatre and Crisis 1632–1642* (Cambridge University Press, 1984); Susan Wiseman, *Drama and Politics in the English Civil War* (Cambridge University Press, 1998); and Janet Clare (ed.), *Drama of the English Republic, 1649–60* (Manchester University Press, 2002).

honoured and almost adored by us, as they deserve', but they left their successors in a sad state:

> We acknowledge them our fathers in wit, but they have ruined their estates themselves, before they came to their children's hands. There is scarce an humour, a character, or any kind of plot, which they have not blown upon. All comes sullied and wasted to us: and were they to entertain this age, they could not make so plenteous treatments out of such decayed fortunes. This, therefore, will be a good argument to us, either not to write at all, or to attempt some other way.[3]

Dryden returned to the topic often. In a dedicatory verse prefixed to the first edition of William Congreve's *The Double Dealer* (1694), Dryden claims that, with Congreve's play, Restoration drama's great predecessors – 'the giant race, before the flood' – have finally been equalled and excelled. In *The Double Dealer*, Congreve matches Jonson in 'judgement', exceeds Fletcher in 'wit', and has as much 'genius' as Shakespeare.[4]

The relationship between the new plays of the 1660s and the pre-1642 drama is a topic of much scholarly debate. When the theatres re-opened, a number of plays from the previous era were available to serve as models: the works of Francis Beaumont and John Fletcher, Ben Jonson, Philip Massinger, Thomas Middleton, and James Shirley were represented, and Shakespeare's *Othello*, *1 Henry the Fourth*, and *The Merry Wives of Windsor* were all performed before the end of 1660.[5] Noting this, and seeing borrowings and adaptations from older drama in the new plays, critics have emphasised continuity in the English dramatic tradition.[6]

By contrast, other commentators characterise Restoration theatre as a break from earlier dramatic styles, taking a cue from Dryden's avowed sense

[3] John Dryden, *Of Dramatic Poesy: An Essay* (London, 1668; Wing D2327), I4v–K1r. Other Restoration playwrights bemoaned the exhaustion of literary resources more generally. In an epistle to his readers, John Wilson writes 'There is hardly anything left to write upon, but what either the ancients or moderns have some way or other touched on': *The Cheats* (London, 1664; Wing W2916), A3r.

[4] John Dryden, 'To my dear friend Mr. Congreve', in William Congreve, *The Double Dealer* (London, 1694; Wing C5847), a2r–v.

[5] Barbara A. Murray, *Restoration Shakespeare: Viewing the Voice* (Madison: Farleigh Dickinson University Press, 2001), 16.

[6] Representative examples include A. C. Sprague, *Beaumont and Fletcher on the Restoration Stage* (Cambridge, MA: Harvard University Press, 1926); John Harold Wilson, *The Influence of Beaumont and Fletcher on Restoration Drama* (Columbus: Ohio State University Press, 1928); James G. McManaway, 'Philip Massinger and the Restoration Drama', *ELH* 1 (1934), 276–304; Robert D. Hume, 'Diversity and Development in Restoration Comedy, 1660–1679', *Eighteenth-Century Studies* 5.3 (1972), esp. 388; Richard W. Bevis, *English Drama: Restoration and Eighteenth Century, 1660–1789* (London: Longman, 1988), 6, 10; and Brian Corman, *Genre and Generic Change in English Comedy, 1660–1710* (University of Toronto Press, 1993), 15, 20.

that he and his fellow playwrights had a distinct advantage over their pre-decessors in the 'native language' of the day, which was now 'more refined and free' and with 'more wit in conversation' than in the writing of the older poets.[7] In comedy, for example, Renaissance 'humour' and 'innate genius' gave way to Restoration 'wit' and 'external form', as the 'national' comedy of the earlier period become more 'local', focusing on the 'fash-ionable intrigue' of London 'society comedy' and the courtly 'comedy of manners'.[8] Scholars also cite Restoration authors who argued that Renais-sance drama did not conform to the rules prescribed by the French theatre critics of the day, and thus could be regarded as obsolete.[9] Others point to changes in the material conditions of the theatre to explain the appar-ent stylistic division between Renaissance and Restoration drama. Harold Love, for example, argues that a new technology of illusion in the theatre after the Restoration 'predetermined many aspects of the verbal texts of the plays': wing-and-shutter scenery was used for the first time, women's roles were now played by women, parts were no longer doubled, and actors were much more static on stage, enhancing a focus on verbal artistry. Allied to this was a strong sense that this was a new era and '[e]verything was to be reformed in the light of up-to-date values'.[10]

This chapter compares the style of the first crop of Restoration plays with the earlier tradition. Did the writers of the 1660s take up where the dramatists of the 1630s and earlier 1640s left off? Did they return to some earlier celebrated styles like that of Shakespeare, or did they perhaps depart entirely from the 'giant race' and 'attempt some other way', as Dryden suggests? We take ten comedies from the 1660s, each by a different author, and eight tragicomedies from the same period, again with eight different authors, and use methods of computational stylistics to map the dialogue styles of these plays against a large set of earlier plays (243 in total). These plays are listed in Appendix A.

[7] John Dryden, 'Defence of the Epilogue', in *The Conquest of Granada* (London, 1672; Wing D2256), V4r.

[8] George Henry Nettleton, *English Drama of the Restoration and Eighteenth Century (1642–1780)* (New York: Macmillan, 1914), 72. See also Emrys Jones, 'The First West End Comedy', *Proceedings of the British Academy* 68 (1982), 215–58.

[9] Maximilian E. Novak, for example, situates the reception of Shakespeare at the time in a political context in which Whig critics praised Shakespeare and Tory critics supported a rules-based model for artistic creation; see 'The Politics of Shakespeare Criticism in the Restoration and Early Eighteenth Century', *ELH* 81 (2014), 115–42. See also Kathleen M. Lynch, *The Social Mode of Restoration Comedy* (New York: Macmillan, 1926), for a useful account of early criticism.

[10] Harold Love, 'Restoration and Early Eighteenth-Century Drama', in John Richetti (ed.), *The Cambridge History of English Literature, 1660–1780* (Cambridge University Press, 2005), 109–10.

Previous scholarship has typically focused on the themes and attitudes of the plays rather than the patterns of their language – on the participation of a 1660s play about *Henry the Fifth*, for instance, in 'the Restoration moment'.[11] Instead, our interest here is in the style of the plays, lying somewhere between *form*, as in the adoption of heroic couplets, and *themes*, as in implied support for one side or other of an ideological divide. The analysis we present in this chapter suggests that 1660s comedy and tragicomedy reflect continuity with older English drama rather than a new beginning. When the new plays are mapped onto the old, they take their place comfortably with earlier plays in their respective genres. Comedies of the 1660s in particular are aligned with the plays of the 1630s and early 1640s, and we discuss the characteristics of this evolved Caroline dramatic style. Then, turning to authors, we show that the language patterns of the 1660s comedies bring them closest to Richard Brome's style, whether taking the genre aspect into consideration or disregarding it. The style of the 1660s tragicomedies comes closest to James Shirley, again when comparing tragicomedies alone or dealing with a mixed group. We do not find a 'doubling back' in style to earlier periods in pre-1642 drama, therefore, and the plays of the 1660s emerge as natural successors to those of the 1630s and 1640s.

Mapping 1660s Comedies

To compare the styles of the 1660s comedies with patterns in the earlier plays, we perform a Principal Components Analysis (PCA) using the 100 most common function words in the 243 professional-company plays from 1580–1642,[12] applied to a combined set of the 243 plays and 10 1660s comedies – 253 plays in all. Figure 7.1 shows how the play-texts scored on the first and second principal components.

The data-points for 1660s comedies are marked by crosses, late plays from the 1630–42 period with black disks, and comedies from among the 1580–1642 plays with extra circles. The 1660s comedies form a distinctive group on the first principal component (PC1), all to the higher end of the

[11] Tracey E. Tomlinson, 'The Restoration English History Plays of Roger Boyle, Earl of Orrery', SEL: Studies in English Literature, 1500–1900, 43.3 (2003), 564.

[12] The words are, in order of descending frequency: *the, I, and, of, a, you, is, my, to*$_{infinitive}$, *it, in*$_{preposition}$, *not, to*$_{preposition}$, *will*$_{verb}$, *me, your, be, but, with, have, this, he, for*$_{preposition}$, *his, as, what, all, him, thou, that*$_{relative}$, *are, shall, if, do, that*$_{demonstrative}$, *now, thy, we*$_{truePlural}$, *by*$_{preposition}$, *no*$_{adjective}$, *or, that*$_{conjunction}$, *thee, they, at, she, would, so*$_{adverbDegree}$, *then, am, was, here, how, from, there, our*$_{truePlural}$, *her*$_{adjective}$, *o, them, more, their, on*$_{preposition}$, *well, her*$_{personalPronoun}$, *may, for*$_{conjunction}$, *must, when, yet, one, which*$_{relative}$, *us*$_{truePlural}$, *so*$_{adverbManner}$, *were, why, can, should, too, ye, had, than, upon*$_{preposition}$, *such, an, these, out, never, some, hath, where, like*$_{preposition}$, *up*$_{adverb}$, *did, much, most, mine, nor, any, has,* and *no*$_{exclamation}$.

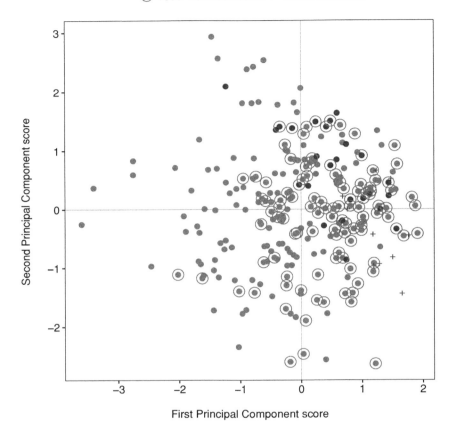

Figure 7.1 PCA scatterplot of 243 plays from 1580 to 1642 and 10 comedies from the
1660s, using the 100 most common function words.

x-axis, and some among the very highest. PC1 would seem to have a *chronol-ogy* component – the 1630–42 plays are mostly, if not all, to the higher end of this axis – as well as a *genre* component, since comedies also cluster to the higher end. This configuration is compatible with the chronology analysis presented in Chapter 5, of a marked temporal effect which runs through a good part of the 1580–1642 set but which peters out in the last four half-decades.

The 1660s comedies are not so sharply different that they form an entirely separate cluster. PC1 is not a '1660s comedies versus the rest' factor.

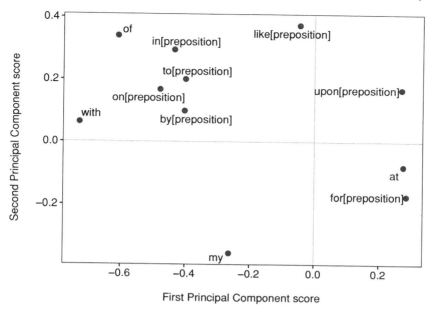

Figure 7.2 Scatterplot of PCA weightings for 11 prepositions in the 100 most common function words across 243 plays from 1580 to 1642 and 10 comedies from the 1660s.

Yet, on a component that has a strong genre and chronology aspect, they are clustered towards one end. Along this axis they are more tightly grouped and generally higher scoring than the 1630–42 plays, perhaps partly because they – unlike the 1630–42 group – are all comedies, and there is a genre aspect to PC1. It may also be perhaps because the 1660 comedies are an extension of a 'drift' in style which had plateaued in the last part of the 1580–1642 period.

The words *with, thy, hath, from, of, the, his, our*trueplural, *their*, and *that*relative had the lowest weightings on PC1 – *with* having the very lowest – and thus are more common in the plays to the lower end of this component in Figure 7.1. The words *it, I, have, you, has, is, a, there, am*, and *would* had the highest weightings and are more common in the plays to the upper end of PC1, with *it* as the highest. This confirms the notion that this component is closely related to the component highlighted in Chapter 5 – with prepositions and *with* in particular at one end, and *I, you*, and auxiliary verbs at the other.

Closer inspection of the PCA weightings of the word-variables thus reveals three large sub-sets: prepositions, verbs, and nouns. Figure 7.2 shows the PCA weightings for the 11 prepositions in the set of the 100 most

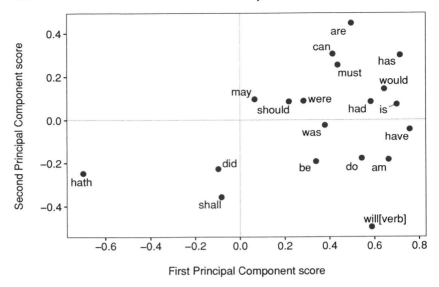

Figure 7.3 Scatterplot of PCA weightings for 19 verbs in the 100 most common function words across 243 plays from 1580 to 1642 and 10 comedies from the 1660s.

common function words. A group of prepositions clusters to the lower end of PC1: *with*, *on*, and *of* are very heavily weighted in a negative direction; *upon*, *at*, and *for* are to the positive end, it is true, but only with medium to low weightings.

The opposite pattern appears in the PCA weightings of the 19 verbs in the 100 most common function words. As shown in Figure 7.3, most have positive weightings on PC1: while *hath* is heavily weighted in the negative direction, complementing *has* in the positive direction, and *did* and *shall* are just to the low side of the PC1 axis, the rest of the verbs cluster to the positive end. *Has*, as already mentioned, *would*, *had*, *is*, *have*, *am*, and *will*$_{verb}$ (as distinguished from the noun form) are among the most heavily weighted variables of all on PC1.

Twenty-three pronouns make up the third large sub-set in the 100 most common function words. Figure 7.4 shows the weightings for this group on PC1 and PC2. The older forms *thy*, *thou*, and *thee* are to the lower end on both axes, and the more modern forms *you* and *your* are to the higher, matching the pattern for *hath* and *has* (Figure 7.3). All the possessives apart from *your* are to the lower end. Evidently, the chronology factor outweighed the possessive factor in this one case. All the subject and object forms apart from *thou*, *thee*, *we*$_{truePlural}$, and *us*$_{truePlural}$ are to the higher end. *It*, *you*, and

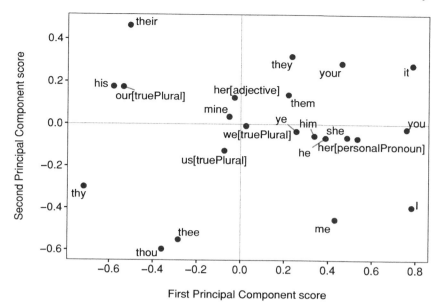

Figure 7.4 Scatterplot of PCA weightings for 23 pronouns and possessives in the 100 most common function words across 243 plays from 1580 to 1642 and 10 comedies from the 1660s.

I are very heavily weighted to the positive end. Generally, a style oriented to reflection, narrative, and description would favour possessives, and a simplified direct style, focused on action and interaction, would favour subject and object pronouns.

To explore further the contrast in style which underlies PC1, we sample the kinds of dialogue that attract high and low scores. We divide the plays into 500-word segments, incorporate any residues into the last segment of a play, and use the word counts for these segments to find them a score along PC1 by multiplying each of the proportional counts for the 100 words by the PC1 weightings for the relevant variable. Each of the 9,823 segments in the 253-play set then has a PC1 score, from the highest, which happens to be the seventh segment of *Love's Cruelty*, to the lowest, the thirteenth segment of *David and Bethsabe* – which was also the lowest in the projection of the 50-word component which arranged the eight half-decades 1585–1624 in chronological order in Chapter 5.

The seventh segment of *Love's Cruelty* has Hippolito receive instruction from a fencer, suffer interruption by a page announcing the arrival of Clariana, and then exchange courtship banter with Clariana. All three kinds of discourse bring clipped, unadorned speech stripped to not much more than verbs and pronouns. The page tells the fencer 'you and I will try a *veny* below',[13] and Clariana declares of her beauty, ''tis as it is, I cannot help it; yet I could paint, if I list' (C3r). When Hippolito asks about her name she replies, 'What would you do with it, if I told you?' (C3r). By contrast, the dialogue in the *David and Bethsabe* segment is rich in elaboration, specification, and illustration. David is as sure of the help of God now as when 'our young men, by the pool of Gibeon, | Went forth against the strength of Ishboseth, | And twelve to twelve did with their weapons play'.[14] Jonadab announces that 'there hath great heaviness befall'n | In Amnon's fields by Absalon's misdeed; | And Amnon's shearers and their feast of mirth | Absalon hath o'erturned with his sword' (7. 73–6). Instead of smart, witty exchanges, there is circumstance and unfolding narrative.

The 1660s comedies fall decisively at the latter end of this axis between a style heavy in prepositions and possessives and one turning on taut, active auxiliary verbs and staccato *I, you,* and *it*. Examining the 1660s comedy segments falling at the upper end of the component, those that have a concentrated version of this style, helps illustrate what the contrasts identified by the statistical analysis mean in terms of dramatic practice.

The forty-fourth 500-word segment of John Wilson's *The Cheats* has a score of 19.41 on PC1 – the highest of the 1660s comedies segments. It comprises the end of Act 5, Scene 3 and the beginning of Scene 4. These unconnected scenes both include exchanges about money: one farcical (Major Bilboe offering the landlord a thousand pounds on behalf of a protesting Alderman Whitebroth), and the other more straightforward (Jolly pressing money on his friend Runter). These are distinctly quotidian exchanges, with fragmented utterances, as in this prose speech of Bilboe's: 'He shall, he shall. Burn it, 'tis but an old house – giv't him. Troth, I was afraid we should not have got him so low! You heard what he said – 'twas for my sake, too. I hope you'll consider it'.[15]

Segment 28 of Dryden's *An Evening's Love* has a score of 19.28 on PC1, the next highest for this group. It comprises Jacinta's demand of 300 pistols from her *inamorato* Wildblood as a gambling stake, and the banter that follows. This is a quarrel in smart dialogue, intimate and insistent. Along the way, Wildblood accuses his man, Maskall, of taking his gold: 'I'll be hanged if he have not lost my gold at play; if you have, confess, and

[13] James Shirley, *Love's Cruelty* (London, 1640; STC 22449), C2v. The word '*veny*', from the French *venue* ('coming on') and misprinted as 'veine' (for 'venie') in the 1640 edition, is a fencing term for a 'hit' or 'thrust'.
[14] George Peele, *David and Bethsabe*, in Fraser and Rabkin (eds.), *Drama*, 1: 7.17–19.
[15] John Wilson, *The Cheats* (London, 1664; Wing W2916), K2v.

perhaps I'll pardon you, but if you do not confess, I'll have no mercy.'[16] This is verisimilar, rather than poetic, dialogue, but supple and witty. The characters make direct demands of each other, and resist just as directly.

The next highest 1660s comedies segment is segment 14 of Thomas Shadwell's *The Sullen Lovers*, which has a PC1 score of 19.19. Huffe, a 'hector' or professional bully, asks Stanford for a loan, is roundly refused, and withdraws. Stanford's man, Roger, then enters and torments him with elaborate preliminaries, which Stanford angrily interrupts – 'one similitude more, and I'll break that fool's head of yours' – finally forcing his message out of him:

> STANFORD. You dog! Tell me quickly or I'll cut your ears off.
> ROGER. Why, Master Lovell would have you come to him.
> What would you have?[17]

The effect is quotidian and colloquial, not exotic. Speakers are direct, aggressive, and impatient. There are unadorned exchanges with inferiors, as with many of the segments with high scores along the component.

Segment 14 of James Howard's *The English Monsieur* is the next highest of the 1660s plays, with a PC1 score of 18.89. It covers a transaction between Vain, his servant Jack, and another hector, in which Vain offers the hector money to refrain from beating him, first through Jack. The dialogue is plain and to the point: Jack inquires, 'An please you, sir, are not you employed as being a stout man to beat a gentleman here this evening?' The hector replies, 'Aye, boy. It is your master then, it seems.'[18]

The next highest 1660s comedies segment is segment 26 of Shadwell's *Sullen Lovers*, with a PC1 score of 18.78. The 'sullen' or inhibited lovers of the title, Stanford and Emilia, discuss how to escape the attentions of the foolish obsessive characters, while expressing their admiration of each other in asides. This is a jerky dialogue of farcical distractions. Here, for example, Stanford fends off the attentions of Sir Positive At-all, who interrupts the lovers' exchange:

> SIR POSITIVE. Jack? Hark ye?
> STANFORD. For Heaven's sake! I have business.
> SIR POSITIVE. 'Tis all one for that, sir. Why, I'll tell you –
> STANFORD. Another time; I beseech you, don't interrupt me now.
> SIR POSITIVE. 'Faith, but I must interrupt you.

> (G1r)

[16] John Dryden, *An Evening's Love* (London, 1671; Wing D2273), F3v.
[17] Thomas Shadwell, *The Sullen Lovers* (London, 1668; Wing S2878), D3v–D4r.
[18] James Howard, *The English Monsieur* (London, 1674; Wing H2980), D4r.

The last part of the segment is an exchange between the play's more conventional lovers, Lovell and Emilia's sister, Carolina, on their marriage plans. Here the wit flows more smoothly, but the focus is still on immediate contingencies, rather than recollection or narrative:

> CAROLINA. I know you cannot love me; she's [= Lady Vain] your delight.
> LOVELL. Yes, yes, I delight in her as I do in the toothache! I love her immoderately, as an English tailor loves a French tailor that's set up the next door to him.
>
> (G1v)

The next highest of this group, and the last we shall discuss here, is segment 7 of William Cavendish's *The Humorous Lovers*, which has a PC1 score of 18.40. A flowery exchange between the lovers Courtly and Emilia is overheard by Colonel Boldman and the widow Lady Pleasant. Boldman's reaction to the lovers' talk is gruff:

> What language is this, madam? The Devil take me if I know what it is . . . [I]t has a touch here and there of English; I would you could make me understand it, madam.[19]

The exchanges of this second couple occupy most of the segment. The widow is frank and outspoken; the colonel sceptical and sardonic, speaking in a manner described by the widow as the 'rougher dialect' of a soldier (C2v). After some verbal skirmishing, Lady Pleasant directly declares her love for Boldman: 'Why then, 'tis that I love you' (C3r). The effect is of verisimilitude through a conscious contrast with the poetical, and a striking frankness.

The dialogue of the 1660s comedies is clipped and staccato compared with pre-1642 drama in general, distinctly colloquial and shorn of elaboration and detail. In this, it fits a tendency in genre and chronology already present in the earlier drama, rather than standing outside it. To confirm this finding, we repeat the experiment using the 100 most common lexical rather than function words.[20] Figure 7.5 shows the resulting PCA scatterplot. Once again, the 1660s comedies score highly on the first principal component and are plotted to the right-hand end of the chart.

---

[19] William Cavendish, *The Humorous Lovers* (London, 1677; Wing N883), C2v.
[20] In descending order of frequency, the 100 most common lexical words are: *go, say, tell, men, lady, away, death, father, aye, two, god, madam, beast, old, little, better, yes, friend, stand, call, else, gentleman, indeed, noble, once, part, set, friends, thought, face, therefore, welcome, fortune, gentlemen, full, words, cause, marry, husband, honest, makes, sister, daughter, came, new, end, three, farewell, state, care, pardon, will*$_{noun}$, *thoughts, heard, nature, strange, thousand, sent, kind, sword, earth, matter, alas, gold, pleasure, work, trust, body, answer, brave, run, reason, company, happy, next, beauty, fathers, worth, charge, command, together, told, like*$_{verb}$, *sit, alone, content, just, gentle, hell, wench, youth, present, base, given, whole, cast, presently, excellent, land*, and *remember*.

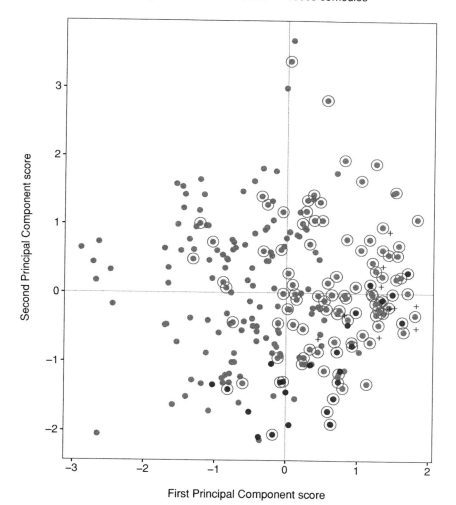

Figure 7.5 PCA scatterplot of 243 plays from 1580 to 1642 and 10 comedies from the 1660s, using the 100 most common lexical words.

Figure 7.6 shows the weightings for these lexical words on the two principal components, with the ten most heavily weighted words in each direction labelled.

The words at the extreme lower (left-hand) end of the first component (*earth* and *death*) relate to elemental forces. Other words at the lower

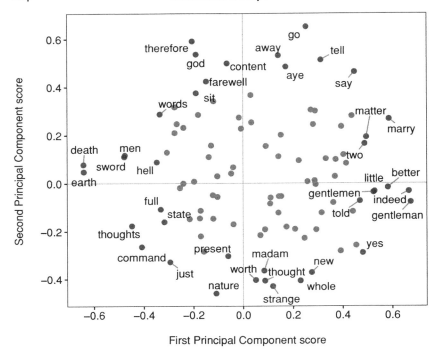

Figure 7.6 Scatterplot of PCA weightings for the 100 most common lexical words in 243
plays from 1580 to 1642 and 10 comedies from the 1660s.

end relate to armies and battle (*men*, *sword*, and *command*), and suggest
reflexiveness about solemn thinking and speaking (*thoughts* and *words*) and
heightened emotions (*full*, *base*, and *hell*). These are opposed on this axis
to words used in gossip and commonplace exchanges (*indeed*, *marry*, *little*,
yes, *better*, and *matter*) and words marking social distinction (*gentleman* and
gentlemen). Although not especially characteristic of the 1630–42 plays, as
Figure 7.5 shows, these words are generally associated with comedy. The
1660s comedies take to extremes the characteristics of pre-1642 comedy,
and, by the same token, are more remote from sombre and violent preoccupations than the earlier comedies, or the plays of the last decade before
the closing of the theatres.

Mapping 1660s Tragicomedies

To compare the styles of the 1660s tragicomedies with patterns in the earlier
plays, we repeat the procedures above, beginning with a PCA using the

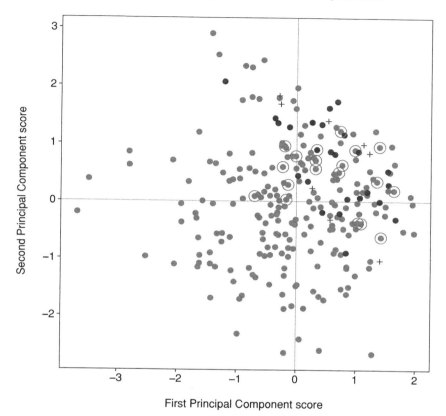

Figure 7.7 PCA scatterplot of 243 plays from 1580 to 1642 and 8 tragicomedies from the 1660s, using the 100 most common function words.

100 most common function words in the 243 professional-company plays from 1580 to 1642, applied to a combined set of the 243 plays and eight 1660s tragicomedies – 251 plays in all. Figure 7.7 shows how the plays scored on the first and second principal components.

The 1660s tragicomedies appear at the right-hand, higher-scoring end of PC1, but share an area of the chart with 1630–42 plays and with pre-1642 tragicomedies. In this assay of style, the 1660s tragicomedies present continuity with the earlier patterns rather than any marked departure. One play, James Howard's *All Mistaken*, stands outside the main cluster, to the high end of PC1 and lower than the other 1660s tragicomedies on PC2. *Henry the Fifth* by Roger Boyle, Earl of Orrery, is to the opposite extreme, plotted as a cross in the top left of the chart. The contrast here is between the public focus of Boyle's history play and the more private orientation of Howard's, which is likely to score it lower on PC2. *All Mistaken* also has a strong comic element through its 'carnivalesque' sub-plot, which is likely to score it higher along PC1.[21]

As before, we perform a PCA using the 100 most common lexical words, rather than function words (shown in Figure 7.8), accompanied by a scatterplot of PCA weightings for these words on the two principal components, with the ten most heavily weighted words in each direction labelled (Figure 7.9).

In this analysis, the 1660s tragicomedies are clustered to the low-scoring end of PC2, with the exception of one play – James Howard's *All Mistaken*, plotted with a cross in the upper right of Figure 7.8. As the most heavily weighted words labelled in Figure 7.9 suggest, PC2 seems to range from philosophical preoccupations (*nature, strange, thought*) and address to a senior female (*madam*) at the lower end, to a focus on immediate interpersonal activity (*go, away, tell*), and an abusive and emphatic element (*god, base*) at the higher end.

Edward Howard's 1660s tragicomedy, *The Change of Crowns*, is the lowest-scoring play on PC2 and the anonymous 1580s history play, *The Famous Victories of Henry the Fifth*, the highest-scoring. If we project 500-word segments on PC2, we find segment 37 of Jonson's *The Devil is an Ass* at the bottom, followed by segment 13 of Shirley's *The Royal Master* and then segment 4 of Howard's *Change of Crowns*. The Jonson segment has Lady Eitherside and Lady Tailbush discuss cosmetics and then entertain what they think is a Spanish lady, in fact Wittipol in disguise. Pretentious courtesy abounds. The Shirley passage covers the end of one scene, another short scene, and the beginning of a third – all courtly exchanges on the subject of courtship and love. The passage from *Change of Crowns* is also set in a court, with an emissary from the King of Lombardy presenting a proposal of marriage to the Queen of Naples, followed by a courtier with news of the Queen's sister, Ariana, after which Ariana enters and learns that her father is dead, with all that that implies about the succession to the kingdom.

By contrast, the highest-scoring 500-word segments are from *Famous Victories* (segments 16 and 2; highest and third highest respectively) and

[21] J. Douglas Canfield, *Tricksters and Estates: On the Ideology of Restoration Comedy* (Lexington: University Press of Kentucky, 1997), 152–3.

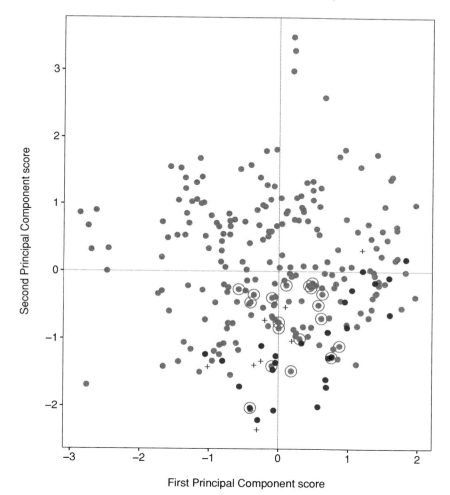

Figure 7.8 PCA scatterplot of 243 plays from 1580 to 1642 and 8 tragicomedies from the 1660s, using the 100 most common lexical words.

2 Henry the Sixth (segment 36; second highest). Segment 16 of *Famous Victories* covers the recruiting activities of a captain meeting reluctance from a cobbler and a thief – plain, angular encounters. The second segment has the Prince conversing with his tavern companions. The passage from

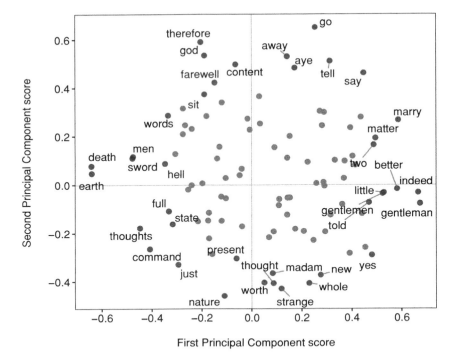

Figure 7.9 Scatterplot of PCA weightings for the 100 most common lexical words in 243
plays from 1580 to 1642 and 8 tragicomedies from the 1660s.

2 Henry the Sixth comprises Jack Cade interviews with various followers
and opponents – generally combative, abrupt, and abusive.

The 1660s tragicomedies are generally to the lower end of PC2, marked
out among the generality of 1580–1642 drama as notably courtly and reflective. Four Shirley plays appear among the lowest seven on the component.

1660s Comedies and Tragicomedies and pre-1642 Authors

In addition to mapping the comedies and tragicomedies of the 1660s
using PCA in relation to each other and pre-1642 drama, we can also use
Delta to place the 1660s plays in relation to playwrights from the earlier
period.

Delta is more typically used in attribution studies, but this experiment
is not intended to establish authorship, which is not contested for any of
the plays (and the pre-1642 playwrights would not be candidates in any

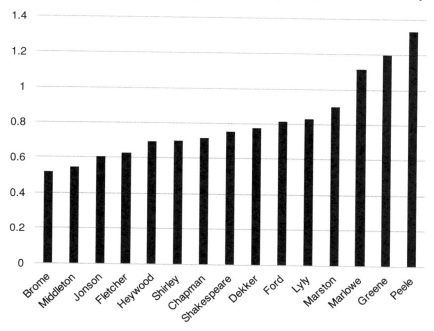

Figure 7.10 Delta distances between a composite text of 10 1660s comedies and 15 playwrights with 4 or more pre-1642 plays, using the 100 most common function words.

case). Rather, the idea is to establish stylistic likeness. This is a matter of relative closeness only, since one playwright will necessarily be judged closest regardless of closeness in any absolute sense.

For this experiment, we treat the ten 1660s comedies as a single test text, averaging their word counts for the list of the 100 most common function words already used earlier in this chapter, and calculate a distance between each playwright with four or more pre-1642 plays and this combined text. Figure 7.10 shows the results.

Brome is the closest author to the composite text of 1660s comedies, followed by Middleton and Jonson. Peele, Greene, and Marlowe, all writing in the 1580s and 1590s, have high Delta scores – that is, are judged to be stylistically different from the 1660s comedies.

We repeat the procedure, this time using the 100 most common lexical words. As shown in Figure 7.11, Brome remains the closest author to the composite text of 1660s comedies, with the lowest Delta score. While order changes, the three highest-scoring and three lowest-scoring authors are the same as in Figure 7.10. Among the fifteen authors we tested, Brome is the

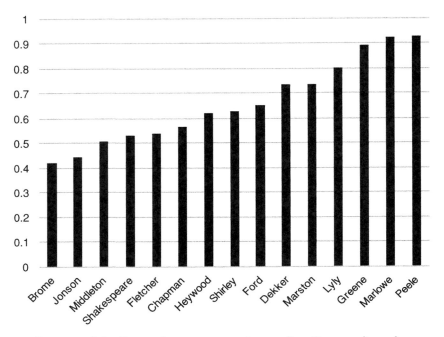

Figure 7.11 Delta distances between a composite text of 10 1660s comedies and 15 playwrights with 4 or more pre-1642 plays, using the 100 most common lexical words.

closest stylistic match with the composite 1660s comedies text, with both function and lexical words.

Mindful of genre factors, we ran the same tests with comic plays, including all the plays in the set defined by the *Annals* as 'Comedy', 'Comic Pastoral', 'Classical Legend (Comedy)', 'Domestic Comedy', and 'Romantic Comedy'. Ten authors have four or more comic plays by this definition, comprising eighty plays in all. For both tests, Brome was the closest author. Lyly was the most distant, corresponding to Figure 7.11 (since Marston, Marlowe, Greene, and Peele did not have enough comic plays in their canons to figure in the comic-plays set).[22]

Brome is placed closest to the 1660s comedies each time. His comedy shows citizens aspiring to the world of fashion.[23] This is satiric rather than

[22] In ascending order of Delta scores, the playwrights were Brome, Middleton, Chapman, Jonson, Fletcher, Shakespeare, Dekker, Shirley, Marston, and Lyly when using the 100 most common function words, and Brome, Jonson, Shakespeare, Middleton, Chapman, Fletcher, Marston, Shirley, Dekker, and Lyly when using the 100 most common lexical words.

[23] Lynch, *Social Mode*, 34.

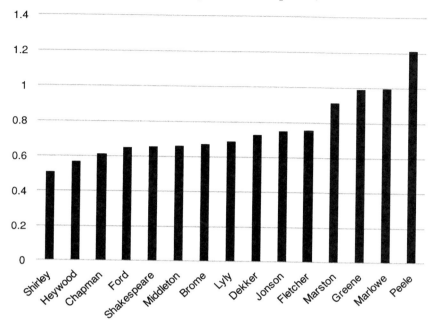

Figure 7.12 Delta distances between a composite text of 8 1660s tragicomedies and 15 playwrights with 4 or more pre-1642 plays, using the 100 most common function words.

romantic comedy, with contemporary urban settings. Once the alignment is posited by the analysis, it is possible to see a likeness between this blend and the 1660s comedies, which are also urban, satiric, and contemporary, and to accept that of the fifteen mixed-genre and ten comic-play playwrights, Brome might be on balance the best match.

As before, we repeat the procedure, substituting tragicomedies for comedies and treating the eight 1660s tragicomedies as a composite text. After averaging their word counts for the list of the 100 most common function words, we calculate a distance between each playwright with four or more pre-1642 plays and this combined 1660s tragicomedies text (Figure 7.12).

This time, Brome is the seventh closest author and Shirley the closest. The three authors with the highest scores (and thus the least similar in style) are the familiar trio of Peele, Marlowe, and Greene. When lexical rather than function words are used (Figure 7.13), Shirley is again the closest and Peele the most distant, but the order of the others is considerably different.[24]

---

[24] Jonson, for instance, moves from tenth closest in Figure 7.12 to the second closest in Figure 7.13.

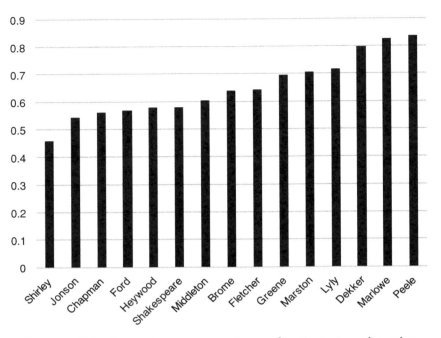

Figure 7.13 Delta distances between a composite text of 8 1660s tragicomedies and 15 playwrights with 4 or more pre-1642 plays, using the 100 most common lexical words.

Shirley's plays depict polite society with a moralising overlay, which may explain why they align so strongly with the 1660s tragicomedies, but less so with the 1660s comedies, which have a stronger satiric thrust.[25] A. H. Nason described Shirley as 'the prophet of the Restoration',[26] and G. K. Hunter argued that Shirley arrived at 'the very threshold of Restoration comedy'.[27] Our analysis supports this connection, but only in relation to tragicomedy, given that Shirley is placed in the middle ranks or with the more remote authors in the four tests with the 1660s comedies described above.

Conclusion

In this chapter, we address a commonly asked question – how do Restoration plays relate in style to pre-1642 drama? – but we frame the question in

[25] Lynch, *Social World*, 42–3.
[26] A. H. Nason, *James Shirley, Dramatist: A Biographical and Critical Study* (New York: A. H. Nason, 1915), 1.
[27] G. K. Hunter, *English Drama*, 415.

a very specific way. How do select groups of plays, namely a set of ten 1660s comedies and one of eight 1660s tragicomedies, relate to a mixed group of pre-1642 plays?

Existing commentary has tended to focus on an individual predecessor such as Shakespeare, Jonson, or Fletcher, or on a wider sweep of Restoration drama, such as from 1660 to Congreve's *The Way of the World* (1700), or on selected Restoration authors such as Dryden or Etherege. Thus we are answering a question about Restoration drama not previously asked in this precise way. However, there are some general observations to be made. Our study supports continuity rather than rupture as a literary history connecting pre-1642 and 1660s English drama. Comedy of the 1660s aligns with the 1630–42 plays, and a number of ways to characterise the style of this alignment emerge. Tragicomedy of the 1660s fits the wider pattern of pre-1642 drama as well as it does plays of the 1630–42 period, and is as much traditional as modern. The analysis highlights Brome as a fore-runner of 1660s comedy, and puts Shirley to the fore as a precursor of 1660s tragicomedy.

Overall, the analysis suggests that the plays of the 1660s fit comfortably as successors to their forebears from the 1620s, 1630s, and 1640s. Despite the eighteen-year theatrical hiatus, the vastly changed social and political context, and developments in staging and dramaturgy, the plays of the 1660s take their place as the natural heirs of Caroline drama. In style, they neither revert back to earlier phases of pre-war drama – showing no special likeness to Shakespeare, for instance, despite his critical reputation in the period – nor take off in a new direction. The 1660s comedies are notably colloquial and clipped in their dialogue. The 1660s tragicomedies belong at the reflective and philosophical end of a spectrum between courtly and abrupt exchanges. Looking from the end of the pre-war era, they would seem modern, but not outlandish. The next question is whether, after this conservative beginning, change accelerated in the next decades of the Restoration, but this takes us beyond the limits of this particular study and beyond the ambit of our book.

Coda

In an oft-cited lecture on 'The Application of Thought to Textual Criticism', A. E. Housman remarked:

> A textual critic engaged upon his business is not at all like Newton investigating the motions of the planets: he is much more like a dog hunting for fleas. If a dog hunted for fleas on mathematical principles, basing his researches on statistics of area and population, he would never catch a flea except by accident. They require to be treated as individuals; and every problem which presents itself to the textual critic must be regarded as possibly unique.[1]

While the practice may not have been widespread in the 1920s when Housman was writing, biological researchers now routinely track the movement and behaviour of fleas using mathematical models.[2] Despite our best efforts, dogs remain frustratingly unable to perform even rudimentary statistics.

In fact, the groundwork for such investigations had been in place since 1907, when the Dutch physicists Paul and Tatiana Ehrenfest introduced a statistical model to describe the jumps of a given population of fleas between two dogs,[3] a model praised as 'probably one of the most instructive

---

[1] A. E. Housman, 'The Application of Thought to Textual Criticism', *Proceedings of the Classical Association* 18 (1921), 68–9.

[2] Representative studies include Sergei Petrovskii, Natalia Petrovskaya, and Daniel Bearup, 'Multiscale Approach to Pest Insect Monitoring: Random Walks, Pattern Formation, Synchronization, and Networks', *Physics of Life Reviews* 11.3 (2014), 467–525; Frédéric Beugnet et al., 'Use of a Mathematical Model to Study the Dynamics of *Ctenocephalides Felis* Populations in the Home Environment and the Impact of Various Control Measures', *Parasite* 11.4 (2004), 387–99; and Jim Hanan et al., 'Simulation of Insect Movement with Respect to Plant Architecture and Morphogenesis', *Computers and Electronics in Agriculture* 35.2–3 (2002), 255–69.

[3] Paul and Tatiana Ehrenfest, 'Über zwei bekannte Einwände gegen das Boltzmannsche H-Theorem', *Physikalische Zeitschrift* 8 (1907), 311–14. On the Ehrenfest dog–flea model, see also Vinay Ambegaokar, *Reasoning about Luck: Probability and Its Uses in Physics* (Cambridge University Press, 1996), 172–7; and Christoph Hauert, Jan Nagler, and Heinz Georg Schuster, 'Of Dogs and Fleas: The Dynamics of N Uncoupled Two-State Systems', *Journal of Statistical Physics* 116.5–6 (2004), 1453–69.

models in the whole of Physics'[4] and 'mentioned in almost every textbook of probability, stochastic processes and statistical physics'.[5]

Although he may not have been familiar with the statistical physics literature of his day, Housman was no luddite; he was simply refuting the idea that the work of the textual critic was essentially systematic and a matter of following abstract rules. Given its materials, textual criticism, according to Housman, must be a series of separate individual responses to unrelated local problems. In stylistics, as in textual criticism, each problem has aspects unique to itself. Yet each one also has enough aspects in common with others (we believe) to make comparison and aggregation feasible. Acknowledging these two truths, our own research practice is to combine the traditional methods of the literary historian (some of which, like close reading and analytical bibliography, overlap with methods Housman would recognise) with new modes of analysis (e.g. text mining and data visualisation, computational stylistics, multivariate statistical analysis, and algorithmic criticism), and to do so critically, aiming to apply the logic and common sense to which Housman appeals.

This combination of qualitative and quantitative methods allows us to shift between microscopic and macroscopic modes of inquiry – to zoom in on an individual flea in isolation, to zoom out to observe relationships between groupings of fleas, or to zoom out further to appreciate the larger ecology of the dog – to explore the fine details, as well as their contexts.

Clifford Geertz describes this 'characteristic intellectual movement' as 'a continuous dialectical tacking between the most local of local detail and the most global of global structures in such a way as to bring them into simultaneous view'. For Geertz, this 'inward conceptual rhythm',

> Hopping back and forth between the whole conceived through the parts that actualize it and the parts conceived through the whole that motivates them, we seek to turn them, by a sort of intellectual perpetual motion, into explications of one another.[6]

We are aware that our work is a long way short of offering a unified theory of dramatic language, or of early modern drama – that we have remained

---

[4] Mark Kac, 'Probability in Some Problems of Classical Statistical Mechanics', in his *Probability and Related Topics in Physical Sciences* (New York: Interscience Publishers, 1959), 73.
[5] Domenico Costantini and Ubaldo Garibaldi, 'A Stochastic Foundation of the Approach to Equilibrium of Classical and Quantum Gases', in Claudio Garola and Arcangelo Rossi (eds.), *The Foundations of Quantum Mechanics: Historical Analysis and Open Questions* (New Jersey: World Scientific Publishing Co., 2000), 137.
[6] Clifford Geertz, '"From the Native's Point of View": On the Nature of Anthropological Understanding', in his *Local Knowledge: Further Essays in Interpretive Anthropology* (New York: Basic Books, 1983), 69.

closer, perhaps, to the flea-biting dog than to Newton describing planetary motion. Nevertheless, we have tried to combine the local and the general in the way Geertz describes. We have also tried to work between the qualitative and quantitative poles of method. In this spirit, we like to think that our findings about particular areas — about when verse and prose contrast in dramatic style, and when not; about the separate stylistic identity of dramatic characters; about the distribution of props by author, genre, and company; about collective stylistic changes over time; about company style; and about the way 1660s plays map onto Elizabethan, Jacobean, and Caroline drama — may be of interest to those who will never conduct a t-test or a PCA. Better yet, our findings may even prompt some readers to try an experiment of their own to test our claims. Our hope is that the chapters of this book serve to illustrate the possibilities for a future mobile criticism, in which mainstream and computational methods will be able to test and invigorate each other, lead to better answers to some specific literary questions, and uncover hitherto hidden aspects of the working of literary language.

APPENDIX A

Play-Texts in the Full Corpus

For the following list, our main bibliographical source is the second edition of the *Annals of English Drama, 975–1700*. 'Date' refers to date of first performances, unless marked with an obelisk ('†') to indicate date of composition or with a diesis ('‡') to indicate date of revision. Copy-texts for printed playbooks are cited by STC and Wing reference, whereas copy-texts for plays in manuscript are sourced from later print editions, typically the Malone Society Reprints ('MSR') editions where available.

Author	Play	Date	Copy-text	Copy-text date	Genre
Armin, Robert	The Two Maids of Mortlake	1608	STC 773	1609	Comedy
Barkstead, William; Machin, Lewis; Marston, John	The Insatiate Countess	1610	STC 17476	1613	Tragedy
Barry, Lording	Ram Alley	1608	STC 1502	1611	Comedy
Beaumont, Francis	The Knight of the Burning Pestle	1607	STC 1674	1613	Burlesque romance
Beaumont, Francis; Fletcher, John	A King and No King	1611	Wing B1582	1679	Comedy
Beaumont, Francis; Fletcher, John	The Maid's Tragedy	1610	STC 1676	1619	Tragedy
Boothby, Frances	Marcelia	1669	Wing B3742	1670	Tragicomedy
Boyle, Roger	Henry the Fifth	1664	Wing O480	1668	Tragicomedy
Brandon, Samuel	The Virtuous Octavia	1598†	STC 3544	1598	Tragicomedy (Closet)
Brome, Richard	The City Wit	1630	Wing B4870	1653	Comedy
Brome, Richard	The Court Beggar	1640	Wing B4870	1653	Comedy
Brome, Richard	Covent Garden Weeded	1632	Wing B4872	1658	Comedy

(cont.)

227

(cont.)

Author	Play	Date	Copy-text	Copy-text date	Genre
Brome, Richard	*The Damoiselle*	1638	Wing B4870	1653	Comedy
Brome, Richard	*A Jovial Crew*	1641	Wing B4873	1652	Comedy
Brome, Richard	*A Mad Couple Well Matched*	1639	Wing B4870	1653	Comedy
Brome, Richard	*The New Academy*	1635	Wing B4872	1658	Comedy
Brome, Richard	*The Northern Lass*	1629	STC 3819	1632	Comedy
Brome, Richard	*The Novella*	1632	Wing B4870	1653	Comedy
Brome, Richard	*The Sparagus Garden*	1635	STC 3820	1640	Comedy
Cary, Elizabeth	*The Tragedy of Mariam*	1604†	STC 4613	1613	Tragedy (Closet)
Cary, Henry	*The Marriage Night*	1663	Wing F315	1664	Tragicomedy
Cavendish, William; others (?)	*The Humorous Lovers*	1667	Wing N883	1677	Comedy
Chapman, George	*All Fools*	1604	STC 4963	1605	Comedy
Chapman, George	*1 The Blind Beggar of Alexandria*	1596	STC 4965	1598	Comedy
Chapman, George	*Bussy D'Ambois*	1604	STC 22302	1607	Foreign history
Chapman, George	*Byron's Conspiracy*	1608	STC 4968	1608	Tragedy
Chapman, George	*Byron's Tragedy*	1608	STC 4968	1608	Tragedy
Chapman, George	*Caesar and Pompey*	1605	STC 4993	1631	Classical history
Chapman, George	*The Gentleman Usher*	1602	STC 4978	1606	Comedy
Chapman, George	*An Humorous Day's Mirth*	1597	STC 4987	1599	Comedy
Chapman, George	*May Day*	1602	STC 4980	1611	Comedy
Chapman, George	*Monsieur D'Olive*	1604	STC 4984	1606	Comedy
Chapman, George	*The Revenge of Bussy D'Ambois*	1610	STC 4989	1613	Tragedy
Chapman, George	*Sir Giles Goosecap*	1602	STC 12050	1606	Comedy
Chapman, George	*The Widow's Tears*	1605	STC 4994	1612	Comedy
Chettle, Henry	*The Tragedy of Hoffman*	1602	STC 5125	1631	Tragedy
Cooke, John (?)	*Greene's Tu Quoque*	1611	STC 5673	1614	Comedy
Daborne, Robert	*A Christian Turned Turk*	1610	STC 6184	1612	Tragedy
Daniel, Samuel	*Cleopatra*	1607‡	STC 6240	1607	Tragedy (Closet)
Davenant, William	*The Unfortunate Lovers*	1638	Wing D348	1643	Tragedy

Author	Play	Date	Copy-text	Copy-text date	Genre
Day, John	*Humour Out of Breath*	1608	STC 6411	1608	Comedy
Day, John	*The Isle of Gulls*	1606	STC 6412	1606	Comedy
Dekker, Thomas	*2 The Honest Whore*	1605	STC 6506	1630	Comedy
Dekker, Thomas	*If It Be Not Good, the Devil Is In It*	1611	STC 6507	1612	Comedy
Dekker, Thomas	*1 Old Fortunatus*	1599	STC 6517	1600	Comedy
Dekker, Thomas	*The Shoemaker's Holiday*	1599	STC 6523	1600	Comedy
Dekker, Thomas	*The Whore of Babylon*	1606	STC 6532	1607	Allegorical history
Dekker, Thomas; Webster, John	*Sir Thomas Wyatt*	1604	STC 6537	1607	History
Dryden, John	*An Evening's Love*	1668	Wing D2273	1671	Comedy
Dryden, John	*The Rival Ladies*	1664	Wing D2346	1664	Tragicomedy
Etherege, George	*The Comical Revenge*	1664	Wing E3367	1664	Comedy
Field, Nathan	*Amends for Ladies*	1611	STC 10851	1618	Comedy
Field, Nathan; Fletcher, John; Massinger, Philip	*The Honest Man's Fortune*	1613	Wing B1581	1647	Tragicomedy
Fletcher, John	*Bonduca*	1613	Wing B1581	1647	Tragedy
Fletcher, John	*The Chances*	1625	Wing B1581	1647	Comedy
Fletcher, John	*The Faithful Shepherdess*	1608	STC 11068	1610	Pastoral
Fletcher, John	*The Humorous Lieutenant*	1619	Wing B1581	1647	Tragicomedy
Fletcher, John	*The Island Princess*	1621	Wing B1581	1647	Tragicomedy
Fletcher, John	*The Loyal Subject*	1618	Wing B1581	1647	Tragicomedy
Fletcher, John	*The Mad Lover*	1617	Wing B1581	1647	Tragicomedy
Fletcher, John	*Monsieur Thomas*	1615	Wing B1581	1647	Comedy
Fletcher, John	*The Pilgrim*	1621	Wing B1581	1647	Comedy
Fletcher, John	*Rule a Wife and Have a Wife*	1624	Wing B1582	1679	Comedy
Fletcher, John	*Valentinian*	1614	Wing B1581	1647	Tragedy
Fletcher, John	*A Wife for a Month*	1624	Wing B1581	1647	Comedy
Fletcher, John	*The Wild-Goose Chase*	1621	Wing B1616	1652	Comedy
Fletcher, John	*The Woman's Prize*	1611	Wing B1581	1647	Comedy

(cont.)

(cont.)

Author	Play	Date	Copy-text	Copy-text date	Genre
Fletcher, John	*Women Pleased*	1620	Wing B1581	1647	Tragicomedy
Fletcher, John; Beaumont, Francis (?)	*The Captain*	1612	Wing B1581	1647	Comedy
Fletcher, John; Massinger, Philip	*The Double Marriage*	1620	Wing B1581	1647	Tragedy
Fletcher, John; Massinger, Philip; others (?)	*The Bloody Brother*	1619	STC 11064	1639	Tragedy
Fletcher, John; Shakespeare, William	*Henry the Eighth*	1613	STC 22273	1623	History
Fletcher, John; Shakespeare, William	*The Two Noble Kinsmen*	1613	STC 11075	1634	Tragicomedy
Fletcher, John; Shirley, James (?)	*Wit Without Money*	1614	STC 1691	1639	Comedy
Ford, John	*The Broken Heart*	1629	STC 11156	1633	Tragedy
Ford, John	*The Fancies Chaste and Noble*	1635	STC 11159	1638	Comedy
Ford, John	*The Lady's Trial*	1638	STC 11161	1639	Comedy
Ford, John	*Love's Sacrifice*	1632	STC 11164	1633	Tragedy
Ford, John	*The Lover's Melancholy*	1628	STC 11163	1629	Tragicomedy
Ford, John	*Perkin Warbeck*	1633	STC 11157	1634	History
Ford, John	*'Tis Pity She's a Whore*	1632	STC 11165	1633	Tragedy
Goffe, Thomas	*The Courageous Turk*	1618	STC 11977	1632	Tragedy
Greene, Robert	*Alphonsus, King of Aragon*	1587	STC 12233	1599	Heroical romance
Greene, Robert	*Friar Bacon and Friar Bungay*	1589	STC 12267	1594	Comedy
Greene, Robert	*James the Fourth*	1590	STC 12308	1598	History
Greene, Robert	*Orlando Furioso*	1591	STC 12265	1594	Romantic comedy
Greene, Robert; Lodge, Thomas	*A Looking Glass for London and England*	1590	STC 16680	1598	Biblical Moral
Greville, Fulke	*Mustapha*	1596†	STC 12362	1608	Tragedy (Closet)

Author	Play	Date	Copy-text	Copy-text date	Genre
Haughton, William	*The Devil and His Dame*	1600	Wing G1580	1662	Comedy
Haughton, William	*Englishmen for My Money*	1598	STC 12931	1616	Comedy
Heywood, Thomas	*A Challenge for Beauty*	1635	STC 13311	1636	Tragicomedy
Heywood, Thomas	*The English Traveller*	1625	STC 13315	1633	Tragicomedy
Heywood, Thomas	*1 The Fair Maid of the West*	1610	STC 13320	1631	Comedy
Heywood, Thomas	*2 The Fair Maid of the West*	1631	STC 13320	1631	Comedy
Heywood, Thomas	*The Four Prentices of London*	1600	STC 13321	1615	Heroical romance
Heywood, Thomas	*1 If You Know Not Me You Know Nobody*	1604	STC 13328	1605	History
Heywood, Thomas	*2 If You Know Not Me You Know Nobody*	1605	STC 13336	1606	History
Heywood, Thomas	*The Rape of Lucrece*	1607	STC 13363	1638	Tragedy
Heywood, Thomas	*The Wise Woman of Hoxton*	1604	STC 13370	1638	Comedy
Heywood, Thomas	*A Woman Killed with Kindness*	1603	STC 13371	1607	Tragedy
Heywood, Thomas; others (?)	*1 Edward the Fourth*	1599	STC 13341	1599	History
Heywood, Thomas; others (?)	*2 Edward the Fourth*	1599	STC 13341	1599	History
Howard, Edward	*The Change of Crowns*	1667	Boas (ed.)	1949	Tragicomedy
Howard, James	*All Mistaken*	1667	Wing H2979	1672	Tragicomedy
Howard, James	*The English Monsieur*	1663	Wing H2980	1674	Comedy
Howard, Robert	*The Committee*	1662	Wing H2995	1665	Comedy
Jonson, Ben	*The Alchemist*	1610	STC 14755	1612	Comedy
Jonson, Ben	*Bartholomew Fair*	1614	STC 14753.5	1631	Comedy

(cont.)

Author	Play	Date	Copy-text	Copy-text date	Genre
Jonson, Ben	The Case is Altered	1597	STC 14757	1609	Comedy
Jonson, Ben	Catiline His Conspiracy	1611	STC 14759	1611	Tragedy
Jonson, Ben	Cynthia's Revels	1601	STC 14773	1601	Comedy
Jonson, Ben	The Devil is an Ass	1616	STC 14754	1640	Comedy
Jonson, Ben	Epicene	1609	STC 14751	1616	Comedy
Jonson, Ben	Every Man in His Humour	1598	STC 14766	1601	Comedy
Jonson, Ben	Every Man Out of His Humour	1599	STC 14767	1600	Comedy
Jonson, Ben	The Magnetic Lady	1632	STC 14754	1640	Comedy
Jonson, Ben	The New Inn	1629	STC 14780	1631	Comedy
Jonson, Ben	The Poetaster	1601	STC 14781	1602	Comedy
Jonson, Ben	The Sad Shepherd	1637	STC 14754	1640	Comic pastoral
Jonson, Ben	Sejanus His Fall	1603	STC 14782	1605	Tragedy
Jonson, Ben	The Staple of News	1626	STC 14753.5	1631	Comedy
Jonson, Ben	The Tale of a Tub	1633	STC 14754	1640	Comedy
Jonson, Ben	Volpone	1606	STC 14783	1607	Comedy
Killigrew, William	Selindra	1662	Wing K470	1665	Tragicomedy
Kyd, Thomas	Soliman and Perseda	1590	STC 22894	1592?	Tragedy
Kyd, Thomas	The Spanish Tragedy	1587	STC 15086	1592	Tragedy
Kyd, Thomas (trans.)	Cornelia	1594†	STC 11622	1594	Tragedy (Closet?)
Lacy, John	The Old Troop	1664	Wing L114	1672	Comedy
Lodge, Thomas	The Wounds of Civil War	1588	STC 16678	1594	Classical history
Lyly, John	Campaspe	1584	STC 17088	1632	Classical legend (comedy)
Lyly, John	Endymion	1588	STC 17050	1591	Classical legend (comedy)
Lyly, John	Galatea	1585	STC 17080	1592	Classical legend (comedy)
Lyly, John	Love's Metamorphosis	1590	STC 17082	1601	Pastoral
Lyly, John	Midas	1589	STC 17088	1632	Comedy

Author	Play	Date	Copy-text	Copy-text date	Genre
Lyly, John	*Mother Bombie*	1589	STC 17084	1594	Comedy
Lyly, John	*Sappho and Phao*	1584	STC 17086	1584	Classical legend (comedy)
Lyly, John	*The Woman in the Moon*	1593	STC 17090	1597	Comedy
Machin, Lewis; Markham, Gervase	*The Dumb Knight*	1608	STC 17399	1608	Comedy
Markham, Gervase; Sampson, William	*Herod and Antipater*	1622	STC 17401	1622	Tragedy
Marlowe, Christopher	*Edward the Second*	1592	STC 17437	1594	History
Marlowe, Christopher	*The Massacre at Paris*	1593	STC 17423	1594?	Foreign history
Marlowe, Christopher	*1 Tamburlaine the Great*	1587	STC 17425	1590	Heroical romance
Marlowe, Christopher	*2 Tamburlaine the Great*	1588	STC 17425	1590	Heroical romance
Marlowe, Christopher; Nashe, Thomas (?)	*Dido, Queen of Carthage*	1587	STC 17441	1594	Classical legend (tragedy)
Marlowe, Christopher; others (?)	*The Jew of Malta*	1589	STC 17412	1633	Tragedy
Marlowe, Christopher; others	*Doctor Faustus*	1592	STC 17429	1604	Tragedy
Marmion, Shackerley	*The Antiquary*	1635	Wing M703	1641	Comedy
Marston, John	*Antonio and Mellida*	1599	STC 17473	1602	Tragicomedy
Marston, John	*Antonio's Revenge*	1600	STC 17474	1602	Tragedy
Marston, John	*The Dutch Courtesan*	1604	STC 17476	1605	Comedy
Marston, John	*Jack Drum's Entertainment*	1600	STC 7243	1601	Domestic comedy
Marston, John	*The Malcontent*	1604	STC 17479	1604	Tragicomedy
Marston, John	*Parasitaster*	1605	STC 17484	1606	Comedy

(*cont.*)

(*cont.*)

Author	Play	Date	Copy-text	Copy-text date	Genre
Marston, John	*Sophonisba*	1605	STC 17488	1606	Tragedy
Marston, John	*What You Will*	1601	STC 17487	1607	Comedy
Marston, John (?)	*Histriomastix*	1599	STC 13529	1610	Comedy
Mason, John	*The Turk*	1607	STC 17617	1610	Tragedy
Massinger, Philip	*The Roman Actor*	1626	STC 17642	1629	Tragedy
Massinger, Philip	*The Unnatural Combat*	1626	STC 17643	1639	Tragedy
Middleton, Thomas	*A Chaste Maid in Cheapside*	1611	STC 17877	1630	Comedy
Middleton, Thomas	*A Game at Chess*	1624	MSR 151	1990	Political satire
Middleton, Thomas	*Hengist, King of Kent*	1618	MSR 167	2003	Tragedy
Middleton, Thomas	*A Mad World, My Masters*	1606	STC 17888	1608	Comedy
Middleton, Thomas	*Michaelmas Term*	1606	STC 17890	1607	Comedy
Middleton, Thomas	*More Dissemblers Besides Women*	1615	Wing M1989	1657	Comedy
Middleton, Thomas	*No Wit, No Help Like a Woman's*	1613	Wing M1985	1657	Comedy
Middleton, Thomas	*The Phoenix*	1604	STC 17892	1607	Comedy
Middleton, Thomas	*The Puritan*	1606	STC 21531	1607	Comedy
Middleton, Thomas	*The Revenger's Tragedy*	1606	STC 24149	1607	Tragedy
Middleton, Thomas	*The Second Maiden's Tragedy*	1611	MSR 17	1909	Tragedy
Middleton, Thomas	*A Trick to Catch the Old One*	1605	STC 17896	1608	Comedy
Middleton, Thomas	*The Widow*	1616	Wing J1015	1652	Comedy
Middleton, Thomas	*The Witch*	1615	MSR 89	1948	Tragicomedy
Middleton, Thomas	*Women Beware Women*	1621	Wing M1989	1657	Tragedy
Middleton, Thomas	*A Yorkshire Tragedy*	1606	STC 22340	1608	Tragedy
Middleton, Thomas	*Your Five Gallants*	1605	STC 17907	1608	Comedy
Middleton, Thomas; Rowley, William	*The Changeling*	1622	Wing M1980	1653	Tragedy

Author	Play	Date	Copy-text	Copy-text date	Genre
Middleton, Thomas; Fletcher, John (?)	*The Nice Valour*	1616	Wing B1581	1647	Comedy
Munday, Anthony; others	*Sir Thomas More*	1595	MSR 28	1911	History
Nashe, Thomas	*Summer's Last Will and Testament*	1592	STC 18376	1600	Comedy
Peele, George	*The Arraignment of Paris*	1581	STC 19530	1584	Classical legend (Pastoral)
Peele, George	*The Battle of Alcazar*	1589	STC 19531	1594	Foreign history
Peele, George	*David and Bethsabe*	1587	STC 19540	1599	Biblical History
Peele, George	*Edward the First*	1591	STC 19535	1593	History
Peele, George	*The Old Wife's Tale*	1590	STC 19545	1595	Romance
Phillip, John	*Patient and Meek Grissel*	1559	STC 19865	1569?	Comedy
Porter, Henry	*1 The Two Angry Women of Abingdon*	1588	STC 20121.5	1599	Comedy
Porter, Thomas	*A Witty Combat*	1663	Wing P2998	1663	Comedy
Rowley, Samuel	*When You See Me You Know Me*	1604	STC 21417	1605	History
Rowley, William	*All's Lost by Lust*	1619	STC 21425	1633	Tragedy
Rowley, William	*A New Wonder, a Woman Never Vexed*	1625	STC 21423	1632	Comedy
Shadwell, Thomas	*The Sullen Lovers*	1668	Wing S2878	1668	Comedy
Shakespeare, William	*All's Well That Ends Well*	1602	STC 22273	1623	Comedy
Shakespeare, William	*Antony and Cleopatra*	1607	STC 22273	1623	Tragedy
Shakespeare, William	*As You Like It*	1599	STC 22273	1623	Comedy
Shakespeare, William	*The Comedy of Errors*	1592	STC 22273	1623	Comedy
Shakespeare, William	*Coriolanus*	1608	STC 22273	1623	Tragedy
Shakespeare, William	*Cymbeline*	1609	STC 22273	1623	Tragicomedy

(cont.)

(cont.)

Author	Play	Date	Copy-text	Copy-text date	Genre
Shakespeare, William	*Hamlet*	1601	STC 22276	1604	Tragedy
Shakespeare, William	*Henry the Fifth*	1599	STC 22273	1623	History
Shakespeare, William	*1 Henry the Fourth*	1597	STC 22280	1598	History
Shakespeare, William	*2 Henry the Fourth*	1597	STC 22288	1600	History
Shakespeare, William	*Julius Caesar*	1599	STC 22273	1623	Tragedy
Shakespeare, William	*King John*	1596	STC 22273	1623	Tragedy
Shakespeare, William	*King Lear*	1605	STC 22292	1608	Tragedy
Shakespeare, William	*Love's Labour's Lost*	1595	STC 22294	1598	Comedy
Shakespeare, William	*The Merchant of Venice*	1596	STC 22296	1600	Comedy
Shakespeare, William	*The Merry Wives of Windsor*	1600	STC 22299	1602	Comedy
Shakespeare, William	*A Midsummer Night's Dream*	1595	STC 22302	1600	Comedy
Shakespeare, William	*Much Ado About Nothing*	1598	STC 22304	1600	Comedy
Shakespeare, William	*Othello*	1604	STC 22305	1622	Tragedy
Shakespeare, William	*Richard the Second*	1595	STC 22307	1597	History
Shakespeare, William	*Richard the Third*	1593	STC 22314	1597	History
Shakespeare, William	*Romeo and Juliet*	1595	STC 22323	1599	Tragedy
Shakespeare, William	*The Taming of the Shrew*	1594	STC 22273	1623	Comedy
Shakespeare, William	*The Tempest*	1611	STC 22273	1623	Comedy
Shakespeare, William	*Troilus and Cressida*	1602	STC 22331	1609	Tragedy
Shakespeare, William	*Twelfth Night*	1600	STC 22273	1623	Comedy
Shakespeare, William	*The Two Gentlemen of Verona*	1593	STC 22273	1623	Comedy
Shakespeare, William	*The Winter's Tale*	1610	STC 22273	1623	Tragicomedy

Author	Play	Date	Copy-text	Copy-text date	Genre
Shakespeare, William; Middleton, Thomas	*Macbeth*	1606	STC 22273	1623	Tragedy
Shakespeare, William; Middleton, Thomas	*Measure for Measure*	1604	STC 22273	1623	Comedy
Shakespeare, William; Middleton, Thomas	*Timon of Athens*	1607	STC 22273	1623	Tragedy
Shakespeare, William; others	*1 Henry the Sixth*	1592	STC 22273	1623	History
Shakespeare, William; others	*2 Henry the Sixth*	1591	STC 22273	1623	History
Shakespeare, William; others	*3 Henry the Sixth*	1591	STC 22273	1623	History
Shakespeare, William; others (?)	*Arden of Faversham*	1591	STC 733	1592	Realistic tragedy
Shakespeare, William; Peele, George	*Titus Andronicus*	1594	STC 22328	1594	Tragedy
Shakespeare, William; Wilkins, George	*Pericles, Prince of Tyre*	1608	STC 22334	1609	Tragicomedy
Sharpham, Edward	*Cupid's Whirligig*	1607	STC 22380	1607	Comedy
Sharpham, Edward	*The Fleer*	1606	STC 22384	1607	Comedy
Shirley, James	*The Brothers*	1641	Wing S3486	1653	Comedy
Shirley, James	*The Cardinal*	1641	Wing S3461	1652	Tragedy
Shirley, James	*The Gamester*	1633	STC 22443	1637	Comedy
Shirley, James	*Love's Cruelty*	1631	STC 22449	1640	Tragedy
Shirley, James	*The Opportunity*	1634	STC 22451	1640	Comedy
Shirley, James	*The Royal Master*	1637	STC 22454	1638	Comedy
Shirley, James	*The Sisters*	1642	Wing S3486	1653	Comedy
Shirley, James	*The Traitor*	1631	STC 22458	1635	Tragedy
Stapylton, Robert	*The Slighted Maid*	1663	Wing S5260A	1663	Tragicomedy
Suckling, John	*Aglaura*	1637	STC 23420	1638	Tragedy

(cont.)

(cont.)

Author	Play	Date	Copy-text	Copy-text date	Genre
Tatham, John	*The Rump*	1660	Wing T233	1660	Topical comedy
Tourneur, Cyril	*The Atheist's Tragedy*	1609	STC 24146	1611	Tragedy
Uncertain	*Appius and Virginia*	1564	STC 1059	1575	Classical moral
Uncertain	*Captain Thomas Stukeley*	1596	STC 23405	1605	History
Uncertain	*Edmond Ironside*	1595	MSR 61	1927	History
Uncertain	*Edward the Third*	1590	STC 7501	1596	History
Uncertain	*Every Woman in Her Humour*	1607	STC 25948	1609	Comedy
Uncertain	*Fair Em*	1590	STC 7675	1591?	Romantic comedy
Uncertain	*The Family of Love*	1603	STC 17879	1608	Comedy
Uncertain	*The Famous Victories of Henry the Fifth*	1586	STC 13072	1598	History
Uncertain	*George-a-Greene*	1590	STC 12212	1599	Romantic comedy
Uncertain	*The Hector of Germany*	1614	STC 22871	1615	Pseudo-history
Uncertain	*1 Hieronimo*	1604	STC 15085	1605	Pseudo-history
Uncertain	*John a Kent and John a Cumber*	1589	MSR 54	1923	Pseudo-history
Uncertain	*John of Bordeaux*	1592	MSR 79	1935	Comedy
Uncertain	*King Leir*	1590	STC 15343	1605	Legendary history
Uncertain	*A Knack to Know a Knave*	1592	STC 15027	1594	Comedy
Uncertain	*A Knack to Know an Honest Man*	1594	STC 15028	1596	Tragicomedy
Uncertain	*A Larum for London*	1599	STC 16754	1602	History
Uncertain	*Look About You*	1599	STC 16799	1600	Comedy
Uncertain	*(The Rare Triumphs of) Love and Fortune*	1582	STC 24286	1589	Mythological moral
Uncertain	*1 Selimus*	1592	STC 12310a	1594	Heroical romance
Uncertain	*The Taming of a Shrew*	1592	STC 23667	1594	Comedy
Uncertain	*Thomas Lord Cromwell*	1600	STC 21532	1602	History

Author	Play	Date	Copy-text	Copy-text date	Genre
Uncertain	*The Trial of Chivalry*	1601	STC 13527	1605	Pseudo-history
Uncertain	*The Troublesome Reign of King John*	1588	STC 14644	1591	History
Uncertain	*The True Tragedy of Richard the Third*	1591	STC 21009	1594	History
Uncertain	*The Valiant Welshman*	1612	STC 16	1615	History
Uncertain	*A Warning for Fair Women*	1599	STC 25089	1599	Tragedy
Uncertain	*The Wars of Cyrus*	1588	STC 6160	1594	Classical history
Uncertain	*The Weakest Goeth to the Wall*	1600	STC 25144	1600	Pseudo-history
Uncertain	*The Wisdom of Doctor Dodypoll*	1600	STC 6991	1600	Comedy
Webster, John	*The Devil's Law-Case*	1617	STC 25173	1623	Tragicomedy
Webster, John	*The Duchess of Malfi*	1614	STC 25176	1623	Tragedy
Webster, John	*The White Devil*	1612	STC 23178	1612	Tragedy
Wilmot, Robert; others	*Tancred and Gismund*	1566	STC 25764	1591	Senecan tragedy
Wilson, John	*The Cheats*	1663	Wing W2916	1664	Comedy
Wilson, Robert	*The Cobbler's Prophecy*	1590	STC 25781	1594	Comedy
Wilson, Robert	*The Three Ladies of London*	1581	STC 25784	1584	Moral
Wilson, Robert	*The Three Lords and Three Ladies of London*	1588	STC 25783	1590	Moral
Wilson, Robert; Drayton, Michael; Munday, Anthony; Hathaway, Richard	*1 Sir John Oldcastle*	1599	STC 18795	1600	History
Yarington, Robert (?)	*Two Lamentable Tragedies*	1594	STC 26076	1601	Tragedy

Characters with ≥ 2,000 Words of Dialogue from 243 Plays Performed on the Commercial Stage, 1580–1642

Play	Characters
Armin, *The Two Maids of Mortlake*	Humil, Sir William Vergir
Barkstead, Machin & Marston, *The Insatiate Countess*	Claridiana, Isabella
Barry, *Ram Alley*	Throat, William Smallshanks
Beaumont, *The Knight of the Burning Pestle*	Citizen, Rafe, Wife
Beaumont & Fletcher, *A King and No King*	Arbaces, Bessus, Mardonius
Beaumont & Fletcher, *The Maid's Tragedy*	Amintor, Evadne, Melantius
Brome, *The City Wit*	Crasy, Pyannet
Brome, *Covent Garden Weeded*	Will Crosswill, Mihil Crosswill, Nicholas Rooksbill
Brome, *A Jovial Crew*	Oldrents, Randall, Springlove
Brome, *A Mad Couple Well Matched*	Alicia Saleware, George Careless, Lady Thrivewell, Thomas Saleware
Brome, *The Northern Lass*	Mistress Fitchow, Sir Paul Squelch, Trainwell, Tridewell, Widgine
Brome, *The Sparagus Garden*	Friswood, Gilbert Goldwire, Samson Touchwood, Sir Hugh Moneylacks, Tim Hoyden, Will Striker
Chapman, *All Fools*	Cornelio, Gostanzo, Rynaldo, Valerio
Chapman, *1 The Blind Beggar of Alexandria*	Irus
Chapman, *Bussy D'Ambois*	Bussy D'Ambois, Montsurry, Monsieur, Tamyra
Chapman, *Byron's Conspiracy*	Byron, Savoy, Henri IV
Chapman, *Byron's Tragedy*	Byron, Henri IV
Chapman, *The Gentleman Usher*	Bassiolo, Margaret, Strozza, Vincentio
Chapman, *An Humorous Day's Mirth*	Lemot
Chapman, *May Day*	Angelo, Lodovico, Lorenzo, Quintiliano
Chapman, *Monsieur D'Olive*	D'Olive, Vandome
Chapman, *The Revenge of Bussy D'Ambois*	Baligny, Clermont
Chapman, *Sir Giles Goosecap*	Clarence, Lord Monford, Sir Giles Goosecap
Chapman, *The Widow's Tears*	Lysander, Tharsalio
Chettle, *Hoffman*	Clois Hoffman, Lorrique

Play	Characters
Cooke (?), *Greene's Tu Quoque*	Bubbles, Spendall, Joyce, Sir Lionell, Staines, Will Rash
Daborne, *A Christian Turned Turk*	Ward
Davenant, *The Unfortunate Lovers*	Altophil
Day, *Humour Out of Breath*	Aspero, Florimell, Octavio
Day, *The Isle of Gulls*	Dametas, Lisander
Dekker, *1 Old Fortunatus*	Andelocia, Fortune, Old Fortunatus, Shadow
Dekker, *2 The Honest Whore*	Bellafront, Hippolito, Lodovico, Mattheo, Orlando Frescobaldo
Dekker, *If It Be Not Good*	Alphonso, Bartervile
Dekker, *The Shoemaker's Holiday*	Firk, Simon Eyre
Dekker, *The Whore of Babylon*	Cardinal Como, Empress of Babylon, Paridel, Third King, Titania
Dekker & Webster, *Sir Thomas Wyatt*	Sir Thomas Wyatt
Field, *Amends for Ladies*	Bold, Widow
Field, Fletcher & Massinger, *The Honest Man's Fortune*	Laverdure, Longavile, Montaigne
Fletcher, *Bonduca*	Caratach, Petillius
Fletcher, *The Chances*	Don Frederic, Don John
Fletcher, *The Faithful Shepherdess*	Amaryllis, Clorin, Perigot
Fletcher, *The Humorous Lieutenant*	Celia, Demetrius, Humorous Lieutenant, King Antigonus, Leontius
Fletcher, *The Island Princess*	Armusia, Governor, Pyniero, Quisara
Fletcher, *The Loyal Subject*	Alinda, Archas, Duke, Theodor
Fletcher, *The Mad Lover*	Chilax, Memnon
Fletcher, *Monsieur Thomas*	Sebastian, Thomas
Fletcher, *The Pilgrim*	Alinda, Alphonso, Juletta, Pedro, Roderigo
Fletcher, *Rule a Wife and Have a Wife*	Donna Margarita, Estifania, Leon, Michael Perez
Fletcher, *Valentinian*	Aetius, Lucina, Maximus, Valentinian
Fletcher, *A Wife for a Month*	Evanthe, Frederick, Sorano, Valerio
Fletcher, *The Wild-Goose Chase*	Belleur, Lillia-Bianca, Mirabel
Fletcher, *The Woman's Prize*	Bianca, Maria, Pedro, Petruccio, Rowland
Fletcher, *Women Pleased*	Penurio, Silvio
Fletcher & Beaumont (?), *The Captain*	Fabritio, Father, Jacomo, Lelia
Fletcher & Massinger, *The Double Marriage*	Virolet, Juliana, Martia, Sesse
Fletcher & Shakespeare, *Henry the Eighth*	Cardinal Wolsey, King Henry, Queen Katherine
Fletcher & Shakespeare, *The Two Noble Kinsmen*	Arcite, Emilia, Jailor's Daughter, Palamon, Theseus
Fletcher & Shirley (?), *Wit Without Money*	Isabel, Valentine, Widow
Fletcher, Massinger & others (?), *The Bloody Brother*	Aubrey, Latorch, Rollo

(cont.)

Play	Characters
Ford, *The Broken Heart*	Bassanes, Ithocles, Orgilus, Penthea
Ford, *A Challenge for Beauty*	Bonavida, Ferrars, Petrocella, Valladaura
Ford, *The Fancies Chaste and Noble*	Livio, Troylo-Savelli
Ford, *The Lady's Trial*	Auria
Ford, *The Lover's Melancholy*	Meleander
Ford, *Love's Sacrifice*	Biancha, Ferentes, Phillippo Caraffa, Roderico D'Avolos
Ford, *Perkin Warbeck*	Henry VII, Perkin Warbeck
Ford, *'Tis Pity She's a Whore*	Arabella, Giovanni, Poggio
Greene & Lodge, *A Looking Glass for London*	Clown, Rasni
Greene, *Alphonsus, King of Aragon*	Alphonsus
Greene, *Friar Bacon and Friar Bungay*	Friar Bacon, Margaret
Greene, *James the Fourth*	Ateukin, Dorothea, James IV
Greene, *Orlando Furioso*	Orlando
Haughton, *The Devil and His Dame*	Belphagor, Grim, Marian
Haughton, *Englishmen for My Money*	Anthony, Frisco, Pisaro
Heywood, *The English Traveller*	Clown, Reignald, Young Geraldine
Heywood, *1 The Fair Maid of the West*	Bess Bridges
Heywood, *2 The Fair Maid of the West*	Bess Bridges, Duke of Florence, Goodlack, Spencer
Heywood, *The Four Prentices of London*	Charles, Eustace, Godfrey, Guy
Heywood, *1 If You Know Not Me*	Elizabeth
Heywood, *2 If You Know Not Me*	Hobson, John, Thomas Gresham
Heywood, *The Rape of Lucrece*	Brutus, Lucretia, Sextus
Heywood, *The Wise Woman of Hoxton*	Chartley, Wise Woman
Heywood, *A Woman Killed with Kindness*	Frankford, Sir Charles Mountford
Heywood & others (?), *1 Edward the Fourth*	Falconbridge, Hobbs, King Edward, Mayor
Heywood & others (?), *2 Edward the Fourth*	Jane Shore, King Edward, Matthew Shore
Jonson, *The Alchemist*	Face, Mammon, Subtle
Jonson, *Bartholomew Fair*	Lantern/Leatherhead, John Littlewit, Adam Overdo, Humphrey Wasp, Bartholomew Cokes, Quarlous
Jonson, *The Case is Altered*	Ferneze, Jaque de Prie, Juniper, Peter Onion
Jonson, *Catiline His Conspiracy*	Catiline, Cicero
Jonson, *Cynthia's Revels*	Amorphus, Crites, Cupid, Mercury
Jonson, *The Devil is an Ass*	Fitzdottrel, Merecraft, Pug, Wittipol
Jonson, *Epicene*	Clerimont, Dauphine, Morose, Truewit
Jonson, *Every Man in His Humour*	Bobadilla, Cob, Doctor Clement, Lorenzo Junior, Musco, Prospero, Thorello
Jonson, *Every Man Out of His Humour*	Carlo Buffone, Cordatus, Fastidius Brisk, Fungoso, Macilente, Puntarvolo, Sogliardo
Jonson, *The Magnetic Lady*	Compass, Polish, Moth Interest

Play	Characters
Jonson, *The New Inn*	Frances, Host, Lovel, Prudence
Jonson, *Poetaster*	Crispinus, Horace, Tucca
Jonson, *Sejanus His Fall*	Arruntius, Sejanus, Siblius, Tiberius
Jonson, *The Staple of News*	Pennyboy Canter, Pennyboy Junior, Pennyboy Senior
Jonson, *The Tale of a Tub*	Tobie Turfe
Jonson, *Volpone*	Corvino, Mosca, Sir Politic Would-Be, Volpone
Kyd, *The Spanish Tragedy*	Hieronimo, Lorenzo
Kyd, *Soliman and Perseda*	Basilisco, Erastus, Soliman
Lodge, *The Wounds of Civil War*	Marius, Sulla
Lyly, *Campaspe*	Alexander
Lyly, *Endymion*	Cynthia, Endymion, Tellus
Lyly, *Midas*	Midas, Petulus
Lyly, *Mother Bombie*	Dromio
Lyly, *The Woman in the Moon*	Pandora
Machin & Markham, *The Dumb Knight*	Epire, King of Cyprus, Mariana
Markham & Sampson, *Herod and Antipater*	Antipater, Herod
Marlowe, *Edward the Second*	Edward II, Mortimer, Queen Isabella
Marlowe, *The Massacre at Paris*	Anjou, Guise
Marlowe, *1 Tamburlaine the Great*	Tamburlaine
Marlowe, *2 Tamburlaine the Great*	Tamburlaine
Marlowe & Nashe (?), *Dido, Queen of Carthage*	Aeneas, Dido
Marlowe & others, *Doctor Faustus*	Faustus
Marlowe & others (?), *The Jew of Malta*	Barabas
Marmion, *The Antiquary*	Aurelio, Lionel, Lorenzo, Lucretia, Petruchio
Marston, *Antonio and Mellida*	Antonio
Marston, *Antonio's Revenge*	Antonio, Piero
Marston, *The Dutch Courtesan*	Cocledemoy, Young Freevill
Marston, *Jack Drum's Entertainment*	Sir Edward Fortune
Marston, *The Malcontent*	Malevole, Mendoza
Marston, *Parasitaster*	Gonzago, Hercules, Zuccone
Marston, *Sophonisba*	Massinissa, Sophonisba, Syphax
Marston, *What You Will*	Quadratus
Mason, *The Turk*	Borgias, Mulleasses, Timoclea
Massinger, *The Roman Actor*	Caesar, Paris
Massinger, *The Unnatural Combat*	Belgarde, Malefort Senior, Montreville
Middleton, *A Chaste Maid in Cheapside*	Allwit, Touchwood Senior
Middleton, *A Game at Chess*	Black Bishop's Pawn, Black Knight, White Queen's Pawn
Middleton, *Hengist, King of Kent*	Hengist, Horsus, Simon, Vortiger
Middleton, *A Mad World, My Masters*	Follywit, Sir Bounteous

(cont.)

(*cont.*)

Play	Characters
Middleton, *Michaelmas Term*	Easy, Quomodo, Shortyard
Middleton, *More Dissemblers Beside Women*	Cardinal, Dondolo, Duchess, Lactantio
Middleton, *No Wit, No Help Like a Woman's*	Mistress Low-Water, Savourwit, Sir Oliver, Weatherwine, Widow
Middleton, *The Phoenix*	Phoenix, Falso, Tangle
Middleton, *The Puritan*	Pyeboard, Sir Godfrey Plus
Middleton, *The Revenger's Tragedy*	Lussorioso, Vindice
Middleton, *The Second Maiden's Tragedy*	Govianus, Tyrant, Votarius
Middleton, *A Trick to Catch the Old One*	Hoard, Lucre, Witgood
Middleton, *The Widow*	Francisco, Martino, Philippa, Ricardo
Middleton, *The Witch*	Francisca, Gasparo, Sebastian
Middleton, *Women Beware Women*	Bianca, Leantio, Livia
Middleton, *A Yorkshire Tragedy*	Husband
Middleton, *Your Five Gallants*	Fitzgrave, Frip, Goldstone, Pursenet, Tailby
Middleton & Fletcher (?), *The Nice Valour*	La Nove, Lapet, Shamont
Middleton & Rowley, *The Changeling*	Beatrice, DeFlores, Lollio
Munday & others, *Sir Thomas More*	Sir Thomas More
Peele, *David and Bethsabe*	David
Peele, *Edward the First*	Edward I, Elinor, Hugh ap David, Lluellen
Porter, *1 The Two Angry Women of Abingdon*	Barnes, Dick Coomes, Frank Goursey, Mall Barnes, Mistress Barnes, Phillip Barnes
Rowley (W), *A New Wonder, a Woman Never Vexed*	Bruyne, Old Foster, Stephen Foster, Widow
Rowley (S), *All's Lost by Lust*	Julianus, Lothario
Rowley (S), *When You See Me You Know Me*	Henry VIII, Will Sommers
Shakespeare, *All's Well That Ends Well*	Bertram, Countess, Helen, King, Paroles
Shakespeare, *Antony and Cleopatra*	Antony, Caesar, Cleopatra
Shakespeare, *As You Like It*	Celia, Orlando, Rosalind, Touchstone
Shakespeare, *The Comedy of Errors*	Adriana, Antipholus of Syracuse, Dromio of Syracuse
Shakespeare, *Coriolanus*	Aufidius, Martius, Menenius, Volumnia
Shakespeare, *Cymbeline*	Belarius, Cloten, Cymbeline, Giacomo, Innogen, Posthumus
Shakespeare, *Hamlet*	Claudius, Hamlet, Polonius
Shakespeare, *Henry the Fifth*	Fluellen, King Harry
Shakespeare, *1 Henry the Fourth*	Falstaff, Hotspur, King Henry, Prince Harry
Shakespeare, *2 Henry the Fourth*	Falstaff, King Henry, Prince Harry
Shakespeare, *Julius Caesar*	Antony, Brutus, Cassius
Shakespeare, *King John*	Bastard, Constance, King John
Shakespeare, *King Lear*	Edgar, Edmund, Gloucester, Kent, King Lear
Shakespeare, *Love's Labour's Lost*	Armado, Biron, King, Princess
Shakespeare, *The Merchant of Venice*	Bassanio, Portia, Shylock

Play	Characters
Shakespeare, *The Merry Wives of Windsor*	George Page, Mistress Ford, Sir John Falstaff
Shakespeare, *Much Ado About Nothing*	Beatrice, Benedick, Don Pedro, Leonato
Shakespeare, *Othello*	Desdemona, Iago, Othello
Shakespeare, *Richard the Second*	Bullingbroke, Richard II, York
Shakespeare, *Richard the Third*	Buckingham, Richard III
Shakespeare, *Romeo and Juliet*	Capulet, Friar, Juliet, Mercutio, Nurse, Romeo
Shakespeare, *The Taming of the Shrew*	Petruccio, Tranio
Shakespeare, *The Tempest*	Prospero
Shakespeare, *Troilus and Cressida*	Cressida, Pandarus, Thersites, Troilus, Ulysses
Shakespeare, *Twelfth Night*	Feste, Malvolio, Olivia, Sir Toby, Viola
Shakespeare, *The Two Gentlemen of Verona*	Julia, Proteus, Valentine
Shakespeare, *The Winter's Tale*	Autolycus, Camillo, Leontes, Paulina
Shakespeare & Middleton, *Macbeth*	Macbeth
Shakespeare & Middleton, *Measure for Measure*	Angelo, Duke, Isabella, Lucio
Shakespeare & Middleton, *Timon of Athens*	Timon
Shakespeare & others (?), *Arden of Faversham*	Alice, Arden, Black Will, Mosby
Shakespeare & others, *1 Henry the Sixth*	Talbot
Shakespeare & others, *2 Henry the Sixth*	Gloucester, Jack Cade, King Henry, Queen Margaret, Suffolk, York
Shakespeare & others, *3 Henry the Sixth*	Warwick, King Edward, King Henry, Queen Margaret, Richard
Shakespeare & Peele, *Titus Andronicus*	Aaron, Marcus, Titus
Shakespeare & Wilkins, *Pericles*	Gower, Pericles
Sharpham, *Cupid's Whirligig*	Lady Troublesome, Timothy Troublesome, Wages, Young Lord Nonsuch
Sharpham, *The Fleer*	Antifront
Shirley, *The Brothers*	Don Carlos, Fernando, Luys
Shirley, *The Cardinal*	Cardinal, Duchess, Hernando
Shirley, *The Gamester*	Hazard, Wilding
Shirley, *Love's Cruelty*	Bellamente, Clariana, Hippolito
Shirley, *The Opportunity*	Aurelio, Duchess, Pisauro
Shirley, *The Royal Master*	Domitilla, King of Naples, Montalto
Shirley, *The Sisters*	Piperello
Shirley, *The Traitor*	Lorenzo, Sciarrha
Suckling, *Aglaura*	Zorannes
Tourneur, *The Atheist's Tragedy*	Charlemont, D'Amville
Uncertain, *Captain Thomas Stukeley*	Thomas Stukeley
Uncertain, *Edmond Ironside*	Canutus, Edmond Ironside, Edricus
Uncertain, *Edward the Third*	Edward III, Prince Edward
Uncertain, *Every Woman in Her Humour*	Acutus

(cont.)

Play	Characters
Uncertain, *The Family of Love*	Gerardine, Glister, Lipsalve
Uncertain, *The Famous Victories of Henry the Fifth*	Henry V
Uncertain, *George-A-Greene*	George-A-Greene
Uncertain, *John a Kent and John a Cumber*	John a Kent
Uncertain, *John of Bordeaux*	Friar Bacon
Uncertain, *King Leir*	King Leir, Messenger, Ragan
Uncertain, *A Knack to Know a Knave*	Honesty, King Edgar
Uncertain, *A Larum for London*	Sancho D'Avila, Stump
Uncertain, *Look About You*	Falconbridge, Gloucester, Old King, Prince John, Prince Richard, Skink
Uncertain, *(The Rare Triumphs of) Love and Fortune*	Bomelio, Hermione
Uncertain, *1 Selimus*	Acomat, Bajazet, Selimus
Uncertain, *The Taming of a Shrew*	Ferando
Uncertain, *Thomas Lord Cromwell*	Cromwell
Uncertain, *The Troublesome Reign of King John*	Bastard, King John, Shrieve
Uncertain, *The True Tragedy of Richard the Third*	Richard
Uncertain, *The Valiant Welshman*	Caradoc
Uncertain, *A Warning for Fair Women*	George Brown, Anne Drury, Anne Sanders
Uncertain, *The Wars of Cyrus*	Araspas, Cyrus
Webster, *The Devil's Law-Case*	Ariosto, Leonora, Romelio
Webster, *The Duchess of Malfi*	Antonio, Bosola, Duchess, Ferdinand
Webster, *The White Devil*	Brachiano, Flamineo, Francisco, Monticelso, Vittoria
Wilson, *The Cobbler's Prophecy*	Ralph
Wilson, *The Three Ladies of London*	Conscience, Lady Lucre, Simplicity
Wilson, *The Three Lords and Three Ladies of London*	Policy, Simplicity
Wilson, Drayton, Munday & Hathaway, *1 Sir John Oldcastle*	King Harry, Sir John Oldcastle
Yarington (?), *Two Lamentable Tragedies*	Alinso, Fallerio, Thomas Merry

Plays First Appearing on the Commercial Stage 1590–1609, with Totals for Prop-Types and Lines Spoken

The source for the following list is *British Drama, 1533–1642: A Catalogue*. Chapter 4 discusses the rationale for departing from our usual bibliographical source, the *Annals* (see page 117–18). 'Date' refers to date of first performance.

Author	Play	Date	Genre	Total prop-types	Total lines spoken
Armin, Robert	*The Two Maids of Mortlake*	1608	Comedy	28	2339
Barnes, Barnabe	*The Devil's Charter*	1606	Tragedy	81	2986
Barry, Lording	*Ram Alley*	1608	Comedy	21	2570
Beaumont, Francis	*The Knight of the Burning Pestle*	1607	Comedy	40	2444
Beaumont, Francis; Fletcher, John	*The Coxcomb*	1609	Comedy	24	2555
Beaumont, Francis; Fletcher, John	*Cupid's Revenge*	1607	Tragedy	18	2674
Beaumont, Francis; Fletcher, John	*Philaster*	1609	Tragicomedy	14	2606
Beaumont, Francis; Fletcher, John (?)	*The Woman Hater*	1606	Comedy	13	2750
Chapman, George	*All Fools*	1604	Comedy	21	2250
Chapman, George	*Byron's Conspiracy*	1608	History	7	2057
Chapman, George	*Byron's Tragedy*	1608	Tragedy	18	2301
Chapman, George	*1 The Blind Beggar of Alexandria*	1596	Romance	16	1575
Chapman, George	*Bussy D'Ambois*	1604	Tragedy	19	2402

(cont.)

(cont.)

Author	Play	Date	Genre	Total prop-types	Total lines spoken
Chapman, George	*Caesar and Pompey*	1606	Tragedy	15	2322
Chapman, George	*The Gentleman Usher*	1602	Comedy	22	2418
Chapman, George	*An Humorous Day's Mirth*	1597	Comedy	31	2063
Chapman, George	*May Day*	1604	Comedy	17	2586
Chapman, George	*Monsieur D'Olive*	1605	Comedy	11	1962
Chapman, George	*Sir Giles Goosecap*	1602	Comedy	17	2591
Chapman, George	*The Widow's Tears*	1605	Comedy	18	2618
Chapman, George; Jonson, Ben; Marston, John	*Eastward Ho!*	1605	Comedy	24	2670
Chettle, Henry	*Hoffman*	1603	Tragedy	34	2426
Chettle, Henry; Day, John	*The Blind Beggar of Bethnal Green*	1600	Comedy	27	2563
Chettle, Henry; Dekker, Thomas; Haughton, William	*Patient Grissil*	1600	Comedy	36	2687
Daniel, Samuel	*Philotas*	1604	Tragedy	4	2131
Day, John	*Humour Out of Breath*	1607	Comedy	14	1692
Day, John	*Isle of Gulls*	1606	Comedy	13	2149
Day, John	*Law-Tricks*	1604	Comedy	22	2006
Day, John; Rowley, William; Wilkins, George	*The Travels of the Three English Brothers*	1607	History	20	2059
Dekker, Thomas	*1 Old Fortunatus*	1599	Romance	29	2845
Dekker, Thomas	*2 The Honest Whore*	1605	Comedy	28	2820
Dekker, Thomas	*Blurt Master Constable*	1601	Comedy	31	1918
Dekker, Thomas	*Satiromastix*	1601	Comedy	41	2610
Dekker, Thomas	*The Shoemaker's Holiday*	1599	Comedy	23	2122
Dekker, Thomas	*The Whore of Babylon*	1606	History	35	2402
Dekker, Thomas; Middleton; Thomas	*1 The Honest Whore*	1604	Comedy	48	2730

Author	Play	Date	Genre	Total prop-types	Total lines spoken
Dekker, Thomas; Webster, John	*Northward Ho!*	1605	Comedy	17	2244
Dekker, Thomas; Webster, John	*Sir Thomas Wyatt*	1602	History	18	1412
Dekker, Thomas; Webster, John	*Westward Ho!*	1604	Comedy	30	2408
Dekker, Thomas; Haughton, William; Day, John	*Lust's Dominion*	1600	Tragedy	31	2503
Field, Nathan	*A Woman is a Weathercock*	1609	Comedy	31	2038
Fletcher, John	*The Faithful Shepherdess*	1608	Tragicomedy	30	2637
Greene, Robert	*James the Fourth*	1590	Romance	18	2344
Greene, Robert	*Orlando Furioso*	1591	Romance	17	1479
Haughton, William	*The Devil and His Dame*	1600	Comedy	28	2031
Haughton, William	*Englishmen For My Money*	1598	Comedy	19	2554
Heywood, Thomas	*1 If You Know Not Me You Know Nobody*	1604	History	33	1427
Heywood, Thomas	*2 If You Know Not Me You Know Nobody*	1604	History	25	2554
Heywood, Thomas	*The Four Prentices of London*	1602	Romance	25	2640
Heywood, Thomas	*How a Man May Choose a Good Wife from a Bad*	1601	Comedy	25	2426
Heywood, Thomas	*The Rape of Lucrece*	1607	Tragedy	28	2492
Heywood, Thomas	*The Royal King and Loyal Subject*	1606	Romance	19	2347
Heywood, Thomas	*A Woman Killed with Kindness*	1603	Tragedy	34	1983
Heywood, Thomas; others (?)	*1 Edward the Fourth*	1599	History	27	2791
Heywood, Thomas; others (?)	*2 Edward the Fourth*	1599	History	43	2998

(cont.)

(cont.)

Author	Play	Date	Genre	Total prop-types	Total lines spoken
Jonson, Ben	*The Case is Altered*	1597	Comedy	15	2356
Jonson, Ben	*Cynthia's Revels*	1600	Comedy	30	2975
Jonson, Ben	*Every Man in His Humour*	1598	Comedy	29	2921
Jonson, Ben	*Every Man Out of His Humour*	1599	Comedy	43	4210
Jonson, Ben	*Poetaster*	1601	Comedy	35	3108
Jonson, Ben	*Sejanus His Fall*	1603	Tragedy	25	3250
Jonson, Ben	*Volpone*	1606	Comedy	35	3095
Lyly, John	*Love's Metamorphosis*	1590	Comedy	19	1263
Machin, Lewis; Markham, Gervase	*The Dumb Knight*	1607	Comedy	17	2202
Marlowe, Christopher	*Edward the Second*	1592	History	35	2638
Marlowe, Christopher	*The Massacre at Paris*	1593	Tragedy	25	1312
Marston, John	*Antonio and Mellida*	1599	Comedy	29	1861
Marston, John	*Antonio's Revenge*	1600	Tragedy	42	1942
Marston, John	*The Dutch Courtesan*	1604	Comedy	28	2117
Marston, John	*Jack Drum's Entertainment*	1600	Comedy	27	2017
Marston, John	*The Malcontent*	1603	Tragicomedy	25	1894
Marston, John	*Parasitaster*	1605	Comedy	19	2534
Marston, John	*Sophonisba*	1605	Tragedy	32	1591
Marston, John	*What You Will*	1601	Comedy	33	2090
Mason, John	*The Turk*	1607	Tragedy	8	2153
Middleton, Thomas	*A Mad World, My Masters*	1605	Comedy	25	2153
Middleton, Thomas	*Michaelmas Term*	1604	Comedy	15	2348
Middleton, Thomas	*The Phoenix*	1604	Comedy	18	2479
Middleton, Thomas	*The Puritan*	1606	Comedy	15	1995
Middleton, Thomas	*The Revenger's Tragedy*	1606	Tragedy	20	2447
Middleton, Thomas	*A Trick to Catch the Old One*	1605	Comedy	22	2099
Middleton, Thomas	*A Yorkshire Tragedy*	1605	Tragedy	17	804

Author	Play	Date	Genre	Total prop-types	Total lines spoken
Middleton, Thomas	*Your Five Gallants*	1607	Comedy	38	2393
Munday, Anthony	*1 Robin Hood*	1598	Comedy	46	2612
Munday, Anthony; Chettle, Henry	*2 Robin Hood*	1598	Tragedy	36	2822
Munday, Anthony; others	*Sir Thomas More*	1601	History	29	2132
Peele, George	*David and Bethsabe*	1590	History	23	1917
Peele, George	*Edward the First*	1591	History	41	2716
Peele, George	*The Old Wife's Tale*	1592	Romance	34	1077
Porter, Henry	*1 The Two Angry Women of Abingdon*	1598	Comedy	11	2970
Rowley, Samuel	*When You See Me You Know Me*	1604	History	30	3015
Shakespeare, William	*All's Well That Ends Well*	1605	Comedy	10	2691
Shakespeare, William	*Antony and Cleopatra*	1606	Tragedy	21	3009
Shakespeare, William	*As You Like It*	1600	Comedy	7	2692
Shakespeare, William	*The Comedy of Errors*	1593	Comedy	10	1764
Shakespeare, William	*Coriolanus*	1608	Tragedy	24	3366
Shakespeare, William	*Hamlet*	1600	Tragedy	34	3698
Shakespeare, William	*Henry the Fifth*	1599	History	17	3213
Shakespeare, William	*1 Henry the Fourth*	1597	History	20	2788
Shakespeare, William	*2 Henry the Fourth*	1597	History	26	3055
Shakespeare, William	*Julius Caesar*	1599	Tragedy	22	2459
Shakespeare, William	*King John*	1596	History	15	2569
Shakespeare, William	*King Lear*	1605	Tragedy	29	3019
Shakespeare, William	*Love's Labour's Lost*	1596	Comedy	17	2579

(cont.)

(*cont.*)

Author	Play	Date	Genre	Total prop-types	Total lines spoken
Shakespeare, William	*The Merchant of Venice*	1596	Comedy	16	2474
Shakespeare, William	*The Merry Wives of Windsor*	1597	Comedy	29	2659
Shakespeare, William	*A Midsummer Night's Dream*	1595	Comedy	13	2116
Shakespeare, William	*Much Ado About Nothing*	1598	Comedy	14	2496
Shakespeare, William	*Othello*	1604	Tragedy	17	3020
Shakespeare, William	*Richard the Second*	1595	History	20	2751
Shakespeare, William	*Richard the Third*	1593	History	28	3569
Shakespeare, William	*Romeo and Juliet*	1595	Tragedy	33	2966
Shakespeare, William	*The Taming of the Shrew*	1592	Comedy	26	2594
Shakespeare, William	*Troilus and Cressida*	1602	Tragedy	9	3202
Shakespeare, William	*Twelfth Night*	1601	Comedy	14	2465
Shakespeare, William	*The Two Gentlemen of Verona*	1594	Comedy	12	2202
Shakespeare, William; Middleton, Thomas	*Macbeth*	1606	Tragedy	48	2166
Shakespeare, William; Middleton, Thomas	*Measure for Measure*	1603	Tragicomedy	7	2615
Shakespeare, William; Middleton, Thomas	*Timon of Athens*	1607	Tragedy	28	2293
Shakespeare, William; others	*Edward the Third*	1593	History	20	2491
Shakespeare, William; others	*1 Henry the Sixth*	1592	History	23	2676
Shakespeare, William; others	*2 Henry the Sixth*	1591	History	11	3096

Author	Play	Date	Genre	Total prop-types	Total lines spoken
Shakespeare, William; others	*3 Henry the Sixth*	1591	History	15	2901
Shakespeare, William; Peele, George	*Titus Andronicus*	1592	Tragedy	45	2429
Shakespeare, William; Wilkins, George	*Pericles*	1607	Romance	28	2309
Sharpham, Edward	*Cupid's Whirligig*	1607	Comedy	14	2751
Sharpham, Edward	*The Fleer*	1606	Comedy	11	1993
Uncertain	*Arden of Faversham*	1590	Tragedy	28	2457
Uncertain	*Captain Thomas Stukeley*	1596	History	27	2747
Uncertain	*Edmond Ironside*	1597	History	19	1943
Uncertain	*Every Woman in Her Humour*	1607	Comedy	15	2147
Uncertain	*Fair Em*	1590	Comedy	5	1474
Uncertain	*The Fair Maid of Bristol*	1604	Tragicomedy	10	1201
Uncertain	*The Fair Maid of the Exchange*	1602	Comedy	12	2596
Uncertain	*The Family of Love*	1607	Comedy	16	2335
Uncertain	*George-a-Greene*	1591	Romance	17	1233
Uncertain	*1 Hieronimo*	1600	Tragedy	16	1209
Uncertain	*Jack Straw*	1590	History	10	913
Uncertain	*John a Kent and John a Cumber*	1590	Comedy	13	1574
Uncertain	*John of Bordeaux*	1591	Romance	12	1423
Uncertain	*A Knack to Know a Knave*	1592	Moral	18	1864
Uncertain	*A Knack to Know an Honest Man*	1594	Comedy	17	1686
Uncertain	*A Larum for London*	1599	History	20	1578
Uncertain	*Liberality and Prodigality*	1601	Moral	14	1247
Uncertain	*Locrine*	1591	Tragedy	27	2092
Uncertain	*The London Prodigal*	1604	Comedy	18	1894
Uncertain	*Look About You*	1599	Comedy	49	3010

(cont.)

(cont.)

Author	Play	Date	Genre	Total prop-types	Total lines spoken
Uncertain	The Maid's Metamorphosis	1600	Romance	10	1671
Uncertain	The Merry Devil of Edmonton	1603	Comedy	6	1470
Uncertain	Mucedorus	1591	Romance	6	1370
Uncertain	Nobody and Somebody	1605	History	16	2039
Uncertain	1 Selimus	1591	Tragedy	19	2416
Uncertain	Thomas Lord Cromwell	1601	History	22	1658
Uncertain	The Trial of Chivalry	1599	Romance	25	2406
Uncertain	A Warning for Fair Women	1597	Tragedy	38	2446
Uncertain	The Weakest Goeth to the Wall	1599	Comedy	29	2312
Uncertain	The Wisdom of Doctor Dodypoll	1600	Comedy	20	1675
Wilkins, George	The Miseries of Enforced Marriage	1606	Tragedy	18	2797
Wilson, Robert	The Cobbler's Prophecy	1592	Moral	29	1497
Wilson, Robert; Drayton, Michael; Munday, Anthony; Hathaway, Richard	1 Sir John Oldcastle	1599	History	41	2580

Distribution of 691 Prop-Types across 160 Plays First Appearing on the Commercial Stage, 1590–1609

adder (1)	agate (2)	ale (8)	almanac (6)	altar (2)	apparel-dirty (1)
apparel-unspecified (2)	apple-johns (1)	apples (5)	apples-little (1)	apricots (1)	aqua-vitae (1)
arbour (1)	armour (2)	arras (9)	arrow (8)	asp (1)	ass (1)
axe (9)	baby (10)	backsword (1)	bag (9)	baggage (2)	ball-barber (1)
balls-bowling (2)	balm (1)	balsam (1)	band (1)	banderoll (1)	bank (8)
bank-river (1)	banner (1)	banquet (24)	bar (5)	bar-judicial (2)	barrel (1)
basin (10)	basket (12)	bat (1)	beads (2)	beaker (2)	beard (3)
beard-brush (1)	bed (23)	bedpan (1)	bedstaff (1)	beef (1)	beer (7)
bench (3)	bench-judicial (3)	berries (1)	bible (5)	bier (1)	bill (12)
bindings (22)	bird (1)	blanket (1)	block-chopping (4)	blood (54)	blotting-materials (1)
board-tally (1)	bodkin (1)	bond (5)	bonnet (1)	book (43)	book-account (3)
book-magic (2)	book-prayer (7)	book-primer (1)	book-table (6)	boots (1)	bottle (15)
bottle-casting (2)	bow (11)	bowl (15)	box (11)	bracelet (4)	branches (4)
brazier (1)	bread (11)	briar (1)	bricks (1)	bridle (2)	brooch (1)
broom (2)	broth (2)	brush (1)	buck-basket (1)	buckler (15)	budget (1)
bush (7)	butter (1)	caduceus (3)	cake (3)	caliver (2)	can (1)
candle (14)	candlestick (3)	cannon-shot (3)	canopy (7)	cap (4)	cap-case (1)

(cont.)

cape (1)	capon (3)	carcanet (2)	carpet (4)	case-pistol (1)	cask (1)
casket (8)	cat (1)	cauldron (1)	censer (3)	chafing-dish (2)	chain (13)
chains (2)	chair (47)	chalice (1)	chambers-shot (2)	chariot (3)	charm (1)
cheese (3)	cherries (2)	chess-pieces (1)	chessboard (2)	chest (2)	chit (1)
clap-dish (2)	claret (2)	cleaning-materials (1)	cloak (8)	cloth (6)	clothing-women's (1)
club (10)	coal (1)	coals (3)	cobweb (1)	codpiece (1)	coffer (1)
coffin (15)	collar (1)	comb (2)	commission (4)	contract (2)	cord (1)
cordial (1)	corn (2)	coronet (2)	corpse (8)	corpse-headless (1)	cosmetics (3)
couch (2)	counter (2)	cowl-staff (2)	cradle (2)	cream (2)	crocodile (1)
crosier-staff (3)	cross (1)	cross-keys (1)	crossbow (4)	crossroads (1)	crowbar (2)
crown (13)	crown-papal (1)	crucifix (5)	crutches (5)	cudgel (10)	cup (43)
cupboard (1)	curtain (28)	cushion (17)	cutlass (2)	cutlery (1)	dag (1)
dagger (38)	dais (2)	dart (2)	deed (1)	degrees (1)	desk (2)
diamond (13)	diary (1)	dice (9)	dish (14)	distaff (5)	document (54)
dog (5)	doublet (1)	dove (2)	drink-sack (12)	drink-unspecified (2)	dust (1)
eagle (1)	ear-ring (2)	ear-severed (1)	edict (1)	effigy-wax (1)	eggs (2)
embroidery (1)	ensign (12)	entrails (2)	ewer (1)	eye-newt (1)	fabric (2)
fabric-calico (1)	fabric-cambric (4)	fabric-holland (2)	fabric-lawn (2)	faggots (1)	falcon (1)
fall (2)	fan (12)	fardel (1)	fasces (3)	favour (3)	feast (1)
feather (2)	featherbed (1)	fetters (1)	finger-severed (1)	fire (12)	flag (3)
flagon (2)	flail (2)	flowers (17)	foil (2)	food-unspecified (12)	form (2)
fountain (1)	fruit (2)	fustian (1)	gag (6)	gage (5)	gall (1)
galley-pot (1)	gallipot (1)	gallows (5)	game-board (1)	game-pieces (1)	garland (7)

garment-bloody (1)	garments (1)	garter (4)	gauntlet (1)	gift (3)	ginger (2)
glaive (1)	glass (7)	glass-broken (1)	globe (3)	glove (18)	goat (1)
goblet (4)	goose (1)	gown (10)	gown-pilgrim (1)	gown-russet (1)	gown-shepherd (1)
grapes (2)	grease (1)	greyhound (1)	gum (1)	gunpowder (1)	hair (1)
halberd (16)	half-pike (2)	halter (21)	hammer (1)	hand-basket (1)	hand-severed (2)
handkerchief (15)	handkerchief-bloody (2)	hangings (6)	hat (8)	hay (1)	head-bear (1)
head-severed (17)	head-stag (1)	headdress (1)	hearse (10)	heart (1)	heart-gold (1)
helmet (2)	hemlock (1)	hemp (1)	herbs (6)	herring-red (1)	hill (1)
hippocras (1)	honey (2)	horoscope (1)	horse-dung (1)	horseshoe (1)	hose (1)
hound (2)	hourglass (4)	hurdle (1)	images-catholic (1)	impresa (10)	imprese (1)
incense (1)	indenture (1)	indictment (4)	ink (33)	inkhorn (2)	inventory (2)
irons (2)	jack (2)	javelin (2)	jewel (31)	jug (6)	key (38)
knife (29)	knife-wooden (1)	ladder (17)	lamp (1)	lance (5)	lance-broken (1)
lancet (1)	lantern (10)	laurel-wreath (3)	leaves (2)	leek (1)	leg-lizard (1)
leg-severed (1)	letter (102)	libel (1)	light (27)	lightning (11)	limb-severed (1)
linen (3)	link (1)	linstock (3)	lion (1)	lips-severed (1)	liquor (14)
liquorice (1)	list (1)	litter (1)	liver (1)	log (1)	looking-glass (8)
lotion (1)	louse (1)	luggage (2)	lure (1)	mace (6)	mallet (1)
mandrake (1)	mantle (2)	map (2)	mask (3)	match (1)	mattock (2)
maw-shark (1)	meat (8)	meat-dog (1)	medicine (2)	mess (2)	military-colours (25)
milk (2)	milk-pail (1)	mirror (9)	molehill (2)	money (116)	money-bag (14)

(cont.)

(cont.)

monkey (1)	mound-crystal (1)	muckender (1)	muffler (1)	mummia (1)	musical-bell (3)
musical-cittern (1)	musical-cornet (2)	musical-drum (48)	musical-drum-kettle (1)	musical-fiddle (8)	musical-fife (4)
musical-flute (1)	musical-harp (4)	musical-horn (11)	musical-lute (10)	musical-lyre (1)	musical-pipe (1)
musical-pipes (3)	musical-recorder (1)	musical-stringed (4)	musical-tabor (3)	musical-theorbo (1)	musical-trumpet (25)
musical-unspecified (13)	musical-viol (5)	musket (5)	muster-roll (1)	mutton (2)	napkin (13)
necklace (3)	needle (4)	needlework (13)	net (3)	nightcap (1)	nightgown (1)
nose-severed (1)	nosegay (1)	note (11)	notebook (1)	nutmeg (1)	nuts (3)
oar (1)	oblations (1)	oil (3)	ointment (4)	opiate (1)	oracle (1)
ordnance (2)	ornament-silver (1)	ornaments-triumphal (1)	ox-horns (1)	pack (1)	pack-pedlar (1)
paintbrush (3)	paints (4)	pan (1)	pan-dripping (1)	pantables (1)	pantofle (1)
papal-bull (1)	paper (71)	parchment (6)	pardon (3)	partisan (3)	patent (4)
pavilion (2)	pearl (11)	pen (44)	pencil (2)	pendant (1)	penknife (1)
pennon (1)	pentacle (1)	perfume (7)	petition (11)	petronel (1)	petticoat (1)
phial (1)	pickaxe (1)	picture (21)	pie (1)	pigeon (1)	pike (7)
pikestaff (2)	pill (1)	pillow (5)	pin (3)	pincers (1)	pint (1)
pistol (16)	pitcher (4)	pitchfork (1)	plague-bill (1)	plaster (1)	plate (4)
playing-cards (7)	plums (2)	point (1)	point-silk (1)	poison (14)	poking-stick (1)
pole-barber (1)	poleaxe (4)	poniard (7)	pork-loin (1)	porridge (1)	porringer (1)
portrait (1)	posset (2)	posy (1)	pot (8)	poting-stick (1)	potion (3)
pottle (1)	pottle-pot (1)	powder (5)	powder-flask (1)	precept (1)	proclamation (4)
prospective-glass (1)	pudding (1)	pumps (1)	purse (50)	purse-money (1)	quart (1)
quill (2)	quiver (2)	racket (4)	rapier (45)	rattle (1)	razor (1)
rebato (3)	reel-fishing (1)	reprieve (2)	ring (34)	ring-signet (8)	robe (3)

rock-large (2) | rod (6) | rod-fishing (2) | root (1) | roots (1) | rope (8)

rosa-solis (1) | rosary-beads (2) | ruby (3) | ruff (1) | ruff-bloody (1) | rushes (5)

sack (3) | salad (1) | salmon-jowl (1) | salt (2) | salt-cellar (2) | sapphire (1)

sarcenet (1) | satchel (1) | saucer (1) | scaffold (4) | scale-dragon (1) | scales (1)

scarf (8) | sceptre (8) | sceptre-broken (1) | scimitar (4) | sconce (1) | scrip (1)

scroll (8) | scutcheon (3) | scuttle (1) | scythe (1) | seal (8) | seat (22)
seat-judgement (1) | seating (67) | seven-headed-beast (1) | shackles (3) | shears (2) | sheep-hook (1)

sheephook (1) | shield (16) | shirt (1) | shoes (4) | shop (2) | shrine (1)
shuttle-cock (1) | siletto (1) | silk (2) | siquisses (1) | skeleton (1) | skull (6)

sledgehammer (1) | sleeve (1) | slippers (1) | smock (1) | smoke (2) | snake (3)

soap (2) | socks (1) | spade (6) | spear (4) | spice (1) | spindle (2)
spit (4) | spoils (2) | spoon (5) | sprig (1) | spring (1) | spurs (1)
staff (27) | staff-broken (1) | stall (1) | standish (4) | star-blazing (3) | statue (2)

statute (1) | stick (2) | stocking (1) | stockings (2) | stocks (5) | stones (4)
stool (28) | stool-joint (2) | stopple (1) | stoup (1) | strands-gold (1) | strap (1)

streamer (1) | sugar (2) | suit (2) | supplication (2) | sweetmeats (6) | sword (119)

sword-broken (2) | sword-long (3) | sword-short (7) | syringe (1) | table (55) | tablecloth (9)
tankard (3) | taper (15) | target (6) | teeth (2) | tennis-ball (1) | tent (3)

testern (1) | thread (4) | thread-ball (1) | throne (21) | thumb-severed (1) | thurible (1)

tires (1) | title-board (7) | toad (1) | tobacco (11) | tobacco-pipe (13) | toe-frog (1)

token (4) | tomb (11) | tongue-adder (1) | tongue-severed (2) | tool-barber (2) | tool-builder (1)

tool-cobbler (5) | tool-cutting (4) | tool-surgical (1) | top (1) | torch (42) | torch-staff (1)
tortoise-shell (1) | torture-device (4) | towel (6) | towel-bloody (1) | toy-bubble-blower (1) | tree (15)

(cont.)

(cont.)

tree-golden (1)	tree-small (1)	trencher (2)	trick-chair (1)	trident (1)	trowel (1)
truncheon (5)	trunk (5)	tun (2)	turf (1)	tweezers (1)	twig (1)
urinal (2)	urine (1)	urn (1)	venison (1)	vessel (1)	vial (5)
viand (1)	voider (1)	waistcoat (1)	walking-stick (1)	wallet (1)	wand (7)
warder (2)	warrant (14)	watch (11)	water (16)	wax (4)	wax-tablet (1)
weapon-bill (15)	weapon-blade (28)	weapon-goad (1)	weapon-projectile (1)	weapon-unspecified (40)	well (2)
wheel (1)	wheel-spinning (1)	whip (7)	wig (1)	will (3)	wine (62)
wing-owlet (1)	wiper (1)	wood (1)	wool (2)	writ (1)	writing-materials (7)
yardstick (3)					

APPENDIX E

A List of 221 Function Words

a	about	above	after	again	against	all
almost	along	although	am	among	amongst	an
and	another	any	anything	are	art	as
at	back	be	because	been	before	being
besides	beyond	both	but	by$_{adverb}$	by$_{preposition}$	can
cannot	canst	could	dare	darest	dareth	did
didst	do	does	doing	done	dost	doth
down	durst	each	either	enough	ere	even
ever	every	few	for$_{adverb}$	for$_{conjunction}$	for$_{preposition}$	from
had	hadst	has	hast	hath	have	having
he	hence	her$_{adjective}$	her$_{personalPronoun}$	here	him	himself
his	how	I	if	in$_{adverb}$	in$_{preposition}$	into
is	it	itself	least	like$_{adjective}$	like$_{adverb}$	like$_{preposition}$
likest	liketh	many	may	mayst	me	might
mightst	mine	most	much	must	my	myself
neither	never	no$_{adjective}$	no$_{adverb}$	no$_{exclamation}$	none	nor
not	nothing	now	O	of	off	oft
often	on$_{adverb}$	on$_{preposition}$ one	only	or	other	
our$_{royalPlural}$	our$_{truePlural}$	ourselves	out	over	own	past
perhaps	quite	rather	round	same	shall	shalt
she	should	shouldst	since	sith	so$_{adverbDegree}$	so$_{adverbManner}$
so$_{conjunction}$	some	something	somewhat	still	such	than
that$_{conjunction}$	that$_{demonstrative}$	that$_{relative}$	the	thee	their	them
themselves	then	there	these	they	thine	this
those	thou	though	through	thus	thy	thyself
till	to$_{adverb}$	to$_{infinitive}$	to$_{preposition}$	too	under	until
unto	up$_{adverb}$	up$_{preposition}$	upon$_{adverb}$	upon$_{preposition}$	us$_{royalPlural}$	us$_{truePlural}$
very	was	we$_{royalPlural}$	we$_{truePlural}$	well	were	wert
what	when	where	which$_{interrogative}$	which$_{relative}$	while	whilst
who$_{interrogative}$	who$_{relative}$	whom	whose	why	will$_{verb}$	with
within	without	would	wouldst	ye	yet	you
your	yours	yourself	yourselves			

Works Cited

SIXTEENTH- AND SEVENTEENTH-CENTURY NON-DRAMATIC TEXTS[1]

Dryden, John. *Of Dramatic Poesy: An Essay*. London, 1668. Wing D2327.
Gosson, Stephen. *Plays Confuted in Five Actions*. London, 1589. STC 12095.
Greene, Robert. *Menaphon*. London, 1599. STC 12272.
Oldham, John. *The Works*. London, 1684. Wing O225.
Peele, George. *A Farewell*. London, 1589. STC 19537.
Shakespeare, William. *Poems*. London, 1640. STC 22344.

LATER EDITIONS OF EARLY MODERN TEXTS

Brome, Richard. *Richard Brome Online*. Richard Allen Cave (gen. ed.). Sheffield: HRI Online. 2010–.
Chapman, George. *The Conspiracy and Tragedy of Byron*. Ed. John Margeson. Manchester University Press, 1988.
    The Widow's Tears. Ed. Akihiro Yamada. London: Methuen, 1975.
Clare, Janet, ed. *Drama of the English Republic, 1649–60*. Manchester University Press, 2002.
Day, John. *The Works of John Day*. Ed. A. H. Bullen. Rev. Robin Jeffs. London: Holland Press, 1963.
Dekker, Thomas, and Thomas Middleton. *1 The Honest Whore*. Ed. Joost Daalder. Digital Renaissance Editions, 2015.
Fletcher, John. *The Island Princess*. Ed. Clare McManus. London: Arden Shakespeare, 2013.
    The Wild-Goose Chase. Ed. Sophie Tomlinson. In: *Three Seventeenth-Century Plays on Women and Performance*. Ed. Hero Chalmers, Julie Sanders, and Sophie Tomlinson. Manchester University Press, 2006.
Fraser, Russell A., and Norman Rabkin, eds. *Drama of the English Renaissance*. 2 vols. New York: Macmillan, 1976.

---

[1] Unless otherwise stated, all citations in this section refer to facsimiles of individual copies of a particular edition accessed using *Early English Books Online*. Appendix A provides bibliographical details for dramatic texts from the period.

Greg, W. W., ed. *Henslowe Papers*. London: A. H. Bullen, 1907.

Henslowe, Philip. *Henslowe's Diary*. Ed. W. W. Greg. 2 vols. London: A. H. Bullen, 1904 and 1908.

Heywood, Thomas. *A Woman Killed with Kindness*. Ed. R. W. van Fossen. London: Methuen, 1961.

Howard, Edward. *The Change of Crowns*. Ed. F. S. Boas. Oxford University Press [for The Royal Society of Literature], 1949.

Jonson, Ben. *The Cambridge Edition of the Works of Ben Jonson*. David Bevington, Martin Butler, and Ian Donaldson (gen. eds.). 7 vols. Cambridge University Press, 2012.

King Leir. Ed. Donald M. Richie. New York: Garland, 1991.

King Leir. Ed. Tiffany Stern. London: Nick Hern, 2003.

Kyd, Thomas. *Soliman and Perseda*. Ed. Lukas Erne. Manchester University Press, 2014.

Lodge, Thomas. *The Wounds of Civil War*. Ed. Joseph W. Houppert. Lincoln, NE: University of Nebraska Press, 1969.

Marlowe, Christopher. *Dido, Queen of Carthage and The Massacre at Paris*. Ed. H. J. Oliver. London: Methuen, 1968.

Edward the Second. Ed. Charles R. Forker. Manchester University Press, 1994.

[1 and 2] Tamburlaine the Great. Ed. J. S. Cunningham. Manchester University Press, 1981.

Marston, John. *Antonio and Mellida*. Ed. W. Reavley Gair. Manchester University Press, 1991.

The Dutch Courtesan. Ed. David Crane. London: A&C Black, 1997.

The Works of John Marston. Ed. A. H. Bullen. 3 vols. London: Nimmo, 1887.

Middleton, Thomas. *Thomas Middleton: The Collected Works*. Gary Taylor and John Lavagnino (gen. eds.). Oxford University Press, 2007.

Morris, E. C., ed. *'The Spanish Gipsie' and 'All's Lost by Lust'*. Boston: D. C. Heath & Co., 1908.

Peele, George. *The Battle of Alcazar*. In: *The Stukeley Plays*. Ed. Charles Edelman. Manchester University Press, 2005.

Puttenham, George. *The Art of English Poesy*. Ed. Frank Whigham and Wayne A. Rebhorn. Ithaca: Cornell University Press, 2007.

Rowley, William. *'All's Lost by Lust' and 'A Shoemaker, a Gentleman'*. Ed. C. W. Stork. Philadelphia: University of Pennsylvania Press, 1910.

Shakespeare, William. *The Complete Works*. Ed. Stanley Wells and Gary Taylor. 2nd edn. Oxford University Press, 2005.

The First Folio of Shakespeare: The Norton Facsimile. Ed. Charlton Hinman. New York: W. W. Norton, 1968.

Hamlet: The Texts of 1603 and 1623. Ed. Ann Thompson and Neil Taylor. London: Arden Shakespeare, 2006.

Henry the Fourth, Part Two. Ed. Jonathan Bate and Eric Rasmussen. Basingstoke: Palgrave Macmillan, 2009.

Henry the Fourth, Part Two. Ed. David Bevington. Oxford University Press, 1994.

Henry the Fourth, Part Two. Ed. Rosemary Gaby. Peterborough: Broadview Press, 2013.

Henry the Fourth, Part Two. Ed. David Scott Kastan. London: Arden Shakespeare, 2002.

Henry the Fourth, Part Two. Ed. Herbert Weil and Judith Weil. Cambridge University Press, 1997; rev. edn 2007.

The Works of Shakespear in Six Volumes. Ed. Alexander Pope. 6 vols. London, 1723–5.

Sharpham, Edward. *A Critical Old Spelling Edition of the Works of Edward Sharpham.* Ed. Christopher Gordon Petter. New York: Garland, 1986.

DATABASES AND OTHER ELECTRONIC RESOURCES

DEEP: Database of Early English Playbooks. Ed. Alan B. Farmer and Zachary Lesser. 2007–.

Digital Renaissance Editions [DRE]. Brett Greatley-Hirsch (co-ord. ed.). 2015–.

Early English Books Online [EEBO]. Chadwyck-Healey (ProQuest LLC). 2001–.

Intelligent Archive. Dev. Hugh Craig, R. Whipp, Michael Ralston, and Jack Elliott. Centre for Literary and Linguistic Computing, University of Newcastle. 2007–.

Literature Online [LION]. Chadwyck-Healey (ProQuest LLC). 1998–.

Lost Plays Database. Ed. Roslyn L. Knutson, David McInnis, and Matthew Steggle. 2009–.

R. R Foundation for Statistical Computing. 1994–.

SPSS [= IBM SPSS Statistics]. IBM Corporation. 1968–.

VARD. Dev. Alistair Baron. Lancaster University. 2006–.

CRITICAL BIBLIOGRAPHY

Abrams, Richard. '"Exercise in this Kind": Shakespeare and the "Funeral Elegy" for William Peter'. *Shakespeare Studies* 25 (1997): 141–70.

Adamson, Sylvia. 'Understanding Shakespeare's Grammar: Studies in Small Words'. In: *Reading Shakespeare's Dramatic Language: A Guide.* Ed. Sylvia Adamson, Lynette Hunter, Lynne Magnusson, Anne Thompson, and Katie Wales. London: Arden Shakespeare, 2001. 210–36.

Alt, Mick. *Exploring Hyperspace: A Non-Mathematical Explanation of Multivariate Analysis.* Maidenhead: McGraw-Hill, 1990.

Ambegaokar, Vinay. *Reasoning about Luck: Probability and Its Uses in Physics.* Cambridge University Press, 1996.

Anderson, Thomas, and Scott Crossley. '"Rue with a Difference": A Computational Stylistic Analysis of the Rhetoric of Suicide in *Hamlet*'. In: *Stylistics and Shakespeare's Language: Transdisciplinary Approaches.* Ed. Mireille Ravassat and Jonathan Culpeper. London: Continuum, 2011. 192–214.

Antonia, Alexis, Hugh Craig, and Jack Elliott. 'Language Chunking, Data Sparseness, and the Value of a Long Marker List'. *Literary and Linguistic Computing* 29.2 (2014): 147–63.

Archer, Dawn, and Derek Bousfield. '"See Better, Lear?" See Lear Better! A Corpus-Based Pragma-Stylistic Investigation of Shakespeare's *King Lear*'. In: *Language and Style*. Ed. Dan McIntyre and Beatrix Busse. Basingstoke: Palgrave, 2010. 183–203.

Argamon, Shlomo. 'Interpreting Burrows's Delta: Geometric and Probabilistic Foundations'. *Literary and Linguistic Computing* 23.2 (2008): 131–47.

Ascari, Maurizio. 'The Dangers of Distant Reading: Reassessing Moretti's Approach to Literary Genres'. *Genre* 47.1 (2014): 1–19.

Astington, John H. *Actors and Acting in Shakespeare's Time: The Art of Stage Playing*. Cambridge University Press, 2010.

Barber, Charles. *Early Modern English*. Edinburgh University Press, 1997.

Barish, Jonas A. *Ben Jonson and the Language of Prose Comedy*. Cambridge, MA: Harvard University Press, 1960.

'Hal, Falstaff, Henry V, and Prose'. *Connotations* 2.3 (1992): 263–8.

Baron, Alistair, Paul Rayson, and Dawn Archer. 'Word Frequency and Key Word Statistics in Historical Corpus Linguistics'. *Anglistik* 20.1 (2009): 41–67.

Bennett, Tony. 'Counting and Seeing the Social Action of Literary Form: Franco Moretti and the Sociology of Literature'. *Cultural Sociology* 3.2 (2009): 277–97.

Beugnet, Frédéric, Thibaud Porphyre, Paul Sabatier, and Karine Chalvet-Monfray. 'Use of a Mathematical Model to Study the Dynamics of *Ctenocephalides Felis* Populations in the Home Environment and the Impact of Various Control Measures'. *Parasite* 11.4 (2004): 387–99.

Bevington, David. *Action is Eloquence: Shakespeare's Language of Gesture*. Cambridge, MA: Harvard University Press, 1984.

Bevis, Richard W. *English Drama: Restoration and Eighteenth Century, 1660–1789*. London: Longman, 1988.

Biber, Douglas. *Variation across Speech and Writing*. Cambridge University Press, 1988.

Bickley, Pamela, and Jenny Stevens. *Shakespeare and Early Modern Drama: Text and Performance*. London: Bloomsbury Arden Shakespeare, 2016.

Binongo, José Nilo G., and M. W. A. Smith. 'The Application of Principal Component Analysis to Stylometry'. *Literary and Linguistic Computing* 14.4 (1999): 445–65.

Blake, N. F. *Shakespeare's Language: An Introduction*. London: Macmillan, 1983.

Bly, Mary. *Queer Virgins and Virgin Queans on the Early Modern Stage*. Oxford University Press, 2000.

Booth, Stephen. 'A Long, Dull Poem by William Shakespeare'. *Shakespeare Studies* 25 (1997): 229–37.

Borish, M. E. 'John Day's *Humour Out of Breath*'. *Harvard Studies and Notes in Philology and Literature* 16 (1934): 1–11.

Bosonnet, Felix. *The Function of Stage Properties in Christopher Marlowe's Plays.* Bern: Francke Verlag, 1978.

Boyd, Brian. 'Getting It All Wrong: The Proponents of Theory and Cultural Critique Could Learn a Thing or Two from Bioculture'. *The American Scholar* 1 Sept. 2006.

Boyd, Ryan L. and James W. Pennebaker. 'Did Shakespeare Write *Double Falsehood?* Identifying Individuals by Creating Psychological Signatures with Text Analysis'. *Psychological Science* 26.5 (2015): 570–82.

Bradley, A. C. *Shakespearean Tragedy.* London: Macmillan, 1904.

Breiman, Leo. 'Random Forests'. *Machine Learning* 45.1 (2001): 5–32.

Brook, G. L. *The Language of Shakespeare.* London: André Deutsch, 1976.

Brown, Bill. 'Thing Theory'. *Critical Inquiry* 28.1 (2001): 1–22.

Brown, Roger, and Albert Gilman. 'The Pronouns of Power and Solidarity'. In: *Style in Language.* Ed. Thomas A. Sebeok. Cambridge, MA: MIT Press, 1960. 253–76.

Bruster, Douglas. 'Christopher Marlowe and the Verse/Prose Bilingual System'. *Marlowe Studies* 1 (2011): 141–65.

'The Dramatic Life of Objects in the Early Modern English Theater'. In: *Staged Properties in Early Modern English Drama.* Ed. Jonathan Gil Harris and Natasha Korda. Cambridge University Press, 2002. 67–96.

'The Politics of Shakespeare's Prose'. In: *Rematerializing Shakespeare: Authority and Representation on the Early Modern English Stage.* Ed. Bryan Reynolds and William N. West. New York: Palgrave Macmillan, 2005. 95–114.

Shakespeare and the Question of Culture: Early Modern Literature and the Cultural Turn. New York: Palgrave, 2003.

Bruster, Douglas, and Geneviève Smith. 'A New Chronology for Shakespeare's Plays'. *Digital Scholarship in the Humanities* 31.2 (2016): 301–20.

Burlinson, Christopher. 'Money and Consumerism'. In: *Ben Jonson in Context.* Ed. Julie Sanders. Cambridge University Press, 2010. 281–8.

Burns, Michael. 'Why No *Henry VII?* (With a Postscript on Malvolio's Revenge)'. In: *Manner and Meaning in Shakespeare: Stratford Papers 1965–67.* Ed. B. A. W. Jackson. Hamilton: McMaster University Library Press, 1969. 208–31.

Burrows, John. *Computation into Criticism: A Study of Jane Austen and an Experiment in Method.* Oxford: Clarendon Press, 1987.

'Delta: A Measure of Stylistic Difference and a Guide to Likely Authorship'. *Literary and Linguistic Computing* 17.3 (2002): 267–86.

Jane Austen's 'Emma'. Sydney University Press, 1968.

'Questions of Authorship: Attribution and Beyond'. *Computers and the Humanities* 37.1 (2003): 5–32.

Burrows, John, and D. H. Craig. 'Lyrical Drama and the "Turbid Mountebanks": Styles of Dialogue in Romantic and Restoration Tragedy'. *Computers and the Humanities* 28 (1994): 63–86.

Burton, Dolores M. *Shakespeare's Grammatical Style: A Computer-Assisted Analysis of 'Richard II' and 'Antony and Cleopatra'.* Austin: University of Texas Press, 1973.

Busse, Ulrich. *Linguistic Variation in the Shakespeare Corpus: Morpho-Syntactic Variability of Second Person Pronouns*. Amsterdam: John Benjamins, 2002.

Butler, Martin. *Theatre and Crisis 1632–1642*. Cambridge University Press, 1984.

Canfield, J. Douglas. *Tricksters and Estates: On the Ideology of Restoration Comedy*. Lexington: University Press of Kentucky, 1997.

Cathcart, Charles. 'Authorship, Indebtedness, and the Children of the King's Revels'. *SEL: Studies in English Literature 1500–1900* 45.2 (2005): 357–74.

Marston, Rivalry, Rapprochement, and Jonson. Aldershot: Ashgate, 2008.

Chambers, E. K. *William Shakespeare: A Study of Facts and Problems*. 2 vols. Oxford: Clarendon Press, 1930.

Chapman, R. W., ed. *Jane Austen's Six Novels*. 5 vols. 3rd illus. edn. Oxford University Press, 1932–5.

Chatfield, Christopher, and Alexander J. Collins. *Introduction to Multivariate Analysis*. New York: Chapman & Hall, 1980.

Clare, Janet. *Shakespeare's Stage Traffic: Imitation, Borrowing and Competition in Renaissance Theatre*. Cambridge University Press, 2014.

Clemen, Wolfgang. *English Tragedy before Shakespeare*. London: Routledge, 1961.

Collins, Eleanor. 'Richard Brome and the Salisbury Court Contract'. *Richard Brome Online*. Richard Allen Cave (gen. ed.). 2010.

'Richard Brome's Contract and the Relationship of Dramatist to Company in the Early Modern Period'. *Early Theatre* 10.2 (2007): 116–28.

Connors, Louisa. 'Computational Stylistics, Cognitive Grammar, and *The Tragedy of Mariam*: Combining Formal and Contextual Approaches in a Computational Study of Early Modern Tragedy'. Ph.D. thesis: University of Newcastle, 2013.

Cook, Ann Jennalie. *The Privileged Playgoers of Shakespeare's London, 1576–1642*. Princeton University Press, 1981.

Corman, Brian. *Genre and Generic Change in English Comedy, 1660–1710*. University of Toronto Press, 1993.

Costantini, Domenico, and Ubaldo Garibaldi. 'A Stochastic Foundation of the Approach to Equilibrium of Classical and Quantum Gases'. In: *The Foundations of Quantum Mechanics: Historical Analysis and Open Questions*. Ed. Claudio Garola and Arcangelo Rossi. New Jersey: World Scientific Publishing Co., 2000. 137–50.

Craig, Hugh. 'A and *an* in English Plays, 1580–1639'. *Texas Studies in Literature and Language* 53.3 (2011): 273–93.

'Authorial Attribution and Computational Stylistics: If You Can Tell Authors Apart, Have You Learned Anything about Them?' *Literary and Linguistic Computing* 14.1 (1999): 103–13.

'Grammatical Modality in English Plays from the 1580s to the 1640s'. *English Literary Renaissance* 30.1 (2000): 32–54.

'Is the Author Really Dead? An Empirical Study of Authorship in English Renaissance Drama'. *Empirical Studies in the Arts* 18.2 (2000): 119–34.

'Plural Pronouns in Roman Plays by Shakespeare and Jonson'. *Literary and Linguistic Computing* 6 (1991): 180–6.

'Shakespeare's Vocabulary: Myth and Reality'. *Shakespeare Quarterly* 62.1 (2011): 53–74.

'"Speak, That I May See Thee": Shakespeare Characters and Common Words'. *Shakespeare Survey* 61 (2008): 281–8.

'Style, Statistics, and New Models of Authorship'. *Early Modern Literary Studies* 15.1 (2009–10): 1–42.

Craig, Hugh, and R. Whipp. 'Old Spellings, New Methods: Automated Procedures for Indeterminate Linguistic Data'. *Literary and Linguistic Computing* 25.1 (2010): 37–52.

Crystal, David. *'Think on My Words': Exploring Shakespeare's Language*. Cambridge University Press, 2008.

Culpeper, Jonathan. 'Keywords and Characterization: An Analysis of Six Characters in *Romeo and Juliet*'. In: *Digital Literary Studies: Corpus Approaches to Poetry, Prose and Drama*. Ed. David L. Hoover, Jonathan Culpeper, and Kieran O'Halloran. New York: Routledge, 2014. 9–34.

Cutts, John P. 'Thomas Heywood's "The Gentry to the King's Head" in *The Rape of Lucrece* and John Wilson's Setting'. *Notes & Queries* 8.10 (1961): 384–7.

de Man, Paul. 'Literary History and Literary Modernity'. *Daedalus* 99.2 (1970): 384–404.

Desmet, Christy. *Reading Shakespeare's Characters: Rhetoric, Ethics, and Identity*. Amherst: University of Massachusetts Press, 1992.

Dessen, Alan, and Leslie Thomson. *A Dictionary of Stage Directions in English Drama, 1580–1642*. Cambridge University Press, 1999.

Dixon, Peter, and Marisa Bortolussi. 'Fluctuations in Literary Reading: The Neglected Dimension of Time'. In: *The Oxford Handbook of Cognitive Literary Studies*. Ed. Lisa Zunshine. Oxford University Press, 2015. 541–56.

Dobson, James E. 'Can an Algorithm Be Disturbed?: Machine Learning, Intrinsic Criticism, and the Digital Humanities'. *College Literature* 42.4 (2015): 543–64.

Downer, Alan S. 'The Life of Our Design: The Function of Imagery in the Poetic Drama'. *The Hudson Review* 2.2 (1949): 242–63.

Duncan-Jones, Katherine. 'Who Wrote *A Funerall Elegie?*' *Shakespeare Studies* 25 (1997): 192–210.

Dutton, Richard, ed. *The Oxford Handbook of Early Modern Theatre*. Oxford University Press, 2008.

Edmondson, Paul, and Stanley Wells. *Shakespeare Bites Back: Not So Anonymous*. Stratford-upon-Avon: Shakespeare Birthplace Trust, 2011.

Egan, Gabriel. 'What Is Not Collaborative about Early Modern Drama in Performance and Print?' *Shakespeare Survey* 67 (2014): 18–28.

Ehrenfest, Paul, and Tatiana Ehrenfest. 'Über zwei bekannte Einwände gegen das Boltzmannsche H-Theorem'. *Physikalische Zeitschrift* 8 (1907): 311–14.

Eliot, T. S. 'The Function of Criticism' (1923). In: *Selected Essays*. 2nd edn. London: Faber and Faber, 1932. 23–34.

Poetry and Drama. London: Faber and Faber, 1951.

Elliott, Jack. 'Patterns and Trends in Harlequin Category Romance'. In: *Advancing Digital Humanities: Research, Methods, Theories*. Ed. Paul Longley Arthur and Katherine Bode. New York: Palgrave, 2014. 54–67.

Elliott, Jack, and Brett Greatley-Hirsch. '*Arden of Faversham*, Shakespeare, and "the print of many"'. In: *The New Oxford Shakespeare: Authorship Companion*. Ed. Gary Taylor and Gabriel Egan. Oxford University Press, 2017. 139–81.

Elliott, Ward E. Y., and Robert J. Valenza. 'Oxford by the Numbers: What Are the Odds that the Earl of Oxford Could Have Written Shakespeare's Poems and Plays?' *The Tennessee Law Review* 72.1 (2004): 323–453.

'Shakespeare's Vocabulary: Did It Dwarf All Others?' In: *Stylistics and Shakespeare's Language: Transdisciplinary Approaches*. Ed. Mireille Ravassat and Jonathan Culpeper. London: Continuum, 2011. 34–57.

Engle, Lars. *Shakespearean Pragmatism: Market of His Time*. University of Chicago Press, 1993.

Enkvist, Nils Erik. 'On Defining Style: An Essay on Applied Linguistics'. In: *Linguistics and Style*. Ed. Nils Erik Enkvist, John Spencer, and Michael Gregory. Oxford University Press, 1964. 1–56.

Erne, Lukas. *Beyond 'The Spanish Tragedy': A Study of the Works of Thomas Kyd*. Manchester University Press, 2001.

Fish, Stanley E. 'Mind Your P's and B's: The Digital Humanities and Interpretation'. *Opinionator* 23 Jan. 2012.

'What Is Stylistics and Why Are They Saying Such Terrible Things about It?' In: *Approaches to Poetics: Selected Papers from the English Institute*. Ed. Seymour Chatman. New York: Columbia University Press, 1973. 109–52.

'What Is Stylistics and Why Are They Saying Such Terrible Things about It? Part ii'. In: *Is There a Text in This Class?* Cambridge, MA: Harvard University Press, 1980. 246–67.

Floridi, Luciano. *Information: A Very Short Introduction*. Oxford University Press, 2010.

Forker, Charles R. 'Marlowe's *Edward II* and Its Shakespearean Relatives: The Emergence of a Genre'. In: *Shakespeare's English Histories: A Quest for Form and Genre*. Ed. John W. Velz. Binghamton: Medieval and Renaissance Texts and Studies, 1996. 55–90.

Foster, Donald W. '*A Funeral Elegy*: W[illiam] S[hakespeare]'s "Best-Speaking Witnesses"'. *PMLA* 111.5 (1996): 1080–105.

'*A Funeral Elegy*: W[illiam] S[hakespeare]'s "Best-Speaking Witnesses"'. *Shakespeare Studies* 25 (1997): 115–40.

'The Text of *A Funeral Elegy* by W. S.'. *Shakespeare Studies* 25 (1997): 95–114.

Frow, John. *Genre*. New York: Routledge, 2006.

Gair, Reavley. *The Children of Paul's: The Story of a Theatre Company, 1553–1608*. Cambridge University Press, 1982.

Geertz, Clifford. *Local Knowledge: Further Essays in Interpretive Anthropology*. New York: Basic Books, 1983.

Gibbons, Brian. 'Romance and the Heroic Play'. In: *The Cambridge Companion to English Renaissance Drama*. Ed. A. R. Braunmuller and Michael Hattaway. Cambridge University Press, 1990. 207–36.

Gleick, James. *The Information: A History, a Theory, a Flood.* New York: Pantheon, 2011.

Gombrich, Ernst H. 'Style'. In: *International Encyclopedia of the Social Sciences.* Ed. David L. Sills. 18 vols. New York: Macmillan, 1968–79. Vol. xv: 352–61.

Goodwin, Jonathan, and John Holbo, eds. *Reading Graphs, Maps, Trees: Responses to Franco Moretti.* Anderson: Parlor Press, 2011.

Graves, R. B. *Lighting the Shakespearean Stage, 1567–1642.* Carbondale: Southern Illinois University Press, 1999.

Greenacre, Michael. *Biplots in Practice.* Bilbao: Fundación BBVA, 2010.

Greene, Thomas. 'The Flexibility of the Self in Renaissance Literature'. In: *The Disciplines of Criticism.* Ed. Peter Demetz, Thomas Greene, and Lowry Nelson, Jr. New Haven: Yale University Press, 1968. 241–64.

Griffith, Eva. *A Jacobean Company and Its Playhouse: The Queen's Servants at the Red Bull Theatre (c. 1605–1619).* Cambridge University Press, 2013.

Gurr, Andrew. *The Shakespeare Company, 1594–1642.* Cambridge University Press, 2004.

 Shakespeare's Opposites: The Admiral's Company, 1594–1625. Cambridge University Press, 2012.

 The Shakespearian Playing Companies. Oxford University Press, 1996.

Haaker, Ann. 'The Plague, the Theater, and the Poet'. *Renaissance Drama* 1 (1968): 283–306.

Hacking, Ian. *The Taming of Chance.* Cambridge University Press, 1990.

Hadfield, Andrew. *Shakespeare and Republicanism.* Cambridge University Press, 2005.

Hanan, Jim, Przemyslaw Prusinkiewicz, Myron Zalucki, and David Skirvin. 'Simulation of Insect Movement with Respect to Plant Architecture and Morphogenesis'. *Computers and Electronics in Agriculture* 35.2–3 (2002): 255–69.

Harbage, Alfred, and Samuel Schoenbaum. *Annals of English Drama, 975–1700.* 2nd edn. Philadelphia: University of Pennsylvania Press, 1964.

Hartman, Geoffrey. 'Toward Literary History'. *Daedalus* 99.2 (1970): 355–83.

Harris, Jonathan Gil, and Natasha Korda, eds. *Staged Properties in Early Modern English Drama.* Cambridge University Press, 2002.

Hauert, Christoph, Jan Nagler, and Heinz Georg Schuster. 'Of Dogs and Fleas: The Dynamics of N Uncoupled Two-State Systems'. *Journal of Statistical Physics* 116.5–6 (2004): 1453–69.

Heffner, Hubert C. 'Pirandello and the Nature of Man'. *Tulane Drama Review* 1.3 (1957): 23–40.

Hieatt, Charles W., Kent Hieatt, Sidney Thomas, James Hirsh, and Donald W. Foster. 'Forum: Attributing *A Funeral Elegy*'. *PMLA* 112.3 (1997): 429–34.

Higdon, David Leon. 'The Concordance: Mere Index or Needful Census?' *Text* 15 (2003): 51–68.

Hirsch, Brett D. 'Moving Targets: Constructing Canons, 2013–2014'. *Early Theatre* 18.1 (2015): 115–32.

Holbrook, Peter. *English Renaissance Tragedy: Ideas of Freedom*. London: Arden Shakespeare, 2015.

Holmes, David I. 'The Evolution of Stylometry in Humanities Scholarship'. *Literary and Linguistic Computing* 13.3 (1998): 111–17.

Hoover, David L. 'Corpus Stylistics, Stylometry, and the Styles of Henry James'. *Style* 41.2 (2007): 174–203.

'Testing Burrows's Delta'. *Literary and Linguistic Computing* 19.4 (2004): 453–75.

Hope, Jonathan. *The Authorship of Shakespeare's Plays: A Socio-Linguistic Study*. Cambridge University Press, 1994.

Hope, Jonathan, and Michael Witmore. 'The Hundredth Psalm to the Tune of "Green Sleeves": Digital Approaches to Shakespeare's Language of Genre'. *Shakespeare Quarterly* 61.3 (2010): 357–90.

Hotelling, Harold. 'Analysis of a Complex of Statistical Variables into Principal Components'. *Journal of Educational Psychology* 24.6 (1933): 417–41.

Housman, A. E. 'The Application of Thought to Textual Criticism'. *Proceedings of the Classical Association* 18 (1921): 67–84.

Hume, Robert D. 'Diversity and Development in Restoration Comedy, 1660–1679'. *Eighteenth-Century Studies* 5.3 (1972): 365–97.

Hunter, G. K. *English Drama, 1586–1642: The Age of Shakespeare*. Oxford University Press, 1997.

Lyly and Peele. London: Longman, 1968.

Hunter, Lynette, and Peter Lichtenfels. *Negotiating Shakespeare's Language in 'Romeo and Juliet': Reading Strategies from Criticism, Editing and the Theatre*. Farnham: Ashgate, 2009.

Ilsemann, Hartmut. 'More Statistical Observations on Speech-Lengths in Shakespeare's Plays'. *Literary and Linguistic Computing* 23.4 (2008): 397–407.

Jackson, MacDonald P. *Determining the Shakespeare Canon: 'Arden of Faversham' and 'A Lover's Complaint'*. Oxford University Press, 2014.

Jannidis, Fotis, and Gerhard Lauer. 'Burrows's Delta and Its Use in German Literary History'. In: *Distant Readings: Topologies of German Culture in the Long Nineteenth Century*. Ed. Matt Erlin and Lynne Tatlock. Rochester: Camden House, 2014. 29–54.

Jolliffe, I. T. *Principal Component Analysis*. New York: Springer, 1986.

Jones, Emrys. 'The First West End Comedy'. *Proceedings of the British Academy* 68 (1982): 215–58.

Kac, Mark. *Probability and Related Topics in Physical Sciences*. New York: Interscience Publishers, 1959.

Kant, Immanuel. 'Idee zu einer allgemeinen Geschichte in weltbürgerlicher Absicht' = 'Idea of a Universal History on a Cosmo-Political Plan'. Trans. Thomas de Quincy. *The London Magazine* Oct. 1824: 385–93.

Kastan, David Scott. 'The Body of the Text'. *ELH* 81.2 (2014): 443–67.

Kaufer, David, Suguru Ishizaki, Brian Butler, and Jeff Collins. *The Power of Words: Unveiling the Speaker and Writer's Hidden Craft*. Mahwah: Lawrence Erlbaum Associates, 2004.

Kaufmann, R. J. *Richard Brome, Caroline Playwright*. New York: Columbia University Press, 1961.

Kay, W. David. 'The Shaping of Ben Jonson's Career: A Reexamination of Facts and Problems'. *Modern Philology* 67.3 (1970): 224–37.

Keenan, Siobhan. *Acting Companies and Their Plays in Shakespeare's London*. London: Arden Shakespeare, 2014.

Kermode, Frank. *Shakespeare's Language*. London: Penguin, 2000.

Kirkup, Les, and Bob Frenkel. *An Introduction to Uncertainty and Measurement*. Cambridge University Press, 2006.

Kirsch, Adam. 'Technology Is Taking over English Departments: The False Promise of the Digital Humanities'. *New Republic* 2 May 2014.

Klarer, Mario. *An Introduction to Literary Studies*. 3rd edn. New York: Routledge, 1999.

Knutson, Roslyn L. *Playing Companies and Commerce in Shakespeare's Time*. Cambridge University Press, 2001.

   The Repertory of Shakespeare's Company, 1594–1613. Fayetteville: University of Arkansas Press, 1991.

   'The Start of Something Big'. In: *Locating the Queen's Men, 1583–1603*. Ed. Helen Ostovich, Holger Schott Syme, and Andrew Griffin. Farnham: Ashgate, 2009. 99–108.

Kolb, Justin. '"To me comes a creature": Recognition, Agency, and the Properties of Character in Shakespeare's *The Winter's Tale*'. In: *The Automaton in English Renaissance Literature*. Ed. Wendy Beth Hyman. Farnham: Ashgate, 2011. 45–60.

Kramnick, Jonathan. 'Against Literary Darwinism'. *Critical Inquiry* 37.2 (2011): 315–47.

Lake, D. J. 'Three Seventeenth-Century Revisions: *Thomas of Woodstock, The Jew of Malta*, and *Faustus* B'. *Notes & Queries* 30.2 (1983): 133–43.

   'Probing Shakespeare's Idiolect in *Troilus and Cressida*, 1.3.1–29'. *University of Toronto Quarterly* 68 (1999): 728–67.

Lascelles, Mary. *Jane Austen and Her Art*. Oxford: Clarendon Press, 1939.

Leggatt, Alexander. 'The Companies and Actors'. In: *The Revels History of Drama in English*. Ed. Clifford Leech et al. 8 vols. London: Methuen, 1975–83. Vol. III: 95–118.

Logan, Robert A. *Shakespeare's Marlowe: The Influence of Christopher Marlowe on Shakespeare's Artistry*. Aldershot: Ashgate, 2007.

Love, Harold. 'Restoration and Early Eighteenth-Century Drama'. In: *The Cambridge History of English Literature, 1660–1780*. Ed. John Richetti. Cambridge University Press, 2005. 109–31.

Lynch, Kathleen M. *The Social Mode of Restoration Comedy*. New York: Macmillan, 1926.

MacFaul, Tom. *Problem Fathers in Shakespeare and Renaissance Drama*. Cambridge University Press, 2012.

Magnusson, Lynne. 'A Play of Modals: Grammar and Potential Action in Early Shakespeare'. *Shakespeare Survey* 62 (2009): 69–80.

Maguire, Laurie, and Emma Smith. *30 Great Myths about Shakespeare.* Oxford: Blackwell, 2013.

Manley, Lawrence. 'Playing with Fire: Immolation in the Repertory of Strange's Men'. *Early Theatre* 4 (2001): 115–21.

Manley, Lawrence, and Sally-Beth MacLean. *Lord Strange's Men and Their Plays.* New Haven: Yale University Press, 2014.

Marche, Stephen. 'Literature Is Not Data: Against Digital Humanities'. *Los Angeles Review of Books* 28 Oct. 2012.

Margaret of Anjou: A New Shakespeare Play. Dir. Rebecca McCutcheon. Caryl Churchill Theatre, Egham. 8 Mar. 2016.

Marsh, Christopher. *Music and Society in Early Modern England.* Cambridge University Press, 2010.

Masten, Jeffrey. *Textual Intercourse: Collaboration, Authorship, and Sexualities in Renaissance Drama.* Cambridge University Press, 1997.

McCarty, Willard. 'Getting There from Here: Remembering the Future of Digital Humanities'. *Literary and Linguistic Computing* 29.3 (2014): 283–306.

McDonald, Russ. *Shakespeare and the Arts of Language.* Oxford University Press, 2001.

McManaway, James G. 'Philip Massinger and the Restoration Drama'. *ELH* 1 (1934): 276–304.

McMillin, Scott, and Sally-Beth MacLean. *The Queen's Men and Their Plays.* Cambridge University Press, 1998.

McMullan, Gordon. *Shakespeare and the Idea of Late Writing: Authorship in the Proximity of Death.* Cambridge University Press, 2007.

Monsarrat, G. D. '*A Funeral Elegy*: Ford, W. S., and Shakespeare'. *Review of English Studies* 53.210 (2002): 186–203.

Moretti, Franco. 'Style, inc. Reflections on Seven Thousand Titles (British Novels, 1740–1850)'. *Critical Inquiry* 36.1 (2009): 134–58.

Morgann, Maurice. *An Essay on the Dramatic Character of Sir John Falstaff.* London: T. Davies, 1777.

Mosteller, Frederick, and David L. Wallace. *Inference and Disputed Authorship: The Federalist Papers.* Reading: Addison-Wesley, 1964.

Munro, Lucy. *Children of the Queen's Revels: A Jacobean Theatre Repertory.* Cambridge University Press, 2005.

Murray, Barbara A. *Restoration Shakespeare: Viewing the Voice.* Madison: Fairleigh Dickinson University Press, 2001.

Nance, John. 'From Shakespeare "To ye Q"'. *Shakespeare Quarterly* 67.2 (2016): 204–31.

Nason, A. H. *James Shirley, Dramatist: A Biographical and Critical Study.* New York: A. H. Nason, 1915.

Nettleton, George Henry. *English Drama of the Restoration and Eighteenth Century (1642–1780).* New York: Macmillan, 1914.

Nevalainen, Terttu, and Helena Raumolin-Brunberg. *Historical Sociolinguistics: Language Change in Tudor and Stuart England.* London: Longman, 2003.

Nichols, Tom. *The Art of Poverty: Irony and Ideal in Sixteenth-Century Beggar Imagery*. Manchester University Press, 2007.

Novak, Maximilian E. 'The Politics of Shakespeare Criticism in the Restoration and Early Eighteenth Century'. *ELH* 81 (2014): 115–42.

Oras, Ants. *Pause Patterns in Elizabethan and Jacobean Drama: An Experiment in Prosody*. Gainesville: University of Florida Press, 1960.

Orlin, Lena Cowen. 'Things with Little Social Life (Henslowe's Properties and Elizabethan Household Fittings)'. In: *Staged Properties in Early Modern English Drama*. Ed. Jonathan Gil Harris and Natasha Korda. Cambridge University Press, 2002. 99–128.

Ostovich, Helen, Holger Schott Syme, and Andrew Griffin, eds. *Locating the Queen's Men, 1583–1603: Material Practices and Conditions of Playing*. Farnham: Ashgate, 2009.

Palfrey, Simon, and Tiffany Stern. *Shakespeare in Parts*. Oxford University Press, 2007.

Pearson, Karl. 'On Lines and Planes of Closest Fit to Systems of Points in Space'. *Philosophical Magazine* 2.6 (1901): 559–72.

Petersen, Lene B. *Shakespeare's Errant Texts: Textual Form and Linguistic Style in Shakespearean 'Bad' Quartos and Co-Authored Plays*. Cambridge University Press, 2010.

Petrovskii, Sergei, Natalia Petrovskaya, and Daniel Bearup. 'Multiscale Approach to Pest Insect Monitoring: Random Walks, Pattern Formation, Synchronization, and Networks'. *Physics of Life Reviews* 11.3 (2014): 467–525.

Pollard, A. W., and G. R. Redgrave. *A Short-Title Catalogue of Books Printed in England, Scotland, & Ireland and of English Books Printed Abroad, 1475–1640*. 2nd edn. Rev. and enl. W. A. Jackson, F. S. Ferguson, and Katherine F. Panzer. 3 vols. London: Bibliographical Society, 1976–91.

Randall, Dale B. J. *Winter Fruit: English Drama, 1642–1660*. Lexington: University of Kentucky Press, 1995.

Richardson, Catherine. *Shakespeare and Material Culture*. Oxford University Press, 2011.

Rivere de Carles, Nathalie. 'Performing Materiality: Curtains on the Early Modern Stage'. In: *Shakespeare's Theatres and the Effects of Performance*. Ed. Farah Karim-Cooper and Tiffany Stern. London: Bloomsbury Arden Shakespeare, 2013. 51–69.

Roberts, Sasha. '"Let me the curtains draw": The Dramatic and Symbolic Properties of the Bed in Shakespearean Tragedy'. In: *Staged Properties in Early Modern English Drama*. Ed. Jonathan Gil Harris and Natasha Korda. Cambridge University Press, 2002. 153–74.

Robertson, J. M. *The Problem of 'The Merry Wives of Windsor'*. London: Chatto and Windus [for The Shakespeare Association], 1917.

Ronan, Clifford. *'Antike Roman': Power Symbology and the Roman Play in Early Modern England, 1585–1635*. Athens, GA: University of Georgia Press, 1995.

Rosso, Osvaldo A., Hugh Craig, and Pablo Moscato. 'Shakespeare and Other English Renaissance Authors as Characterized by Information Theory Complexity Quantifiers'. *Physica A* 388 (2009): 916–26.

Rutter, Tom. 'Repertory Studies: A Survey'. *Shakespeare* 4.3 (2008): 336–50.

Shakespeare and the Admiral's Men: Reading across Repertories on the London Stage, 1594–1600. Cambridge University Press, 2017.

Rybicki, Jan. 'The Great Mystery of the (Almost) Invisible Translator: Stylometry in Translation'. In: *Quantitative Methods in Corpus-Based Translation Studies*. Ed. Michael P. Oakes and Meng Ji. Amsterdam: John Benjamins, 2012. 231–48.

Salomon, Brownell. 'Visual and Aural Signs in the Performed English Renaissance Play'. *Renaissance Drama* 5 (1972): 143–69.

Satterthwaite, F. E. 'An Approximate Distribution of Estimates of Variance Components'. *Biometric Bulletin* 2.6 (1946): 110–14.

Schoone-Jongen, Terence G. *Shakespeare's Companies: William Shakespeare's Early Career and the Acting Companies, 1577–1594*. Farnham: Ashgate, 2008.

Schopenhauer, Arthur. 'A Few Parables'. *Studies in Pessimism: A Series of Essays*. Trans. T. Bailey Saunders. London: Swan Sonnenschein & Co., 1893. 137–42.

Shannon, C. E. 'A Mathematical Theory of Communication'. *Bell System Technical Journal* 27 (1948): 379–423.

'Prediction and Entropy of Printed English'. *Bell System Technical Journal* 30 (1951), 50–64.

Shapiro, James. *1599: A Year in the Life of William Shakespeare*. London: Faber and Faber, 2005.

Smith, Peter W. H., and W. Aldridge. 'Improving Authorship Attribution: Optimizing Burrows' Delta Method'. *Journal of Quantitative Linguistics* 18.1 (2011): 63–88.

Snedecor, George W., and William G. Cochran. *Statistical Methods*. 8th edn. Ames: Iowa State College Press, 1989.

Snyder, Susan. *The Comic Matrix of Shakespeare's Tragedies*. Princeton University Press, 1979.

Sofer, Andrew. *The Stage Life of Props*. Ann Arbor: University of Michigan Press, 2003.

'"Take up the Bodies": Shakespeare's Body Parts, Babies, and Corpses'. *Theatre Symposium* 18 (2010): 135–48.

Sprague, A. C. *Beaumont and Fletcher on the Restoration Stage*. Cambridge, MA: Harvard University Press, 1926.

Steggle, Matthew. *Richard Brome: Place and Politics on the Caroline Stage*. Manchester University Press, 2004.

'Student' [= W. S. Gosset]. 'The Probable Error of a Mean'. *Biometrika* 6.1 (1908): 1–25.

Tarlinskaja, Marina. *Shakespeare and the Versification of English Drama, 1561–1642*. Farnham: Ashgate, 2014.

Tarrant, Harold, and Terry Roberts. 'Appendix 2: Report of the Working Vocabulary of the Doubtful Dialogues'. In: *Alcibiades and the Socratic Lover-Educator.* Ed. Marguerite Johnson and Harold Tarrant. London: Bristol Classical Press, 2012. 223–36.

Tave, Stuart M. *Some Words of Jane Austen.* University of Chicago Press, 1973.

Taylor, Gary. 'The Fly Scene in *Titus*'. Paper presented at Shakespeare 450, Paris, 25 Apr. 2014.

Teague, Frances. *Shakespeare's Speaking Properties.* Cranbury: Associated University Presses, 1991.

Teichmann, Howard, and George S. Kaufman. *The Solid Gold Cadillac: A Comedy.* New York: Random House, 1954.

Timberlake, Philip W. *The Feminine Ending in English Blank Verse.* Menasha: George Banta, 1931.

Tomlinson, Tracey E. 'The Restoration English History Plays of Roger Boyle, Earl of Orrery'. *SEL: Studies in English Literature, 1500–1900*, 43.3 (2003): 559–77.

Trumpener, Katie. 'Paratext and Genre System: A Response to Franco Moretti'. *Critical Inquiry* 36.1 (2009): 159–71.

Tschopp, Elizabeth. *The Distribution of Verse and Prose in Shakespeare's Dramas.* Berne: Francke Verlag, 1956.

van Peer, Willie. 'Quantitative Studies of Literature: A Critique and an Outlook'. *Computers and the Humanities* 23.4–5 (1989): 301–7.

Vickers, Brian. *The Artistry of Shakespeare's Prose.* London: Methuen, 1968.

(ed.), *Seventeenth-Century Prose.* London: Longmans, Green, & Co., 1991.

Wakasa, Tomoko. 'Swords in Early Modern English Plays'. M.Phil. thesis: University of Birmingham, 2011.

Weimann, Robert. *Shakespeare and the Popular Tradition in the Theater: Studies in the Social Dimension of Dramatic Form and Function.* Ed. Robert Schwartz. Baltimore: Johns Hopkins University Press, 1978.

Welch, B. L. 'The Generalization of "Student's" Problem When Several Different Population Variances Are Involved'. *Biometrika* 34.1–2 (1947): 28–35.

Wells, Stanley. '"A Funeral Elegy": Obstacles to Belief'. *Shakespeare Studies* 25 (1997): 186–91.

Werstine, Paul. *Early Modern Playhouse Manuscripts and the Editing of Shakespeare.* Cambridge University Press, 2013.

Whitworth, Charles W. '*The Wounds of Civil War* and *Tamburlaine*: Lodge's Alleged Imitation'. *Notes & Queries* 22 (1975): 245–7.

Wiggins, Martin, in association with Catherine Richardson. *British Drama, 1533–1642: A Catalogue.* 10 vols. Oxford University Press, 2011–.

Wilson, John Harold. *The Influence of Beaumont and Fletcher on Restoration Drama.* Columbus: Ohio State University Press, 1928.

Wing, Donald. *Short-Title Catalogue of Books Printed in England, Scotland, Ireland, Wales and British America and of English Books Printed in Other Countries, 1641–1700.* 2nd edn. Rev. and enl. John J. Morrison, Carolyn W. Nelson, and Matthew Seccombe. 4 vols. New York: Modern Language Association of America, 1972–98.

Wiseman, Susan. *Drama and Politics in the English Civil War*. Cambridge University Press, 1998.

Witmore, Michael, and Jonathan Hope. 'Shakespeare by the Numbers: On the Linguistic Texture of the Late Plays'. In: *Early Modern Tragicomedy*. Ed. Subha Mukherji and Raphael Lyne. Woodbridge: Boydell & Brewer, 2007. 133–53.

Index

(*The Rare Triumphs of*) *Love and Fortune*, 57
A Larum for London, 94, 95, 114, 117, 154
Adamson, Sylvia, 18
Admiral's (Nottingham's) Men, 166, 170–81
Anderson, Thomas and Scott Crossley, 20
Annals of English Drama, 975–1700, 29, 94, 118,
    156, 182, 187, 220
Archer, Dawn and Derek Bousfield, 20
Arden of Faversham, 86
Argamon, Shlomo, 44
Astington, John H., 164
Austen, Jane
    Emma, 12
    Persuasion, 15
authorial style
    and attribution study, 7, 9–11
    effect of repertory company on. *See* Chapter 6
    in translation, 2
    late style, 2, 166

Barber, Charles, 137
Barish, Jonas A., 55, 58, 76
Barnes, Barnabe
    The Devil's Charter, 120, 125
Baron, Alistair, 29
Barry, Lording
    Ram Alley, 186
Bate, Jonathan and Eric Rasmussen, 57
Beeston's Boys, 188–99
Bennett, Tony, 22
Bevington, David, 56, 115
Bevis, Richard W., 203
Biber, Douglas, 161–2
Blake, N.F., 76
Bly, Mary, 164, 181
Borish, M.E., 187
Bosonnet, Felix, 115
Boyle, Roger
    Henry the Fifth, 216
Bradley, A.C., 81
Breiman, Leo, 39

Brome, Richard
    A Mad Couple Well Matched, 88, 191–4, 196
    and Salisbury Court, 197
    Covent Garden Weeded, 191–4
    in comparison with Restoration drama,
        218–22
    The City Wit, 191–4
    The Demoiselle, 194–6
Brook, G.L., 55, 59
Brown, Roger and Albert Gilman, 21
Bruster, Douglas
    on prose and verse, 55, 57–8
    on stage properties, 21, 111–13, 116–17
Bruster, Douglas and Geneviève Smith, 20
Bullen, A.H., 92
Burlinson, Christopher, 125
Burrows, John
    and Principal Components Analysis, 12–16
    Computation into Criticism, 2, 13, 17, 22–3
    Delta. *See* Delta
    development of computational stylistics,
        12–17
    on counting and interpreting, 15
Burton, Dolores M., 20
Busse, Ulrich, 20, 55, 57, 70, 71
Butler, Martin, 202

Canfield, J. Douglas, 216
Cathcart, Charles, 166, 187
Cavendish, William
    The Humorous Lovers, 212
Chamberlain's (Hunsdon's) Men, 166, 177
Chambers, E.K., 73
Chapman, George
    Byron's Conspiracy, 82–92, 103, 145
    Byron's Tragedy, 82–92, 145
    in comparison with Restoration drama,
        218–20
    May Day, 105–6
    The Gentleman Usher, 151
    The Widow's Tears, 56

characters
    corpus of dialogue. *See* Appendix B
    linguistic profiles of. *See* Chapter 3
    prose and verse parts of. *See* Chapter 2
    reception of, 79, 98
    Shakespearean character criticism and, 81
    stylistic resemblances between. *See* Chapter 3
Chettle, Henry
    Hoffman, 82–92, 128
Children of Paul's, 170, 177
Children of the King's Revels, 166, 181–7
Children of the Queen's Revels, 166
chronology. *See* quantitative analysis and
    chronology
Clare, Janet, 183, 202
Clemen, Wolfgang, 172
cluster analysis
    definition and demonstration of, 99–100
Clymon and Clamydes, 182
Collins, Eleanor, 197–8
computational stylistics. *See* Burrows, John,
    quantitative analysis, stylistics
concordance
    computer-based, 13
    history of, 3
Congreve, William
    The Double Dealer, 203
    The Way of the World, 223
Connors, Louisa, 18
Cook, Ann Jennalie, 202
coordinates
    definition of, 33
Corman, Brian, 203
corpus
    features excluded, 30
    of character dialogue. *See* Appendix B
    of full-text plays. *See* Appendix A
    of stage properties. *See* Appendices C and D
    text segmentation, 30
    text selection and preparation, 29–30
    treatment of spelling, 29
correlation
    definition of, 5, 30
Craig, Hugh, 10, 12, 20, 65, 145, 163, 167, 199
Crystal, David, 55, 76
Culpeper, Jonathan, 20

Daniel, Samuel
    Philotas, 120
Day, John
    Humour Out of Breath, 105, 186, 187
    Law Tricks, 187
    The Isle of Gulls, 72
de Man, Paul, 1, 3, 21
decision tree. *See* Random Forests

DEEP: Database of Early English Playbooks, 29,
    94
Dekker, Thomas
    1 Old Fortunatus, 94, 101
    and Thomas Middleton
        1 The Honest Whore, 114
    in comparison with Restoration drama,
        218–20
    The Shoemaker's Holiday, 94, 101
    The Whore of Babylon, 92, 103, 163
Delta
    definition and demonstration of, 44–8
Derby's (Strange's) Men, 170–81, 200
Dessen, Alan and Leslie Thomson, 128
dialogue
    collective changes in. *See* Chapter 5
    definition of, 138
Digges, Leonard, 98
distance metrics
    and cluster analysis, 99–100
    types of, 82
DocuScope, 161
dogs
    unable to conduct statistical analysis, 224–5
Dryden, John
    An Evening's Love, 210
    on Renaissance drama, 202–3
    The Conquest of Granada, 203
Dutton, Richard, 164

Early English Books Online, 29
Edelman, Charles, 173
Edmondson, Paul, 9
Edmond Ironside, 114
Egan, Gabriel, 10, 166, 199
Ehrenfest, Paul and Tatiana Ehrenfest, 224
Eliot, T.S., 17, 21, 60, 75, 76–7
Elliott, Jack, 8
Elliott, Jack and Brett Greatley-Hirsch, 39,
    44
Elliott, Ward E.Y., and Robert J. Valenza, 77
Engle, Lars, 27
English language
    as analytic, 17
    countable features of, 21–3
    definite article, 18
    evolution of, 136–7 *See also* Chapter 5
    modal verbs, 18
    pronoun system, 18
    tagging of homograph forms, 18, 30
    thou and you, 21, 70
    variability and predictability of, 24–8
    word types and tokens in, 17, 21
Enkvist, Nils Erik, 5
Erne, Lukas, 29, 136

Fair Em, 120
Farmer, Alan B., and Zachary Lesser. *See DEEP: Database of Early English Playbooks*
Federalist Papers, 13
Fish, Stanley, 5, 22
fleas
    textual critics and, 224–5
Fletcher, John
    in comparison with Restoration drama, 218–22
    Monsieur Thomas, 72
    The Faithful Shepherdess, 158
    The Humorous Lieutenant, 86–8, 102
    The Island Princess, 148
    The Loyal Subject, 153
    The Wild-Goose Chase, 72, 86–8, 145
Floridi, Luciano, 48
Ford, John
    The Broken Heart, 82–92
Foucault, Michel, 165
Frow, John, 22
function words
    definition of, 13, 16–17
    list of. *See* Appendix E
    skip n-grams of, 74
    style and, 16–19

Gaby, Rosemary, 57
Gair, Reavley, 164
Geertz, Clifford, 225
Gibbons, Brian, 174
Gombrich, Ernst H., 5, 9
Gosset, W.S. *See t-*tests
Gosson, Stephen, 111
Graves, R.B., 126
Greene, Robert
    Alphonsus, 144
    Friar Bacon and Friar Bungay, 86
    in comparison with Restoration drama, 218–22
    Orlando Furioso, 156
Greg, W.W., 1
Griffith, Eva, 164
Gurr, Andrew, 164

Haaker, Ann, 197, 198, 199
Hacking, Ian, 25
Hadfield, Andrew, 173
Harbage, Alfred and Samuel Schoenbaum. *See Annals of English Drama, 975–1700*
Hartman, Geoffrey, 1
Heffner, Hubert C., 84
Henslowe, Philip, 113
Heywood, Thomas
    1 and 2 Edward the Fourth, 82–92, 101

A Woman Killed with Kindness, 125
    The English Traveller, 86
    The Rape of Lucrece, 150
Hirsch, Brett D., 10
Holbrook, Peter, 163
Holmes, David I., 16
Hoover, David L., 2, 44
Hope, Jonathan and Michael Witmore
    on Shakespearean genre, 11, 20, 161
Hotelling, Harold, 14
Housman, A.E., 224
Howard, Edward
    The Change of Crowns, 216
Howard, James
    All Mistaken, 215
    The English Monsieur, 211
Hume, Robert D., 203
Hunter, G.K., 137, 163, 171, 200, 222

Ilsemann, Hartmut, 20
Intelligent Archive, 30, 32

Jack Straw, 120
Jackson, MacDonald P., 19
Jannidis, Fotis and Gerhard Lauer, 44
John of Bordeaux, 118
Jones, Emrys, 204
Jonson, Ben
    Bartholomew Fair, 82–8, 92
    Catiline, 82–92
    Cynthia's Revels, 137
    Every Man in His Humour, 136
    Every Man Out of His Humour, 95, 100, 120, 136
    in comparison with Restoration drama, 218–22
    Sejanus, 82–92
    The Devil is an Ass, 216
    The Magnetic Lady, 82–92
    Volpone, 82–92

Kant, Immanuel, 25–6
Kastan, David Scott, 56, 165
Kaufmann, R.J., 194
Kay, W. David, 136
Keenan, Siobhan, 164, 200
Kermode, Frank, 63, 75
King Leir, 183
King's Men, 188–99
King's Revels Company, 188–99
Knutson, Roslyn L., 164, 167, 199
Kyd, Thomas
    Soliman and Perseda, 29
    The Spanish Tragedy, 136

Lake, D.J., 94
Lascelles, Mary, 15
Leggatt, Alexander, 1
Leslie, Michael, 191
literary Darwinism, 7
literary history
  and fragmentary evidence, 1
  quantitative turn in, 2, 138
Literature Online, 29
Lodge, Thomas
  The Wounds of Civil War, 170–3, 177
Logan, Robert A., 136
logarithm
  definition of, 49
Look About You, 95
Lost Plays Database, 95, 114
Love, Harold, 204
Lyly, John
  Galatea, 46
  in comparison with Restoration drama,
    218–20
  Love's Metamorphosis, 118
  Mother Bombie, 35
  The Woman in the Moon, 70, 72

MacFaul, Tom, 183
Machin, Lewis and Gervase Markham
  The Dumb Knight, 186
Magnusson, Lynne, 18
Maguire, Laurie and Emma Smith, 121,
  166
Manley, Lawrence, 200
Manley, Lawrence and Sally-Beth MacLean,
  164
Markham, Gervase and William Sampson
  Herod and Antipater, 82–92
Marlowe, Christopher
  1 and 2 Tamburlaine the Great, 35, 57, 82–92,
    136, 170–3, 177
  and others
    Doctor Faustus, 82–92, 115
  and Thomas Heywood (?)
    The Jew of Malta, 41, 47, 82–92
  and Thomas Nashe (?)
    Dido, Queen of Carthage, 106
  Edward the Second, 35, 106–8
  in comparison with Restoration drama,
    218–22
  The Massacre at Paris, 106–8
Marsh, Christopher, 130
Marston, John
  Antonio and Mellida, 80, 94, 95
  in comparison with Restoration drama,
    218–22
  Jack Drum's Entertainment, 137

Sophonisba, 92
  The Dutch Courtesan, 53–4
Martin, Randall, 136
Masten, Jeffrey, 165
Maxwell, James Clerk, 26
McDonald, Russ, 56
McManaway, James G., 203
McMillin, Scott and Sally-Beth MacLean, 164,
  167, 181, 182, 184
McMullan, Gordon, 166
Methods. *See* cluster analysis, Delta, distance
  metrics, Principal Components Analysis,
  Random Forests, Shannon entropy,
  t-tests
Middleton, Thomas
  A Game at Chess, 145, 147, 163
  A Mad World, My Masters, 147
  A Trick to Catch the Old One, 82–92
  in comparison with Restoration drama,
    218–20
  Michaelmas Term, 82–92, 149
  The Phoenix, 147
  The Revenger's Tragedy, 147
  The Second Maiden's Tragedy, 147
  The Widow, 92, 147
  Your Five Gallants, 147
Monsarrat, G.D., 11
Moretti, Franco, 6, 18
Morgann, Maurice, 81
Mosteller, Frederick and David L. Wallace, 12
Munday, Anthony
  1 Robin Hood, 113, 114
Munro, Lucy, 164, 187, 200
Murray, Barbara A., 203

Nance, John, 77
Nashe, Thomas
  on Senecan tragedy, 137
Nason, A.H., 222
Nettleton, George Henry, 204
Nevalainen, Terttu and Helena
  Raumolin-Brunberg, 137
Newton, Isaac, 26
Nichols, Tom, 125
normal distribution
  definition of, 50
Novak, Maximilian E., 204

Oldham, John, 110
Oras, Ants, 20
Oxford Dictionary of Biography, 159
Oxford's Boys, 170

Palfrey, Simon and Tiffany Stern, 79
Pearson, Karl, 14

Peele, George
  A Farewell, 173
  David and Bethsabe, 92, 102, 145, 148–9,
    209
  Edward the First, 86
  in comparison with Restoration drama,
    218–22
  The Battle of Alcazar, 154–5, 170–3, 177
Petersen, Lene B., 21
Petter, Christopher Gordon, 187
Pope, Alexander, 56
Porter, Henry
  1 The Two Angry Women of Abingdon, 86–8,
    103
Principal Components Analysis
  definition and demonstration of, 14, 30–9
  history of, 14
  interpreting biplots of, 35–8
  interpreting scatterplots of, 33–5
props. *See* stage properties
Puttenham, George, 4, 26, 55

quantitative analysis
  and chronology, 11
  and the counter-intuitive, 7–9
  assumptions and bias, 7–9, 141
  authorship. *See* authorial style
  classification and description, 6
  danger of over-fitting, 41, 141
  distant reading, 6
  in literary studies, 3
  nature of findings, 3, 27–8
  of multivariate and univariate data, 31
  previous studies of early modern drama,
    19–21
  relationship to qualitative analysis, 3–4, 7,
    225
  supervised and unsupervised, 31, 41
Queen Elizabeth's Men, 165, 167, 170–87
Queen Henrietta Maria's Men, 197

Randall, Dale B.J., 202
Random Forests
  definition and demonstration of, 39–42
readers
  human versus computer, 2–3
repertory companies
  distinct styles of. *See* Chapter 6
  studies of, 164–70
Restoration drama
  corpus of. *See* Appendix A
  critical appraisal of, 203–4
  in comparison with Renaissance drama. *See*
    Chapter 7
Richardson, Catherine, 110

Richie, Donald M., 184
Rivere de Carles, Nathalie, 116
Roberts, Sasha, 129
Ronan, Clifford, 173
Rutter, Tom, 164, 199
Rybicki, Jan, 2

Salomon, Brownell, 115
Schoone-Jongen, Terence G., 164
Selimus, 182
Shadwell, Thomas
  The Sullen Lovers, 211–12
Shakespeare, William
  1 Henry the Fourth, 56, 58–63, 76, 82–92,
    105–6
  2 Henry the Fourth, 58–63, 82–92
  A Midsummer Night's Dream, 55, 116,
    150
  and George Peele
    Titus Andronicus, 7, 133, 150
  and George Wilkins
    Pericles, 86
  and John Fletcher
    Henry the Eighth, 86
  and others
    2 Henry the Sixth, 217
    3 Henry the Sixth, 106–8
    Sir Thomas More, 86
  and Thomas Middleton
    Macbeth, 49
    Measure for Measure, 58–63
  Antony and Cleopatra, 86, 114
  As You Like It, 56, 73, 150
  authorship of *A Funeral Elegy*, 10
  Coriolanus, 105
  Cymbeline, 118
  Double Falsehood, 5
  Hamlet, 27, 58–63, 75, 105, 137, 153
  Hamlet, 76
  Henry the Fifth, 82–92, 94, 103
  in comparison with Restoration drama,
    218–20
  Julius Caesar, 94, 95–9, 153
  King Lear, 49, 55, 58–63
  Much Ado About Nothing, 105
  Othello, 11, 58–63, 155–6
  Restoration revivals and adaptations of,
    203
  Richard the Third, 35, 42, 82–92
  Romeo and Juliet, 52, 56, 106
  The Merchant of Venice, 58–63, 117, 153
  The Tempest, 21
  The Winter's Tale, 125, 153
  Troilus and Cressida, 152
  Twelfth Night, 49, 73, 152, 153

Shannon, Claude. *See* Shannon entropy
Shannon entropy
  definition and demonstration of, 48–9
Shapiro, James, 94, 100
Sharpham, Edward
  Cupid's Whirligig, 186, 187
Shirley, James
  in comparison with Restoration drama,
    218–22
  Love's Cruelty, 209–10
  The Opportunity, 88
  The Royal Master, 216
skip n-grams, 74
Snyder, Susan, 11
Sofer, Andrew, 110, 132
Sprague, A.C., 203
stage properties
  ambiguous references to, 114–15
  authorial practice and, 112, 116–17, 121–2
  chronology and, 111, 112, 121
  corpus of. *See* Appendices C and D
  counting of, 116–17
  definitions of, 115–16
  effect of genre on, 111, 112, 116, 121,
    122–33
  play length and, 119–20
  quantitative analysis of. *See* Chapter 4
  sources for, 113–14
  Thing Theory and, 116
  types and tokens of, 118
standard deviation
  definition and demonstration of, 44, 45,
    50
Steggle, Matthew, 191
Stern, Tiffany, 184
style
  authorial. *See* authorial style
  definitions of, 4–6, 167
  neutral, 5
  physiognomic fallacy and, 5
  prose and verse. *See* Chapter 2
    attribution study, 77
    compositorial practice, 56, 64
    previous studies, 55–6
stylistics
  and function words, 13–16
  and style, 4
  objections to, 21–4
Sussex's Men, 177

Tarlinskaja, Marina, 20
Tave, Stuart M., 12
Taylor, Gary, 7
Teague, Frances
  on stage properties, 21, 111, 116–17
  The Famous Victories of Henry the Fifth, 182, 216
  The Valiant Welshman, 145
  The Weakest Goeth to the Wall, 133
Thing Theory
  definition of, 115
Timberlake, Philip W., 20
Tomlinson, Tracey E., 205
Tschopp, Elizabeth, 57
t-tests
  definition and demonstration of, 50–2

van Peer, Willie, 21
VARD, 29
Vickers, Brian, 55, 57, 76

Webster, John
  The Devil's Law-Case, 103, 144
  The Duchess of Malfi, 82–92, 163
  The White Devil, 82–92, 163
Weil, Herbert and Judith Weil, 56
Weimann, Robert, 63, 163
Welch, B.L. *See t*-tests
Wells, Stanley, 9
Werstine, Paul, 30
Whitworth, Charles W., 173
Wiggins, Martin
  British Drama, 1533–1642, 29, 94, 117–18, 182,
    187
Wilson, John
  The Cheats, 203, 210
Wilson, John Harold, 203
Wilson, Robert
  and Michael Drayton, Anthony Munday,
    and Richard Hathaway
    1 Sir John Oldcastle, 94, 100
  The Cobbler's Prophecy, 133
  The Three Lords and Three Ladies of London,
    184
Wiseman, Susan, 202
Witmore, Michael and Jonathan Hope. *See*
  Hope, Jonathan and Michael Witmore
Wright, Frank Lloyd, 27

Yamada, Akihiro, 57